Habitat
for Humanity®

HOW TO BUILD
A HOUSE

Habitat
for Humanity®

HOW TO BUILD
A HOUSE

REVISED & UPDATED

LARRY HAUN

WITH VINCENT LAURENCE AND TIM SNYDER

The Taunton Press

 The Taunton Press

The Taunton Press, Inc., 63 South Main Street, PO Box 5506, Newtown, CT 06470-5506
e-mail: tp@taunton.com
Distributed by Ingram Services

Editors: Vincent Laurence and Tim Snyder
Copy editor: Seth Reichgott
Indexer: Cathy Goddard
Cover design: Renato Stanisic
Front cover photograph: Roe Osborn, courtesy *Fine Homebuilding* magazine, © The Taunton Press, Inc.
Back cover photographs: Randy O'Rourke (top), courtesy HFHI (bottom)
Interior design and layout: Renato Stanisic
Illustrator: Mario Ferro (except p. 238, illustration by Charles McCausland, courtesy
    Fine Homebuilding magazine)
Photographer: Randy O'Rourke (except where noted). Photographs p. ii, iii courtesy HFHI

Library of Congress Cataloging-in-Publication Data:
Haun, Larry.
  Habitat for Humanity how to build a house / Larry Haun. -- Rev. and expanded.
    p. cm.
  Includes index.
  ISBN 978-1-56158-967-8
  1. House construction--United States--Amateurs' manuals. 2. Habitat for Humanity, inc.--Amateurs' manuals.
I. Habitat for Humanity, inc. II. Title. III. Title: How to build a house.

TH4815.H38 2008
690'.837--dc22

                    2007051045

Printed in the United States of America
10 9 8 7 6 5 4 3 2 1

The following brand names/manufacturers appearing in *How To Build a House* are trademarks: Barricade®, Dalluge®, Durabond®, Gore-Tex®, Lego®, Lincoln Logs™, L.L. Bean®, Milwaukee®, Porta Potti®, Sawzall®, Sheetrock®, Skyhook®, Smartside®, Spackle®, Speed® square, Stiletto®, Surform®, Typar®, Tyvek®

Homebuilding is inherently dangerous. From accidents with power tools or hand tools to falls from ladders, scaffolds, and roofs, builders and homeowners risk serious injury and even death. We try to promote safe work practices throughout this book, but what is safe for one builder or homeowner under certain circumstances may not be safe for you under different circumstances. So don't try anything you learn about here (or elsewhere) unless you're certain that it's safe for you. If something doesn't feel right, don't do it. Look for another way. Please keep safety foremost in your mind whenever you're working.

To all the beautiful hands that help build decent, affordable houses.

ACKNOWLEDGMENTS

I didn't find it easy to write this book, mainly because of the amount of material it covers and because I have tried to write it for a national audience. I was able to do it because hundreds of people helped me. This book is not the work of one person. My name may be on the cover, but the contents belong to a large group of wonderful people who gave willingly of their time and knowledge.

Let me begin by offering a deeply felt thanks to those who I won't be able to mention by name.

Thanks also to my wife, Mila, and my brothers and sisters, Margaret, Jim, Loretta, and Joe, good-hearted, helping people.

Thanks to Anna Carter from Charlotte, North Carolina, for the hours she freely gave to make this book accurate and comprehensive.

The helpful people from Habitat for Humanity make up a long list. Many thanks to Nevil Eastwood and all the Habitat folks.

To everyone who answered my phone calls and e-mails, thanks.

Give credit to the editors, Vincent Laurence and Tim Snyder, for the consistency and coherency in this book. They deserve special thanks. And thanks to the people at Taunton Press, including Carol Kasper, Meredith DeSousa, Stefanie Ramp, Wendi Mijal, Jennifer Renjilian, Courtney Jordan, and Steve Culpepper.

CONTENTS

5 SHELTER

A Roof Overhead 112

Roof Trusses 113

Photos this spread courtesy HFHI

6 CLOSING IN

Windows, Doors, Siding, and Exterior Trim 146

Vinyl Siding 148

7 BUILDING AN OUTDOOR ROOM

Basic Design for Porches, Decks, and Landings 176

Design Ideas for Decks and Porches 177

Photos this spread courtesy HFHI

FOREWORD

Not everyone is a master carpenter. Fortunately for most of us, it's possible to learn. And that's the inspiration for *How to Build a House*. It is designed to teach various building techniques to people with a wide range of backgrounds, skills, and interests. My hope is that in the following pages you'll find the "tools" you need to complete your next project competently, safely, and efficiently, whether it's your personal project or as a volunteer.

As chief executive officer of the nonprofit house-building ministry Habitat for Humanity, I've seen countless volunteers bring to Habitat building projects around the world an eagerness to learn new construction skills. Some may be seasoned pros, with many building experiences under their belts. Some may be first-timers who have never picked up a hammer, trowel, or tape measure. What all share, however, is the commitment to learn, the passion to serve, and the drive to make a difference.

That kind of spirit has enabled Habitat for Humanity throughout the United States and across the globe to build more than 225,000 modest, affordable homes—hand in hand with volunteers and low-income families who needed a better place to live. That means more than

1 million people are living today in Habitat for Humanity homes—which they've helped build and then bought on terms they could afford. Habitat for Humanity, as you may know, is not a give-away program, but rather a "hand up" that lets families in need become part of their own decent housing solution.

Given the immense need in our world for decent shelter, we need all the support we can get. If you've never experienced the meaning and excitement of a Habitat build, I invite you to join us. You can learn more by visiting us online at www.habitat.org or calling (800) HABITAT. Either way, please know that you're helping us help others simply by purchasing this book. That's because a portion of the proceeds from each book sale support the important, life-changing work we are doing with so many hard-working families in so many parts of the world.

So thank you for buying, thank you for building . . . and good luck with your project!

Jonathan T. M. Reckford
Chief Executive Officer
Habitat for Humanity International

INTRODUCTION

Since this book was first published in 2002, the need for decent, affordable housing in this country (and throughout the world) has only increased. It is astonishing, but millions of families spend over one-third of their income on housing alone. Even families with steady middle-class incomes struggle to purchase homes and make mortgage payments on time. Money that used to go toward medical care, food, and a child's education is now spent so families can keep a roof over their heads.

I was born and raised in a wood-frame house sited high on the short-grass prairies of western Nebraska, that huge inland sea of grass where the only constant is the wind whistling across the snow-covered, sagebrush hills. Aged, warped, unpainted clapboard siding hardly slowed the wind and cold. It was an uninsulated farmhouse with no central heating, no electricity, no indoor plumbing, and windows that let in more wind than light. Just 3 ft. from the iron stove in the kitchen, it was freezing. In our bedrooms, even when Mother warmed the sheets with her flat iron, the temperature never got much above what it was outside. Wallpaper, as the saying goes, was used not for decoration, but for insulation.

After high school, I headed south. The first framing job I worked on was in Los Angeles in

1950. There were lots of carpenters, all wearing white overalls, cutting different pieces of wood with sharp handsaws and nailing them together with 16-oz. curved-claw hammers. The pace was slow and methodical. A wall chalkline would be snapped on the floor. The bottom plate was nailed to the line. Corner posts were then set and a string pulled taut over posts from corner to corner. The length of each wall stud was measured from that string. Once the studs were cut and toenailed to the bottom plate, we would stand on ladders and nail on the top plate. It took a month or so to frame a house.

Six months later, I was one of a small crew, all wearing jeans and nail aprons and wielding long-handled, 20-oz. framing hammers. GIs were returning from the war by the millions and the postwar housing boom was underway. We were framing tract houses, one every couple of days. Those were affordable housing units, decent homes in decent communities, two- and three-bedroom houses with about 1,000 sq. ft. of living space. They were definitely not mansions. In 1951, my brother Jim moved into one of those houses with his family. It cost him $400 down, with monthly payments of $63, which included taxes and insurance. Fifty years later, those houses are still standing, and they have seen more than one generation of children grow up, move on, and start families of their own. We do know how to build affordable housing.

Habitat for Humanity (HFH) is one group that not only knows this to be true but also is doing something with that knowledge. All across this country, in hundreds of towns and cities, people like you and me are working with our neighbors to build decent, affordable housing. In the past 30 years, more than 225,000 affordable houses have been built in America and in other countries by HFH affiliates. Families that otherwise would not have even dared to dream of owning their own homes have been given a "hand up" to dwellings that they can actually afford. But make no mistake: This isn't charity—the houses are not given away. Rather, in addition to shouldering a modest mortgage, the new homeowners put in around 500 hours of "sweat equity," working with volunteers who help them build their house. In the few years I have lived here in Coos Bay, Oregon, we have built 17 houses that have become homes for the families who worked with us. Because of all the volunteer labor, we are able to build these houses for about $55,000, including land, which results in a mortgage that even low-income families can handle.

If HFH can build an affordable house, why can't anyone? First of all, others are doing it. More than 175,000 owner-builders create new housing units each year. It takes a significant amount of courage, effort, and time, not to mention a piece of land, some money, and help from friends—but it can and is being done. How to build a simple house is not a mystery. It's rather like putting together Lego® blocks or Lincoln Logs™, one piece at a time. Many of you already have the basic skills needed to build a simple house. Just look at the thousands of people who flood places like home improvement stores to buy tools and materials for working around their homes.

If you're considering building your own home, keep in mind that it is also possible to build a home that is beautiful but, in the long run, is neither decent nor affordable. Decent housing, for example, doesn't have leaks that can cause mold and rot, compromising both your health and your home. Neither is decent housing full of toxic fumes, which can come from paint, carpet, and a host of other common, seemingly innocuous materials. A decent, affordable home is energy efficient, well ventilated, and comfortable; built from safe, health-preserving materials; and requires a minimum of upkeep or maintenance. It can also be built from forest products and other materials that are sustainable, so that we don't further lay waste to our homeland. Building such a home isn't impossible, but it does take some careful planning.

So, where do you start? There is an old saying, "You can hear a lot just by listening." Talk to neighbors, contractors, carpenters, building inspectors, and the staff at your local building-supply store. Contact your local Habitat affiliate or Habitat for Humanity International for information. Read the how-to information that comes with many building materials, study this book and others, and check out the numerous how-to-build sites on the Web (see Resources on p. 279). Ask questions, work out details and ideas on paper, and gradually the big picture will start to get clearer. Although no single book can answer all the questions you're likely to have on the subject, it's my intent to provide a step-by-step guide that will take you from basic planning and design through the actual construction of a simple, decent, affordable house.

Photo courtesy HFHI

GETTING STARTED

Site, Design, Permits, and Preparation

Building a house is a long journey, and one of the most important characteristics you can possess is optimism. In this context, I often think about President Jimmy Carter, who has done so much to promote the work of Habitat for Humanity. Over the years, he and his wife Rosalynn have helped build nearly 3,000 houses in the sincere belief that decent housing can be made available to every human being. As you take your first steps toward building a house, remember Mr. Carter's optimistic attitude, and make it your own.

The homebuilding process can be intimidating, especially if you haven't been through a house construction project from start to finish. This book is here to help you. By gaining a good understanding of when, why, and how things are done, you'll also gain confidence in your ability to build a house that's comfortable, functional, and affordable. Take care, and hold on to your optimistic attitude. Enjoy the step-by-step journey and all the people who help out along the way.

STEP 1 OBTAIN A SITE

The first step in building a house is finding a place to put it. This is not a step to be taken lightly. There are many factors to consider, not the least of which are the exact location of property lines, the setback and other zoning requirements (the distance a house must be set back from property lines), and whether there are any easements or restrictions on what or where you can build.

Soil characteristics are important when choosing a building site. We once built a house in Montana where 6 in. of topsoil hid large boulders, making it impossible to dig trenches by hand. Building on expansive clay soil requires

Former President Jimmy Carter and his wife Rosalynn—Habitat for Humanity volunteers. [Photos courtesy HFHI (above and inset facing page)]

BUILDING A HOUSE IS A TEAM EFFORT

Working together builds more than houses. Every Habitat project offers a unique opportunity to make new friends and build a new beginning.

TIP Get help from the EPA. If you suspect that your building site may have been contaminated with hazardous materials, contact your local chapter of the Environmental Protection Agency or order an environmental site assessment from an environmental professional.

extra precautions. Learn about the lot's zoning, whether it's situated in a flood plain or on a wetland, and whether any hazardous materials are, or have ever been, present. Removing asbestos debris or an underground oil tank can be very expensive.

Also check to see whether utilities are in place—water, water meter, sewer or septic system, electricity, gas, and telephone and cable lines. When we first moved to Oregon, I inquired about a two-acre site near where we now live. The city water lines stopped ¼ mile away from the property, and to drill a deep well or extend water lines to the new site would have

cost a small fortune. We looked elsewhere. Be sure to check with the local building department (as well as the health, zoning, wetlands, and any other local departments that must issue approval for a construction project) about any potential lot. This investigative work can save you a lot of time and money. Make sure you've done all your homework to determine a lot's suitability before you buy.

Particularly in cities, finding a suitable lot can be a daunting task. The price of the property can sometimes be the biggest impediment to building an affordable house. I know of a couple of marginally suitable building lots in the Bel Air section of Los Angeles that recently sold for $258,000 each. Both of those lots are pitched so steeply that each one will require at least $150,000 just to prepare for construction. That's $400,000 before the owners can even start building! Obviously, most of us have to look elsewhere. There's no easy way to find the "perfect" lot. Check with realtors, follow up on newspaper and online ads, let friends

Heavy equipment readies the site. Initial site preparation is usually done with heavy equipment because of the sheer difficulty of clearing, grading, and digging by hand.
[Photo © Larry Haun]

HIRING A CONTRACTOR

If you're building a house, somewhere along the line you'll likely need to hire a contractor. Whether it's a surveyor, excavator, foundation contractor, plumber, electrician, or other tradesperson, you'll want to choose carefully. Regardless of the job, always get bids from at least three contractors. Ask questions about their work, ask to see other work they have done, and ask for names of former clients, then follow up by talking with some of their previous clients. Make sure the contractor you choose is fully insured and bonded. Finally, before hiring anyone, call your state contractor's board to see whether any complaints have ever been filed against your prospective contractor. (Look in the blue pages of the phone book for the appropriate department within your state's consumer-protection division.)

When you interview each contractor, pay attention to his or her attitude. You want someone who listens to you. What you don't need is someone who acts as though he or she knows what you need better than you do. Get a written cost quote that includes a detailed description of the work to be done and a completion date. Make sure all the quotes you receive are for identical work.

Most contractors are in business because they do competent work for a fair price. But this is the real world and, unfortunately, not every contractor is honest. I recently received a call from a distraught couple who had given a roofing contractor a $2,000 deposit to have their house reshingled. When the couple called to find out why the contractor hadn't shown up to do the work, the phone number provided by the "contractor" turned out to be disconnected. So please, take care.

TIP Protect trees and vegetation. If you want trees, vegetation, and other site features to be preserved during the construction process, rope them off before the work begins. Heavy equipment can damage roots that are close to the surface. It can also compact soil, limiting water absorption.

know you're looking for land, and focus on the outskirts of the town or city where you'd like to build. But above all, be persistent. Keep your energy and optimism high and you'll find the right piece of land.

STEP 2 PREPARE THE SITE

Site preparation can mean many things (see the photo on the facing page). In Oregon, for example, you're likely to have a huge tangle of blackberry vines to subdue. In the southeast, your land may be covered with kudzu. I once built a house on what looked like an old junkyard—the lot was strewn with a dozen dismantled cars and several old motorcycles, which had to be removed before we could start the construction process. Removing vegetation or junk from a lot may be just the beginning, though. Another possibility is that you might encounter hard rock, which may require blasting. In any case, you'll most likely need to hire a contractor to level the land, establish proper drainage, put in a septic tank or sewer connection, prep the driveway, or dig trenches for the foundation footing. If you bring in heavy equipment, do your best to communicate to the operator that you want to save existing trees and to work native plants into the landscape when the project is finished.

Run power to the site

Before you can build, you'll need to run electrical power to the site. Most builders contact the power company to arrange for a temporary power pole to be set up on the site (see the photo on p. 10). Another option is to ask a neighbor

The power pole is an interim system. Mounted on a post, this temporary setup consists of a meter to measure power consumption, a service panel to turn electricity on and off, an outdoor receptacle where extension cords can be plugged in, and conduit that runs back to the main power lines. [Photo © Larry Haun]

to allow you to use—and pay for—electricity while you are building.

Remember, you're going to live in this neighborhood. There's no time like the present to be friendly and to get to know your neighbors. If you're building in a remote area, you'll probably need a generator to get electricity to the site. I've built many houses using a portable, gas-powered generator. Make sure your generator is capable of supplying power to several tools at once.

Provide a fence for safety and security

Installing a fence around your site is a good idea. It can deter or prevent the theft of tools and building materials. It also makes the site safer by discouraging unauthorized visits.

Liability insurance is also a good idea, and it may even be required if you're borrowing money from a bank. Always work to keep your site safe, organized, and free of debris, especially boards with nails protruding from them. Stack unused materials neatly, keep trenches covered, and limit access to any unsafe areas. One nail in a worker's foot or a bad ankle sprain from tripping into a trench can cost a lot of time in medical attention and recovery.

STEP 3 DESIGN THE HOUSE

The bumper-sticker slogan, "Live Simply That Others May Simply Live," speaks to the design aspects of an affordable house. To increase the cost of a house, all you need to do is complicate its design. Affordable housing is, by nature, small and simple. The same formula that makes for a safe house in earthquake country—small, low, and light—makes for an affordable house anywhere in the country.

Money-saving design ideas

The houses featured throughout this book are some of the most cost-efficient designs you can build (see the photo on the facing page). This single-story structure has a simple gable roof

Neatness counts. A clean, well-organized job site enhances safety and improves construction efficiency. [Photo © Roger Turk]

TIP Practice building with a scale model. By assembling a scale model of your house, you can troubleshoot the building process, solving problems before you begin full-scale construction. You can buy balsa wood in different dimensions and other model-making supplies from a well-stocked hobby shop or craft supply store.

Habitat houses are affordable and easy to build. Like most Habitat houses, this one (in Charlotte, N.C.) is designed to make economical use of basic building materials.

that extends over a small porch, where the main entry is located.

On a small lot, where setbacks seriously limit the footprint of the house, you may need to consider a small, two-story design. Habitat for Humanity has a good selection of basic house plans that fit the needs of most families (see Resources on p. 279). Admittedly, the bedrooms are not discothèque size, but you can do your dancing in the living and dining room. In a house, quantity of space doesn't necessarily translate into quality of life. When my children were young, I enclosed our front porch and made two 5-ft. by 9-ft. rooms. They were cozy, sun-filled spaces; one was used for study, one for music. To my surprise, those two tiny rooms became the most popular parts of the house. A well-sited, well-designed house elicits that kind of reaction (see the sidebar at right).

Another way to conserve space and save money is to choose a floor plan that reduces or eliminates hallways. As you look over a house design, remember that doorways need to be at least 32 in. wide—36 in. for easy wheel-

ON THE JOB

SITING A HOUSE

Often, especially in the city, houses are just plopped down square on the lot with a 15-ft. setback from the street and a 5-ft. side yard to meet building-code requirements. Such a building is a stranger to its land. Sometimes we can do better than that. Ideally, a house should be of the land, not merely on the land. Pay attention to the natural lay of the land, the path the sun takes overhead, the direction from which the prevailing wind blows, the good views that long to be seen, and the bad views that really should be hidden. Try to position the house so that you bring some of the outdoors in, but take into account the landscape's features. In high-wind areas, the gable end of a house should be turned so it isn't exposed to the prevailing winds. A great way to get information and inspiration for a new home design is to camp out on your building site. You'll learn about the path of the sun, prevailing breezes, and nice views.

But building is more than just a physical and intellectual feat. Open your heart, and let it tell you what feels good. Trust your intuition. You'll wind up with a much better house.

Small is beautiful. With some thoughtful design, a small house can have a warm, cozy feel while still offering plenty of convenience and privacy.

chair accessibility. And keep in mind that the direction in which a door swings can affect how well a room works and where you can place the furniture.

Other cost-saving strategies have more to do with materials and energy use. Keep the kitchen and the bath on the same side of the house to minimize rough plumbing expenses. In cold regions of the country, run plumbing lines in interior walls and enclose the porch as a mudroom to minimize heat loss when coming and going. To find out which house designs work well in your area, seek advice from local builders, building inspectors, designers, or architects. You'll find it's not too difficult to modify basic plans to suit your needs and meet building-code requirements in your region (see Resources on p. 279).

Check with your building department to see whether your house is required to have a garage. Habitat for Humanity's policy is to "build for people, not cars," but some municipalities require garages. Sometimes, however, you can get a variance to build off-street parking rather than a garage.

Design for the future

Consider building a wheelchair ramp leading to an entry or at least providing room for a ramp to be built in the future. An accessible ramp has a 1-in-12 rise (1 ft. of rise for every 12 ft. of length). When designing a house, it's smart to look beyond what your needs are today. Try to think about and allow for expansion in the future. An addition to the family—whether a new child or an elderly parent—often requires adding a bedroom. If you plan ahead, you'll have room to expand when you need to. This can save a lot of work and money down the line.

Small doesn't mean boring

Whether we admit it or not, we all respond emotionally to our surroundings. Buildings create interior environments that can be drab, distinctive, inspiring, or discouraging. How a building looks, how it's laid out, the materials used—all these influence how we feel. I've visited huge, expensive homes that were not very inviting. Just because a house is big does not mean that it is warm and attractive.

Even a small, plain house can be made to feel inviting and uplifting, giving us pleasure, raising our spirits, and making us feel safe and secure (see the photo on the facing page). In the years that I've been a Habitat volunteer, I've had the opportunity to give a few humble houses a bit more personality and life than they'd otherwise have had. In this book, I've tried to include many of the lessons I've learned—things such as ensuring that there are two sources of light in every room. For example, add an easy-to-install tube skylight in a dark area. Simple things like this can help make rooms bright and cheery.

Ask the right questions

Getting the details right will make life more convenient when you move into your house. Details also present many opportunities to make spaces special by using color schemes, hardware, unique materials, and built-in features (see the photo at left). As you're working out your house's design, ask yourself these key questions: "Is there a place to set groceries when I enter? Where will we hang up our coats or take off our boots when we come inside in the winter? Is it easy to get food to the table and to clear the dishes?" More than anything else you do, thinking about how you will actually live in the house will help you refine its design and ensure that the experience of living in it is a pleasant one.

STEP 4 SECURE THE BUILDING PERMITS

It's not uncommon for builders or owner-builders to view the local building department as enemy turf. Let me suggest that your building experience will be immeasurably more positive, productive, and efficient if you view the building department as a resource and think of the building inspector as someone who can help you. Certainly there are exceptions, as there are in any field, but, by and large, building departments and building inspectors exist to protect prospective homeowners from unscrupulous or incompetent builders and owner-builders from themselves. The building inspector knows the building codes, which have been developed over the years to ensure that safe, durable houses are built. Your building inspector has the same

Details make a difference. Built-in drawers, painted wood paneling, and a well-crafted valance above the window make this small space extra special. [Photo © Richard Stringer]

FLOOR PLAN

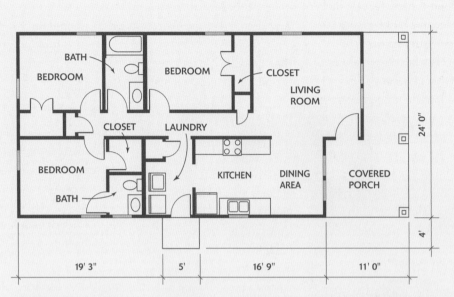

BATH

BEDROOM

BEDROOM

CLOSET

LIVING ROOM

24' 0"

CLOSET

LAUNDRY

BEDROOM

KITCHEN

DINING AREA

COVERED PORCH

BATH

4'

19' 3" 5' 16' 9" 11' 0"

This is the floor plan for a simple three bedroom house. With it you can see the size of the building, the arrangement of the living spaces, and the location of doors and windows.

FOUNDATION PLAN: CRAWL SPACE

38 ft.

TRUSS JOISTS @ 24 IN. O.C.

4x6 GIRDER   6 FT.   6 FT.

24 FT.

CONCRETE FOUNDATION 6 IN. WIDE AND 18 IN. HIGH

12 IN. x 12 IN. PIERS

6 FT.

10 FT.

Using this plan, a concrete contractor can build a crawl-space foundation for your house. Other foundations can be on a slab or include a basement.

PLOT OR SITE PLAN

A plot plan lets you see, from above, the size of the lot and where your house will be placed on the land. It also shows where utilities like water and electricity are located.

36'-0"   15'-0"

EDGE OF THE ROOF   GUTTER   ELECTRIC METER

5'-0"

DS   DS

BLDG. LINE BELOW RIDGE

DOWN SPOUT

REDWING STREET

25'-0"

WATER METER

6'-0"   5'-0"

DS   DS

15'-0"

GUTTER

TELEPHONE TELEVISION

EAST SUN AVE.

PROPERTY LINE

PLOT or SITE PLAN   NORTH   ADDRESS: 44 EAST SUN AVE.

goals that you do. He or she wants a house that doesn't leak, isn't a fire hazard, complies with zoning requirements, and can stand up to everyday use and all but the most severe natural disasters. Building inspectors really are on your side.

Taking the plans to a building department to request permits need not be a big affair. I have often submitted basic plans on 11-in. by 14-in. sheets of paper. Plans do need to be drawn to scale, and the most common scale is ¼ in. = 1 ft.; this means that 1 in. on a plan equals 4 ft. in the actual house. Using graph paper can help with preliminary designing, but an inexpensive computer-aided design (CAD) program makes professional-looking plans that are simple to draw and easy to change. For a simple house, most building departments need the basic types of drawings shown on pp. 14, 16, and 17:

- Plot or site plan to give an overall view from above, showing the shape and dimensions of the property and the size and location of the building.

- Foundation plan to show the location and size of the concrete footings, walls, and piers that will support the floor frame.

- Floor plan to provide a bird's-eye view of the size and arrangement of living spaces. The floor plan shows the location and size of doors and windows and often the location of electrical, plumbing, and heating system components (see the symbols explained in the sidebar at right). Even the location, spacing, and direction of the roof trusses can be found here.

- Wall sections to show the "guts" of the floors, walls, or ceilings. Think of a wall section drawing as an apple that's been sliced in half to reveal its core (see the drawing on p. 16). Both section and detail plans (see p. 17) are sometimes drawn at a larger scale to better identify the details that wouldn't show up as clearly in a smaller scale.

- Elevation plan to show how each side of the house will look. Elevation drawings show the foundation, wall height, siding and trim, roof

READING FLOOR PLANS

Building a house requires that you learn more than one new language. Besides the terminology of building (plates, braces, lined walls, plumb, toenail, and the like), there's also the visual vocabulary of lines, symbols, and notations found on building plans. Fortunately, most of these symbols are fairly easy to understand (see the illustration below). It's important to become familiar with building plans so that you can begin to visualize, from a two-dimensional representation, what the house will look like with the walls framed and the fixtures and appliances in place. It's far easier (and less expensive) to make a change at the planning stage than after the walls and rough plumbing are in place.

SYMBOLS USED ON FLOOR PLANS

Wall	
Window	
Door (and direction it opens)	
Sliding doors	
Bifold doors	
Insulation	
Sink and Lavatory	Sink / Lav
Bathtub	
Shower	
Toilet	
Stove	
Refrigerator	
Washer and Dryer	
Water heater	WH
Furnace	F (or FAU, for Forced-Air Unit)

We see symbols on our highways that tell us of an approaching curve or that children are nearby. Symbols are also used on plans to tell us where to place a window or where a water heater goes or when to install a bifold door, for example.

WALL SECTION

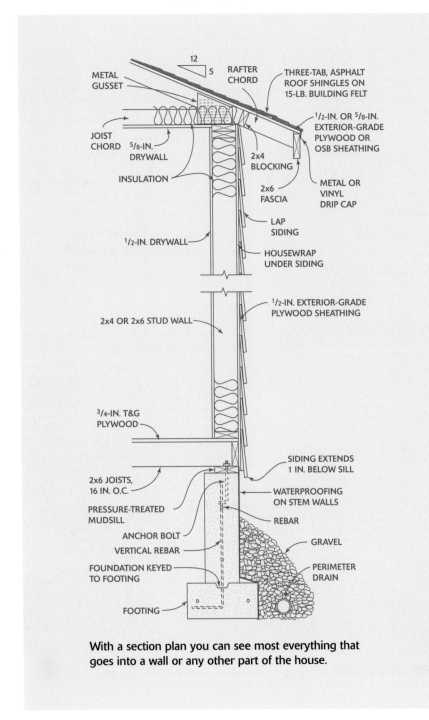

METAL GUSSET

12
5

RAFTER CHORD

THREE-TAB, ASPHALT ROOF SHINGLES ON 15-LB. BUILDING FELT

1/2-IN. OR 5/8-IN. EXTERIOR-GRADE PLYWOOD OR OSB SHEATHING

JOIST CHORD

5/8-IN. DRYWALL

2x4 BLOCKING

INSULATION

2x6 FASCIA

METAL OR VINYL DRIP CAP

LAP SIDING

1/2-IN. DRYWALL

HOUSEWRAP UNDER SIDING

1/2-IN. EXTERIOR-GRADE PLYWOOD SHEATHING

2x4 OR 2x6 STUD WALL

3/4-IN. T&G PLYWOOD

SIDING EXTENDS 1 IN. BELOW SILL

2x6 JOISTS, 16 IN. O.C.

WATERPROOFING ON STEM WALLS

PRESSURE-TREATED MUDSILL

REBAR

ANCHOR BOLT

VERTICAL REBAR

GRAVEL

FOUNDATION KEYED TO FOOTING

PERIMETER DRAIN

FOOTING

With a section plan you can see most everything that goes into a wall or any other part of the house.

TIP Improve your design skills. Check with your local community college if you're interested in learning how to read house plans or design a house. Most community colleges offer courses in computer-aided design, drafting, and construction management.

style and pitch, and roof overhang at the eaves.

• Detail plans to provide close-up views of small sections of the house. These are useful for providing clarification or additional detail that isn't shown in the other drawings.

If you can draw it, you can build it

If you're drawing your own plans, the process—though slow and often frustrating—will give you a clearer understanding of your house than many builders ever have. It can save you from making costly mistakes and will likely contribute to building a better house.

A good way to test your ability to visualize a house design based on plans is to visit some building sites where you can examine both the plans and the actual construction details as the house goes up. If you've bought stock plans, they may seem bewildering initially; as you work with them, they'll become much easier to read and understand. The ability to both draw and read plans gets easier with experience.

STEP 5 GET ORGANIZED TO BUILD

Building a house is a process that consists of a seemingly endless number of steps. Knowing which step follows which—for example, when to call the electrical company to install a temporary power pole, when to call the plumber to install drains and vents in the joist system—is key to organizing tasks and materials so that work isn't held up. This knowledge comes primarily from experience, but for the first-time builder I've listed most of the steps in the process (see pp. 18–23).

When my brothers and I were building houses, we spent many hours planning and organizing so that we always knew what to do next, who would do it, and when and how it would be done. Organizing time and materials is an essential skill for any builder, whether that builder is working with professionals, friends, family, or Habitat volunteers. Staying organized and on top of the situation is

ELEVATION PLAN

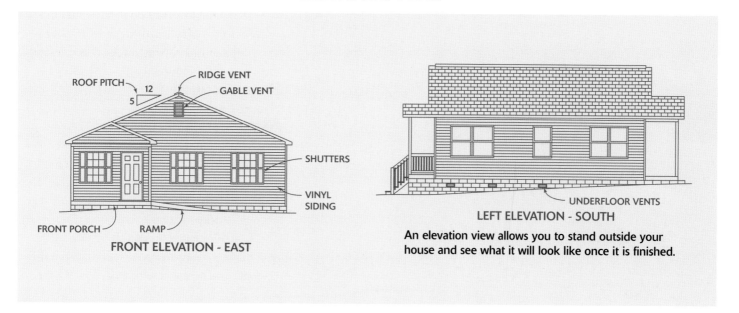

ROOF PITCH
12
5
RIDGE VENT
GABLE VENT
SHUTTERS
VINYL SIDING
FRONT PORCH
RAMP

FRONT ELEVATION - EAST

UNDERFLOOR VENTS

LEFT ELEVATION - SOUTH

An elevation view allows you to stand outside your house and see what it will look like once it is finished.

---

especially important when working with volunteers and unskilled helpers. Careful planning, good organization, and effective communication will ensure that less-experienced workers are able to contribute meaningfully and feel good about the work they are doing.

Display patience, understanding, and openness

People of all ages and abilities come to Habitat job sites wanting to work. Try to give them work that they can do successfully, so that more than just a house is built. Sometimes it's easy to get along with your coworkers; at other times, it's quite challenging. You'll find this to be true on a Habitat project, on your own construction site, and in every situation in life. We all know what it's like to work with people who are arrogant, have an attitude, or are unwilling to listen and learn. We also know what's it's like to work with people who treat us as equals, listen to us, show patience when we are trying to learn a new skill, and praise our efforts even when we fall short of expectations. Try to be the latter, and have patience with the former.

DETAIL PLAN

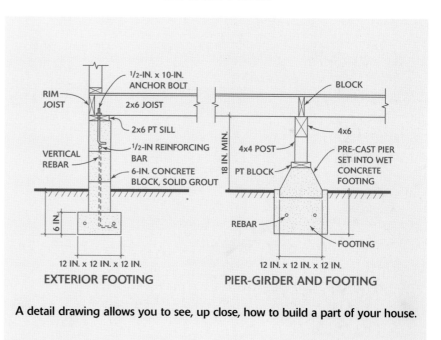

RIM JOIST
1/2-IN. x 10-IN. ANCHOR BOLT
2x6 JOIST
2x6 PT SILL
VERTICAL REBAR
1/2-IN REINFORCING BAR
6-IN. CONCRETE BLOCK, SOLID GROUT
6 IN.
12 IN. x 12 IN. x 12 IN.

EXTERIOR FOOTING

BLOCK
4x6
18 IN. MIN.
4x4 POST
PT BLOCK
PRE-CAST PIER SET INTO WET CONCRETE FOOTING
REBAR
FOOTING
12 IN. x 12 IN. x 12 IN.

PIER-GIRDER AND FOOTING

A detail drawing allows you to see, up close, how to build a part of your house.

TIP Rent a power pole. Most equipment rental dealers have a temporary power pole that you can set up at the job site. Mount the service panel, which the electric utility will install, on the power pole.

Many hands, one goal. Working together gets the job done.
[Photo by HFHI/Gregg Pachkowski]

Habitat for Humanity®

SHARING A VISION

It is important to have a decent place to live. Most of us don't want to live in a mansion. We only want a clean, safe place where we can live and raise our children. A decent house uplifts our spirits and provides dignity and hope for the future.

It is hard for many people to realize what it's like to live in a moldy, leaky house with rat holes in the wall and plumbing that's inadequate or nonexistent. Yet that is the condition of millions of people living around the world today. Poor housing is not just somewhere else. Every city in this country has its share.

Habitat for Humanity has a goal of eliminating poor housing by working with families who need a hand up. There is no magic wand to wave that will produce a new home. Decent housing is built because people like you and me roll up our sleeves, pick up our hammers, and start building. What we may not be able to do alone can be accomplished when we work together. Lots of sweat, a little skill, and a shared vision get the job done.

During this process of working together, we build much more than houses. We meet all kinds of interesting people and develop close friendships as we work side by side, take breaks together, and share stories.

A guide for the first-time builder

The checklist on the following pages contains most of the major steps involved in building a small house. Naturally, there will always be unforeseen or site-specific steps, but this list should serve as a fairly thorough guide to building a house, from raw idea to move-in day.

Getting started

- Look for land and determine whether you can build on it.
- Acquire a piece of land.
- Survey your land to confirm the boundaries.
- Buy or draw up plans or acquire plans through Habitat (see Resources on p. 279).
- Obtain permits from the building department and other departments, if necessary.

Preparing the site.

Readying the foundation for floor framing.

- Consider an environmental site assessment.
- Contact subcontractors for the foundation, plumbing, electrical, heating, lumber, and material companies. Get bids on work and materials. Select subcontractors and suppliers. Schedule work and deliveries.
- Take out liability insurance.
- Contact the gas, electric, and telephone companies to locate on-site utilities.
- Prepare the site.
- Bring in temporary electrical power.

Sheathing the floor.

Foundation

- Trench and prepare for concrete footings and a foundation or slab.
- Before pouring concrete, lay down a gravel bed and install a plastic moisture barrier, if necessary.
- Call the building department to schedule an inspection of the concrete foundation footing and reinforcing steel.
- Have the footings and then the foundation or slab poured.

Subfloor

- Have the floor framing and sheathing materials delivered.
- Frame the subfloor.
- Install the rough plumbing (water, gas, and waste lines) and heating pipes.
- Call the building department for the floor joist framing, rough plumbing, and heating inspections.
- Sheathe the floor.

Raising the walls.

Walls

- Have the wall framing and wall sheathing materials delivered.
- Place chalklines on the floor to show the wall locations.
- Plate the walls, then cut and locate the headers. Frame and erect the walls.
- Brace the walls straight and plumb.
- Place the shower-tub units in the bathrooms; cover them to protect the fiberglass.
- Sheathe the walls, if necessary.

Nailing up sheathwall.

TIP Schedule inspections ahead of time. To avoid delays, contact the building inspector several days before you expect each inspection to take place.

Installing roof trusses.

Sheathing the roof.

Porch

- Have materials delivered for the exterior porch, deck, and stairs. Build the porch, deck, and stairs. After they're built, cover the deck and stairs with scraps of OSB to protect them until the job is finished.

Roof

- Order the roof trusses at least two weeks in advance of your anticipated need.
- Have the roof sheathing, fascia, and trusses delivered and set on framed walls.
- Install the trusses.
- Install the fascia or gutter board and the barge rafters.
- Install the roof sheathing on the trusses and the felt underlay on the sheathing.
- If required, have the roof sheathing inspected.
- Call the plumber to put vent and exhaust pipes through the roof.
- Shingle the roof. Install the ridge vent.

Doors, windows, siding, and paint

- Order the windows and exterior doors two to three weeks before your anticipated need.

- Install the housewrap and exterior vapor barrier where needed.
- Plumb the trimmers and install the windows and doors.
- Have the siding and trim delivered; cover them with plastic for protection. Prime both sides of the wood siding and trim. Install the siding.
- Paint the exterior.
- Install the gutters.

Systems

- Install the rough electrical, heating and/or cooling ductwork, and gas lines.
- Install the cables for the telephone, television, and doorbell.
- Schedule and have inspections for the rough framing and the electrical, plumbing, and heating systems.

Finishing vinyl-siding work.

Installing a window. [Photo courtesy HFHI]

Installing fiberglass batt insulation.

Nailing up drywall.

Insulation and ventilation

- Insulate the walls, ceilings, and floors.
- Install the interior vapor barrier where needed.
- Schedule the insulation and vapor barrier inspections.

Drywall and paint

- Have the drywall delivered. Install drywall on the walls and ceilings.
- Schedule and have the drywall nailing (or screw) inspection.
- Tape and finish the drywall.
- Paint the interior ceilings and walls.

Finish floors

- Install the underlayment for the vinyl floor covering.
- Put down the vinyl floors.

- Install all remaining finish floors (wood, tile, etc.) except for carpeting.
- Protect the floors until construction is completed and all major appliances are installed.

Built-ins and trim

- Install the cabinets and countertops.
- Order prehung interior doors two weeks before your anticipated need. Install the doors.
- Have the trim—door and window casings, baseboards, windowsills, aprons, and closet shelves and poles—delivered. Install the trim.

Installing an interior prehung door.

- Prime, paint, and finish-coat the doors and trim. Touch up where necessary.

Finishing touches

- Install the finish plumbing and the electrical and heating units.
- Install the door locks.
- Install the medicine cabinet, towel bars, closet poles, and other hardware and fixtures.
- Lay wall-to-wall carpeting.
- Complete the work on the driveway and walkways (where applicable).
- Put on the house number. Set up the mailbox.
- Grade around the house so the ground slopes and drains water away from the house.
- Landscape. Plant trees, grass, shrubs, and flowers.
- Schedule the final inspection.

Installing a wall cabinet.

BUILDING BASICS

Getting Acquainted with Tools and the Parts of a House

The craft of carpentry has a long and honorable heritage. Ages before we began recording our history, our ancestors were shaping and joining materials to create various types of shelters. Today, we are the fortunate inheritors of centuries of accumulated knowledge, experience, skills, and tools. Although carpentry continues to be transformed by technology (from computer-aided design programs to cordless tools and pneumatic nailers), many basic tools and techniques remain unchanged.

It still takes a human hand wrapped around a hammer handle to build a decent place to live. Like basic carpentry tools, many parts of the house have stayed the same over the years. Technology has improved some of the parts, as well as created new ones. But the house is still the same basic structure it always was. Before you start building a house, it's essential to learn the common language spoken on construction sites and in home centers, lumberyards, and building-supply stores.

Tool-Buying Tips

When I started working as a carpenter in the late 1940s, almost every task was done with hand tools. I remember spending hours cutting a pile of 2×4s to length with a crosscut saw. Floors were sheathed with 1×6s, both ends of which had to be cut at 45-degree angles. Cutting all the pieces of a house by hand was a big job, to say the least. In 1950, when I bought my first circular saw, my world as a carpenter changed forever.

But what began as a boon (the proliferation of new and better tools) has over the years also become downright bewildering. These days, the number of

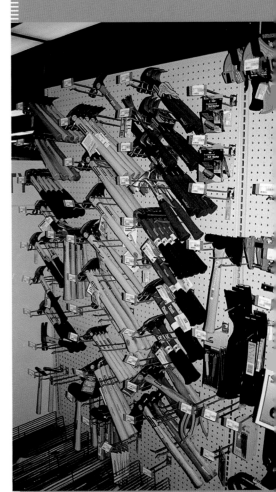

Photo by Larry Haun (above), photo courtesy HFHI (facing page)

TIP Avoid overloading. As you move from one phase of construction to another, make sure you're not carrying around unnecessary tools or nails in your tool belt. The added weight can tire you.

Have a good job-site handsaw. A compact, tool-box-size handsaw is good to have around in case someone else is using the circular saw or you have just a few boards to cut.

tools on the market can make buying tools a difficult task. Each time I walk into a tool center or receive a tool catalog in the mail, I am amazed by the dizzying array of carpentry tools offered for sale. When there are 50 different models, even buying something as basic as a hammer can be frustrating.

Try before you buy

So what do you look for when buying a tool? Well, it helps to remember that tools are not like stretch socks, where one size fits all. A circular saw, for example, may have the right combination of power and weight but still feel out of balance or awkward when you hold it. A tool that's not comfortable is like a shoe that is one size too small. It's never a bargain, regardless of price. A tool that feels good in your hands will most likely be easy and safe to use. So, whenever possible, try before you buy. Visit home centers

and tool dealers that have good selections of tools. Grip the tool to test its balance and feel. If you have small hands, rule out tools that aren't easy to hold comfortably. Try the controls and adjustments, too. Use this hands-on information to make your selections.

Get advice from the pros

Talk to carpenters, who use tools daily, and ask them for their preferences. Research magazines, such as *Fine Homebuilding* and the *Journal of Light Construction*, which evaluate tools. And always buy the best quality you can afford. Most of us know the experience of wishing we had bought quality rather than a piece of junk. Professional tools cost more initially, but they are more durable, more powerful, and easier and safer to use. Ironically, they make it easier to be a beginner.

Buy tools as you need them

If you're intending to work professionally as a carpenter, you'll eventually acquire quite a large collection of tools. If, however, you're only planning to build one house or work with Habitat as a weekend volunteer, a small kit of essential tools should stand you in good stead. In addition to the basics described on the following pages, you can acquire more specialized tools as you need them, which is the best way to do it anyway. Otherwise, you may wind up with unnecessary tools that clutter your tool belt, your storage bucket, and your life. You can also rent specialized tools if you plan to use them just a few times.

Essential Hand Tools

The fundamental tasks of carpentry are measuring, marking, cutting, and joining. And though circular saws and power drill-drivers have largely replaced handsaws, braces, and screwdrivers, many carpentry tasks can still be done with hand tools (see the photo above). Like power tools, many hand tools have improved over the years.

READING A TAPE MEASURE

A measuring tape is simply a long ruler in a convenient, easy-to-use package. Just like a ruler, a tape is laid out in feet, inches, and fractions of inches. Knowing how to read a tape quickly and accurately is an essential skill for anyone involved in the building trades.

The key to being able to read a tape is learning and understanding all the subdivisions of an inch (see the illustration at right). Each inch is divided into halves, quarters, eighths, and sixteenths. Once you can discern the meaning of all these little marks, you'll have no problem measuring 13 ft., 9³⁄₁₆ in., or any other odd dimension. Study the drawing and your own tape until you can rattle off accurate readings at a glance.

In addition to feet and inches, a tape also has special marks at 16 in., 32 in., and so on to indicate the layout of most floor joists and wall studs. Some tapes also have decimal equivalents and a metric conversion scale on the back.

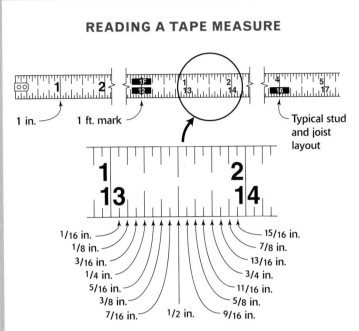

READING A TAPE MEASURE

1 in. — 1 ft. mark — Typical stud and joist layout

1/16 in. — 1/8 in. — 3/16 in. — 1/4 in. — 5/16 in. — 3/8 in. — 7/16 in. — 1/2 in. — 9/16 in. — 5/8 in. — 11/16 in. — 3/4 in. — 13/16 in. — 7/8 in. — 15/16 in.

It's important to know at a glance what the different marks on a tape measure mean. Practice using a tape so your measurements will be accurate.

Tape measures

Just as I sometimes enjoy writing letters on my old manual typewriter, it's also fun to measure with my old 6-ft. wooden folding rule. Flexible steel tapes have replaced old-fashioned wooden rules, because they're more compact and capable of measuring much longer distances quickly and accurately. Steel tapes come in many sizes and lengths, but the most common are 16-ft., 25-ft., and 30-ft. models. I prefer a 16-ft. tape, because it feels better in my hand. A 100-ft. tape is useful for checking building lines and squaring foundations. Tape measures have moving parts and receive heavy use, so use the following tips to treat them with special care:

Measuring and marking. A steel tape measure is one of the most-used tools in a carpenter's kit.

TIP Check a level for level. To check a level's accuracy, place it edge to edge against another level and against a flat surface that's close to level. If the level vials on both tools read the same, you can assume both levels are accurate. Test the vials that read for plumb in the same way.

- Don't leave a tape extended open on the floor, where it could be stepped on and creased. A creased tape will never work properly.
- If a tape is allowed to retract too quickly, the hook can break off when it hits the case. Learn to slow the tape with your fingers as the hook approaches the case.
- Clean any tape that gets gummed with wood pitch, tar, or caulk. A soft rag dampened with mineral spirits works well to remove those materials.
- When working in wet weather, wipe the tape dry with a cloth before reeling it into the case. Moisture inside the tape case can cause rust and friction, which can shorten the tape's life span.

Pocket calculators

Building a house involves math problems galore. Whether figuring out the amount of concrete needed for a driveway, the square footage of floor space in a house, the number of studs for a wall, or the amount of shingles needed for the roof, these are not numbers you want to leave to

Horizontal and vertical. Available in different lengths, levels can quickly test for plumb (vertical) and level (horizontal). [Photo by HFHI/David Spielman]

chance. Math challenged or not, I recommend using a small hand-held calculator. There are several on the market, and they work in feet, inches, and fractions (see Resources on p. 279).

Levels

Checking for level (horizontal) and plumb (vertical) are construction tasks that carpenters do every day. Both 2-ft. and 4-ft. levels are good to have around. The 2-ft. model allows you to get into tighter spaces—to check a header or rough sill for level, for example. A 4-ft. or 6-ft. model provides greater accuracy across longer distances, such as when checking walls for plumb. More so than perhaps any other carpentry tool, a level must be treated with loving care to remain useful (an inaccurate level does you no favors). Check your levels for accuracy before you put them to work (see the tip at top left).

New calculators that work in feet and inches make it easy to solve many construction problems. [Photo by Don Charles Blom]

Small laser units are available to help you build straight, square, and plumb. [Photo by Don Charles Blom]

Lasers

Everyone wants a house that is built straight, plumb, and square. This may be why lasers are now almost as common as hammers on the job site. Small, self-leveling laser units cast a beam of light that can help ensure accurate measurements. Some of these laser units are small enough to fit in the palm of your hand (see Resources on p. 279).

Squares

Most things a carpenter builds are either square or rectangular. With a good square or two, you can mark square lines exactly and make square cuts precisely. These days, the most useful square is a small rafter square, often called a Speed® square—the brand name of a popular model (see the photo at left). This triangular square fits conveniently inside a nail bag. It's rugged and easy to use and lets you lay out almost any desired angle, in addition to the usual 45-degree and 90-degree angles.

Get the right angle. A small, triangular rafter square is designed to lay out 90-degree and 45-degree angles quickly, but it's also capable of laying out just about any angle you might need.

Snap a line. Loaded with powdered chalk, a chalkline stretched tightly between two points is snapped to make straight lines quickly and accurately.

Marking tools

Once you've measured, it's time to mark. A carpenter's pencil and a lumber crayon, or keel, are the two most common marking tools you'll need. A carpenter's pencil is flat (so it won't roll away if you set it down), and it's less apt to break than a regular pencil. A keel marks easily where pencils can't—on materials such as tarpaper, housewrap, and concrete. It's waterproof, too.

A chalkline is also essential. The first chalkline I used was simply a string pulled through a solid chunk of chalk. Today's chalklines come in cases or reels that hold both

USING A HAMMER

Just like hitting a solid line drive or delivering a blazing tennis serve, driving nails quickly and accurately takes time and practice to master. Like most athletic endeavors, efficient nailing has at least as much to do with rhythm and coordination as it does with power and force. Learn to nail using your entire body; make a fluid shoulder, elbow, and forearm movement that ends with a decisive snap of the wrist (see the illustration at right). Practice your technique. Grasp the handle near the end with an easy, firm grip, making sure your thumb is wrapped around it. Buy a box of 8d or 16d framing nails, find a hunk of wood, and start driving nails. In time, you'll be amazed at the speed and force with which you can drive nails.

When pulling nails with a wooden-handled hammer, hook the nail and push the hammer to one side and then the other, rather than straight back (see the photo at left). Otherwise, you could break the handle right at the hammer's head. To pull nails with a metal-handled hammer, you can lever the hammer sideways or backward. To increase your leverage, put a block under the head of the hammer.

NAILING WITH A HAMMER

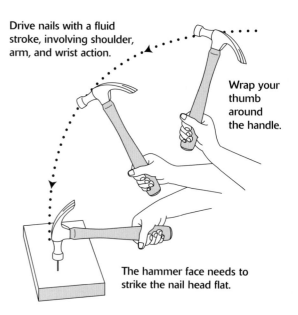

Drive nails with a fluid stroke, involving shoulder, arm, and wrist action.

Wrap your thumb around the handle.

The hammer face needs to strike the nail head flat.

Driving nails is sort of like swinging a tennis racket. Your grip on the handle should be secure but relaxed, and the swing should involve your entire arm and wrist.

Hammers have different heads and handles. A corrugated face on the head (far left hammer) is the best choice for framing, because it tends to slip less on nail heads. For finish work, you'll need a smaller hammer with a smooth face.

a string and a supply of powdered chalk. You pull the chalk-covered string out of the case, snap your line, and then rewind the string inside the case, where it becomes covered in chalk again, ready for the next line. The chalk comes in many colors, including a few neon shades. Chalk that leaves a permanent line is good for working in rainy weather.

Hammers

Carpenters can be a bit touchy about their hammers. You may have more luck borrowing a carpenter's pickup truck than a favorite hammer. These days, most framers west of the Mississippi prefer a 21-oz. hammer with a serrated face and a 16-in.- or 18-in.-long wooden handle. My preference is the well-balanced Dalluge® hammer. Women friends in the trade tell me they like the Stiletto®, a 14-oz. framing hammer made of titanium with a steel face. East of the Mississippi, I see carpenters mostly using smooth-faced hammers with metal or fiberglass handles.

Hammer faces and weights vary greatly (see the photo above). The best advice I can give is to select a professional-grade hammer that feels

good to you. Definitely check out a hammer in person before you buy it. It should match your physical strength, feel well balanced, and be comfortable in your hand. When I bring a new hammer home, I usually reinforce the upper part of the wooden handle by wrapping it with electrical tape.

Utility knives and tinsnips

A few more essential tools round out a carpenter's basic, must-have kit. Perhaps foremost on this list is a utility knife. On the job site, a utility knife may be used to open packages or cut building paper, fiberglass insulation, shingles, vinyl, or drywall. You'll also need it several times a day to sharpen a carpenter's pencil. I recommend using a knife with a retractable, replaceable blade and a handle with space inside to hold several replacement blades. When a blade becomes dull, replace it or restore its edge with a whetstone. A dull blade doesn't cut as neatly and is dangerous because of the extra force required to make it cut.

You'll need a good pair of tinsnips to cut steel packaging bands around lumber. Snips are

TIP Shrink-wrap strengthens a wooden handle. Available from electrical suppliers, plastic shrink-wrap can add strength to a wooden hammer handle right where it counts—where the handle meets the head. Slip a 6-in.-long piece of the plastic wrap onto the handle, then shrink it in place with a hair dryer.

Stay sharp. A good, sharp utility knife has many uses on a construction site, from sharpening a pencil to trimming shingles to opening packing material.

A flat bar has many uses. Here, a volunteer uses a flat bar to help slip a piece of aluminum cladding under the roof's drip edge.

also essential when working with aluminum cladding and vinyl siding. Be careful when using these cutting tools. Accidents with utility knives are common.

Cat's paws and flat bars

These prying tools really come in handy during new construction and remodeling work. Your hammer's claw will generally work fine for removing exposed nails. When a nail is buried, though, a cat's paw is the tool to use. With a couple of hammer blows, you can sink the cat's paw into a board, grab the head of a nail, and lever it above the surface. From there, your hammer takes over to completely remove the nail.

A flat bar can also be used to pull nails, or it can be used as a prybar. In new construction, I often use a flat bar to separate boards that have been temporarily nailed together and to slip aluminum or vinyl trim under a drip edge (see the photo at right).

Create a tote for tools. Fitted with a pouch-covered canvas or nylon insert, a 5-gal. plastic bucket replaces an old-fashioned carpenter's toolbox.

Tool Carriers

Once you have a few tools, you'll need to carry them with you as you frame walls and install siding or shingles. It doesn't work well to carry a measuring tape in your jeans and to fish nails from a shirt pocket. Fifty years ago, when I started working as a carpenter, we wore white carpenter's overalls with a lot of little pockets for nails and tools. Those soon gave way to cloth aprons, which were replaced by heavy leather aprons with a wide leather belt. Today, nylon pouches seem to be taking over, and for good reason: The best versions are lighter than leather and just as durable. As with tools, the selection of tool belts, pouches, and holders can be confusing. There are good belt and pouch systems for both men and women. Inexpensive versions are available for novice and occasional builders. If you're serious about construction work, consider some of the tool belt systems that allow you to add pouches and holders as you need them.

For larger items or for tools that are used only occasionally, the traditional carpenter's toolbox has given way to the carpenter's tool bucket (see the photo at left). This is just a 5-gal. bucket fitted with a bag insert that allows

WORKING SAFELY ON A CONSTRUCTION SITE

Working on a construction site is not a sunny stroll in the park. There are all kinds of unusual, uncomfortable, and potentially hazardous conditions you may encounter—uneven ground, troublesome weather, boards with protruding nails, and sloped roof surfaces that challenge your balance. Learning how to work safely and effectively in a construction environment is just one more skill that you need to acquire, such as hammering a nail or sawing a board. Here are some basic suggestions to keep you safe and productive:

- Wear good shoes, clothes that fit well, long-sleeved shirts, long pants, a hat with a brim, and sunscreen. (see Resources on p. 279). Leave jewelry at home, and bunch up long hair, so it doesn't get caught in a power tool.
- Protect your eyes with safety glasses or goggles when sawing or nailing.
- Protect your ears. Hearing damage is cumulative and permanent; once you've damaged your ears, you can't undo it. I keep a few sponge earplugs in a 35mm film canister stored in my tool bucket.
- Protect your lungs with a dust mask.
- To prevent back injuries, remember to lift with your legs, not your back. If you'll be working on your knees, wear kneepads.
- To reduce the risk of tripping or stepping on a nail, keep your work area clean.
- If you see any nails sticking out of boards, either bend the nails or remove them.
- Never throw anything off a roof without looking to see whether anyone is below.
- Don't drink (or do drugs) while doing construction work.
- No one under 18 years of age should be permitted on a construction site with hazardous materials.
- No one under 16 years of age should ever be permitted on a construction site.
- Work with a clear head and pay attention to what

you and others around you are doing. Be especially careful toward the end of the day, when you are physically tired.

- Pay attention to your inner voice. If you feel that something might be dangerous, ask for help or figure out a better way to do it.
- Don't forget to rest and drink plenty of water. Your body can become dehydrated rapidly on a hot, dry day. If you aren't visiting the Porta Potti® regularly, you aren't drinking enough water.
- Keep your tools sharp and clean, take care of them, and treat them well.
- Take a course in basic first aid.

SAVING YOUR BACK WHEN LIFTING A LOAD

Start off squatting, with your back straight and your knees bent, then grasp the load.

Begin to lift, keeping your back straight, and gradually straighten your legs.

Finish with both your back and your knees straight, but don't lock your knees.

One of the reasons so many carpenters have lower back pain is that they never learned to lift heavy loads properly.

TIP Keep portable power tools accessible. Instead of storing your circular saw on the ground or subfloor, fasten a stick to a stud or sawhorse to keep the tool handy. That way, you won't have to bend over every time you need to make a cut.

you to carry many individual tools. For organizing specialized tools (collections of drill bits, chisels, or screwdrivers, for example), inexpensive storage boxes in many sizes are available from supply stores. Label the boxes so you know what's inside.

Power Tools

Although power tools can't replace hand tools, they sure do make construction work easier and more efficient. It can be a real timesaver to not have to drag a cord behind you and yet have a tool with enough power to do a professional job. Nowadays there are numerous cordless tools powered by lithium-ion batteries that would be an asset when constructing a house. These include screwdrivers, reciprocating saws, and even circular saws. For years such tools were designed primarily for homeowner use, but today they are used on almost every jobsite. I wouldn't want to be without them.

Circular saws

The circular saw has been around since the 1920s, but it didn't really catch on until the housing boom began after World War II.

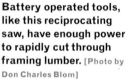

Battery operated tools, like this reciprocating saw, have enough power to rapidly cut through framing lumber. [Photo by Don Charles Blom]

Direct-drive saw. Sometimes referred to as a side-winder saw, a direct-drive saw is a type of circular saw. Its motor is on the side, in line with the blade. [Photo by HFHI/Will Crocker]

Worm-drive saw. Larger and heavier than a side-winder saw, a worm-drive saw has its motor to the rear of the blade.

These days, many homeowners have one in the garage. For a builder, this portable power tool is indispensable. The most popular circular saws are designed to hold 7¼-in.-dia. blades. In the eastern part of the United States, most carpenters prefer direct-drive saws, often referred to as sidewinders (see the top photo on the facing page). In the West, carpenters mainly use the heavier worm-drive models (see the bottom right photo on the facing page). Check out both to see which one you prefer. Above all, buy quality. Light, low-priced homeowner models aren't in the same league with professional models.

Here are some tips for using your saw safely and accurately. Some of them apply to other power tools as well. As with any power tool, be sure to study and follow the instructions in the manual.

- Make sure the blade guard works freely before using the tool.
- Use the right blade for the job, and replace a dull blade with a new one. Carbide-tipped blades are best for most wood-cutting work.
- To reduce friction when cutting, apply paste wax to both sides of the blade, or spray it with silicone.
- Adjust the saw's cutting depth according to the thickness of the material. If you are cutting ½-in.-thick material, set the cutting depth at no more than ¾ in. (see the top photo on p. 36). The less amount of blade that's exposed, the less potential for injury should something go wrong.
- Always unplug your saw when changing blades and adjusting the cutting depth or angle.
- Make sure the stock is adequately supported. With proper support, the cut won't bind on the blade, and the cut-off end will fall free.
- To begin a cut, place the saw base on the stock with the blade about 1 in. from the edge of the wood, aligned with the cut line. Hold the saw with both hands, pull the switch, and slowly push the blade into the wood, following the cut line. Go slowly, guiding the saw, and let it do the work. Eventually, you will

MAKING A PLUNGE CUT

Sometimes it's necessary to cut a hole in the middle of a board or a panel. You can do this with your circular saw if you know how to make a plunge cut. (Don't attempt this unless you're an experienced circular-saw user.) Start by leaning the saw forward over the cut line. Rest the front edge of the saw base on the wood, and hold the blade about 1 in. from the surface. Use the lever on the blade guard to lift the guard and expose the blade. Make sure that the blade is aligned over the cut line. Start the saw and use the front edge of the base as the pivot point. Lower the blade into the wood, using both hands to control the saw and complete the cut. When you are finished, turn off the saw and let the blade stop spinning before pulling it out. Another way to make a plunge cut is to loosen the lever that controls the cutting depth and raise the blade completely above the board. Set the saw base in position over the cut line, loosen the depth adjustment lock, and slowly lower the blade into the material.

learn to cut with one hand on the saw and the other hand on the material.
- Don't try to hold a short or small piece with one hand while guiding the saw with the other. Instead, use a clamp to secure the workpiece while you make the cut.

AVOIDING KICKBACK

When the blade of a circular saw gets pinched by the wood, the power of the motor can force the saw backward—a safety hazard called kickback. In extreme cases, the saw can jump away from the material with the blade still spinning, harming anything in its path. To prevent kickback when using a circular saw, follow these guidelines:

- Use a sharp, carbide-tipped blade.
- Cut in a straight line.
- Let the saw do the cutting—don't force it. Forcing the cut can cause the blade to bind and kick back.
- Always provide proper support for the stock. Avoid setups that allow the material being cut to pinch the blade (see the illustration below).
- If a kickback does occur, release the saw trigger immediately and let the blade stop. As long as the blade guard is working properly, there is little danger of injury. Don't resume cutting until the cause of the kickback is determined and corrected.

Adjust the cutting depth. Always set the cutting depth so that the saw just barely cuts through the material. [Photo © Tony Mason]

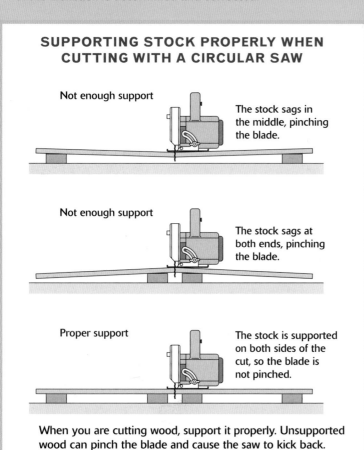

SUPPORTING STOCK PROPERLY WHEN CUTTING WITH A CIRCULAR SAW

Not enough support

The stock sags in the middle, pinching the blade.

Not enough support

The stock sags at both ends, pinching the blade.

Proper support

The stock is supported on both sides of the cut, so the blade is not pinched.

When you are cutting wood, support it properly. Unsupported wood can pinch the blade and cause the saw to kick back.

A reciprocating saw gets into tight places. This saw moves its blade back and forth, as if you were cutting with a handsaw. It's useful for cutting in tight places. Here, a worker removes the bottom plate from a doorway opening.

Reciprocating saws

Another frequently used tool is the reciprocating saw, also called a sabersaw or a Sawzall®—the name given to Milwaukee's® popular saw (see the bottom photo on the facing page). This tool allows you to cut in tight places and make curved cuts. Different blades are available for cutting through wood, metal, plaster, and plastic. For general use, I buy 6-in. bimetal blades, which cut through both wood and metal.

Chopsaws

The power-miter saw (generally referred to as a chopsaw) has revolutionized finish carpentry just as the circular saw revolutionized rough-framing carpentry. With a chopsaw, you can make precise square and angled cuts in framing lumber, door and window casings, and base-board trim. These saws are rugged and easy to use. When equipped with a fine blade, they can make glass-smooth cuts.

Sliding compound miter saw

This tool, the sliding compound miter saw, is a trim worker's dream. It is essentially a chop saw that can cut angles across wide boards. I use it not only to cut baseboards and door casings, but also to cut across wide boards used in closets, blocks, headers, and cripples used in a house frame (see Resources on p. 279).

Lightweight tablesaw

It wasn't long ago that tablesaws were cumbersome, heavy, and anything but portable. But times have changed. Now an on-site tablesaw can be moved easily by just one or two workers. But don't be fooled by the lightweight label. These saws are well built, accurate, and with reasonable care will last for years (see Resources on p. 279).

Drills

An electric drill is a versatile tool on any job site. It's capable of boring holes in all sorts of material and can also be used for driving screws and mixing paint or drywall compound. Most

Use a chopsaw for speed and accuracy. With a chopsaw, it's easy to make precise cuts at different preset angles. This type of saw must be set on a good worktable, with outboard supports for longer boards. [Photo by HFHI/Steffan Hacker]

The sliding compound miter saw makes short work of anything from 4× header stock to a small piece of door trim. [Photo by Don Charles Blom]

TIP A hook can be helpful. Some new saws come with a built-in hook that allows you to hang the saw over a joist or a rafter when you're working up high. A Skyhook accessory is also available to retrofit on saws that lack this convenient feature (see Resources on p. 279).

USING DRILLS

Old drills were made with enclosed trigger guards like those on firearms. Carpenters had their trigger fingers caught and broken from time to time, such as when a drill bit got hung up on a knot in a board and spun suddenly. For safety reasons, workers often used a hacksaw to cut out the trigger guards. These days, manufacturers have eliminated trigger guards, but that doesn't mean drills can't do you harm. To use a drill safely, follow these guidelines:

- Use clean, sharp bits.
- Don't force the drill; let it cut at its own pace.
- Use a slower speed when drilling harder materials, and coat the bit with wax or silicone to reduce resistance.
- When drilling thick material, hold the drill with both hands, and use the side handle if the drill comes with one.
- If you're drilling a deep hole, pull the bit out of the hole from time to time to clear debris from the bit and the hole.
- Don't rely on hand pressure alone to hold the workpiece in which you're drilling. Instead, clamp the workpiece to a sawhorse or a workbench.
- Be especially careful when drilling from a ladder. Make sure you have proper balance.
- Release the trigger immediately if the bit begins to bind or catch.

New, lightweight tablesaws can be brought to the job site with ease. [Photo by Don Charles Blom]

carpenters have at least two drills on a job site. A corded drill is best for mixing paint and drywall compound and boring holes in concrete, framing lumber, and metal.

There are numerous tools out there that can be used to drive screws or drill holes. One of the newer models on the market allows you to drive multiple screws in decking material with no fuss. A cordless impact-driver is another tool that makes driving screws "a walk in the park." It can set screws with a circular motion or, like a jackhammer, an up-and-down motion that "drives" screws into hard wood or other material.

When you have multiple screws to drive into decking material, try one of these stand-up screw guns.
[Photo by Don Charles Blom]

Whether corded or cordless, a drill is usually described by the maximum capacity of its chuck (bit holder). A ⅜-in. model can handle a bit shank diameter of up to ⅜ in. For general carpentry work, buy either a ⅜-in. or a ½-in. drill. Look for a model with a reverse switch (so you can remove screws) and variable speed control. A good cordless drill will also have a clutch, which makes it easier to drive screws of different sizes. A low clutch setting (1 to 3) is good for driving small screws. Higher settings are used for bigger screws.

Air compressors

For almost sixty years I have been using an air compressor to power the various pneumatic tools used on a job site. The early models took a team of mules to haul around, but many of the compressors we have today can be carried with one arm or have been put on wheels to make maneuvering easier. With the proliferation of air-driven tools, a good air compressor, along with an air hose or two, is a valuable asset. Just make sure workers are given basic safety training and guidelines to avoid injury (see Resources on p. 279).

Accessories for workers

When it comes to tools, work clothes, or tool kits, one size fits all is a thing of the past. These days there are numerous companies (see Resources on p. 279) that offer a good line of work accessories that are tailored for both men and women.

Extension cords

Power tools need adequate power to operate properly, and that means you need good-quality extension cords. The smaller the gauge number marked on the cord, the heavier the wire. The three most common gauges are 12, 14, and 16 (12 is the heaviest). From time to time, I've seen carpenters run a circular saw with a 100-ft. 16-gauge extension cord. That's like watering a lawn with a hose the diameter of a drinking straw. Not much water (or, in the case of an extension cord, electricity) comes through. With

Many of today's tools are powered by compressed air. Lightweight compressors are easy to move around a job site. [Photo by Don Charles Blom]

a light extension cord, you risk burning out the motor. To prevent that, always use the shortest cord that will do the job. There's no need to use a 50-ft. cord if you are working just 15 ft. from an outlet. Here's a rule you can use for selecting the proper extension cord: Use 16-gauge wire for a 25-ft. (or shorter) cord, 14-gauge wire for a 50-ft. cord, and 12-gauge wire for a 100-ft. cord.

TIP Cord awareness is important. When using a portable power tool, make sure there's enough slack in the power and extension cords so that you can maneuver the tool freely. It's also good to know exactly where the cord is, so you won't cut into it while you're using the tool.

Tool kits, nail bags, and pockets for buckets are available to help keep tools handy and in order. [Photo by Don Charles Blom]

Current issues. Extension cords for builders are designed for outdoor use, with properly sized wires. One good way to store a long cord is to loop it together in a daisy chain.

Proper care of cords is essential. Looping a cord into a daisy chain, or a simple crochet stitch, makes for easy storage (see the photo at left). If a cord is frayed or nicked, repair it. A cord with exposed wires can be extremely dangerous. If that happens, the cord should be cut and rewired with new plugs. You can buy a cord equipped with a built-in ground-fault circuit interrupter (GFCI). In the event of a short, the GFCI automatically shuts off power, preventing electrical shock.

TIP Nominal versus actual size. When you shop for lumber, remember the difference between nominal and actual measurements. If you buy a 2×4, you'll get a 1½-in. by 3½-in. board. If you buy a 2×6, you'll get a 1½-in. by 5½-in. board.

PARTS OF A HOUSE

Wall studs

Top cripples

Double top plate

Top plate

Metal angle brace

Header

King stud

Roof trusses

Metal gusset

Catwalk

Webbing

Floor sheathing

Door trimmer

Barge rafter

Roof sheathing

Rim joist

Fascia

Sill

Screened vents

Bottom plate

Wall sheathing

Block

Sway brace helps hold trusses plumb.

Girder

Foundation wall

Post

Block

Footing

Top cripples

Pier block

Pier

Header

Footing

Bottom cripples

Floor joist

Rough sill

Footing

Lookouts support barge rafter.

Study this drawing. It includes the name of most every part used in a wood-frame house.

The Parts of a House

When you decide to build a house, there's a whole new vocabulary you have to master. Every part of a house has a name and, as with most endeavors, learning the lingo will take you a long way toward getting the job done. There are plenty of terms that intuitively make sense, such as header, footing, cladding, brace, and sheathing. In other cases, you'll find that some parts have several names. The illustration on the facing page, combined with the definitions on the following pages, will give you a good basic working vocabulary that we'll build on in later chapters.

Sill or sole plates

These are generally pressure-treated (PT) 2×4s or 2×6s that are bolted to the concrete foundation and support the floor joists. However, in areas where earthquakes or high winds occur, new codes can require these plates to be made of heavier stock than a 2×6 to prevent the sill plates from being ripped off the foundation. Check with your building department before putting down sills to be sure.

Construction basics. Joists are the framing members that lie across a foundation and support the subfloor.

PRESSURE-TREATED LUMBER

In areas where the termites are especially hungry (Hawaii and some southern states), entire house frames can be built of pressure-treated wood. Pressure-treatment technology was developed to repel termites and inhibit rot, and it does so effectively. During the treatment process, a preservative compound is forced under pressure into raw lumber, penetrating deeply into each board.

For many years the main ingredient used in treated wood was arsenic. A dangerous poison, arsenic was effective in repelling termites but also harmed the workers who manufactured and used these construction materials. The EPA eventually banned the use of arsenic in PT wood, and suppliers replaced the arsenic with copper and other less harmful chemicals. Copper is what gives PT lumber its distinctive green or brown color. Because copper is quite corrosive, nails and metal fasteners had to be redesigned. It's best to used hot-dipped galvanized nails (rather than regular steel nails) when working with pressure-treated wood. Always check with your supplier to make sure you use nails and metal fasteners that won't corrode easily.

To avoid injury when handling and cutting PT lumber, it's important to follow these safety precautions:

- Use gloves when working with PT wood.
- If you handle PT wood with bare hands, wash your hands before eating.
- Don't burn scrap PT lumber in your woodstove or anywhere else.
- When cutting more than a few PT boards, wear a dust mask.

Posts, girders, and beams

Posts are vertical supports for horizontal pieces, which are called girders or beams. These major horizontal members support floor joists. Posts that sit on concrete piers are often made of PT wood.

Joists

Typically spaced 16 in. or 24 in. o.c., joists are installed parallel to each other and support the subfloor and rough plumbing. They span the entire house, running from one outside sill, across any interior girders, to the other

Plates and studs are nailed together and raised upright to form a wall.

Materials matter. Builder's felt, sometimes called tar paper, is rolled over the roof sheathing before asphalt shingles are installed.

outside sill. Most often they are made from 2×-dimension lumber (such as 2×8s, 2×10s, or 2×12s) or from manufactured, wooden I-beam joists.

Floor sheathing

Floors are usually sheathed with ⅝-in.- or ¾-in.-thick, 4-ft. by 8-ft. sheets of tongue-and-groove plywood or oriented strand board (OSB). Better sheets have their edges treated with paint to inhibit moisture absorption in wet weather.

Wall plates

These are the 2×4 or 2×6 horizontal members that hold together the parts of a wall. Each wall has three plates—one on the bottom and two on the top. The two uppermost plates are called the top plate and the double top (or cap) plate. When framing on a concrete slab, the bottom plate is made of PT wood.

Studs

Studs are the vertical wall members nailed to the plates, and they are typically spaced either 16 in. or 24 in. o.c. The standard, precut stud length in many parts of the country is 92¼ in. That stud, along with three 1½-in.-thick wall plates (one on the bottom and two at the top), creates a framed wall that is 96¾ in. high. That leaves room for ½-in. or ⅜-in. drywall on the ceiling and full 8-ft. sheets on the walls. In addition to solid 2× lumber, you may also encounter finger-jointed studs, which are manufactured from shorter pieces of wood glued end to end. Some houses are being built with metal studs.

Headers, trimmers, and cripples

The weight from above a window or door opening is transferred around the hole by a header nailed horizontally between studs. Trimmers nailed to the studs at both ends of the header support the header. Cripples, or jack studs, extend from the top of a header to the top plate, as well as from the bottom plate to the underside of rough windowsills.

Roof trusses

Each of these factory-made assemblies typically consists of a bottom chord (or joist chord), a top chord (rafter or rafter chord), and interior webbing. Trusses are often engineered to carry the entire weight of a roof's load, transferring it to the exterior walls. That load can be considerable in snowy parts of the country. Trusses allow roof construction to be done quickly and easily. Most trusses for residential construction are spaced 24 in. o.c.

Fascia and gutter boards

These terms are often used interchangeably, but a gutter board is technically distinct from a fascia board. Both parts are installed over the ends of the rafter tails. A gutter board is nailed directly to the rafter tails, and it is covered by aluminum or vinyl cladding or by a fascia board that serves as the finished exterior's trim surface. For more details, see Chapter 6.

Roof and wall sheathing

Roofs and walls are usually sheathed with ½-in.- or ⅝-in.-thick OSB. In some parts of the country, exterior walls, along with their gable trusses, are sheathed before they are raised upright. In earthquake and high wind areas, you are often required to sheathe some interior walls to help withstand lateral forces that can tear buildings apart. Take a look at the damage caused by Hurricane Katrina in the Gulf states and you begin to get the picture.

Housewrap and felt paper

Housewrap or felt paper is placed under siding

and shingles to prevent wind and water from entering stud cavities or the attic. You can also use a rain screen behind siding to help prevent moisture from getting trapped in these areas, which can cause mold.

Sealants

Construction adhesives, caulk, and other sealants are ever present on job sites. Most of those products come in cylindrical cartridges that fit inside a caulking gun, which is used to apply the caulk or sealant. Construction adhesives can be used to bond different materials together—floor sheathing to floor joists, for example. To prevent water leakage, caulks are used to seal around windows and doorframes, at siding joints, and where a bathtub meets the floor. They can be used under wall plates and around pipe holes to block out cold air. Gaps between baseboards and walls or door casings can be filled with caulk before painting. Be sure to buy the right type of caulk. Don't use a basic latex painter's caulk around exterior doors and windows, for example. Silicone caulks offer much better protection in these areas.

Make sure that every window and door has proper flashing and caulking before setting them in place.
[Photo by Don Charles Blom]

In earthquake and high wind areas, it's important to tie different parts of a building together. [Photo by Don Charles Blom]

Nails

The most commonly used framing nails are 8d (the "d" stands for "penny") and 16d sinkers, or vinyl-coated nails. The vinyl coating makes the nails drive easier and hold better, but don't hold them in your mouth. In damp locales, on sites near the ocean, or when using PT wood, use hot-dipped galvanized or stainless-steel nails.

Screws

Drywall screws are the most universally used screws in house construction. But thanks to the popularity of cordless drill-drivers, all kinds of screws are now being used to build houses. Corrosion-resistant screws are available for deck construction and other outdoor applications. Other types of screws are used to install cabinets, built-ins, and hardware. Screws are typically described by head type (main types include flat, round, pan, and hex); length (given in inches); gauge, or shank, diameter (usually between 4 and 10); and typical use (drywall, wood, sheet metal, and so on). Although popular for general-purpose use, drywall screws aren't strong enough to support heavy loads, such as wall cabinets.

Other fasteners

Toggle bolts, molly bolts, hollow-wall anchors, and other fasteners are used to help secure items, such as wire shelving to drywall panels. When fastening materials to a masonry surface

ON THE JOB

DEALING WITH SUPPLIERS AND SCHEDULING DELIVERIES

Estimating lumber and materials for a small, affordable house is fairly simple, but it does take some experience to get it right. If you are building a Habitat house, you can call or e-mail affiliates and ask them to share their lists with you (check the Habitat website for the affiliate in your area). You can also take a set of plans to a local supplier. Most building-supply outlets will create a materials list and give you a bid on what everything will cost. Always get bids from more than one supplier. Just make sure every supplier understands the type and grade of each item.

If you don't make your own list, take the opportunity to inspect the plans closely. Get acquainted with the house and all its parts before you start. Remember that a lumber list is only an estimate of materials that will be needed for a particular job. You may need to order a few more items as you build, or

you may need to send some materials back to the supplier. Find out ahead of time whether your suppliers charge a restocking fee for returned materials.

Most builders have materials delivered as needed, rather than all at once. You should do the same. That way, you won't have to worry as much about storage problems. Also, ask your supplier to stack the lumber load in the order in which it will be used.

Some materials (especially trim, doors, and unpainted siding) should be stored indoors. When storing material outside, set it on blocks above the ground and cover it with plastic to keep it dry. Be specific about where you want the lumber company to drop the wood, and pick a level, accessible location close to where it will be used. Hauling lumber by hand from any distance is hard, time-consuming work.

or adding bolts through a sill into the foundation, threaded replacement bolts or epoxy works well (see Resources on p. 279).

Special hardware

If you live in earthquake or hurricane country, you will be using lots of metal hardware to help hold your house together. Earthquakes can be catastrophic events. Properly installed straps, braces, and hold-downs can mean the difference between life and death. To hold the sill plates in place atop foundation walls, anchor bolts are usually embedded in the foundation during its construction. The threaded ends of those bolts extend through the sill plates and are held fast with washers and nuts. Metal angle braces (10 ft. to 12 ft. long) are used as permanent braces to help hold walls plumb. Metal hangers are used to support joists around openings, such as stairways. Metal straps are sometimes needed to attach the house frame to the sill and the foundation or to tie plates together. Code may also require that hold-down hardware, such as metal angles, be fastened to framing members and the foundation.

These hold-downs are attached to long bolts embedded in the concrete. They tie into the house frame and help keep a building on the foundation where it belongs. [Photo by Don Charles Blom]

AN OPPORTUNITY FOR A NEW START

Salvador and Sara Arevalo almost decided not to participate in the Jimmy Carter Work Project when it came to Los Angeles, CA, in 2007.

"We had another engagement," Salvador said, laughing. "But the affiliate urged us to attend."

During the event, the Arevalos (along with 29 other families) were given the opportunity to build a home for themselves in just a matter of days. It was a family wish fulfilled.

Before their involvement with Habitat, the Arevalos never believed they would own a home in Los Angeles. The high cost of housing in the city left them with few options. Until recently they

Photo courtesy HFHI

occupied a one-bedroom fourplex, in urgent need of repair, with their three teenage daughters. Katy, soon to be a freshman in college, and Lesly, her youngest sister, slept in bunk beds in the dining room. Laria, 14, slept in a converted storage closet that she lovingly decorated.

When the opportunity arrived to work with Habitat, Salvador, who works in building maintenance, was eager to build his family's home. Since the house's completion, Salvador has dedicated himself to customizing and personalizing the residence and making improvements when necessary.

"We are grateful to everyone who has made it possible for us to realize our dream of owning a house," he said.

Sara, who is quiet and reserved, was quick to answer when asked what advice she would give to someone considering a partnership with Habitat—"I would tell them not to miss the opportunity."

—*Heather Myers*

FIRM, FLAT, LEVEL, AND SQUARE

Foundations and Floors

3

Floors may seem to be the simplest of the challenges facing a new builder, but the importance of establishing a firm, sound, dependable connection between a house, the foundation, and the earth cannot be overstated. Everything rests, quite literally, on the quality of the foundation and framing work done in the first few days or so after the concrete contractor has left. Our first house, in coastal Oregon, had a concrete foundation made from beach sand. Sixty years of wind and rain had washed much of that sand back toward the beach, leaving us with a shaky, tilted floor that wasn't even bolted to the foundation.

Know the Foundation Fundamentals

Take a deep breath. Having found and purchased a lot, bought or drawn up the plans, obtained the permits, cleared the land, run power to the site, and completed the necessary grading, drainage, and excavation work, you're finally ready to begin working on the foundation. You've already come a long way.

Whenever I think about foundations, I can't help but recall being told as a child, "You're on your feet most of the day, so wear good shoes." A foundation is like a pair of shoes—quality makes all the difference. Walk around all day in poor shoes and your whole body feels lousy. Build a house on a poor foundation and the entire house is unstable.

There are quite a few foundations that can be used for houses. The three major types—slabs, crawl spaces, and full basements—are discussed in the sidebar on pp. 50–51. Because many houses have a crawl-space foundation, we'll cover the step-by-step process for this type shortly. The main parts of this

Photo by Don Charles Blom

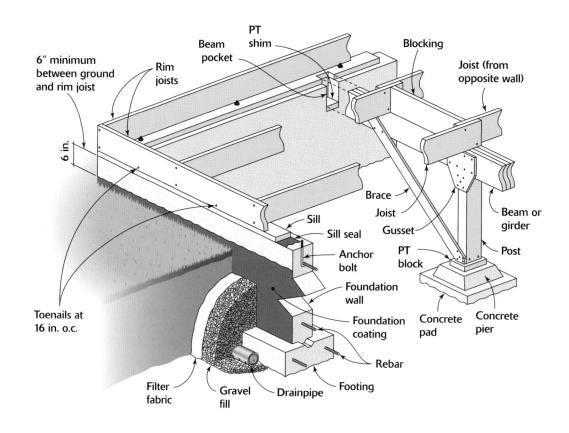

TIP All foundations need proper drainage. In addition to installing drainpipe around the footings, make sure that the finished grade slopes away from the house. If gutters and downspouts are installed, use elbows and splash plates to direct runoff away from foundation walls.

foundation are shown in the illustration above. However, if you're planning to build a house, it's a good idea to consider all your foundation options. Talk to builders and foundation sub-contractors in your area to find out which foundations and special site conditions to consider. If you're building a crawl-space foundation, as we did here, find out about the ventilation requirements. In most areas, vents are required in crawl-space foundations. In some areas, codes have been updated to allow for an unvented crawl space (see the sidebar on the facing page).

Clay can cause problems

Local soil conditions have a lot to do with choosing and constructing a foundation. Extra care must be taken when building on clay-rich soils, which exist in many parts of the country. Clay expands when saturated with moisture.

This can exert tremendous pressure on a foundation. I have seen how this expansive action moves footings, cracks slabs, and causes extensive damage to a house. When builders are aware of the potential problems with clay soil, they can take precautions to avoid damaging effects (see the drainage guidelines discussed in the sidebar on p. 52). I have worked on sites where several feet of clay soil were removed and replaced with nonexpansive soil, which was then compacted before the footings were poured.

Foam forms are worth considering

If you haven't done so already, take a look at the possibilities offered by insulated concrete forms (ICFs). These lightweight foam forms are easy to handle and assemble, and they stay in place to provide wall insulation after the foundation wall is poured (see the sidebar on p. 54). With

VENTING A CRAWL-SPACE FOUNDATION—OR NOT

Until recently, most crawl-space foundations were built with vents to promote air circulation and help prevent damaging levels of moisture from building up beneath the house. In northern states, builders often install vents that can be closed in the winter to keep out cold air. The same is done on the Oregon coast to keep out moist air. Many local building codes require crawl-space ventilation, so be sure to check with your building department to find out which requirements are in effect.

Codes requiring vents usually stipulate that a vent be installed 2 ft. from each corner of the foundation and every 6 ft. on at least three sides of the building. For appearance's sake, most builders try to leave vents off the front of the building.

If you need to install crawl-space vents, there are several ways to do so. Some factory-made vents are designed for installation in openings formed in a poured concrete wall. Others are sized to fit in concrete block walls. For a simple, inexpensive, and attractive vent, cut sections of 3-in.- or 4-in.-dia. plastic pipe and put them in the foundation wall forms before pouring the concrete. Use adhesive to secure pieces of ¼-in. wire mesh (also called hardware cloth) over indoor pipe sections to keep out animals. Still another way to ventilate a crawl space is by cutting openings in the rim joists, as shown in the illustration at right.

Unvented Crawl Spaces

Based on relatively new research, builders in some regions are beginning to eliminate vents and treat crawl spaces like small basements. The idea behind this type of construction is that you start with a dry crawl space and keep it that way. Sealing off a wet crawl space can lead to a moldy disaster, but it is possible to create a warm, dry crawl space by preventing moisture and air from entering. Follow the good drainage guidelines explained in the sidebar on p. 54.

Dirt floors must be sealed with a sheet of 6-mil plastic that laps up onto the foundation and is fastened against it with mastic. Rigid insulation should be used on foundation walls, eliminating the need for insulation in the joist spaces under the floor. With the help of a heating contractor, you can even supply a crawl space with a small heating duct to help keep it dry. You can create access to the crawl space through a trap door framed in the floor of a closet.

CRAWL SPACE VENTILATION

Vent spaces can be built in the foundation wall. If they're not, they can still be cut out of the rim joists.

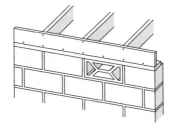

3-in.- or 4-in.-dia. plastic pipe in foundation wall, screen glued to the back

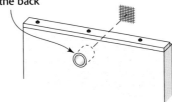

Vents will be screened before subfloor is installed.

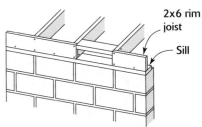

2x6 rim joist

Sill

A 4½-in. by 14½-in. opening is required for standard vents.

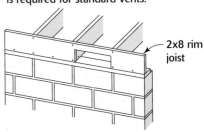

2x8 rim joist

Vents can allow moisture to escape and air to circulate in underfloor areas.

CHOOSING A FOUNDATION

Foundation types vary by region. When deciding which type of foundation to use, consider the cost, climate, and local preferences. The three major foundation types are discussed here.

Concrete Slab

Slab foundations are popular throughout southern sections of the country and in regions where winter temperatures are mild. A concrete slab is more than a foundation; the slab also serves as the rough or finished floor for the first level of the building. This explains why slab foundations are less expensive than other types. Because concrete has poor insulative qualities, slab foundations are often insulated with rigid foam. Plumbing waste lines are typically cast into the slab, so they must be carefully laid out and installed first. Plumbing supply lines can be placed under a slab, and tubes for radiant floor heating can be cast into a slab.

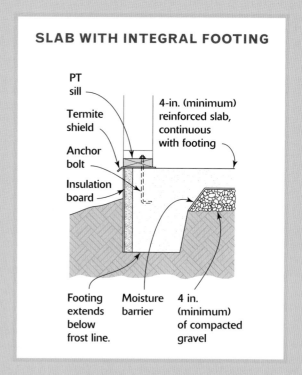

SLAB WITH INTEGRAL FOOTING

PT sill

Termite shield

Anchor bolt

Insulation board

4-in. (minimum) reinforced slab, continuous with footing

Footing extends below frost line.

Moisture barrier

4 in. (minimum) of compacted gravel

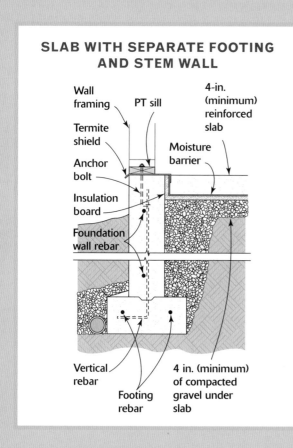

SLAB WITH SEPARATE FOOTING AND STEM WALL

Wall framing

PT sill

4-in. (minimum) reinforced slab

Termite shield

Moisture barrier

Anchor bolt

Insulation board

Foundation wall rebar

Vertical rebar

Footing rebar

4 in. (minimum) of compacted gravel under slab

Types of Slab Foundations

Concrete slabs can be poured inside stem walls that bear on conventional footings. Another construction method is to form and pour the floor and footings together. With this type of slab, the floor is simply thickened at the perimeter of the house (and beneath any load-bearing walls or interior posts) to form the footings. As with other foundations, the footings should extend below the frost line.

Crawl Space

Crawl-space foundations are very compatible with affordable housing. In humid, high-moisture areas (such as the Southeast and Pacific Northwest), this type of foundation raises the living space off the ground, away from wet soil. A house built on floor joists over a crawl space provides a more resilient and more comfortable floor than a slab. It also allows for easy access to plumbing pipes, under-floor insulation, and electrical wiring. If you are planning a crawl-space foundation, decide whether you want the crawl space to be ventilated (see the sidebar on p. 49). You'll also need to decide between poured concrete walls and concrete block.

Basement

Building a house on a full basement provides all the advantages of crawl-space construction with the added benefit of extra room below the main living area. Of course, basement foundations are more expensive than other types, and the living space they provide can be damp and lacking in natural light. To overcome these disadvantages, some basements incorporate window wells—windows located just below grade level—surrounded by a metal or concrete retaining wall on the outside of the foundation. When a basement will be used as a living space, the foundation walls must be waterproofed on the outside, insulated on the outside or on the inside, and finished on the inside. Today, many basement foundations are built with poured concrete walls. Other builders construct basement foundations with concrete block.

CRAWL-SPACE WALL BUILT WITH CONCRETE BLOCKS

Floor joist

Mudsill

Anchor bolt

Backfill

Bond beam with #4 rebar embedded in the top course

18 in. minimum between joists and dirt

Slope the top of footing with mortar to shed water.

Vertical rebar — Footing

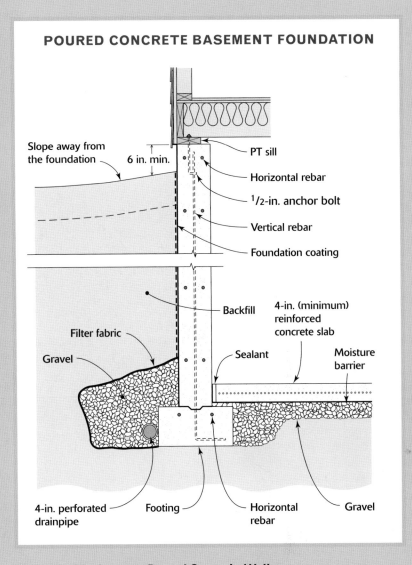

POURED CONCRETE BASEMENT FOUNDATION

Slope away from the foundation

6 in. min.

PT sill

Horizontal rebar

$1/2$-in. anchor bolt

Vertical rebar

Foundation coating

Backfill

4-in. (minimum) reinforced concrete slab

Filter fabric

Sealant

Moisture barrier

Gravel

4-in. perforated drainpipe

Footing

Horizontal rebar

Gravel

Concrete Block versus Poured Concrete Walls

If you have a large crew, like we do on most Habitat projects, it makes sense to build foundation walls with concrete block. All you need are a couple of experienced masons and enough volunteers to keep them supplied with blocks and mortar as they work their way around and up, course by course. A crawl-space foundation can be completed in just a couple of days. When building walls with concrete block, it's easy to form beam pockets and openings for vents, doors, and windows. And by switching to a smaller block just below the planned grade level, you can create a ledge for brick veneer on the outside.

If you want a full basement and you don't have a Habitat-size crew, poured concrete is the way to go. Most basement foundations are built with poured concrete walls that are formed and poured by foundation contractors.

ENSURING PROPER DRAINAGE

We need water. We just don't need it in our basements or under our floors, causing dampness, mold, and rot. We may not be able to hold back the Mississippi when it floods, but we can control most of the rainwater that falls around our homes. Follow the guidelines below and you'll stand a good chance of keeping water on the outside of your foundation.

- Don't build on the lowest part of the lot.
- Seal all holes around the pipes that go through the concrete.
- Install perforated drainpipes at the bottom of the concrete footings around the outside of the foundation (see the photo below).
- Coat the foundation walls with a suitable damp-proofing or waterproofing treatment. Check with builders in your area or the local building department to find out which foundation coatings are recommended. Tar coatings are inexpensive but not as effective as more recently developed waterproofing treatments.
- Compact loose fill as you backfill around the foundation, but be careful, because excessive compaction can damage masonry walls. Make sure that the finished grade (ground level) slopes away from the foundation. But remember that loose fill can settle. A finished grade that slopes away from the house may later slope toward the house should settling occur.

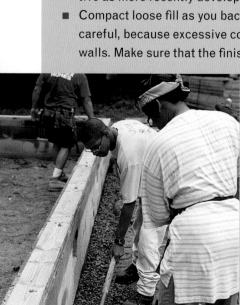

- Use gutters and downspouts to manage high roof water run-off. Make sure you keep gutters unclogged and install downspouts to direct water away from the house.
- Get advice from your building department. The time to protect your house from water infiltration is while you are building. Fixing a leaky basement or a damp crawl space after the house has been built can be very expensive.

an ICF system, laying up foundation walls doesn't demand back-breaking labor. Even so, many homebuilders still prefer to hire a foundation contractor to take on this phase of the construction project, and there's nothing wrong with that choice. The important thing is to begin building on a base that's level, square, and guaranteed to remain solid and stable for many years to come.

STEP 1 FORM AND POUR THE FOOTINGS

Thick, solid, and strong, footings evenly spread the weight of the house (and everything inside it) over a wide area, ensuring that the finished house does not settle. With some slab foundations, it's possible to pour the footings and the slab at the same time. In other cases, the footings and the slab must be formed and poured separately. In many areas, a footing inspection by the building department is required; this must be done before the foundation walls are built.

Footings must be set on solid, undisturbed earth, not on fill dirt. Local soil conditions determine the depth and design of footings. In areas of the country where the ground freezes solid in the winter, footings must extend below the frost line, which can be 4 ft. or deeper in northern regions. This prevents the freeze-thaw cycle from moving the foundation, cracking it, and causing damage throughout the entire house. The building department in your area will know the footing depth that is required. They'll also know about local soil conditions that may require a larger size footing or the use of rebar (steel reinforcing rod) in the footing.

Forms for footings

Footings are typically poured in temporary forms constructed from plywood or 2× lumber. Wood stakes and braces hold the forms in position. The top edges of the footing forms must be level, and the footings must be set to the dimensions specified on the plans. A ready-mix truck is called in to fill the footings with concrete. If the site conditions make it difficult or impossible for the truck to get close to the forms, a mobile concrete pumper can be brought in to pump the concrete from the truck to the forms. Check with your building department about code requirements for footings. It also may be necessary to embed vertical rebar in the footings so that the upper part of the reinforcing rods can extend into the foundation wall.

Pads are poured

It's common practice to pour any pads required in the plans at the same time the footings are poured. In a crawl-space foundation that includes a post-and-girder framework, poured concrete pads provide a base for concrete piers and wood posts (see the illustration on p. 48). A common size for these pads is 16 in. square by 8 in. deep. If you're building a basement foundation, pads are also required to support each post or Lally column. These pads are poured below the level of the basement floor and will be covered when the slab floor is poured. If a wall will provide midspan support for joists, a continuous footing is poured instead of separate pads.

STEP 2 BUILD THE FOUNDATION WALLS

The house shown here has concrete block walls. With a crew of helpers to move blocks and mix mortar, an experienced block mason can erect a simple crawl-space foundation wall in just a couple of days. However, in many parts of the country, poured concrete walls have surpassed concrete block walls in popularity. Subcontractors—specialists who have the equipment and experience to do the job quickly and, hopefully, with a high degree of accuracy—often form and pour concrete walls. If a foundation contractor arrives in the morning with a truckload of wall forms and rebar, he or she will probably have everything erected before the end of the day. Don't forget to have the forms inspected before the ready-mix truck arrives to fill them with concrete.

Forms are usually stripped a day or two after the pour. It takes about a week for concrete to get its first hard set, but you can begin to lay out and install the sills as soon as the forms come off. Even though you may not be forming and pouring the walls yourself, it's useful to know about some aspects of the process. This applies whether you're building the foundation walls with concrete block or with insulated concrete forms.

Anchor bolts and tie-downs

Regardless of the type of foundation, anchor bolts are required around the perimeter to hold the sill plates and the walls securely in place. In earthquake and hurricane zones, the building code may call for additional hold-downs, such as metal straps that are embedded in the concrete and extended to the sills, rim joists, and wall framing (see the illustration on p. 56). Most codes require that a long piece of rebar be planted in the concrete near the planned location of the main electrical panel so that it can be used as a ground for the electrical system.

Beam pockets

Beams or girders that tie into the foundation usually do so by means of pockets built into the foundation walls (see the illustration on p. 48). If a post-and-girder system is planned for a basement or a crawl-space foundation, the beam pockets are located in the end walls, in line with the concrete piers where the posts will be installed. It's critical for the pockets to be correctly sized and located as the foundation walls are built. To hold a 4×6 girder, the pocket should be 4½ in. wide and 5½ in. deep. This provides clearance between the girder and the concrete so that moisture in the concrete doesn't seep into the wood, potentially damaging it. The 5½-in. depth also allows a pressure-treated 2×4 shim to be installed beneath the girder, bringing its top edge flush with the sill.

Pockets are cast into poured concrete walls by fastening pocket-size wood or rigid foam blocking inside the forms. In a concrete block or ICF wall, pockets are created as the walls are laid up.

TIP If the corner of your house is settling, chances are it is on the lot's lowest spot. Every time it rains, water collects there, saturating the ground and causing the foundation to settle. To fix the problem, try pouring a concrete sidewalk, which covers the low spot and causes water to drain away from the house rather than toward it.

BUILDING WALLS WITH INSULATED CONCRETE FORMS

Insulated concrete forms (known as ICFs) offer builders an easy way to build insulated concrete walls for crawl-space and basement foundations. Made from polystyrene or another rigid foam, these forms are designed to stay in place; they aren't stripped off like standard forms.

It doesn't take a lot of building skill to stack these blocks properly. On a recent job in Oregon, we snapped chalklines on the concrete footing to mark where the first course of form blocks would fit. We then started from the corners and laid two courses of blocks to form the crawl-space walls. With four of us working, it took less than two hours to lay the blocks.

Polystyrene blocks interlock, so very little extra bracing is needed to hold them in place as concrete is poured into them. A horizontal 2×4 screwed to the outside or inside of the wall helps hold the forms straight. Drive a stake in the ground every 4 ft. or so, and run a brace between the stake and the horizontal 2×4. This will keep the walls straight throughout the pour. To strengthen the wall and prevent the forms from floating up and away, tie together a network of horizontal and vertical rebar, as shown in the photo below.

There are some concerns with ICF walls. The foam can offer a hidden pathway for subterranean termites. To avoid this, install a metal termite shield under the sill plate. Also, the foam surface is rather soft and can be easily dented and gouged. To prevent this, cover the outside walls with 2-ft. by 8-ft. fiber-cement panels or stucco.

STEP 3 BACKFILL AROUND THE FOUNDATION

The foundation is ready for the floor framing work to begin. But the job site isn't. Backfilling against the walls restores at least some of the site's original contour, making it safer and easier to move around. If you're building a house with a full basement, the backfilling process is usually delayed until after the first floor is framed and sheathed. Because they are taller, basement walls need the extra rigidity provided by the floor framing to ensure that backfilling doesn't damage the foundation. This isn't a major concern with crawl-space walls, so it's good to backfill now. But first, it's important to take care of the following details.

Termite protection

In areas where termite infestation is possible, some builders elect to call in a licensed pest-control contractor to apply pesticide around the base of the foundation before backfilling against the walls. However, if you don't like the idea of putting chemicals in the soil, there are other termite control options to consider (see the sidebar on p. 60).

Foundation coatings

It's important to keep moisture out of the basement or crawl-space area, as well as out of the masonry wall itself. Foundation coatings help accomplish this. Concrete block walls are often parged—covered with a layer of mortar that conceals and protects the joints between the blocks. A waterproof coating should also be applied. Asphalt-type coatings are popular because they are inexpensive and have been used for many years. More effective and more expensive coatings are also available and should be considered when you're building in soil that stays wet for extended periods of time. No matter how good a waterproof coating is supposed to be, it shouldn't be your only line of defense against under-house moisture (see the sidebar at left).

Foundation wall insulation

Foundation insulation isn't used in mild climates. But in areas with frigid winter months, it can improve interior comfort and save on heating costs. Even though it's not required by code in many areas, it's definitely worth installing wherever prolonged freezing temperatures are expected. You can install insulation on the inside or outside of a crawl-space or basement wall. Exterior insulation, in the form of rigid foam boards, is glued to the foundation walls before backfilling. Where they're exposed above the finished grade on the exterior, insulation boards must be protected with siding material or stucco. It's important to remember that any type of foundation insulation can provide a hidden passageway for termites and other insects to enter the house. Make sure you cut off this passageway by installing a termite shield beneath the sill. As shown in the illustrations on pp. 50–51, the shield should be installed between the top of the foundation and the sill.

Drainage around the foundation

After you've taken care of the details, you can begin backfilling around the foundation. Along the footing, install perforated drainpipes in a bed of gravel several inches thick. Cover the pipe with at least several more inches of gravel. To prevent the drainage channel from silting up, cover the top layer of gravel with filter fabric before backfilling it with soil.

STEP 4 ATTACH THE SILLS

Some important carpentry work is about to begin. Whether you are building on a concrete slab, over a crawl space, or over a full basement, the first wooden member that is laid down is called a sill, mudsill, or sole plate. This sill is commonly a pressure-treated 2×4 or 2×6 attached directly to the foundation with anchor bolts embedded in the concrete. Occasionally, it is attached with hardened concrete nails or steel pins shot through the sill and into the concrete by a power-actuated nailer.

ADJUSTING THE MUDSILL TO FIX FOUNDATION WALLS

Unlike nailing together a bunch of 2×4s to frame a wall, pouring a concrete slab is for keeps. That's why most concrete contractors are careful to set up and brace their forms. Still, a perfectly square, parallel, and level foundation is not always a realistic expectation. Fortunately, you can make up for foundation walls or a slab that's less than perfect when you install the sill plates.

Say, for example, that the foundation walls are out of parallel by 1 in. and you're using 2×6s (5½-in.-wide boards) for the sill. At the wide end of the foundation, measure in 5¾ in. from the outside edge at each corner. At the narrow end, measure in 5¼ in. at each corner. Snap a chalkline between the two marks on each side to locate the inside edge of the sill plates. By making just a ¼-in. adjustment at each corner, you gain 1 in. overall, making the walls parallel. For walls that are not square, you can use the same method—moving the two walls slightly in or out, as necessary—to bring them into square.

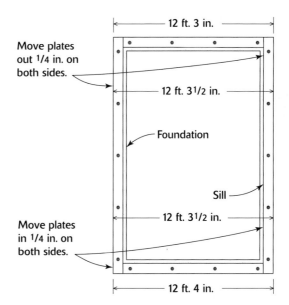

COMPENSATING FOR OUT-OF-PARALLEL WALLS

12 ft. 3 in.

Move plates out ¼ in. on both sides.

12 ft. 3½ in.

Foundation

Sill

12 ft. 3½ in.

Move plates in ¼ in. on both sides.

12 ft. 4 in.

If the walls are out of parallel, you can still start framing from a square base by adjusting the position of the sills to compensate for the error in the foundation. For example, if the foundation is 1 in. wider at one end than the other, simply move the sill in an extra ¼ in. on both sides at the wide end and out an extra ¼ in. on both sides at the narrow end. The sill plates will now be parallel.

FASTENING MUDSILLS WITH METAL STRAPS

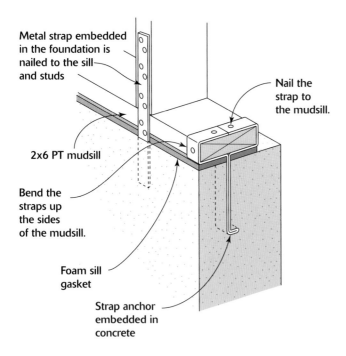

Metal strap embedded in the foundation is nailed to the sill and studs

Nail the strap to the mudsill.

2x6 PT mudsill

Bend the straps up the sides of the mudsill.

Foam sill gasket

Strap anchor embedded in concrete

Metal straps can be embedded in the concrete foundation. After the bottom plate is down, the straps are nailed to it. Metal hardware creates a positive connection between the foundation and the house frame. This is especially important in earthquake and high-wind areas.

TIP Take special care when working in a trench or around a basement wall. Dirt can cave in, fill a trench, and trap you under tons of earth. The rule of thumb is to never get in over your head!

Snap chalkline to lay out the sill. The line shows where the sill's inside edge rests. If the foundation isn't perfectly square, adjust the line's position so that the sills will be. [Photo by Roe A. Osborn, courtesy *Fine Homebuilding* magazine © The Taunton Press, Inc.]

Most codes require that anchor bolts be located 1 ft. from each corner of the foundation, 1 ft. from the ends of each sill plate, and a maximum of 6 ft. o.c. everywhere else. These are minimum requirements. Builders living in earthquake or high-wind areas often use ⅝-in.-dia. anchor bolts rather than ½-in. bolts and reduce the spacing to 4 ft. o.c. or less. As mentioned in Chapter 1, it's important to check with the local building inspector to ensure that the house you're building meets or exceeds code.

Check the foundation first

Unfortunately, you can't assume that your foundation is straight, parallel, square, and level. But here's some good news: If you know how far off it is, you can usually make the appropriate corrections when installing the sills (see the sidebar on p. 55). It's worth it to make the sills as straight, parallel, square, and level as possible. Otherwise, the mistakes made at this preliminary stage tend to become even more troublesome further down the line. Here's how to check the foundation:

STRAIGHT. Check the walls for straightness by stretching a dry line (string) from corner to corner. At this point, you just need to know how straight the top outside edge of the foundation is, because you'll be measuring in from this edge to locate the sill.

PARALLEL. Measure across the walls at both ends and in the middle. All three measurements should be the same. I use ¼ in. over 20 ft. as the tolerance limit for parallel.

SQUARE. Plus or minus ½ in. over 20 ft. is the tolerance that I use for square walls. You can check any rectangular foundation for square simply by comparing the diagonal measurements, which should be equal. When that isn't possible, use the 6-8-10 rule to check for square corners. Measure 6 ft. in from a corner on one side and 8 ft. on the other side (see the photo on the facing page). Then measure between those two points. If the corner is square, the hypotenuse of the triangle should be 10 ft. For smaller buildings, 3 ft. on one side and 4 ft. on the other should yield a 5-ft. hypotenuse. On a large building, use measurements of 12 ft., 16 ft., and 20 ft.

LEVEL. I like to check a foundation for level with a builder's level (especially one with a laser beam) set on a tripod. If you don't have one of these available, an inexpensive water level will work fine (see the illustration below). The walls should be level to within ¼ in. over 20 ft.

Determine the sill's position

Depending on what you find after measuring the foundation, you may need to adjust the sill's position using some of the techniques explained in the sidebar on p. 55. The sill plates are often bolted flush to the outside of the foundation, but there are variations you may want to consider (see the illustration on p. 58). For example, when the walls will be sheathed with ½-in. plywood or OSB, it's best to hold the plates ½ in. inside the foundation. This puts the sheathing flush with the foundation and allows the siding to lap down over the concrete.

The sills must be installed along snapped layout lines on top of the foundation walls. (If

Test for square. One way to test foundation corners for square is to measure 6 ft. from the outside corner along one side and 8 ft. along the other. If the third side of the triangle measures exactly 10 ft., you have a right angle. [Photo © Roger Turk]

USING A WATER LEVEL

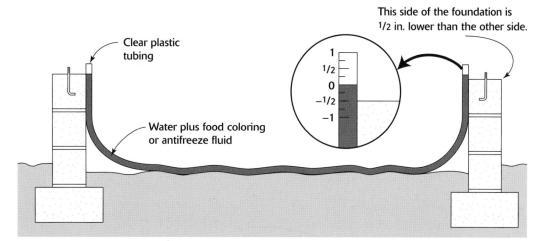

A simple water level can be used to check the foundation for level. These are available at home improvement centers. If the foundation is not level, the sill plate can be shimmed up with pressure-treated shims.

you're building on a slab, the layout lines will be on top of the slab.) The lines identify where the inside edge of the sill will fit.

Taking the width of the sill lumber into account (3½ in. for a 2×4 sill, 5½ in. for a 2×6), snap chalklines around the perimeter to indicate the inside edge of the sill (see the photo on p. 56). Make slight adjustments in the positions of the chalklines, if necessary, so that the sill is straight, square, and parallel.

Locate and drill bolt holes

Anchor bolts sometimes come out of the foundation at odd angles. You can straighten bent bolts with a length of pipe, as shown in the photo at left. Then set long, straight, pressure-treated sill boards in place for marking and drilling. You can use a square and a tape measure to lay out the bolt hole locations

A long pipe straightens a short bolt. A length of 1-in.-dia. pipe straightens any bolts that may have been bent during (or since) the foundation pour. [Photo © Roger Turk]

POSITIONING SILLS ON THE FOUNDATION

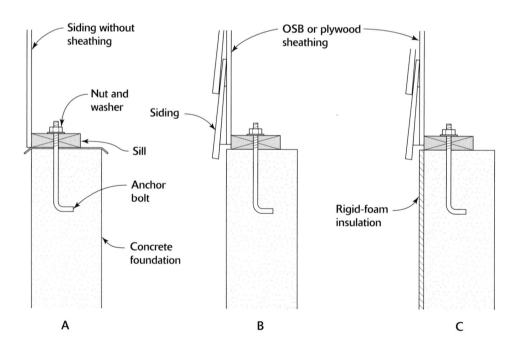

Sill plates can be set flush with the edge of the foundation (A) and the siding nailed directly to the walls. When sheathing the house frame with OSB or plywood, though, hold in the sill plates ½ in. (B). When using rigid foam to insulate a basement or a crawl space (C), position the plates so that the outside face of the sheathing is in plane with the outside face of the foam.

MAKING A BOLT-HOLE MARKER

Select an 18-in. by 1½-in. by ⅛-in. metal plate strap. Cut a notch in one end of the strap so that it will fit around a ½-in. or ⅝-in. bolt. From the center of the notch, measure back 3½ in. for a 2x4 plate and 5½ in. for a 2x6 plate. Drill holes at those points and insert ³/₁₆-in. by ¾-in. stove bolts. Put a bend in the plate strap to make it easier to use.

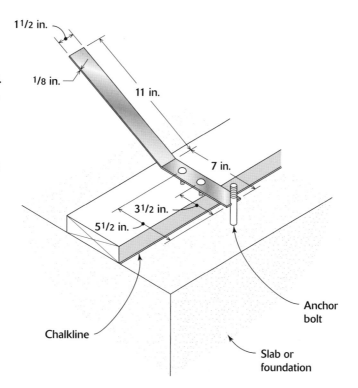

1½ in.

1/8 in.

11 in.

7 in.

3½ in.

5½ in.

Chalkline

Anchor bolt

Slab or foundation

A bolt-hole marker makes it easy to transfer the bolt location to the sill in preparation for drilling a hole.

An electric drill is great for boring holes. Use a spade bit in an electric drill to bore bolt holes through a wood sill.

TERMITE CONTROL

When I was studying at UCLA in the early 1950s, I lived in a small house that was held together by stucco on the outside and plaster on the inside. The wall framing had long been devoured by families of termites. Today, a number of defensive strategies are used to deter termites. Check with the building inspector and with builders in your area to find out which of the following strategies are used locally and how they work with different types of foundations.

Termites like wood. Scrap wood buried at a job site can attract colonies of termites. And once they're finished with that lumber, they'll look for other wood sources, such as any wood siding that is in contact with the ground or even floor joists in the crawl space. Eliminate the supply of unprotected wood and you'll help eliminate any unforeseen termite troubles.

- Pressure-treated wood. Today, most houses are required to have at least some wood that termites don't eat. Pressure-treated wood qualifies, but on most houses it's used only as the mudsill atop the foundation. A more extensive use of pressure-treated wood (in the joists over a crawl space, for example) provides good protection in termite-prone areas.
- Pesticide treatment. A licensed pest-control contractor can apply termiticide (termite-targeting pesticide) around footings and foundations before backfilling to create a barrier that deters insects.
- Termite shields. This metal flashing is installed between the top of the foundation and the mudsill. The shield makes it more difficult for termites to build their earth access tubes between the ground and the floor framing. The shield also makes the tubes easier to spot during an inspection. Remember that these shields are touching PT wood. They need to be galvanized to keep from corroding and deteriorating.

½-in. bolts. For ⅝-in. bolts, use a ¾-in. bit.

Install sill seal and termite shields

Sweep the foundation clean of debris, then put down a layer of sill seal insulation where the sills will be located (see the photo on the facing page). Sill seal does just what its name says. As an alternative, you can run two heavy beads of silicone caulk between the sill plates and the foundation. This also prevents cold air leaks between the foundation and the sill. In areas where termite infestation is a possibility, you'll also need to lay down a termite shield over the foundation bolts and under the sill. As shown in the illustrations on p. 50, the shield edges must extend beyond the foundation (including the foundation insulation) and the sill.

Place the sills over the bolts, put on the washers and nuts, and tighten the nuts with a crescent wrench, taking care to keep the inside edge of the sill on its layout. (Note: When working on a slab, drill holes in the plates but leave them unbolted until after the wall is raised— see Chapter 4 for details.) Codes in earthquake and high-wind areas often require the use of larger washers (galvanized, ¼ in. thick, and 2 in. square). These larger washers help secure the mudsill and keep it from splitting when under pressure from lateral forces.

If the measuring work you did at the beginning of this step told you that parts of the foundation were out of level, you can expect the sills to be that way, too. To correct slight discrepancies (up to ¼ in. or so), you can insert pressure-treated shims underneath the sills. For larger errors, it's best to call in a concrete contractor.

STEP 5 BUILD MIDSPAN SUPPORT FOR JOISTS

Unless you are building on a slab, you'll probably need to provide midspan support for the floor joists. Without additional support somewhere between the sills, the joists can be overspanned, resulting in a finished floor that sags or feels bouncy. A friend once took me through

on the sills, but it's a lot faster to mark the hole locations with a bolt marker. You can make a bolt marker or buy a ready-made version (see the illustration on p. 59 and Resources on p. 279). To use this layout tool, place each plate directly on the inside of the chalkline.

Once the bolt locations are marked, set the sill plates on blocks of wood or sawhorses and drill the holes. Use a ⅝-in. bit to make holes for

Use sill seal to block drafts and insects. Installed between the sill and the foundation, sill seal provides a resilient layer of insulation, filling in small gaps and helping maintain an effective barrier between indoors and out.
[Photo © Mike Guertin]

his 18th-century home in rural Connecticut. The beautiful, hand-hewn floor joists in the basement were fascinating—dry, free from rot and termites—but far overspanned. Upstairs, it felt like walking on ocean waves. Clearly, what was needed was some support to keep the joists from sagging and bouncing in the middle.

Codes require a minimum of 18 in. between the earth and the joists in a crawl space. These days, two systems are commonly used to provide midspan support for the joists: crib walls (also called pony walls) and post-and-girder systems. A crib wall is just a shortened version of a regular stud wall and is supported along a continuous concrete footing. With a post-and-girder system, a solid or built-up girder (also called a beam) is supported by posts every 6 ft. or so, depending on code. The girder usually fits into a recess or pocket where it meets the foundation wall. Joined to the girder by metal connectors or plywood gussets, the posts bear on concrete piers (see the illustration on p. 48).

In both these systems, the joists rest on and are nailed to the top support member. The width of the joists and the length of the span determine how much support is needed. With 2×6 joists, for example, posts and girders are often placed every 6 ft. With 2×12s or

DEALING WITH RADON

Radon is an odorless gas that forms naturally as the uranium in soil and water breaks down. It is found in every state. If comparatively large amounts are present in your region, it can accumulate in closed areas, such as basements and other living spaces. It's always a good idea to check with local authorities, an environmental engineer, and the Environmental Protection Agency before building.

If you live in an area where excessive radon is a problem, you can usually control gas entry into your home with a passive system. Locate a perforated 3-in. PVC "tee" (a plastic pipe fitting) in the gravel below the basement slab or below the 6-mil poly in a crawl space. Seal any holes in the concrete slab or use mastic to affix the poly sheet to the basement or stem walls. Next, attach a 3-in. plastic pipe to the tee, then extend the pipe up through one of the walls and out through the roof. If your house tests positive for radon in the future (test kits are available; see Resources on p. 279), you can always turn this passive system into an active one by installing an in-line exhaust fan to pull the gas to the outside.

I-joists are light, strong, and uniform. Rather than using 2× lumber for joists, most builders prefer to install factory-made I-joists.

Build a crib wall. It's best to use **PT** wood in underfloor areas. Crib walls (also referred to as pony walls) are short, stud-framed walls and can provide midspan support for joists that extend over a crawl space. After bolting the wall's bottom plate to the footing, stretch a line over the sills to measure the length of the crib wall's studs (see the photo above). Place two pieces of top plate stock on the wall's bottom plate and measure up to the line. Toenail the studs to the bottom plate, spacing them 16 in. o.c. or 24 in. o.c. depending on your code requirements (see the photo below). [Photos © Memo Jasso]

Finishing the wall. After nailing both top plates, fasten plywood or **OSB** sheathing to one side to give the wall shear strength. Hold the bottom edge of sheathing panels ½ in. off the concrete. [Photo © Memo Jasso]

MEASURING POST OR PONY-WALL STUD LENGTHS

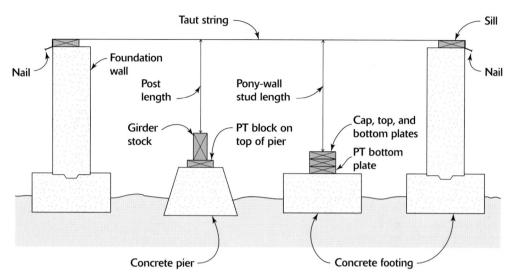

Stretch a string tightly from one sill to another. For the post length, measure from a piece of girder stock to the taut string. To find the stud lengths for a pony wall, measure from the top of a stack of three wall plates to the string.

TIP Wait to carpet over concrete. Make sure you let a concrete slab dry out well (for several months) before laying carpet on it. If you don't, the carpet adhesive may not hold properly and your carpet could rot, possibly posing a health hazard.

engineered I-joists, only one support in the center may be needed.

Crib-wall construction

Just in case a moisture or termite problem develops in the future, I like to build crib walls with pressure-treated wood. To determine the length of the crib wall's studs, first bolt the wall's bottom plate to the footing. Then tightly stretch a string above the crib wall's bottom plate and across the mudsills installed on the stem walls. Set two pieces of top plate stock on the bottom plate. The distance between the top plate stock and the string is the length of the crib wall's studs (see the top right photo on the facing page).

Toenail the studs to the bottom plate, spacing them 24 in. o.c. but leaving a 30-in.-wide opening somewhere in the wall so that plumbers, electricians, and others can get from one side of the crawl space to the other. When toenailing the studs to the crib wall's bottom plate, you can drive either four 8d toenails or three 16d nails per stud. If you're using a pneumatic nailer,

make sure you follow the safety guidelines explained in the sidebar on p. 65.

Once the crib wall's studs are in place, nail on the two top plates. Drive a pair of 16d nails through the first plate into the top of each stud. Secure the double top plate with a single 16d nail at each stud location, and toenail the plate's ends to the sill on the foundation wall at each end of the house. I like to sheathe sections of a crib wall with pressure-treated plywood (my first choice) or OSB to provide good lateral bracing (see the bottom left photo on the facing page). Be sure not to sheathe over the crawl-through opening you framed in the wall. As an alternative to sheathing a crib wall, you can stiffen it with 2× diagonal braces nailed to the top and bottom plates and across at least one stud.

Build a post-and-girder system

Posts used to construct a post-and-girder system can be anchored directly to a metal post base that is set in the concrete footing. You can also use a precast pier with a metal strap that

TOENAILING BASICS

Driving a couple of nails through the side of one 2× into the edge or face of another creates a strong connection. This is a good way to join two 2×s at a right angle. But sometimes this isn't possible, either because the board is too thick or because its face is not exposed. That's when you resort to driving a nail at an angle, or toenailing.

To toenail two boards together, hold the nail at a 60-degree angle and start it about 1 in. from the end of the board. If the nail angle is not correct, the connection between the two pieces of wood will not be as strong. Back up the wood with your foot to hold the board in place as you toenail. With practice, you'll soon gain skill, speed, and confidence.

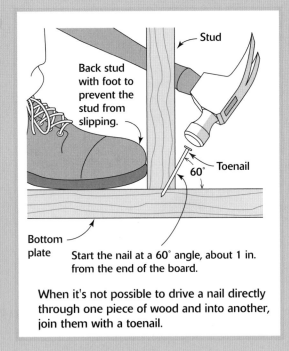

Stud

Back stud with foot to prevent the stud from slipping.

Toenail

60°

Bottom plate

Start the nail at a 60° angle, about 1 in. from the end of the board.

When it's not possible to drive a nail directly through one piece of wood and into another, join them with a toenail.

The girders that support the joists need to break over a post. [Photo by Don Charles Blom]

attaches to the pier post and holds it in position. Secure a 1½-in.-thick pressure-treated pad to the top of the pier if the posts will be cut from untreated lumber. You can measure for the post's length just as you measured for the crib wall's studs, stretching a line above a piece of girder stock placed on the pier. Cut your posts to length, then secure them directly to the piers or toenail them to the blocks attached to the piers. Make sure the posts are plumb and parallel to one another.

Girders must butt together over a post. When the end of a girder fits into a pocket in the foundation, you'll have to shim up the girder to get the top surface level with the top of the sill. The shims used beneath girders will bear the full weight of the floor, so they must be cut carefully from pressure-treated stock. Cut uniformly thick shims instead of tapered ones and make them large enough to fit in the bottom of the foundation pocket. Rather than foundation pockets, we inserted a metal 4× post base in the footing next to the stem wall to hold the end of the girder.

Plywood gussets tie girders securely to their post supports. [Photo by Don Charles Blom]

Because of concrete's ability to absorb moisture, code requires that the end of the girder be held about ½ in. away from the back of the pocket when cutting the girder to fit. If you're not using pressure-treated stock for the girder, you can wrap the end of the girder with builder's felt or sheet metal to give it some protection against moisture damage. Toenail the girders to the posts with either four 8d or three 16d nails. Now brace the posts and splice the girders by nailing the plywood gussets on both sides of the joint (see the illustration on p. 48).

STEP 6 INSTALL THE JOISTS

Joists span a house from edge to edge, providing support (and a nailing surface) for the subfloor and a platform for the walls. Many older houses were built with undersized joists that were unable to keep floors and ceilings from sagging. Building codes today help ensure that joist sizing and spacing are more than adequate to keep floors rock solid yet resilient. Joists are normally spaced to allow for the most efficient use of full-size (4-ft. by 8-ft.) sheets of OSB or plywood. Joists cut from 2× lumber are generally spaced 16 in. or 24 in. o.c. Engineered wood I-joists can be spaced on centers of 12 in., 16 in., 19.2 in., or 24 in.

Solid lumber versus engineered I-joists

Up until 20 years ago, most of the floors in this country were built with standard 2× joists. These days, more floors are being built with engineered I-joists. So named because of their "I" profile, I-joists have plywood top and bottom chords connected by an OSB web (see the top left photo on p. 62). They offer several advantages over solid lumber. Being an engineered product, they are knot-free and can span long distances without interior support. I-joists don't

TIP Patterns save time. When cutting multiple identical pieces of framing members, such as joists, it is common to use a pattern piece. Cut one piece to the correct length, then lay it on top of the next piece to be cut and mark that one. Write the word "pattern" on the original piece.

SAFETY FIRST

PNEUMATIC NAILERS

Volunteers who help build Habitat houses use only hammers to drive nails. But these days, buildings are nailed together with all kinds of pneumatic nailers. These are good, reliable tools, available for framing, finish work, siding, and shingling. However, there are basic safety considerations to keep in mind.

- Treat a pneumatic nailer with respect. Be mindful of what you are doing. Never point a nailer at yourself or at others.
- Read and follow the instruction manual regarding its maintenance and use.
- Don't walk around with your finger on the trigger. You could accidentally fire a nail.
- Adjust the air pressure as needed. Larger nails require more pressure.
- Wear safety glasses or goggles.
- Disconnect the nailer from the air compressor before clearing a jammed nail.
- When nailing on a sidewall, don't hold the nailer in front of your face. Hitting a metal strap or other hardware beneath the surface could cause the nailer to recoil into your face with considerable force.
- Drain moisture from the compressor tank after using it. A rusty, compromised tank can explode under pressure.
- No one under 18 years of age should use a pneumatic nailer.
- Pneumatic nailers should only be used by a trained professional or an experienced volunteer under supervision.

I-JOIST CUTTING GUIDE

I-joists are awkward to cut because the top and bottom chords are wider than the web. To overcome this difficulty, make a simple jig with ¾-in.-thick plywood. Cut a rectangular piece of plywood to fit between the chords and serve as the base of the jig. Screw a longer piece to the first piece, positioning it to guide a 90-degree cut. The edge of the top piece guides the base of the circular saw, as shown in the photo at right. Lay the guide on the I-joist, set the saw on it, and make a square cut. It's that simple.

Cut I-joists with a guide. Scrap sheathing that is nailed or screwed together creates an effective guide for cutting I-joists. [Photo by Roe A. Osborn, courtesy *Fine Homebuilding* magazine © The Taunton Press, Inc.]

Install the rim joists. The outside face of the rim joist (also called a band joist) must be flush with the outside edge of the sill. Toenail each joist to the sill, spacing 16d nails 16 in. o.c.

swell, shrink, crack, or warp the way solid lumber does. They are much lighter and easier to carry than 2× joists. And they're uniform in size. In a load of 2× joists, you might find up to ⅜ in. of variation in joist width. I-joists don't vary; once installed, they create a dead-level floor. Nails driven through the sheathing into the top chord are less likely to come loose and create a squeaky floor, especially when the sheathing is applied with adhesive. In terms of price, they are competitive with standard-

dimension lumber. Installation details for I-joists are slightly different than those for 2× joists. I'll cover those differences just ahead.

Nail rim joists first

Rim joists form the exterior of the building and are the first joists to be installed. The layout of other joist locations are marked on the top edges of the rim joists. Cut the rim joists to length and toenail each one flush with the outside of the sill. I drive one 16d nail every 16 in. around the perimeter (see the photo at left). Don't forget that nails going into PT wood should be hot-dipped galvanized. In earthquake and high-wind areas, code may require that the rim also be secured to the sill with framing anchors, so check with your local building inspector. If there are no vents in the foundation, they can be cut into the rim joists. A standard screened vent fits in a 4½-in. by 14½-in. opening.

If you're framing a floor with I-joists, you'll probably use the specially made OSB rim joists supplied with your I-joist order. Install rim joists along only one side of the house. Then lay the I-joists flat across the sills, butting the end of each joist fast against the installed rim joist. The opposite ends of the joists will extend over the sill at the other side of the house. You can now snap a line across the ends to establish where the I-joists need to be cut. A simple jig, explained in the sidebar on the facing page, makes it easy to cut the joists smoothly and accurately. After cutting the I-joists to length, complete the rim joist installation.

Joist layout goes quickly

When a single joist spans a house from edge to edge, the layout is identical on parallel rims. Just hook a long tape on the end of the rim joist and make a mark on top every 16 in. (32 in., 48 in., etc.) down the entire length. Put an "X" next to each mark to indicate which side of the line the joist goes on.

When the joists lap over a central girder or wall, the layout on the opposing rim joists must be staggered. On one rim joist, mark the 16-in. o.c. locations with an "X" to the right; on the opposite side, lay out the joists with an "X" to the left. This allows the joists to lap and nail over a girder or crib wall, where they will be stabilized with blocks (see the illustration on p. 68).

Your joist layout may include openings (called headouts) for a stairway or to provide clearance for plumbing or vents. Your plans should show these openings, but it's always a good idea (and it could save a lot of time and effort) to check with the plumber. A common mistake is leaving insufficient room between

FRAMING HEADOUTS

Sometimes joists must be cut to allow room for a stairway, a heater vent in the floor, or a tub trap in the bathroom. Such an opening is called a headout. As shown in the illustration below, regular 2× joists (not I-joists) can be cut and supported by a header joist that is fastened to parallel joists. If the opening is larger than 4 ft., double both the side and the header joists. Attach the doubles with 16d nails spaced 16 in. o.c.

A common mistake made by carpenters framing a headout is not taking into account the thickness of the header joists. Remember to factor in these joists when determining the size of your floor opening. If, for example, you need a 2-ft.-long floor opening, cut the joists at 2 ft. 3 in. to leave room for the single-header joist at each end. For double-header joists, cut the joists at 2 ft. 6 in.

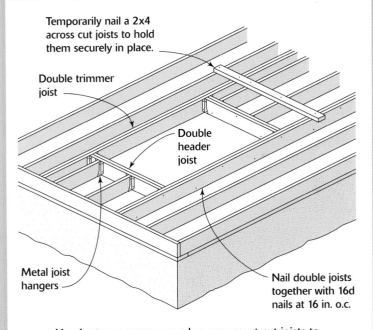

Temporarily nail a 2x4 across cut joists to hold them securely in place.

Double trimmer joist

Double header joist

Metal joist hangers

Nail double joists together with 16d nails at 16 in. o.c.

Headouts are necessary when you must cut joists to make room for a stairway, a heating duct, or plumbing.

With a little training, almost everyone can learn to safely use a nail gun to frame walls, though a trained professional or an experienced volunteer under supervision should use them. [Photo by Don Charles Blom]

JOIST LAYOUT

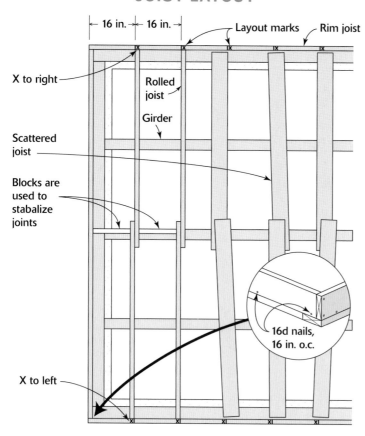

← 16 in. → ← 16 in. →

Layout marks — Rim joist

X to right

Rolled joist

Girder

Scattered joist

Blocks are used to stabalize joints

16d nails, 16 in. o.c.

X to left

If a single joist spans from rim to rim, the layout is identical on each rim. When joists lap midspan, the layout on opposing rim joists must be staggered.

TIP Blocking adds strength. Install blocking between joists directly over the midspan support. Nail the blocking to the joists and to the top of the girder or crib wall.

the joists for the tub's trap and the toilet's drain. You may need to frame a headout to make room for plumbing. For headout framing details, see the sidebar on p. 67. When framing with I-joists, remember that, like any other type of engineered joist, they cannot be notched or cut midspan without destroying their structural integrity.

Cut the joists in place

If you trust your eye, try cutting 2× joists in place rather than measuring each one individually. As you become comfortable using a circular saw, you'll be able make a square cut without using a square (see the sidebar on the facing page). This technique is definitely worth learning. Over the course of framing a house, it will save a significant amount of time.

Roll and nail the joists

Once the joists are cut to length and in position, carpenters say that it's time to "roll" them. This just means setting the joists on edge, aligning them with their layout, and nailing them in place. If you are working with 2× joists, it's important to sight down each joist to see whether there's a bow or a crown, and then set the joist with the crown facing up.

Drive two 16d nails through the rim joist directly into the end of the joist—one nail near the top and one near the bottom (see the photo below). Most codes also require that joists be toenailed (one 16d on each side) to the sill plates and supporting girders. To nail off an I-joist, drive a 16d nail through the rim joist and into each chord, then nail the chord to the sill on both sides of the web.

Make sure that all the joists are nailed securely. This is important for safety reasons, for quality workmanship, and for meeting code requirements. Once all the joists are nailed upright, stop and check for symmetry—make sure the line of one joist is parallel with another.

Nail off 2× joists. To install 2× joists, drive a pair of 16d nails through the rim joist into the end of the joist. Then drive a toenail through each side of the joist into the sill.

CUTTING SQUARE WITHOUT A SQUARE

One of the most important skills a carpenter learns over the years is training and trusting his or her eye. And one of the best ways to develop this capability is to cut square by eye. Instead of using a square to mark a 90-degree cutoff line on a board, simply make a quick pencil mark for length on the board, line up a circular saw, and make the cut. Over the course of framing a floor or a wall, this method can save you plenty of time.

If you're comfortable using a circular saw, it's not difficult to master this technique. Position the saw with the blade aligned on the cutoff mark and the front of the saw's base parallel with the edge of the board. As you make the cut, keep the base parallel with the board's edge. Practice a few times on scrap, check each cut, and adjust the angle of the cut until you've got it right. In time, you'll develop a "feel" for square.

Make square cuts by eye. To make a square cut, put the blade on the cut line and keep the front edge of the saw base parallel with the board.

This is an easy way to spot layout mistakes. Take the time to check the framing against the details shown on the plans. Corrections are much easier to make now than after the floor sheathing is installed. Enjoy the moment. Joists on edge are beautiful in their own right, clearly and unmistakably showing the promise of a new building.

Blocking adds strength. Install blocking between joists directly over the midspan support. Nail the blocking to the joists and to the top of the girder or crib wall. [Photo by Roe A. Osborn, courtesy *Fine Homebuilding* magazine © The Taunton Press, Inc.]

STEP 7 INSTALL EXTRA JOISTS AND BLOCKING

Until recently, extra joists were often required under walls that ran parallel to the joists, because they helped support the roof structure. Most houses built these days use roof trusses, however, which are engineered to span from outside wall to outside wall without the need for interior support. There usually isn't a need to install extra joists under walls, though some local codes still require them. Check with your town or city building department to make sure.

Similarly, wood or metal bridging is no longer required. Installed in crossed pairs between

MAKING A BLOCK-CUTTING TOOL

Many carpenters cut blocks with a chopsaw, which is fine if you have one. But there is another easy way to cut blocks. Try making a simple block-cutting tool to use with a circular saw. Once you have the guide, simply hook it on a 2× and make the cut along the edge.

Make a jig to cut blocks quickly. This simple jig can be made from scrap in just a few minutes. It eliminates all measuring and marking, which saves a great deal of time when cutting blocking.

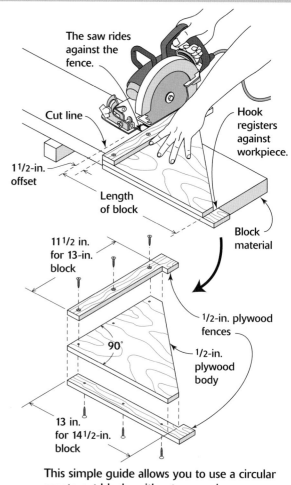

The saw rides against the fence.

Cut line

Hook registers against workpiece.

1 1/2-in. offset

Length of block

Block material

11 1/2 in. for 13-in. block

1/2-in. plywood fences

90°

1/2-in. plywood body

13 in. for 14 1/2-in. block

This simple guide allows you to use a circular saw to cut blocks without measuring.

TIP That empty feeling. When installing sheathing, you can feel when a nail doesn't hit a joist—it goes in too easily. Driving a fresh nail to the left or right of the dud usually results in solid contact.

joists, bridging is often visible between the rim joists and the interior girders or crib walls in the basement or crawl space of an old house. Stress tests have long shown that bridging provides little extra stability to a floor sheathed with plywood or OSB. My experience is that most midspan bridging does little except increase floor squeaks.

Blocking between joists, on the other hand, helps stabilize a building and keeps the joists from falling like dominoes under severe lateral stress, such as that generated by an earthquake

or high winds. Blocking is installed at the bearing points where joists cross girders or crib walls. On many houses, this is also the spot where joists from opposite sides of the building lap against each other (see the illustration on the facing page). To quickly cut identical blocks with a circular saw, use a jig like the one shown in the sidebar above.

If you're building with I-joists, you'll need to determine the length of the blocking on the job site, as I-joist width varies from manufacturer to manufacturer. The most common width for residential I-joists is 9½ in., so you can cut blocking from scrap pieces of I-joists or from 2×10 lumber. Cut the blocking to fit snugly between the chords of adjacent I-joists, and nail the blocking to the chords.

When nailing blocking between joists, it's best to begin at one end of the house and simply work your way toward the opposite end. Sight down the length of the first joist (the one closest to the rim joist) and make sure it is running straight. Measure the first joist space and cut the block to length. Set the block on edge over a girder or a crib wall. Drive two 16d nails into one end of the block and two 16d nails through the floor joist into the opposite end. Then nail the joist directly into the girder with two 16d nails. Finish by nailing the lapping joists together with two more 16d nails.

Once you have a few blocks nailed in place, use a tape measure to make sure the joists are maintaining an accurate 16 in. or 24 in. o.c. layout so that the sheathing will land mid-joist. If necessary, cut the blocks a bit short or long to maintain accurate spacing.

In many parts of the country, rough plumbing and heating ductwork are installed before the floor is sheathed, so be sure to check with those contractors before sheathing. Also, find out whether you need a floor joist inspection before you install the floor sheathing.

STEP 8 INSTALL THE FLOOR SHEATHING

Before plywood and OSB were readily available, we sheathed floors with softwood 1×6s that were cut and nailed diagonally across the joists. To make the joints between the 1×6 boards, the ends of each board were cut at a 45-degree angle. Frequently, the 1×6 lumber was of poor quality and had large knots. I still have scars

Sheathing must be glued and nailed. Use a caulking gun to apply a bead of construction adhesive to the joists' top edges before installing the floor sheathing. The adhesive strengthens the floor and helps reduce squeaking in the future.

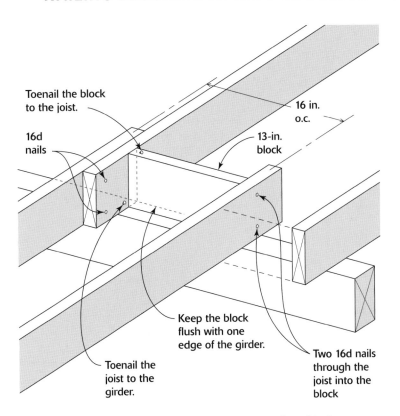

Toenail the block to the joist.

16d nails

16 in. o.c.

13-in. block

Keep the block flush with one edge of the girder.

Toenail the joist to the girder.

Two 16d nails through the joist into the block

Lapped joists spaced at 16 in. o.c. require a block about 13 in. long between the joists.

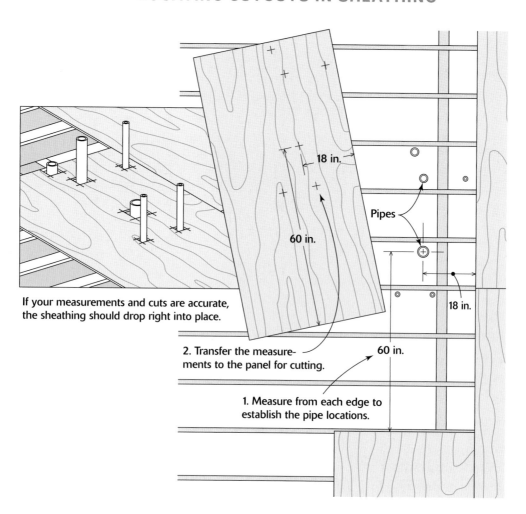

If your measurements and cuts are accurate, the sheathing should drop right into place.

18 in.

60 in.

Pipes

18 in.

60 in.

2. Transfer the measurements to the panel for cutting.

1. Measure from each edge to establish the pipe locations.

TIP You can use ring shank or hot-dipped galvanized nails when nailing off subfloor. These nails, along with the adhesive, will hold the sheathing to the joists and help prevent squeaky floors.

on my lower legs from breaking through subfloors while working on job sites decades ago. The sheathing panels we use today are much better than 1×6 boards—yet another improvement over how houses were built in "the good old days."

Sheathing with 4×8 sheets of tongue-and-groove plywood or OSB is not difficult, though the sheets can be awkward to handle. Carry them with a partner, if necessary, and take care not to damage the tongues or the grooves, which can make it more difficult to fit the sheets together. Be sure to use exterior-grade, ⅝-in.- or ¾-in.-thick sheathing.

Snap a line to lay out the first sheathing course

When laying out long rows of 4×8 sheathing, it's best to start from a control, or reference, line. On one side of the building, measure in 48¼ in. at each end and snap a chalkline across the joists. The first row of sheathing is laid and nailed directly on that line. Getting this first row straight makes it easier to lay all subsequent rows.

Lay down a full ¼-in. bead of construction adhesive on the joists beneath each sheet just before setting it in place (see the photo on p. 71). This makes the floor structurally stronger and cuts down on squeaks in the future. Lay the first sheet with its grooved edge right along the

Without a floor on top, there's just a big empty space inside the foundation walls. Getting all the joists in place seems like a huge job.

The masonry walls look square and level, but we have to check them anyway.

We use pressure-treated 2×6s for the sill plates.

Once they're installed, we begin with all the joists.

There's a rhythm to rolling the joists up onto their lay-out lines and then anchoring them in place by driving nails through the rim joists.

Before long, it's time to start installing the floor sheathing. We're already looking forward to wall framing.

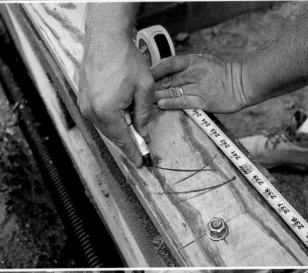

Cut sheets in place at the edge of the floor. With the circular saw's cutting depth set to the thickness of the sheathing, you can trim the excess from a panel directly on the rim joist.

the joints, which makes for a stronger floor. If you're building in a humid climate, leave about ⅛ in. between the ends and the edges of the sheets to allow for expansion. This gap can be gauged by eye or by using an 8d nail as a spacer. The ⅛-in. gap between sheets means that you will have to trim an end now and then so that each sheet lands squarely in the middle of a joist.

When plumbing pipes are installed before the sheathing, you must lay out and cut holes in the sheathing. The easiest way to lay out these cuts is to measure from the edges of sheathing already in place to the center of the pipe, then transfer those measurements to the sheet that the pipe will go through (see the illustration on p. 72). Cut the holes somewhat larger than the pipes, using a circular saw to make a plunge cut, as shown in Chapter 2. This makes it easier to lift the sheet and set it in place over the pipes. Later, seal the holes well to keep cold or moist air from entering the living space from below.

control line, with one end on the center of a rim joist and the other end landing mid-joist—8 ft. to the left or the right. If a sheet doesn't fall on the center of a joist, try pushing the joist over a bit. If this can't be done, mark the sheet to length so the edge will land mid-joist, then snap a chalkline and cut the sheet. Finish sheathing the first row before moving on to the second one.

The second row of sheathing is installed much like the first, except that you begin with half a sheet (a 4-ft. by 4-ft. piece). This staggers

Secure the sheathing to the joists with 8d nails

When the last panel in a course of sheathing extends beyond the rim joist, cut it flush with the rim joist before nailing it down (see the photo at left). The typical nailing schedule for sheathing is 8d nails 6 in. o.c. around the

FITTING SHEATHING

Sometimes a little extra persuasion is needed to unite tongue-and-groove sheathing panels. Have one person stand on the edge of the sheet and hold it flat and snug against the previous row of sheathing. Another person can lay a scrap of 2× (to protect the groove from damage) against the sheet and hit it with a sledgehammer. A couple of licks should bring the two sheets together. If not, check the edge for damage or for an obstruction that may be holding the two sheets apart.

Coax panels into place. A couple of good wallops with a sledge will usually seat even an ornery sheet of tongue-and-groove sheathing. [Photo by Don Charles Blom]

Habitat for Humanity®

HABITAT BUILDS BARRIER-FREE HOMES

Simple, single-story houses are not only less expensive to build but also lend themselves well to barrier-free (handicap-accessible) construction. In addition to the obvious differences that relate to wheelchair accessibility—wider hallways and doorways, a ramp instead of a stairway at the entryway—many other smaller details help make these homes easier for their owners to use and enjoy.

The key to building or retrofitting a house for wheelchair accessibility is recognizing the modified reach of a seated person. You can start by raising the position of electrical outlets and lowering the height of light switches, closet poles, shelves, and countertops. These easily made alterations help make day-to-day life more convenient for someone in a wheelchair.

Bathrooms and kitchens require special attention. Plenty of strategically placed grab bars are important; place them around the toilet and in and around the tub/shower. Extra space in the bathroom—so a wheelchair can get in and maneuver around—is essential, too. In the kitchen, lowered stovetop, sink, and cabinets help make it possible for someone in a wheelchair to prepare and serve meals and clean up.

Modify cabinets for wheelchair access. Lower countertops and desk-type openings can make the kitchen much more accessible. [Photo by Steve Culpepper, courtesy *Fine Homebuilding* magazine © The Taunton Press, Inc.]

Recognizing the increasing need for barrier-free housing, the Knoxville, Tennessee, Habitat affiliate sponsored a contest to design an adaptable, inexpensive, barrier-free house. Two designs were selected as winners; both are available to any affiliate through Habitat for Humanity International. With the leading edge of the baby-boom population already past 60, more and more of us may come to appreciate housing that's flexible enough to adapt to our needs as the years go by.

—*Vincent Laurence*

---

perimeter of the building and at joints between the sheets and 12 in. o.c. in the field (the middle of the sheets). It's best to nail the sheets soon after laying them, especially in hot weather, so that the adhesive doesn't have a chance to set before the sheet is pulled fast to the joists. If necessary, snap chalklines across the panels to show the joist locations for nailing.

An efficient method is to have one team lay sheets and tack them at their four corners, then have another team follow behind, nailing off the sheets completely. In many areas of the country, carpenters use rough-coated, hot-dipped galvanized nails or nails with grooves cut in them (ring-shank nails) to ensure that the sheathing stays firmly secured to the joists.

GOING UP

Walls Create Space

The wall-framing phase of a homebuilding project is an exciting one. Piles of lumber scattered around a flat platform are soon assembled into a complex skeleton that defines the shape and size of a home's interior spaces. For the first time, it's possible to experience the look and feel of a new house. We're still a long way from move-in, but the completed frame is a dramatic step forward.

Framing walls requires an abundance of energy, good teamwork, and real presence of mind. As you'll see on the following pages, it takes quite a few steps to get the walls up and ready for roof trusses. Wall locations must be chalked out on the slab or subfloor; plates must be scattered; headers, rough sills, cripples, and trimmers must be cut; plates must be marked; and the pieces must be nailed together. After the walls are nailed together, they must be raised, braced, connected, plumbed, lined, and sheathed. It all happens fast, though, and before you know it, there's a house standing where there wasn't one before.

As a novice carpenter, I was often afraid that I would make a huge mistake while doing wall layouts. Transferring measurements from the building plans to the floor sheathing or slab seemed like a precise and unforgiving science, the principles of which I didn't fully understand. I knew that once the house was framed, the wall-layout lines would be real spaces—bedrooms, bathrooms, and kitchens—so accuracy seemed critical. After laying out a few houses, however, I learned that, as with most other aspects of carpentry, wall layout just needs to be close—normally within ¼ in. tolerance—not accurate to a machinist's or scientist's tolerances. After I realized that, I was able to relax and get on with the work.

Photo by Don Charles Blom

STEP 1 LAY OUT THE WALLS

I've done plenty of house layouts on my own, but it's better to tackle this job with a helper or two. The work goes faster when you have someone else to hold the other end of the tape or chalkline. More important, your chances of catching mistakes improve significantly.

Read the building plan

A building plan is a guide, just like a road map. There are symbols and measurements to tell you what to do (see the illustration on the facing page). You don't have to visualize every detail on a road map to get from Texas to Maine. Neither do you have to visualize every detail on a plan to be able to build a house. You just have to know how to read the plan, then take it one step at a time.

The most common plan scale uses ¼ in. to equal 1 ft., so 1 in. on a plan equals 4 ft. on a subfloor. Plan dimensions, however, can be labeled as outside to outside, inside to inside, outside to center, or center to center (wall to wall), so you need to pay close attention to this information (see the illustration below). For layout purposes, if you encounter an outside to center (o/s to c) dimension, simply add 1¾ in.—half the width of a 2×4—to the overall measurement to obtain the outside to outside measurement, which you can then transfer to the floor (for a 2×6 wall, add 2¾ in.).

The first layout work involves transferring key information from the building plans to the subfloor or slab. These layout lines enable you to lay down the top and bottom plates for every wall in the house—a process called plating the walls. With each wall's top and bottom plates temporarily tacked together on the subfloor, you can mark up the plates to identify exactly where each stud, king stud, header, and trimmer is located. If you haven't already done so, take the time to familiarize yourself with the various parts that go into a wood-frame wall (see the illustration on p. 87).

Mark wall layouts

Three marking tools are essential: a chalkline, a keel, and a carpenter's pencil. A chalkline and an ample supply of chalk allow you to snap wall layout lines on the subfloor or slab (see the top photo on p. 80). It's not necessary to mark two lines for a wall; instead, use a carpenter's crayon, or keel, to mark an "X" on the side of the line that will be covered by the wall plates. A keel is also useful for labeling parts, writing cripple sizes on headers, and indicating door and window openings.

To make a snapped line easier to find, use a pencil or keel to make a crow's foot, or a large "V" mark, with the point centered on the line. If you snap a line in error, wipe it away with your foot or at least draw a wavy line through it before snapping a line in the correct place. Use another chalk color to snap the correct line. Try to keep all markings clear and simple, and avoid complicating things unnecessarily. The object is to get all the information you

WALL DIMENSIONS ON PLANS

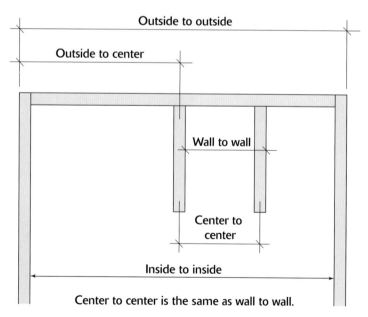

Dimensions on plans can be shown in different ways. Make sure you know the beginning and end points of your measurements before laying out any walls.

FROM PLANS TO PLATES

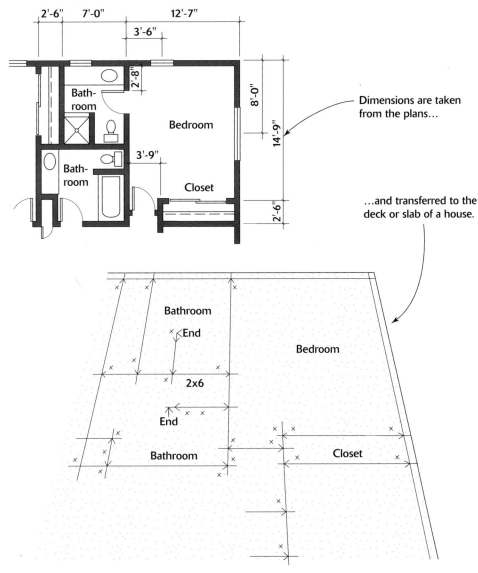

Dimensions are taken from the plans…

…and transferred to the deck or slab of a house.

Chalklines are snapped on the floor to show the location of all the walls. The top and bottom plates will be tacked to the deck along those lines.

TIP **Select the right chalk.** The powdered chalk used for chalklines comes in different colors. Have a second color on hand, in case you need to snap a new chalkline close to an incorrectly snapped line. If you need to lay out walls in wet weather, use water-proof chalk to make sure your lines stay sharp and precise.

need off the plan and onto the floor in an understandable format.

Mark exterior walls first

If the deck perimeter isn't parallel and square, the walls won't be either. Take the time to check this now, following the procedure explained in Chapter 3 (see pp. 56–57). If necessary, fine-tune the exterior wall layout to correct for out-of-square corners or nonparallel walls. The lines you snap define the inside edge of the exterior walls. For 2×4 walls, measure 3½ in. in from the deck edge (slightly more or less if you need to get the walls square and parallel). If the walls will be framed with 2×6s, use a 5½-in. measurement. Instead of measuring this distance, you can simply lay a scrap 2×4 (or 2×6) on the deck and mark against its inside edge.

TIP **Slab plates are important.** If you're framing walls on a concrete slab, re-member that the bottom plate must be made from pressure-treated lumber. A PT bottom plate will repel termites and resist rot when moisture wicks up from the slab.

Layout starts with snapped lines. The floor deck is clear, but not for long. Snapped chalklines and Xs marked with carpenter's crayon identify where the walls will be located.

Mark all the exterior corners to establish the layout marks for snapping the exterior wall lines around the perimeter of the floor (or slab).

When you've marked all the corners, snap lines around the perimeter. If you're working on a concrete slab, you may want to move all these lines in an extra ½ in. so that the wall sheathing can be nailed onto the framed wall flush with the concrete. At this point, pay no attention to the openings for doors and windows—just snap the wall lines right through the openings.

Mark interior walls next

Begin laying out the interior walls by measuring from the exterior walls. For example, the illustration on p. 79 calls for a distance of 12 ft. 7 in. from the outside corner of the house to the center of a partition wall. Add or subtract 1¾ in. from that distance to snap the layout line for the partition wall. Remember to note how measurements are given on the plans. Lay out

long interior walls (such as hallways) first, then do the short walls (such as closets). There is no need to mark the door and wall openings.

For hallways, the minimum width is 37 in. in the rough, which yields a finished width of 36 in. (accounting for ½-in. drywall installed on each side). I sometimes frame hallways 40 in. wide in the rough to create easier passage for a wheelchair (a standard wheelchair is 26 in. wide).

Pay particular attention to squaring bathrooms and kitchens, which makes it easier to set cabinets and install vinyl flooring. When framing on a slab, plumbing lines will have been set in the concrete. If a pipe was placed slightly outside where a wall should be, it's better to move the wall rather than the pipe. If the pipe misses the wall by a lot, you'll need to involve a plumber.

Although a standard bathtub is 60 in. long, I snap wall lines with a 60⅛-in. space for the tub, which makes installation easier for the plumber. I also lay out the bathroom's plumbing wall with a 2×6 wall instead of a 2×4; a wider wall makes it much easier to fit all the bathroom pipes inside.

STEP 2 PLATE THE WALLS

This step involves laying out all of the lumber required for the top and bottom plates, cutting the plates to length, and temporarily tacking them on their layout lines so that matching marks can be made on both plates for the studs, doorways, windows, and intersecting walls. Don't plate, mark, and build one wall at a time. This old method is time-consuming and makes it difficult to frame accurately. Instead, put all the plates down for every wall, beginning with the outside walls.

It's best to plate the long, outside through walls first, then plate the outside butt walls that extend between the through walls. As shown in the illustration on the facing page, through walls have plates that run through from corner to corner. Walls that fit between or intersect other walls are called butt walls. After you

PLATING WALLS

- Plate exterior walls first, beginning with through walls.
- Plate interior butt walls second.
- Use 8d nails to temporarily tack plates in place.
- When possible, tack top plates directly on top of bottom plates.

TIP "Tacking" is temporary. When a framing carpenter uses the word "tack," it means that parts are temporarily nailed together.

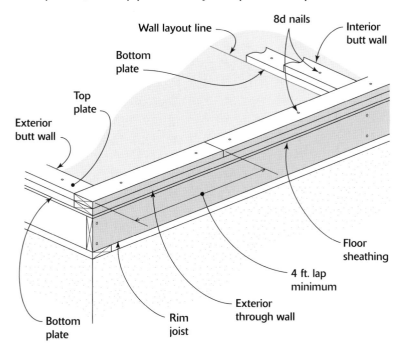

TIP Select straight plates. Check 2× plate lumber for bow and twist and select only the straightest boards for plates. This makes for strong, straight walls.

finish plating the outside walls, you can move inside, beginning with the longest walls and working your way toward the shortest ones.

Stack, tack, and cut

Plating a wall involves three procedures.

STACK THE PLATES. Place two layers of plate stock (2×4s are used for the wall framing on this house) along the layout line for the wall. These layers will become the top and bottom plates. Reserve the straightest 2×4s for the plates, and use the longest plates (typically 16 ft.) on the longest exterior walls. Pay attention to where the top plate stock butts together. These butt joints should be at least 4 ft. away from an intersecting wall.

TACK THE PLATES IN PLACE. After you've distributed the plate stock, you can start tacking it down. Using 8d nails, tack, or

Wall plating is the next step. Carry the plates to the wall lines before cutting them to length and tacking them in place.

WAYS TO PLATE WALLS

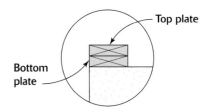

Most walls are plated this way. The bottom plate is tacked to the floor and the second plate is tacked to the first with 8d nails.

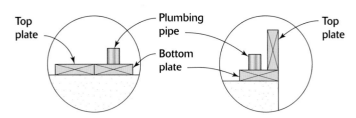

Two ways to plate walls that house pipes

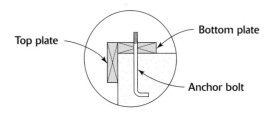

When working on a concrete slab the exterior walls have bolts. In this case, hang the top plate on the outside. Bottom plate is PT.

temporarily nail, the bottom plate to the subfloor right on the line. Drive an 8d nail about 1 ft. from the end of each board and another near each intersecting wall. Tack the top plate directly on top of the bottom plate. Continue stacking and tacking until you reach the end of the wall.

CUT THE PLATES TO LENGTH. As you're stacking and tacking, you'll also be cutting plates to length with a circular saw. Where 2× plate stock butts together, make sure that the ends are square-cut and that they meet snugly. Although it's acceptable for the bottom plate to be a little short, the top plate must be as close as possible to the exact length. The bottom plate of a framed wall is nailed to the subfloor. Roof trusses are nailed to the top plates.

When the outside walls have been plated, you can start scattering plate stock for the interior walls. Don't do this haphazardly. Just as when you were laying out the walls, it's best to plate the long, parallel interior walls first. These long walls become through walls into which shorter walls butt. Plate the shortest walls last. Pay attention to which interior walls are butt walls and which ones are through walls. If the walls are plated properly, it is easier to build and raise them. I run all plates continuously, ignoring door and window openings. The bottom plate will be cut for the door openings later.

CARRYING LUMBER

Framing lumber can be heavy. A 2×4 stud isn't a big deal, but a wet, 16-ft. 2×12 sure is—and there are many boards of that heft even in a small house. Don't carry lumber by holding the board at your waist; this puts undue strain on your elbows and lower back. Instead, grab a long, heavy board at its balance point and, in one fluid motion, lift and flip it gently onto your shoulder. With your entire body helping absorb and distribute the weight, the load is much easier to carry.

Mark the sill plate on the slab with a bolt marker.
[Photo by Don Charles Blom]

Another way to mark the plate is by creating indents of the bolts on the plate. Place the plate over the bolts and apply pressure. [Photo by Don Charles Blom]

Solidly brace the plate while drilling bolt holes with a spade bit. [Photo by Don Charles Blom]

The band joist is nailed on top of the plate. The floor joists are nailed to the band joists. [Photo by Don Charles Blom]

Plating on a concrete slab and around plumbing

Remember to use treated wood when working on concrete. Untreated wood placed next to a slab is an open invitation for hungry termites to move in. When working on a slab with anchor bolts, use an anchor-bolt marker to locate the holes in exterior wall plates (see p. 58 for more on anchor bolts). With a bit of practice, you can also mark the bolt holes by setting the plate di-rectly on the bolts. Just sight down and align the plate edge with the chalkline, then hit the plate with a hammer directly over the bolts.

After the holes are drilled, you can fit the bottom plate on the anchor bolts and nail the top plate along the bottom plate's outside edge (see the illustration on the facing page). It can also be toenailed on edge to the top of the top plate.

If you encounter plumbing pipes in the walls, cut the bottom plate to fit around them.

TIP Add anchor bolts to slabs. Anchor bolts need to be within 1 ft. of the end of a wall plate. If necessary, additional bolts can be epoxied into holes drilled in the slab, or suitable masonry anchor bolts can be installed.

ALL ABOUT HEADERS

Spanning the distance above window and door openings, headers transfer the weight of the roof down through the trimmers, making it possible to have openings in a wall without compromising its strength. There are three things you need to know about headers: length, cross-sectional dimensions, and construction details.

Header Lengths

Window and door manufacturers typically provide recommended rough opening sizes for the prehung units they sell. To determine the length of a window header, you can simply add 3 in. to the rough opening size; this is the combined thickness of the trimmers that support the ends of the header.

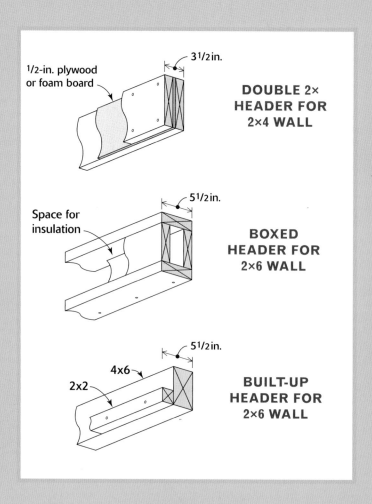

½-in. plywood or foam board

3½ in.

**DOUBLE 2×
HEADER FOR
2×4 WALL**

Space for insulation

5½ in.

**BOXED
HEADER FOR
2×6 WALL**

5½ in.

4×6

2x2

**BUILT-UP
HEADER FOR
2×6 WALL**

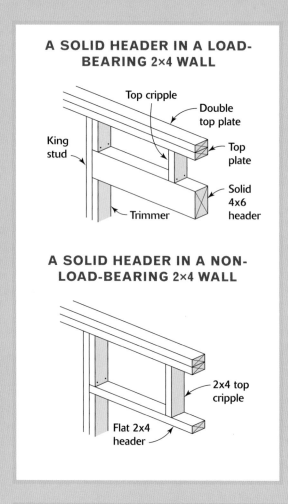

**A SOLID HEADER IN A LOAD-
BEARING 2×4 WALL**

Top cripple

Double top plate

King stud

Top plate

Trimmer

Solid 4x6 header

**A SOLID HEADER IN A NON-
LOAD-BEARING 2×4 WALL**

2x4 top cripple

Flat 2x4 header

- The length of a door header is usually 5 in. greater than the width of the door. Therefore, a 3/0 door (36 in. wide) needs a 41-in. header. The extra 5 in. includes 3 in. for the trimmer thickness, 1½ in. for two ¾-in.-thick door jambs, and ½ in. of clearance space for setting the door plumb.

- A set of sliding doors typically requires a shorter header than a regular door—just 3 in. longer than the combined width of the pair of doors. For example, a set of 5/0 (60-in.) sliding doors requires a 63-in.-long header, which provides 1½ in. on each side for the trimmers. After the trimmers are wrapped with drywall, you're left with a 59-in.-wide opening, which allows the sliding doors to overlap 1 in.

- On the other hand, bifold doors require a header 4¼ in. longer than the actual door size. So 5/0 (60 in.) bifold doors require a 64¼ in. header. The 4¼ in. margin leaves room for two trimmers (3 in.), a layer of drywall (1 in.), and ¼ in. so that the doors will close properly.
- The standard header length for vinyl-framed windows is 3 in. longer than the rough opening (39 in. for a 36 in. window). For wood-frame windows, headers are cut 5 in. longer than the rough opening, just like door headers are. Make sure that the window sizes meet code requirements for daylight, ventilation, and egress.

Header Cross Section and Construction

- The header in a nonbearing wall can be a single 2×. In a load-bearing wall, the length a header spans determines its cross-sectional measurement. For a 3/0 exterior door or a 4/0 window in a 2×4 wall, code requires at least a 4×4 header. A 5/0 or 6/0 window requires a 4×6 header. An 8/0 window needs at least a 4×8 header. In 2×6 walls, simply increase the thickness of the header to 5½ in.
- Headers can be constructed in many ways. They must be as wide as the wall in which they are installed. In cold regions, headers are built with gaps so that foam or fiberglass insulation can be added. Talk to builders in your area to find out what's done locally, and check with the building inspector to make sure the headers you plan to use will meet code.

You can place the top plate alongside the bottom plate or toenail the top plate on edge to the bottom plate. These plating strategies maintain the alignment of the top and bottom plates so that you can accurately mark both plates at once.

Interior walls without bolts can be secured to a slab in various ways. You can drill through the plate and into the concrete with a cement bit. Once the hole is cleaned out, you can secure a bolt in the cement using epoxy or by using a bolt that expands as it is tightened.

Another common way to fasten a plate to a slab is by using a powder-actuated tool that shoots a hardened pin through the wood into the concrete. These tools pack serious power, so take care. Ask for training from your site supervisor before using them. Be sure to wear lenses to protect the eyes and plugs for the ears.

STEP 3 COUNT AND CUT THE HEADERS, ROUGH SILLS, CRIPPLES, AND TRIMMERS

I helped build my first house in 1948. It was a mail-order house brought to our small town by the Chicago and Northwestern Railroad, then to the site by horse and wagon. Every piece of the house frame was precut and tied in bundles. My job was to untie the bundles and bring the pieces to the carpenters who nailed them together.

Today, the same house pieces are needed, but most of them are cut to length on site. Headers are needed over door and window openings to transfer roof loads down to the subfloor and foundation. Rough sills support windows. Cripples or jack studs either support a rough sill or transfer weight from a top plate to a header. Trimmers extend on both sides of door and window openings to support headers (see the illustration on p. 87).

Before you can begin cutting or marking framing members, you need some basic information, including the standard stud length, the height at which headers will be set, the size and location of door and window openings, and

TIP "Scrap" pieces are valuable. It's smart to collect and organize the offcuts that accumulate as you cut plates, sills, and other wall parts. (This is a great job for one or two volunteers who haven't worked on a construction crew before.) Shorter pieces of 2× lumber can be used to make essential small parts, such as top cripples and blocking.

MAKING A STORY POLE

The best way to obtain accurate lengths for cripples and trimmers is to make a story pole. As the name suggests, this straight length of wood (I use a 2×4) tells a story. In this case, it's the description of a wall layout, with the locations of sills and headers for windows and doors providing the measurements for cutting cripples and trimmers. With a story pole, you do all the measuring once, double-check everything, then use the pole as a reference for the entire layout. Instead of repeatedly measuring cripples and trimmers with a tape measure, you simply transfer the layout marks from the story pole.

To make a story pole, select a straight stud and nail a short scrap of 2×4 on one end to act as the bottom plate. Then, measuring upward from the base of the bottom plate, clearly mark the underside of the header at 6 ft. 10 in. (assuming that is the header height). Measure upward another 1½ in. for a single flat header, 3½ in. for a 4×4 header, and 5½ in. for a 4×6 header, making clear marks across the story pole. The distances remaining above the header layout lines are the lengths of the top cripples. Remember that headers for pocket and bifold doors may be higher, so their cripples will be shorter. Label the layout lines on your story pole to avoid confusion.

To locate windowsills, measure the window height down from the bottom of the header. Measure down another 1½ in. for a single 2× rough sill. The amount remaining is the length of the bottom cripples. The trimmer lengths are measured from the bottom plate to the bottom of the header.

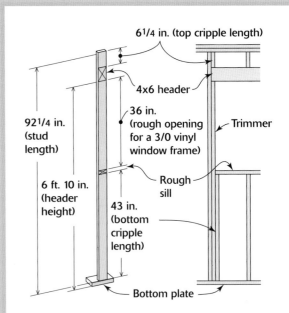

Make a story pole from a 2x stud. This pole will help you accurately lay out trimmers, headers, rough sills, and top and bottom cripples.

the way in which headers will be constructed. A good way to carry around this information is with a story pole, as explained in the sidebar above. Recording wall-building information on a story pole reduces the chance of error and speeds the entire framing process.

Determine dimensions for stud length and header height

Stud length, header height, and other "standard" dimensions vary somewhat from region to region. Find out what is standard in your area. Out west, where I'm accustomed to

framing, we use a stud that is 92¼ in. long. Headers for doors and windows are usually held 6 ft. 10 in. off the subfloor. Check the height in your region, though—in some places, the standard is 6 ft. 10½ in. Headers for pocket doors and closet bifold doors may need to be higher to allow room for an overhead track. Door and window sizes are noted on the plans with designations such as 3/0 × 6/8 (36 in. by 80 in.) or 5/0 × 4/0 (60 in. by 48 in.). Carpenters will say, "There's a three-oh by six-eight door," or "We've got a five-oh by four-oh window going in this wall." The first measurement is the width, the

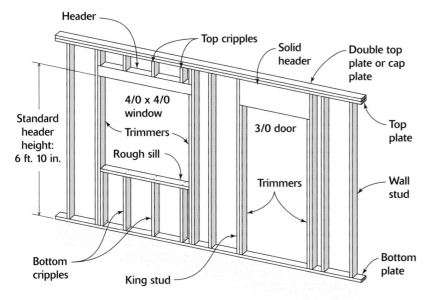

Header

Top cripples

Solid header

Double top plate or cap plate

4/0 x 4/0 window

Trimmers

Rough sill

Standard header height: 6 ft. 10 in.

3/0 door

Trimmers

Top plate

Wall stud

Bottom plate

Bottom cripples

King stud

STUDS are spaced on 16-in. or 24-in. centers. The length of the stud determines the overall height of the wall. Standard stud length is 92¼ in.

KING STUDS are full-length studs used on either side of a door or window opening. They back up trimmer studs and are nailed against the ends of the header and (for window openings) to rough sill.

TRIMMERS (also called trimmer studs) frame the sides of rough openings. They extend along king studs to support ends of headers.

CRIPPLES, often called jack studs, span the distance between top plates and headers and between bottom plates and rough sills.

The **BOTTOM PLATE** is fastened to the floor deck or to a concrete slab floor.

The **TOP PLATE** is nailed to studs and cripples.

The **DOUBLE TOP PLATE** adds rigidity to the top of the wall and overlaps the top plate at wall intersections.

second is the height, and both are expressed in feet/inches. These dimensions are the actual door or window dimensions. To figure out your rough openings, you'll have to add space for the jambs and trimmer studs. This is discussed in the following pages.

After you have a list of headers and all their dimensions for every opening in the house, you can cut and nail them together. Guidelines for sizing and building headers are explained in the sidebar on p. 84. If a door header requires cripples, mark their length on the header, then place the header along the plate where the doorway will be. On window headers, mark the length of the top and bottom cripples, then place each header near the plate location where it will be installed (see the photo at right).

Cut trimmers, rough sills, and cripples

Trimmers are cut and installed in pairs. The two trimmer studs set on the bottom plate support the ends of the header. Trimmers for 6/8 doors and windows are typically 80½ in. long (81 in. in parts of the country where the

header height is 6 ft. 10½ in.). Cut two trimmers for every window less than 8 ft. wide. For windows that are 8 ft. or wider, double up the trimmers on each side. Although you can cut door trimmers at this stage, I prefer to wait until the walls have been raised.

The width of a rough window opening tells you how long to make the rough sill. Taking the

Label the grouped parts. Marked with the top and bottom cripple lengths, the rough sill for a window rests on the header. Both parts are placed on the wall plates where the window will be installed.

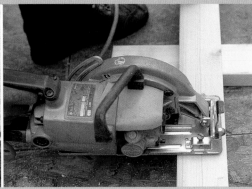

Before the walls go up, we start with a bare floor deck and lots of lumber. Pretty soon there are 2×4s in all directions. Making cuts with a handsaw is no picnic, so be sure to have a good circular saw on hand.

SLIDESHOW

TIP Laying out wall plates begins at the corners of the subfloor or slab. A piece of scrap that is the same width as the plates can be used to mark the corners quickly and accurately.

trimmers into account, the rough still for a window is 3 in. shorter than the window header. A 36 in. window with a 39 in. header gets a 36 in. rough sill. Tack rough sills to the header with one 8d nail, and make sure that the sizes of the window and cripples are marked on the header or sill. For windows that are 6 ft. or wider, you'll need to double up on the rough sills and shorten the cripples by 1½ in.

Cut the cripples after you have cut all the headers, trimmers, and rough sills. Use a story pole, and make sure that your head is clear and your mind is focused. Making a mistake in the cripple length can result in window frames not fitting inside their openings, but you may not know that until all the walls have been built and raised. I once cut all of a house's top cripples 1 in. too long. As a result, I had to remove every door and window header and shorten all of the cripples. Not a good way to start the week.

Cut enough top and bottom cripples to nail one on each end of every header and rough sill and one every 16 in. or 24 in. o.c., depending on the stud spacing. A chopsaw set up on a good work platform is great for cutting cripples (see the photo at right). A stop block, secured to the worktable or to an extension attached to the chopsaw, will enable you to cut identical cripples quickly and precisely.

STEP 4 MARK THE PLATES

Building walls is like baking a cake. Success depends on having all the right ingredients. When you mark the plates, you're setting the exact locations for all of the headers, cripples, studs, corners, and wall intersections associated with each wall in the house.

A chopsaw cuts parts quickly and accurately. To cut a number of framing members quickly and accurately, set up a chopsaw on a large work platform.

Mark corners and channels first

When marking up each plate, start with the locations of corners and wall intersections, which are referred to as channels or tees (see the top illustration at right). As we'll see shortly, corners and channels require extra studs so that the walls can be properly nailed together once they are raised. The extra studs also provide backing for drywall on the inside and siding on the outside. Use a channel marker to mark corners and channels on the plates. Store-bought aluminum markers are available, as shown in the left photo on p. 90. It's also easy to make your own (see the bottom illustration at right).

Take time to make accurate layout marks. Sloppy work at this stage means trouble after the walls have been raised and you begin to plumb and straighten them. Draw accurate lines along all edges of the marker, including the inside edges of the plates, where one wall intersects another. In other words, mark the inside, the outside, and the top surfaces of the through-wall plate. This is important. These corner and channel marks also indicate where the double top (or cap) plates will intersect, tying together through walls and butt walls. Use a keel to mark an "X" on the top plate to let the wall-builder know the location of a corner or channel. Some carpenters write out the word "tee" to note the location of an intersecting channel.

Keep layout marks clean and simple

Methods of marking header locations on plates differ regionally. Whichever system you use, keep it simple. Check the floor plans for each header location, then position the header on the top plate, aligning the sides of the header with the edges of the plate. Mark down from both ends of the header, across both the top and the bottom plates. On outside walls, make these marks on the outside; on interior walls, make marks on the stud layout side.

Next to the end line, mark an "X" on both plates on the side away from the header to indicate the king-stud location (see the photo on p. 91). King studs are nailed alongside headers

MARKING CORNERS AND CHANNELS

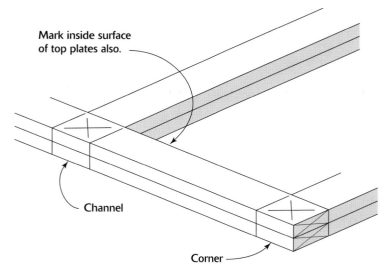

Mark inside surface of top plates also.

Channel

Corner

Be sure to mark the inside, top, and outside of every through-wall plate with the locations of every intersecting wall, both channels and corners.

MAKING A CHANNEL MARKER

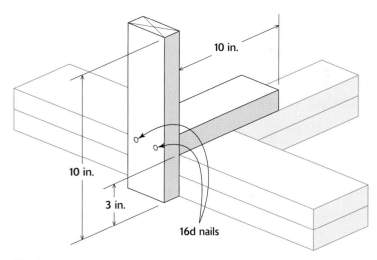

10 in.

10 in.

3 in.

16d nails

The fastest, most accurate way to mark corners and channels is with a tool the same width as the butt walls. In less than a minute, you can cut and nail together such a tool from scrap. Select two pieces of 2x stock about 10 in. long. Turn one piece on end and place the second piece flat against it to form a "T." With the second piece protruding over the first by 3 in., nail the two together with 16d nails.

Mark joining walls with a channel marker. Be sure to make layout marks on all three exposed faces of the plates on the inside, the outside, and the top.

An "X" is easy to spot. Mark an "X" or the word "tee" on the top plate to indicate where one wall intersects another.

BLOCKING IN BATHROOMS AND CLOSETS

Nailed between studs, blocking provides solid backing for items such as towel racks, closet shelves, and safety grab bars. Blocking ensures that the mounting hardware for those devices can be anchored with screws driven into solid wood, so that you don't have to worry about racks, bars, and shelves pulling loose.

It's smart to include blocking when marking up wall plates. Cut blocking boards from 2× scraps. As shown in the illustration at right, blocking is installed so that the face of the 2× is flush with the edges of the studs. To help locate blocking, use these standard heights for common bath, kitchen, and storage fixtures:

- Towel bars: Near the tub and vanity, center blocks 54 in. above the floor.
- Toilet-paper holder: Near the toilet, center blocks 24 in. above the floor.
- Toothbrush and soap holder: Above the sink, center blocks 40 in. above the floor.
- Safety grab bars: Near the toilet and near (or in) the bathtub/shower, center blocks 36 in. above the floor.
- Closet shelf and pole: Block 66 in. above the floor; more blocking may be needed if you install wire shelves.
- Linen-closet shelves: First block above the floor at 20 in., then block every 14 in. thereafter for above-floor measurements of 34 in., 48 in., 62 in., and 76 in. Don't forget to block for a shelf or two in the utility room to hold detergent and other laundry items.

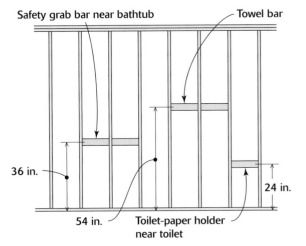

WALL-BLOCK HEIGHTS FOR BATHROOM FIXTURES

Safety grab bar near bathtub — Towel bar

36 in.

54 in. — Toilet-paper holder near toilet

24 in.

All measurements are from the floor to the center of the blocking.

Many fixtures in a bathroom require solid blocking behind the drywall to ensure safe, secure mounting.

- Kitchen cabinets: Block below 36 in. for base cabinets, above 54 in. and below 84 in. for wall cabinets.
- Shutters: Block at the top and bottom of windows at least 12 in. wide.

and hold door and window frames together. On the other side of the line, underneath the header, make a long, straight line along both plates to indicate that there will be an opening at that location and that no studs should be nailed there.

No matter what the plans indicate, keep interior wall headers at least 1½ in. away from corners and channels so you'll have space on which to nail door and window trim. In hurricane and earthquake zones, exterior walls must not have window or door openings less than 4 ft. from an exterior corner, so that these sections of wall can be braced properly.

Above all, mark clearly. These plates will be pulled up and moved during framing. Clear marks improve the odds that all framing members will be attached accurately.

Use special markings to help other tradespeople

It's important to remember that the framing must accommodate plumbing, heating, and electrical features. Talk to the subcontractors

To indicate the position of the king studs, which hold the window and door frames together, mark an "X" on the edges of the top and bottom plates just outside the straight line that indicates where the header goes. The long, straight marks on the plates indicate the door and window openings.

BATHROOM STUD AND BACKING LAYOUT

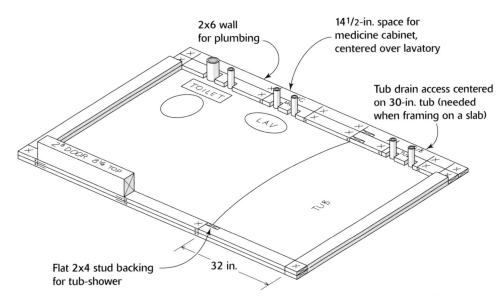

2x6 wall for plumbing

14½-in. space for medicine cabinet, centered over lavatory

Tub drain access centered on 30-in. tub (needed when framing on a slab)

Flat 2x4 stud backing for tub-shower

32 in.

In addition to regular studs, bathroom walls need special layouts for the tub backing, medicine cabinet, and access to the drain.

MAKING A LAYOUT STICK

Whether you use a store-bought layout stick or make your own, this tool will save you a lot of time when marking plates in preparation for wall construction. A stick like the one shown here can be used to lay out studs on 16-in. and 24-in. centers.

To make your own layout stick, cut a series of 1½-in.-wide strips from a panel of ¾-in.-thick plywood. Cut one strip 49½ in. long and five strips 9½ in. long. Glue and nail the short pieces to the long piece at right angles and at the spacing shown in the illustration below. The 3-in. legs allow you to mark top and bottom plates at the same time. The 5-in. legs make it easy to mark two plates side by side and to mark headers and rough sills along with the plates.

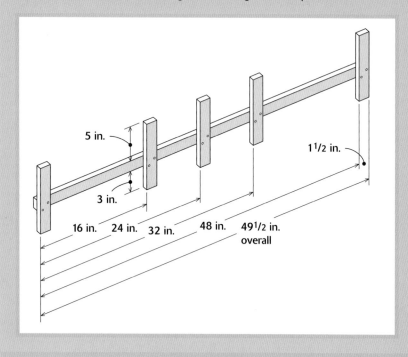

5 in.

1½ in.

3 in.

16 in.   24 in.   32 in.   48 in.   49½ in.
overall

before you even start on the floor. Show them your plans and find out what you can do when it comes time to frame walls so that they can do their work without having to remodel your structure.

You can start by asking the plumber whether there's anything you can do while laying out the bathroom to make it easier to install the pipes. The plate layout for a typical bathroom is shown in the illustration on p. 91. Code requires a mini-

mum of 31 in. from sidewall to sidewall for a toilet. The wall behind a toilet is usually 12½ in. from the center of the waste drain. Standard bathtubs are usually 30 in. wide and 60 in. long. If building on a slab, you may need a 12-in. by 12-in. access hole in the wall so the plumber can hook up or repair the tub trap. Measure 15 in. from the wall to the center of the tub trap and make a mark. Then measure 6 in. to each side of the mark (for a 12-in. hole) and strike lines onto the plates. Mark an "X" on the outside of these lines on both plates to show the studs' positions.

Once a tub/shower unit has been installed, the plumber will nail it in place to a backing stud. Measure 32 in. from the corner and mark both plates with a keel. The stud location falls away from this mark. Toward the inside, mark the location of a flat stud that will be nailed to the first stud. The flat stud provides backing for the tub.

Plans often show an in-wall medicine cabinet centered over the bathroom sink. The standard rough opening for an in-wall medicine cabinet is 14½ in. wide. To accommodate one, measure 7¼ in. in each direction from the center (directly over the sink's drain pipe) and mark across both plates with a keel, making an "X" on the outside of each line to indicate the studs' locations. This will give you a 14½-in.-wide rough opening for the medicine cabinet. Write "MC" on the plates between the two stud locations.

Include blocking requirements when marking up plates. As explained in the sidebar on p. 90, blocking between studs provides solid backing for important items, such as towel bars, built-in shelves, and so on, which will be installed after the interior walls are finished. If you're building a porch, this is also the time to mark the location of any porch beams (see Chapter 6). Porch beams recess 3 in. inside the walls and require two trimmers underneath to support them.

Mark stud locations last

I don't know who made the first layout stick for marking stud locations, but I have been using one for almost 50 years. You can either make

Stud layout is a quick process when you use a layout stick. Position the layout stick 3⁄4 in. beyond a corner on outside walls and mark stud (and cripple) locations every 16 in. or 24 in. o.c.

one (see the sidebar on the facing page) or buy one (see Resources on p. 279). I learned how to do stud layouts with a long tape and a small square, but I think it is faster and easier to use a layout stick.

Take a look at the building plans. Exterior walls generally have studs spaced 16 in. o.c. Interior wall studs may also be spaced 16 in. o.c. but are sometimes 24 in. o.c. When exterior walls are sheathed with plywood or OSB, the studs are spaced to fit these 4-ft. sheets.

Start the stud layout at one end of a long exterior wall. Place the layout stick on the outside edge of the plates, with the first tab 3⁄4 in. beyond the end of the wall. This sets up a 16-in.-o.c. or a 24-in.-o.c. layout that will accommodate the 4-ft.-wide sheathing sheets (see the photo above). Mark both sides of the remaining tabs to note the locations of the next three studs. Move the layout stick, line up the end tab with the last mark, and mark again. If you're nailing a sheet of OSB at the outside corners for bracing, make sure you lay out a stud 4 ft. from each corner in both directions.

Before we can nail the walls together, other parts (top and bottom plates, the studs, and any openings) must be assembled. Raising walls is hard work, but driving nails can be pretty satisfying, whether you use a good, old-fashioned hammer or a pneumatic nailer.

NAILING TOGETHER THE WINDOW FRAME ASSEMBLIES

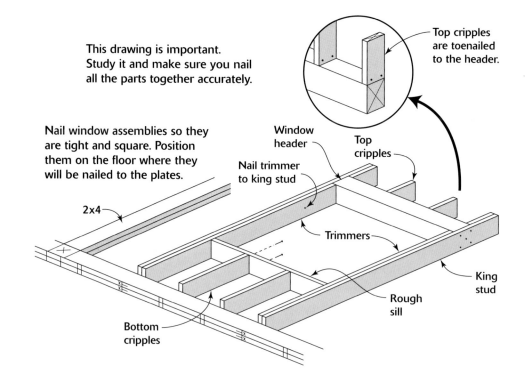

This drawing is important. Study it and make sure you nail all the parts together accurately.

Nail window assemblies so they are tight and square. Position them on the floor where they will be nailed to the plates.

Top cripples are toenailed to the header.

Window header

Nail trimmer to king stud

Top cripples

2x4

Trimmers

King stud

Rough sill

Bottom cripples

TIP Dull tips are useful! When you need to drive a nail near the end of a board, first blunt the tip of the nail. This helps prevent splitting the wood.

When you come to a door or window opening, just continue the stud layout, marking cripple locations on the headers and the rough sills. Lay out all exterior walls and then begin on the interior walls. The layout of interior walls is not as critical as that of exterior walls, because most drywall hangers use long sheets of drywall, which often run from corner to corner. Just put the stick in a corner against a through wall and start marking. Make sure you put the stud markings on the same side of the plates as the header markings. When you encounter rough plumbing, don't put a stud next to a pipe. Give the plumbers room to finish their work. Each intersecting wall automatically has a stud on each end, so there's no need to mark those locations.

Old codes required that a stud be placed under every break in the top plate. Here in the West, this hasn't been a requirement for nearly 40 years, but check with your local building inspector. My guess is that few, if any, areas in the country still require it. As long as you have

a double top plate, locating a stud under a plate break adds little to the structural integrity of the frame.

Because of the sheer number of marks required on walls, it's a good idea to walk through every "room" after you have finished marking all the plates. Visually check whether all of the wall plates, headers, rough sills, corners, and channels are properly marked. The time you take to inspect your work now can save you much more time later. It takes a lot longer to tear out studs and frame a door that was missed during layout than it does to take a leisurely but focused stroll through the house to make sure everything is in order.

STEP 5 BUILD THE WALLS

In addition to being a carpenter for the past 50 years, I've also been a gardener my entire life, and I see a lot of similarities between framing and gardening. If you take the time to prepare the ground, add lots of compost, plant good seeds, mulch well, and nurture young plants, you can't help but grow outstanding vegetables. The situation is similar when you're framing walls. If you take the time to lay out, cut, and correctly position every part of every wall, then the actual framing will go smoothly and you'll produce a quality building.

A Habitat volunteer once said to me, "Now the fun starts," as we began to nail together all the wall pieces. I guess everything in life is relative. If you have to stand out in the blazing sun building walls day in and day out, the joy of framing does eventually wear off. On the other hand, when working as a team, a group of people building walls will see a lot of progress in one day, and that is satisfying.

Before I start building walls, I always begin by cleaning up the work area. Some scrap will have been generated as you cut the parts for the walls and there's no need to leave it lying around for someone to trip over.

Begin with door and window assemblies

I begin framing by building the door and window assemblies. All window headers and most door headers need top cripples (sometimes called jacks) and all rough sills need bottom cripples (see the illustration on the facing page). A chopsaw worker has probably already cut these to size and grouped and labeled them. Grab an armload and carry them to their proper locations. Check to see that the cripples match the lengths written on each header. Every header takes a cripple on each end and one on each layout mark. Pay close attention! Place bottom cripples perpendicular to the wall plates, exactly where they will be nailed in place. I also place a trimmer and a king stud next to each window opening before I do any nailing.

To make toenailing cripples to headers easier, back up the cripple with your foot before starting the first two 8d toenails (see the top photo at right). Make sure each 2× cripple is on its layout mark and flush with the sides of

A work boot does a good job of backing up the cripple as you toenail it to the header.

the header, then drive the nails home. After nailing off one side, toenail two more 8d nails into the other side. Repeat the process until all the top cripples for each wall have been nailed to their headers.

Attaching the bottom cripples to rough windowsills is easier. Move the rough sill to the upper ends of the cripples placed against the plates. There should be one cripple at each end of the sill and one at each layout mark. Drive two

Door and window assemblies are nailed together and ready to be installed between the top and bottom wall plates. [Photo © Larry Haun]

'WE FELT SPECIAL'—A FAMILY SURVIVES KATRINA

Stephanie Jordan was living in a rented house next door to her grandmother's place when Hurricane Katrina struck. Having weathered previous storms like Hurricane Camille, Stephanie's grandmother was determined to stay.

Two-and-a-half feet of water flooded the houses during that scary night. All the Jordan family possessions were ruined except things stored in the uppermost parts of the house. FEMA declared Stephanie's home unsalvageable. She and her children—Tory, 10, and Tyce, 4—were forced to move into a cramped trailer until Christmas 2006, when they moved into their Habitat home.

Each of the children now has a room to themselves—a welcome change for two growing children after more than a year of living in tight quarters. "Before they were always at each other's throats," Stephanie said.

For Stephanie, the added space is just one of the things she likes about her new home. She also likes to cook in her full-size kitchen. "Every time I cooked in the trailer I set off the fire alarm," she laughs. And she loves having a place that she owns. Stephanie, a NASA transportation specialist, says that living in the Habitat home has made her "more relaxed."

In April 2007, President Jimmy Carter visited Stephanie and her Habitat neighbors. "For me and my oldest, it's something that we'll never forget," Jordan said. "It was quite an astounding event for us. We felt special." —*Susan Stevenson*

Tyce Jordan loves playing on the porch of the Habitat house he shares with his mother, Stephanie, and older sister, Tory. [Photo courtesy HFHI]

16d nails about ¾ in. from each edge of the rough sill into each cripple. When nailing near the end of 2× stock, set the nail back from the end and drive it at an angle or blunt the nail point to reduce your chances of splitting the board.

Finish the window-frame assemblies by nailing on the trimmers and king studs. This is easy to do now because you are working flat on the floor. Don't move these units around. Keep them in place where they will be nailed to the plates. Nail the window trimmers flush with the ends of the bottom cripples. Secure the trimmers to the rough sill with just two 16d nails each. Then nail the king studs alongside them so they are flush with the top of the top cripples and with the bottom of the trimmers. Secure the king studs on each side by driving two 16d nails into a 2× header or four or five 16d nails into a larger header. Finally, drive a nail near the top of the trimmer into the king stud. The trimmers will be permanently nailed later, before you install the exterior sheathing or set the windows. As for door trimmers, wait to install them until after the walls have been raised.

With all the walls plated and the window and door frames nailed together, you're ready to frame the walls. At this stage, it's smart to check your work. Make sure that the framing members are flush with each other and nailed tightly together. Keep the door and window frames square. This makes for quality construction and you'll have an easier time nailing the top and bottom plates to wall studs and door and window frames.

Distribute studs, corners, and channels

Ask your crew to distribute studs along one of the exterior through walls, with one stud per layout mark. Place the studs against the two tacked-down plates. Where corners and channels are required, decide which corner style you want to use. The sidebar on the facing page

BUILDING CORNERS AND CHANNELS

Like headers, outside corners and channels can be built in a number of different ways, and preferences tend to be regional. The most common constructions are shown in the illustration below. A two-stud outside corner works well in most cases, but if you are planning to install clapboard or fiber-cement siding directly to the studs (with no exterior sheathing), you'll need more backing at the outside corners. A blocked-up corner provides more backing and makes good use of 2× offcuts. In addition, all of these outside corner configurations provide backing on the inside of the wall for drywall or other wallboard.

Channels (sometimes called tees) are most easily made with a flat stud or blocks nailed between two regular studs. I place a crowned or knot-filled stud between two good studs. In some parts of the country, framers build ladder-type channels to provide backing at intersecting walls. Building ladder backing doesn't save a lot on materials, but it does allow more insulation to be inserted at those spots.

Both corners and channels are nailed together with one 16d nail every 2 ft. o.c. When nailing channels to the top and bottom plates, make sure that the flat stud is oriented correctly to provide backing for an intersecting wall. It's not difficult to put in a channel upside-down.

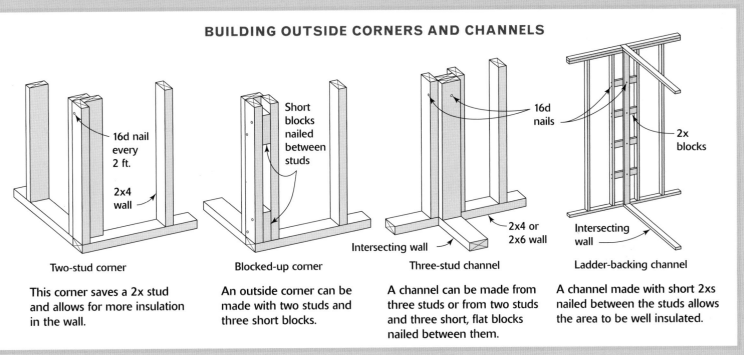

BUILDING OUTSIDE CORNERS AND CHANNELS

Two-stud corner

This corner saves a 2× stud and allows for more insulation in the wall.

Blocked-up corner

An outside corner can be made with two studs and three short blocks.

Three-stud channel

A channel can be made from three studs or from two studs and three short, flat blocks nailed between them.

Ladder-backing channel

A channel made with short 2×s nailed between the studs allows the area to be well insulated.

16d nail every 2 ft.

2×4 wall

Short blocks nailed between studs

Intersecting wall

2×4 or 2×6 wall

16d nails

2× blocks

Intersecting wall

explains the main types of corners and channels. You can build corners and channels in place as you frame the walls, or you can build them all at once in a central location, then distribute them and insert them in the walls as needed.

Keep your eyes open for studs that are bowed, twisted, or crowned. Set them aside to use for blocking and roof braces. This ensures a more uniform finished wall and makes it easier for finish carpenters to install cabinets, countertops, and interior trim. It's always good to think about how to make future tasks easier. So take care to use straight studs in all walls that will hold kitchen cabinets.

Nail on the top and bottom plates

It's finally time to pry apart the two wall plates that were tacked together on the subfloor.

A pneumatic nailer makes quick work of making a channel, which consists of two studs separated by 2×4 blocking.

After separating the top plate from the bottom plate (visible in the background), the top plate can be nailed to the studs, channels, and window and door assemblies. Drive a pair of 16d nails into each stud.

TIP If possible, nail the blocks for cabinets, toilet fixtures, and even the closets to the wall before it has been positioned upright. It's much easier to install the blocks when the wall is flat on the deck.

Working on one wall at a time, separate the top wall plate from the bottom plate, removing the 8d tack nails as you go. Leave the bottom plate tacked to the floor for now. Nail the top plate first, using the bottom plate to keep the studs aligned. Move the top plate straight up to the upper ends of the studs. Don't turn a top plate end for end as you move it into position or you'll have a real mess. The exterior walls can be framed over the interior walls rather than flat on the deck or slab (see the top photo above). This is okay. The most important element in wall framing is to keep the frame reasonably straight and square on the floor.

This is not difficult to do. Take your time until you get it right.

Begin nailing studs to the plate at an outside corner. Make each stud flush with the edge of the plate. Drive a pair of 16d nails through the plate into each stud. You will find that consistently working either from left to right or from right to left has a natural feel. Over time, you will develop a rhythm to nailing studs that involves not just your hands and arms but your entire body.

If you are using a pneumatic nailer, always drive the bottom nail first. Then remove your hand from the stud and drive the top nail. If you keep your hand in place while driving the top nail, sooner or later you will miss and drive a nail into your hand. Unfortunately, I learned this the hard way.

When you come to a door or window opening, be especially careful to nail each king stud on the "X" mark next to the header location. Once all the wall, king, and top cripple studs are nailed to the top plate, pull up the bottom plate and begin nailing it in place, always paying attention to your layout marks. Repeat the process. Nail all wall members to the bottom plate just like you did with the top plate.

I always nail the blocks for a recessed, or in-wall, medicine cabinet while the wall is flat on the floor. At the "MC" marking, hook your tape on the bottom plate and measure up 4 ft. and 6 ft. on the two studs on each side. Nail a flat block below the 4-ft. marks and above the 6-ft. marks. This leaves a clear space of 2 ft., which is the height of a standard recessed medicine cabinet.

Nail on the double top plate

In some parts of the country, carpenters raise the walls before cutting and nailing on the double top plate. In my opinion, the time to nail on the double top plate is now—while the wall is still flat on the floor. Otherwise, you will have to use a ladder. The top plate is an important structural member. It ties the entire frame together. Without it, severe lateral stress from an earthquake or high winds could easily rip apart a building. If you frame with a single top plate, secure them together with metal plate straps.

On a 2×4 butt wall, the double top plate extends beyond the top plate a bit less than 3½ in. (cut it ¼ in. short—about 3¼ in.—to make sure it doesn't protrude beyond the through wall), so that it can tie into the notch in the double top plate of a through wall. On through walls, the double top plate has notches where it receives the double top plates extending from butt or intersecting walls. Now you can see why it was important to mark the plates accurately while locating the corners and channels. You don't need to measure the length of double top plates. All you need to do is set the double top plate on a through wall above the top plate, with one end held back 3½ in. (5½ in. on 2×6 walls) from the end, then cut it to length.

At channel marks, leave a 3¾-in. cutout so that an intersecting wall can comfortably lap over and tie in at that spot (see the photo on p. 100). When cutting and installing double top plates, leave about a 3¾-in. gap where the walls

tie into each other. This makes it easier for the overlapping double top plates to slip into place. This is another one of those times when it's okay to be less than absolutely accurate.

When you nail the double top plate to the top plate, it's important to make sure that there are no gaps in the top plate. The top plate stock must butt tightly together, just as it did when you plated the walls on the subfloor. Nail the double top plate to the top plate with two 16d nails at each end of the wall and at each break in either the top plate or the double top plate. Elsewhere, nail one 16d nail over each stud. It is best not to nail between studs, because electricians and plumbers run wires and pipes through holes drilled in those locations. Hitting a nail while drilling can dull the bit and give your arm a nasty twist.

Brace the walls

The sudden, intense pressure exerted on a wall by a hurricane, tornado, or earthquake can be devastating. To withstand these forces, the walls must be well braced. As a novice carpenter, I

TIP Remove all temporary nails. When prying loose wall plates and other parts that are temporarily tacked together, make sure you remove all "tacking" nails so that they don't cause injuries.

TIP Alignment is important. As volunteers learn to nail studs, they often find it difficult to keep them aligned on their layout marks and to keep their edges flush with the edges of wall plates. For more accurate results, work in teams of two. Have one volunteer hold the stud on its layout while another drives the nails. Use a cat's paw to pry studs and nails loose when the alignment must be corrected.

With the bottom plate nailed off, cut the double top plate in place, following the layout marks on the top plate.

Diagonal metal braces are easy to install and help hold walls plumb. In earthquake and high wind areas it is much better to use sheets of plywood or OSB for braces. Metal braces offer little resistance to strong lateral forces.

used to cut 2× stock with a handsaw and nail them between the studs, running it diagonally from plate to plate. It was a good brace, but it took about an hour to make each one. These days, braces are much easier to install. You can attach L-shaped metal angle braces or nail plywood or OSB sheathing to the frame. Code requirements vary, so be sure to check with your building department to find out how the walls should be braced. In some areas, bracing is also required on certain interior walls.

USING METAL ANGLE BRACES. Metal angle braces are easy to install (see the photos on the facing page). In many areas, they can be used instead of plywood or OSB sheathing. If the finished siding you plan to install can be nailed directly to the studs or furring strips (clapboards and fiber-cement boards are good examples), metal braces can save you the

expense of plywood or OSB sheathing. Every exterior wall should receive a metal brace at every corner as well as every 25 ft. between corners. The typical metal brace has an L-shaped profile; it's designed to be set into a kerf cut diagonally across the wall. Here's how to install one:

1. Position the brace and mark the cut. Lay the brace across a framed wall so that it extends at a 45-degree angle from the bottom plate to the double top plate. Trace a pencil mark along one side, as shown in the far left photo on the facing page.

2. Cut the kerf. With a circular saw, cut a 1-in.-deep slot along the line into the plates and studs.

3. Nail off the bottom of the brace. Slip one flange of the brace into the slot and nail it to the bottom plate with three 8d nails. Drive one more 8d nail through the brace and into the first stud. At the double top plate, start an 8d nail alongside the brace and bend the nail over to hold the brace in place as the wall is raised.

Now you are ready to raise and plumb the wall. It's important not to install the brace completely until after the wall has been raised and plumbed. See pp. 101–108 for details on raising and plumbing walls.

Finish nailing the brace to the studs and plates by driving one 8d nail through the brace and into every stud it crosses. At the top of the wall, drive three nails through the brace and into the top and double top plates. If the top of the brace extends above the double top plate, trim it flush with a hacksaw.

USING PLYWOOD AND OSB BRACING. When nailed properly to wall framing, plywood and OSB provide much stronger racking resistance than metal braces do. Wall sheathing is essential as a substrate for some types of exterior siding. It also acts as a wind and weather barrier. Many codes require that a full sheet of OSB be nailed at each exterior corner and every 25 ft.

Install the double top plate. Gaps in the double top plate allow those in a butt wall to overlap.

1. To mark the cut line, position the brace diagonally across the wall section from the bottom plate to the double top plate, and then pencil a line along one edge of every framing member the brace crosses. [Photo © Larry Haun]

2. Set the blade on a circular saw for a depth of 1 in., then cut the kerf along the marked lines. [Photo © Larry Haun]

3. Slip the brace into the saw kerf and nail it to the bottom plate and the first stud. Then secure the top of the brace with a bent-over nail. You'll finish nailing off the brace after the wall has been raised. [Photo © Larry Haun]

along the wall. The spaces between can be filled with sheets of rigid foam insulation. That's the sheathing strategy we used on this house.

There are different ways to install wood sheathing panels. Sometimes sheathing is positioned to extend over the wall and cover the rim joist. I try to keep OSB ½ in. away from concrete so it won't absorb water. On a one-story building, my preference is to sheathe the walls once they are raised. This is especially true when working on a slab that has plumbing pipes sticking up.

Other builders prefer to sheathe the walls while they are flat on the floor. One of the problems with sheathing the walls before raising them is that they become heavy. To raise a long 2×6 wall fully sheathed with OSB or plywood, you may have to call in the National Guard. Or you could use a wall jack, a device that hooks under a wall and slowly raises it up (see

Resources on p. 279). Sheathing a wall while it's still flat on the subfloor also requires greater accuracy—the wall must be dead-on straight and square before it's sheathed. You can do this by making sure the bottom plate is directly on the chalkline and the end corner studs are flush with the outside of the building. It doesn't hurt to measure from corner to corner to check the wall for square. After the wall is ready, you can attach the required sheets of plywood or OSB (8d nails every 6 in. o.c. around the perimeter, 12 in. o.c. in the field, or middle of the sheet). Be sure to insulate headers, corners, and channels before covering them with sheathing.

STEP 6 RAISE THE WALLS

As with barn raisings of yore, it takes a few warm bodies to raise framed walls. Let one person be the team leader and encourage everyone

TIP Clear the deck. Before raising walls, be sure to clean up loose nails, lumber scraps, and other debris. If a small object lodges beneath the bottom plate of a wall, it can throw the wall plates out of level.

TIP When you re-
move the tem-
porary blocks nailed to the
rim joist, be sure to pull the
nails or bend them over so
that no one gets a nail in
the foot!

The first wall goes up! Make sure you have enough help when you're ready to raise the walls. Have one person take charge, and get everyone to lift in unison. [Photo by HFHI/Will Crocker]

TIP Temporary
braces are im-
portant. After raising a
wall, make sure it is braced
securely with 2× lumber
that extends diagonally
from the rim joist or the
floor to the top of a stud in
the wall. Secure bracing
eliminates the serious injuries that can result from a
falling wall. These braces
also help keep walls
plumb, straight, and ready
for roof trusses.

to work together (see the photo above). Remind people to lift with their legs, not with their backs. In many areas, builders put a heavy bead of caulk or a roll of foam (polystyrene) on the floor or slab under the bottom plate before rais-ing a wall. This helps keep out cold air as well as any bugs that may want to migrate inside. To ensure that the wall won't slip over the outside edge of the building as it's being raised, nail pieces of 2× stock to the rim joist so they stick up a few inches above the floor to catch and hold the bottom plate (see the photo at right). On a slab, bolts hold the bottom plate in place.

Raise exterior through walls first

Start with one of the exterior through walls. Make sure there is no debris beneath the plates before raising the walls upright. If the wall is flat on the deck, stick the claw of a hammer into the double top plate, lift the wall up a bit, and put a 2× block under the wall. This way you can get your fingers under the wall to lift it. Keeping your back straight, use your legs to lift the wall to your waist, then take it overhead using your arms and upper body. Continue to raise the wall by pushing on the studs until it is fully upright. Once the wall is upright, hold

Nailing the bottom plate is best done when one worker nails while others steady the wall. The short 2×4s nailed to the rim joist prevent the bottom plate from sliding off the floor when the wall is raised.

Remember that diagonal braces are important. Both exterior through walls are up; diagonal braces hold them securely while the other walls are raised. Use these temporary braces liberally where needed.

Steel straps provide extra holding power. Metal ties like this one are sometimes required by code or the building engineer. They anchor the wall framing to the floor and foundation, keeping the house together under adverse conditions.

it steady—especially if there's a good wind blowing—until the temporary wall braces are nailed in place.

After the wall is in position, nail a stud to each end as a temporary brace, extending it diagonally from about 6 ft. up on the corner stud down to the rim joist. Drive a couple of 16d nails into each end of the brace. On long walls, nail other braces in the middle from a stud down to the subfloor. Make sure these temporary braces will hold the wall until the butt walls are built and raised against it.

Use a sledgehammer to move the wall until it is right on the chalkline and flush at the ends with the correct marks on the subfloor. After

When raising interior walls, it often helps to tack part of the double top plate to the wall, as shown here, until after the wall has been raised. Later, this short section of double top plate can be positioned to overlap the top plate in an adjacent wall.

TIP Watch your step. Whether you're walking the plates or using a ladder, don't wear slick-soled shoes. Even with good treads on your shoes, be careful on surfaces that are damp or wet.

the wall is in position, nail through the bottom plate and into the subfloor, using one 16d nail between each stud. Be sure to drive a 16d nail close to each king stud. Drive plate nails into the rim joist or into a floor joist. Nails driven through the subfloor alone don't have nearly as much holding power as those embedded in framing lumber. Don't nail in doorways, because you'll be cutting out the plate later when you set the door frame.

When working on a slab, lever the bottom plate into position over the bolts. Slip the end of a 2×4 under the bottom plate to use as a lever. While one person works the 2×4 lever, other crew members can move the bottom plate in or out to align the holes with the installation bolts. In some areas, bottom plates are attached to the slab with concrete nails. In other areas, steel hurricane straps are used to tie wall framing to the floor framing and foundation (see the bottom left photo on p. 103). Now is the time to make sure that these framing connectors are nailed to the wall frame.

Raise exterior butt walls next

Once you've finished with the exterior through walls, it's time to raise the exterior butt walls. Remember that you want the butt walls' double top plates to be about 3¼ in. longer than the top plates (5¼ in. for 2×6 walls) so that they will lap over the through walls' top plates. This can make it difficult to raise the butt walls, though, because the double top plate sticks out at both ends.

There are a couple of tricks for making it easier to raise these and other butt walls. One approach is to double-plate the entire butt wall except for a short section—say, 4 ft. or 5 ft.—at each end. Cut these short pieces and tack them to the wall to keep them close at hand (see the bottom right photo on p. 103). Then nail them on after raising the wall. Alternatively, you can leave off a section of the double top plate from one end of the wall, then jockey the opposite end into position with a couple of helpers. With a little experience, you'll learn these shortcuts.

When the last wall has been raised, something special happens. What was once just a jumble of framing lumber on the deck all of a sudden feels like a house with real rooms.

Raise interior walls from the longest to the shortest

As you raise and position each wall, nail the end stud of each intersecting butt wall flush with the corner or channel on the through wall. Use three 16d nails: one 2 ft. up from the bottom, one 2 ft. down from the top, and one in the center. After all the walls are raised, stop and admire your work. It's like magic: As you stand in individual rooms, you can see the shape of the house.

Tie off the double top plates

Nailing the lapped double plate into the adjoining top plates ties the entire framed structure together. This important task, when done accurately, makes it easy to plumb and straighten the walls. If you are a gymnast, like my carpenter-daughter, you can hop right up on the plates and start tying the walls together. Otherwise, it's best to work on a sturdy ladder.

The corner marks you drew on the plates earlier now serve as guides when nailing off the top plates. Make sure that the double top plate is on these lines and that the top plates of both walls are touching. If necessary, toenail a 16d nail up through the top plate of the through wall into the double top plate of the butt wall to draw everything together, as shown in the bottom right photo. Nail two 16d nails through the lap into the intersecting wall.

STEP 7 PLUMB AND LINE THE WALLS

The word "plumbing," when used in the context of framing a house, means making sure that the walls are standing straight up and down. "Lining" means straightening the top plate along the length of each wall. It's important that all the walls are plumbed and lined accurately. Anything else is unacceptable. Badly plumbed or crooked walls cause significant problems later—cabinets won't fit properly, doors won't close correctly, and finished surfaces

LOCKING WALLS TOGETHER

To tie joining walls together, the double top plate must overlap the top plate at each wall intersection.

- If you're nimble, you can perch on top of the framing to hammer overlapping joints together.
- Otherwise, do the job on a ladder.
- It's good practice to drive a toenail (or two) into the overlapping plate. A toenail pulls the joining walls together before the top is nailed off.

TIP Most walls can be held plumb and straight using 2×4 studs. Properly placed and nailed, a stud, rather than a longer piece of plate stock, will hold a wall in its proper position.

While one person holds the level, another person can nudge the wall to get it plumb, then nail off a diagonal brace to keep it that way. [Photo by Don Charles Blom]

(both inside and outside) will be wavy.

If the exterior walls were squared and sheathed before being raised, they should be plumb. Otherwise, plumb them now that they are upright. To test for plumb, use an accurate level that is at least 4 ft. long or make a plumb stick, as shown in the sidebar on the facing page. Plumbing a wall is best done with two people: one to hold the level and one to move the wall and nail off the bracing.

Plumb the exterior walls first

Hold a level or plumb stick in a corner to see whether the bubble is centered in the vial. If not, the wall must be moved laterally. Sometimes a wall can be moved a bit with a bodily shove. If you can push the wall plumb, install a temporary 2× diagonal brace to keep it that way (see the photo above). If you need

more force, use a push stick, as shown in the top photo on the facing page. Cut a push stick from a 1×4 or 1×6, making it about 116 in. long for an 8 ft. wall. Use the natural flex in the push stick to exert force on the wall. Position the top of the stick under the top plate and against a stud. Diagonally extend the stick down to the floor, as parallel as possible to the wall. Bend the stick down, holding the bottom end against the floor with one foot. Now pull the middle of the stick up. As the board straightens, the wall moves.

After the wall is plumb, finish nailing in the metal braces or use temporary 2× stud braces nailed at an angle to hold the wall plumb until it is sheathed. When the exterior walls are plumb, proceed to the interior walls. You can't straighten a wall until the walls that butt into it have been plumbed.

A small laser can be used to accurately plumb walls. [Photo by Don Charles Blom]

When a wall needs extra coaxing to get it plumb, wedge a 1×4 or 1×6 push stick against the top of a stud. Your foot can anchor the bottom end of the stick. Flexing the stick upward pushes the wall outward.

Stretch a line to get top plates straight

The bottom plates of your walls are straight because they've been nailed to chalklines. The top plates should be fairly straight if you used straight stock when plating. But walls can deviate from straight at the top plate, and that's where we need to check them. The easiest way to line a wall is to hop up on a ladder and look down the top plate to see if it's straight. A lot of carpentry is done by eye. Learn to trust your eye. If something looks good, it is good. On long walls, it may be best to stretch a line (string) the length of the wall, as shown in the top photo on p. 108. Nail a 2× block to each end of the wall and stretch the line tightly from one block to the other. Using another scrap of 2× as a gauge, slide it along the wall and check for a consistent 1½-in. space between the line and the wall.

To straighten a crooked wall, you'll need to move it in or out. To move a wall out, use two 16d nails to secure a 2× brace to the nearest stud at about header height. Pushing on the brace,

MAKING A PLUMB STICK

To plumb walls, you can make a plumb stick from any 2-ft. level and a straight 2×4 stud. Even a battered, inaccurate level can be used. Select the straightest stud you can find and nail a 16-in. 1×2 strip onto each end, letting the strips overhang the stud ends by about 3 in. Use some duct tape to attach a 2-ft. level to the opposite edge of the 2×4 (near the center) and your plumb stick is nearly ready to use (see the photo below).

It's important to check your plumb stick for accuracy. To do so, hold it vertical and flat against a wall. Keep the bottom end fixed in place as you move the top end back and forth until the bubble is exactly centered in the vial. Make pencil marks on the top and bottom of the wall along the 1× extensions. Now turn the plumb stick side for side—not end for end—so that the level is flat against the wall on the other side of the lines you marked. Carefully line up the extensions with the marks on the plates. If the bubble returns to the exact center of the vial, the plumb stick is accurate. (By the way, you can check the accuracy of any level with this method.)

If the bubble is not centered in the tube, the level needs to be adjusted. Stick a wooden shim, a folded piece of paper, or an 8d nail under one end of the level (between the level and the 2×4), and then check the plumb stick again. Keep adjusting the shim thickness until the bubble is centered both ways.

HAMMERING IN A NAIL CLIP

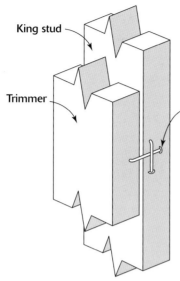

King stud

Trimmer

1. Once the trimmer is plumb, drive an 8d nail into the edge partway and then bend it over, embedding the shank and head in the king stud.

2. Clip the first nail by bending a second nail over it. Hammer the clip until both nails are fully embedded in the wood.

This pair of 8d nails clips one piece of wood next to another. Pairs of nails are frequently used to clip a trimmer stud plumb next to a king stud.

To create a straight reference line, stretch a string tightly around 2× spacer blocks positioned at opposite ends of the wall's top plate. Use another 2× scrap to test for straightness along the top plate. Move the top plate in or out to get the wall straight.
[Photo © Larry Haun]

Walls that need to be moved out slightly can simply be pushed with a stud brace nailed to a wall stud. Nail the brace to the subfloor when the top plate is straight.

move the top plate out until it's straight, then secure the bottom of the brace to the floor with two 16d nails. If you are framing on a slab, first nail a 4-ft. 2× flat on the bottom plate at a right angle to the wall, then nail a brace to the wall and to the flat 2×.

Moving a wall in is a little trickier. Try this: Nail a long 1× or 2× under the top plate and against the subfloor. Then place a short 2× under the center of this diagonal brace and bend the brace upward. As the brace flexes upward, the top plate moves in. This works especially well on a wall that is badly out of line.

Make sure you use enough temporary braces as you plumb and straighten the walls to keep every wall in place. Put braces on straight walls as well. Using plenty of braces ensures that the building will be held plumb and straight. Leave all the braces in place until the roof trusses and sheathing have been installed to prevent any frame movement.

STEP 8 INSTALL AND PLUMB DOOR AND WINDOW TRIMMERS

Many builders—even experienced ones—don't like to spend time plumbing window and door trimmers. But I've found that this step really makes a better building. If the door trimmers are plumb, the door's hinge-side jamb butts solidly against the trimmer along its entire length. There's no need for shims on this side of the door. That means you save time and obtain solid, continuous backing for the jamb that supports the full weight of the door. If the opposite trimmer is also plumb, the shims you install can share the same thickness. There's no fussing to make shims of different sizes. Similarly, window installation benefits from plumb trimmers.

Window trimmers were installed during step 5, when the window assemblies were built on the floor deck. Full-length window trimmers are firmly attached at the bottom corners of the rough window opening, but each trimmer can still be pried away from its king stud to get the trimmer as plumb and straight as possible. Use a straight claw on a framing hammer or a flat bar to pry and a 2-ft. level to test for plumb and straight. When the trimmer is where you want it to be, secure it by toenailing through the header

ON THE JOB

SHEATHING A WALL

When all the walls have been raised, braced, and lined, it's time to attach the sheathing. On this house, two types of sheathing are used. To provide shear bracing, OSB panels are installed on all corners and every 25 ft. along exterior walls. Foam-board sheathing is nailed to the framing between wood panels. It's easier to sheathe right over window and door openings, then cut out the openings from the inside. Foam cuts easily with a handsaw.

with 8d nails. Make sure you toenail from both sides of the wall. To lock a trimmer in straight position, hammer a nail clip into each edge of the trimmer, as shown in the illustration on p. 108.

It's best not to install door trimmers until after the walls have been raised and braced. This way, each trimmer can be measured and cut to fit snugly up against the bottom of the header. I carry two straight studs to each opening, hold them in position under the header, and mark them to length. When the trimmer has been cut for a snug fit, secure it to the king stud with a single 16d nail driven near the center. Don't drive any more nails, because you will need to tap the 2× in or pry it out slightly to get it plumb. Test for plumb with a 6-ft. level. When it is plumb, drive toenails through the header and into the trimmer, then toenail the trimmer to the bottom plate.

SAFETY FIRST

LADDERS

Few things scare me more than working on a ladder. Although they are frequently indispensable, ladders must be treated with the same respect as power saws. Here are a few tips to make working on a ladder safer:

- Don't buy a cheap ladder. I like the heavy-duty fiberglass models. Look for one with a 1A rating (the best) on the label. When buying an extension ladder, be sure to select one that is long enough to extend 3 ft. above the height of your roof.
- Aluminum and wet wood can conduct electricity. It's best to use a fiberglass model when working near electrical wiring.
- Don't stand on the uppermost rungs. Get a longer ladder instead.
- When working on a ladder, you can lose your balance by reaching too far to the side. If your reach starts to feel precarious, it probably is. Get down and move the ladder.
- Don't leave tools sitting on top of an unattended ladder.
- Make sure the ladder's feet are firmly and securely planted on a solid surface before climbing up it. When using an extension ladder, tie it to the building at both the top and the bottom (this is particularly important if it's a windy day).

Finish by getting the trimmer straight, using nail clips, if necessary. When the sheathing is installed, you can lock the trimmers in place by nailing through the sheathing and into the trimmers' edges.

STEP 9 SHEATHE THE WALLS

I lived through the 6.8-magnitude earthquake that hit Northridge, California, in 1992. It made me believe in wall sheathing. A 6.8 quake is not a big one, yet a number of people lost their lives. More lives would have been lost if critical areas in buildings had not been sheathed with plywood or OSB. The buildings that held up best were small, single-story wood-frame houses, such as those built by Habitat. Many were knocked several feet from their foundation, but they didn't collapse on their occupants.

Unlike drywall, stucco, and most exterior siding, plywood and OSB wall sheathing provide both lateral (horizontal) and vertical strength. Sheathing helps hold buildings together and makes a house windproof, which is important if you live in an area where cold winds are a reality.

Because sheathing panels will be covered with finished siding, they don't need to be installed perfectly. Earthquake- and hurricane-country sheathing codes are often quite strict, so check with your local building department before you start covering walls. Again, remember to insulate corners, channels, headers, and behind tubs before you attach wall sheathing.

Install sheathing on the corners first

I always install sheathing on the corners first (see the left photo on p. 109). To hold a sheet in position while you get ready to nail it, try driving a couple of 16d nails near the bottom of the wall. Keep plywood and OSB ½ in. away from a masonry foundation. If the stud layout is correct, the edge of the first panel should fall on a stud 4 ft. from the corner. In humid areas, leave a ⅛-in. expansion gap between sheets. If a sheet doesn't break on the center of a stud, rip the sheet to fit, move the wall stud, or put in an extra stud.

You can sheathe right over windows and doors and cut them out later with a reciprocating saw. Use scrap pieces to fill in gable ends and underneath windows or to cover rim joists.

I also sheathe various walls inside the house, though this goes beyond most codes. I do this because I know that a few extra sheets of OSB might save someone's life during an earthquake or a tornado. Sheathing the back wall of a closet, bathroom, or utility room gives the frame extra lateral stability. In areas prone to serious tornadoes, you may be required to create an entirely sheathed and well-anchored safety room in which household members can gather during a storm.

The nailing schedule for sheathed walls often requires 8d or 10d nails at 4-6-12. This means that nails are spaced 4 in. around the perimeters of walls, 6 in. at the joints between sheathing panels, and 12 in. in the field. Check with your building department for the required nailing schedule in your area.

Install foam sheathing

There are many areas in the country where plywood or OSB sheathing is required only at exterior corners and every 25 ft. along exterior walls. This allows you to install nonstructural sheathing material everywhere else. On this house, we used $1/2$-in. foam sheathing. The foam board is light and easy to handle, though it can be damaged by a stray hammer blow or by someone stepping on it. Attach foam sheathing with $1\frac{1}{2}$-in. roofing nails. Sheathe right over window openings, then go inside the house with a handsaw and cut out the foam from the openings (see the right photo on p. 109).

If you've come this far, congratulations! Make sure you spend some time cleaning up the job site at this point in your project. There are bound to be plenty of offcuts, such as 2× stock, plywood or OSB scraps, and stray fragments of foam sheathing. Remove the debris and get set to raise the roof.

It's exciting to see an entire wall nailed together on the subfloor.

We line up and grab part of the top plate to get ready to lift. Then up it goes.

At first, we're not worried about making sure the walls are plumb or straight—we just keep them up with diagonal braces.

Then we start finding the exact positions with a level.

As soon as the exterior walls are up, we start on the inside.

It's amazing to think that just a short while ago we had only piles of lumber and a bare floor.

This is going to be a great house!

SHELTER

A Roof Overhead

T The walls for our house are up and we now have something to show for our work. At this stage, we can walk through the structure; admire the view through rough window openings; and imagine how the finished siding, painted drywall, and flooring will look. But first, we need to raise the roof.

Before we reach for a hammer, we need to make some decisions about the roof trusses. We also have to prepare the site for their delivery and do some layout work so that the installation process can go smoothly. Once the trusses are installed, we'll move on to the fascia boards, sheathing, and shingling.

Roof Trusses

Early in my building career, I was taught how to lay out rafters with a site-made template containing the plumb and bird's-mouth cuts. You can still cut and frame a roof one rafter at a time (see the illustration on p. 114), but today most roofs are constructed with factory-made trusses. Trusses are designed on a computer, built on an assembly line, and delivered to the job site ready to install. If you're building a simple gable-roof house like the one shown here, roof trusses can save time and keep the construction process simple—something that everyone will appreciate.

Each truss includes a pair of rafters and a bottom chord that functions as a ceiling joist inside the house and as level soffit framing outside the house. Short lengths of wood, called webbing, connect the rafters with the bottom chord; barbed steel gusset plates (gussets, for short) are pressed into place over the joints to hold all the parts together. For a basic look at the different truss configurations, see the illustrations on p. 115. The basic roof installation process that we'll use on this house will be very much the same for other houses, regardless of size.

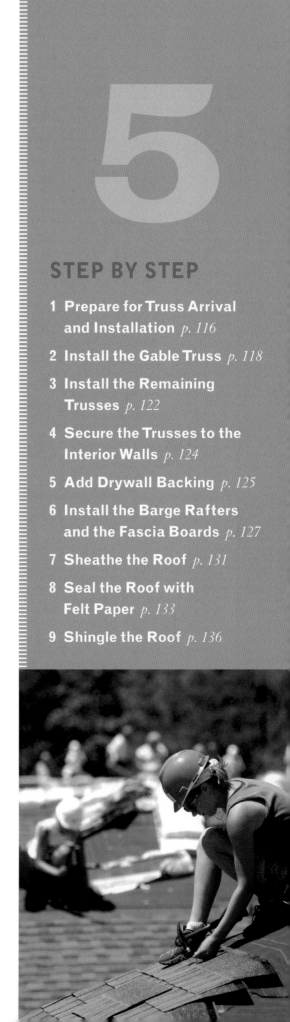

5

STEP BY STEP

Porch considerations

On the house we're building, the main roof extends over a small porch. In this situation, you need to have at least some of the porch framed before installing the roof trusses. Some builders choose to erect temporary posts to support the top beams on which the roof trusses (or rafters) will bear. When the porch is completed later, these temporary posts are replaced with permanent ones. This strategy allows roof framing to follow wall framing directly, without the interruption of porch construction work. For details on how to build a porch or a deck that's attached to the house, see Chapter 7.

Ordering roof trusses

After you make a few basic decisions about the trusses for your house, it's fairly easy to order them. I like the raised-heel design of the trusses we used on this house (see the top illustration on the facing page). This type of truss

Trusses can be made to fit any type of roof. This side porch has trusses that will tie into the main roof. [Photo by Don Charles Blom]

provides an overhang along the eave walls as well as framing for a level soffit. Because the rafter is elevated above the wall's top plate, there's ample room for ceiling insulation and ventilation space above.

However, as shown in the illustration on the facing page, other truss designs are also possible. Depending on your budget and design preferences, you can use a scissor-type truss and have a cathedral ceiling inside the house. Or perhaps you like the rustic appearance of an open soffit and exposed rafter tails along the eaves. A good lumber dealer has different truss designs to show you, and it's worth taking a look. Once you decide, here are the basic specifications the manufacturer needs to design and construct your trusses:

TYPE OF TRUSS. The major types of trusses for gable roofs are shown in the illustrations on the facing page.

SPAN BETWEEN EXTERIOR WALLS. The span is measured from one outside edge of the building to the other.

EAVE DETAILS. The amount of overhang at a building's eaves is usually shown on the plans. The plans should also tell you whether the soffit will

RAFTER AND RIDGE-BOARD FRAMING DETAILS

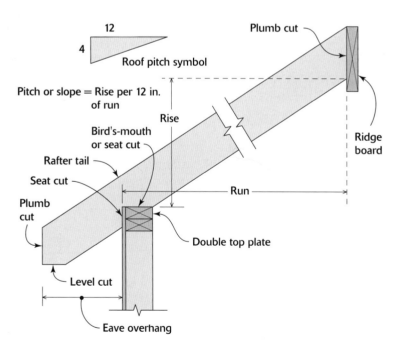

The run of a rafter is half its span. The span is measured from one outside edge of the building to the other. A 4-in-12 roof rises 4 in. vertically for every 12 in. horizontally.

COMMON TRUSSES FOR GABLED ROOFS

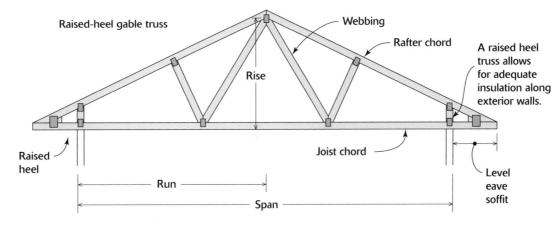

Raised-heel gable truss

Webbing

Rafter chord

A raised heel truss allows for adequate insulation along exterior walls.

Rise

Raised heel

Joist chord

Level eave soffit

Run

Span

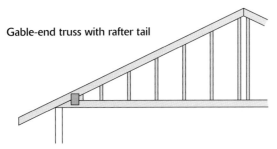

Gable-end truss with rafter tail

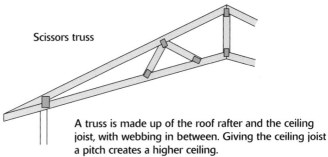

Scissors truss

A truss is made up of the roof rafter and the ceiling joist, with webbing in between. Giving the ceiling joist a pitch creates a higher ceiling.

be open or closed. For details on different ways to finish off an eave, see the sidebar on p. 117.

NUMBER OF TRUSSES. Roof trusses are typically spaced 24 in. o.c. Therefore, if your building is 40 ft. long, you'll need to order 21 trusses. Two of the trusses will be for the gable ends. These trusses have studs rather than webbing to receive the exterior wall covering.

SPECIAL REQUIREMENTS. If your house has a more complex roof, special trusses may be required where one roof section joins another. Often houses are built in a "T" or "L" shape or have a side porch that connects to the main roof. You can cut the rafters needed to tie the porch roof to the main roof. Another option is to have the truss builder look at the plans, check the span of these trusses, and build to your specifications.

ROOF PITCH. Trusses for most small affordable buildings have either a 4-in-12 or a 5-in-12 pitch (see the illustration on the facing page).

Delivery right on the walls. It saves time and energy to have the truss company deliver the trusses and lay them right on the top plate of the framed walls. [Photo © Elmer Griggs]

METAL ROOFS

Metal roofs have been around for a long time. One of the outbuildings at our prairie home had a corrugated metal roof. It was rusty and rattled in the wind, but it shed water. Today, you can buy metal roofs in a variety of colors and styles. They are lightweight and fireproof and don't hold heat the way asphalt shingles do. Metal roofs work well in snow country because they shed snow so well. With extra fasteners, they can be used in high wind areas, too.

The initial cost of a metal roof is greater than that of a shingled roof, but a metal roof will last much longer. Roofs with concealed fasteners usually cost more than those with exposed fasteners. The neoprene gasket on an exposed fastener may leak after several years in the sun, so it will need to be replaced. In general, though, the upkeep on a metal roof is minimal.

Metal roofing panels, ridge vents, and other components can be precut at the factory and installed with basic tools and simple instructions supplied by the manufacturer. The most basic metal roofs are fastened to the roof structure through a standing seam that is raised above the drainage plane to reduce the chance of leaks. Cuts can be made on the job site with tinsnips or electric shears, which are often referred to as nibblers.

TIP Get set for bracing. Before you begin to install roof trusses, have plenty of bracing boards on hand. You'll need some 16-ft. 1×4s to nail across rafters, plus a good supply of 2×4s for sway and other braces.

STEP 1 PREPARE FOR TRUSS ARRIVAL AND INSTALLATION

When roof trusses are delivered to a job site, they can be offloaded onto the ground or onto the framed walls of the building (see the photo on p. 115). The choice depends on the builder's preference and on the delivery truck's capabilities. Experienced builders prefer delivery on the walls because it saves time. Trusses can be long and cumbersome. Putting them up on walls by hand can be difficult, dangerous, and time consuming. Most truss builders deliver the trusses on a boom truck. The boom can be used to set all the trusses directly on the walls. Plan ahead and order truss delivery the day after all the walls are framed and braced.

Whether your trusses are offloaded onto the walls or onto the ground, they need to lie flat. I have seen trusses that were stored on uneven ground come apart at the seams, making them useless within a couple of weeks. Until they are nailed upright in place, braced, and sheathed, trusses are actually quite fragile. Prepare a flat area close to the house where the trusses can be offloaded. The bottom-most truss should not rest directly on the ground but on wood stickers that provide a flat, level base.

Set up work platforms

One of the most difficult parts of roof-truss installation is working high off the ground. It takes skill and practice to be able to stand on a narrow top plate and nail trusses to the wall. If this seems dangerous, or if you're uncomfortable with it, try working on a ladder or a scaffold instead. To make it easy to move trusses into position, I like to build a catwalk, or walkway, over open sections, such as the living room. (For directions on how to erect a catwalk, see the illustration on p. 118.)

Mark truss locations

Before trusses arrive on the job site, take some time to lay out their locations on the top of the wall plates. Hook a long tape on the end of the

A balancing act. The ability to walk on the wall plates is helpful when installing roof trusses, but you can also do the work from a ladder or from staging set up inside the house.

CREATING EXTERIOR SOFFITS

In the dry Southwest, open, exposed rafter tails are preferred. But elsewhere—especially in cold, wet locations—soffits are more popular. Eave soffits are usually vented.

There are quite a few ways to frame soffits. The easiest way is to have the truss company extend the joist chord beyond the building line to form a level overhang. This is called a raised-heel truss.

If the trusses do not have a raised heel, you can still build a soffit easily by sheathing the underside of the sloped rafter tails. For a level soffit, nail a long 2× to the building and sheath between it and the gutter board or subfascia. If only a fascia board is used, cut a groove near the bottom edge to support the outer edge of the soffit board. No matter which type of fascia treatment you choose, make sure you install fire-stops between the studs to help prevent a fire in the wall from spreading into the soffit area. Check with your building department to find out which fire-stop details are required.

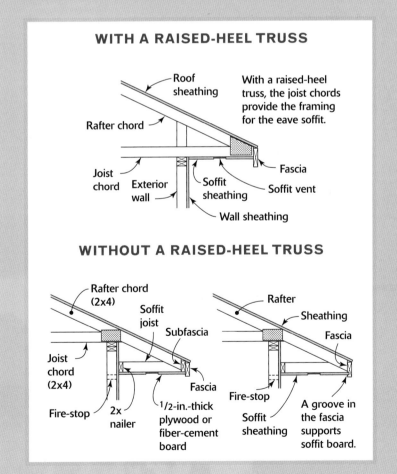

WITH A RAISED-HEEL TRUSS

With a raised-heel truss, the joist chords provide the framing for the eave soffit.

Roof sheathing · Rafter chord · Joist chord · Exterior wall · Soffit sheathing · Wall sheathing · Fascia · Soffit vent

WITHOUT A RAISED-HEEL TRUSS

Rafter chord (2x4) · Soffit joist · Subfascia · Joist chord (2x4) · Fire-stop · 2x nailer · Fascia · 1/2-in.-thick plywood or fiber-cement board

Rafter · Sheathing · Fascia · Fire-stop · Soffit sheathing · A groove in the fascia supports soffit board.

exterior walls and mark the entire length of the building at 2 ft., 4 ft., 6 ft., and so on, putting an "X" on the far side of each mark. Do the same on any long interior walls that run parallel to the outside walls. Mark the same 2-ft. o.c. layout on several straight 16-ft. 1×4 boards. These 1×s will later be nailed near the ridge to hold each truss upright at the proper spacing.

Despite your best efforts to line the walls (as explained in Chapter 4), the exterior eave wall plates may not be totally straight. If you hold the truss overhang to a wall that is not straight, the rafter ends and fascia won't be straight, either. There is an easy way to remedy this. Measure 1 in. in from the outside at each end of the exterior wall's top plate. Snap a chalkline the full length of the wall to create a straight reference line. Make an alignment mark on the joist chord of each truss. Measure in from the end of the truss the planned eave overhang distance plus 1 in. When installing each truss, put the truss mark right on the plate's snapped reference line. As long as the truss fabricators cut all the tails the same length, the truss ends will be aligned.

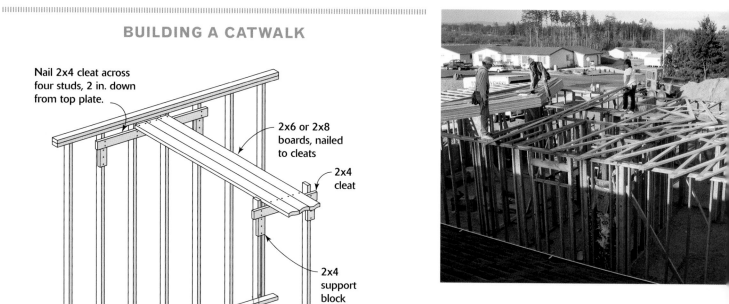

BUILDING A CATWALK

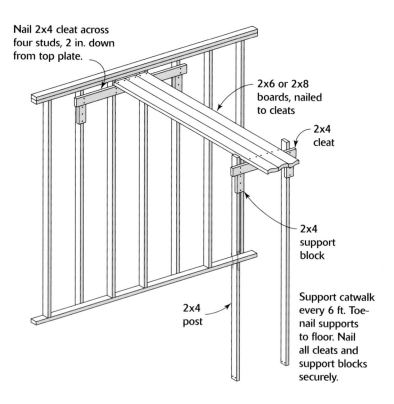

Nail 2x4 cleat across four studs, 2 in. down from top plate.

2x6 or 2x8 boards, nailed to cleats

2x4 cleat

2x4 support block

2x4 post

Support catwalk every 6 ft. Toe-nail supports to floor. Nail all cleats and support blocks securely.

To work on roof framing above a large room, you may need to construct a catwalk. At a wall near the center of the room, securely nail a 2x cleat with 16d nails across four studs about 2 in. down from the top plate. Install a similar cleat on the opposite wall. Build a sturdy 2x support every 6 ft. Lay two or three 2x6 boards flat on this cleat and support and nail them in place.

Spreading the trusses

The temporary catwalk allows you to take a truss from a bundle and move it across the walls. Pull each truss, peak first, and spread it out near its layout mark. Each truss overlaps the previous one like a fallen domino.

STEP 2 INSTALL THE GABLE TRUSS

The first truss to be installed is the gable truss (also called an end truss or a rake truss) that rests on the top plate of an end wall. This truss is usually built differently from regular trusses. Instead of having angled web pieces, these end

Rolling roof trusses. The first truss you should nail in place is the one for the gable end. Then it's just a matter of rolling the remaining trusses in place, setting them on their layout marks, and nailing them down. You can do this while standing on the walls or by working off a ladder. [Photo by Don Charles Blom, courtesy *Fine Homebuilding* magazine © The Taunton Press, Inc.]

trusses often have vertical webbing spaced 16 in. or 24 in. o.c. to allow for easy installation of sheathing or siding.

Some carpenters like to sheathe end trusses with OSB and even finish siding before raising them upright. Another option is to cut all the sheathing pieces on the ground, raise the truss, and then nail the precut sheathing in place. It is certainly easier to sheathe a truss on the ground, but it makes the truss substantially heavier and more difficult, even dangerous, to handle. If you do decide to sheathe the trusses before raising them, let the sheathing lap down below the ceiling joist chord by a couple of inches. The lap will be nailed to the top plates once the gable is raised upright. This helps ensure a strong union between the truss and the wall, which is especially important in windy areas.

Notch the gable-end truss

Notches for lookouts are exceptions to the "never cut a truss" rule. Lookouts hold the barge rafters, which extend beyond the building line at each gable end to create a roof overhang (see the photos at right). Gable trusses are not self-supporting. They can be notched because they are nailed directly over a load-bearing wall. As a result, the entire joist chord of each a gable-end truss is fully supported.

It's best to cut notches for 2×4 lookouts while the gable truss is still lying flat. For the first lookout, measure and mark 48 in. from the end of the truss tail. Cut a 2×4 notch (which is actually 1½ in. deep and 3½ in. wide) below the first 48-in. mark and every 48 in. thereafter (see the illustration on p. 121). With the gutter board or fascia in place, 4-ft.-wide sheathing will fall on the lookouts.

CHOOSING NOT TO NOTCH. Some houses (especially in northern areas) are designed without gable-end overhangs so that more sunlight can get into the house. If this is how you plan to build a house, lookouts or notches are not necessary. Instead, furr out the rake board with 1× lumber, so that the exterior siding tucks under it (see the illustration on p. 120).

Making gable-end notches. Whether you're installing trusses (see the photo below) or traditional rafters and ridge boards (see the photo above), the gable-end rafters require notches every 4 ft. to hold the lookout boards that support the barge rafter. Each lookout butts against the face of the closest inboard rafter, where it's nailed fast. [Top photo © Larry Haun; bottom photo © Roger Turk]

WORK SAFELY ON A ROOF

Keep your wits about you and pay extra attention to what you're doing when you're up on a roof—both to keep yourself safe and to ensure that the integrity of the roof is not compromised. To get on and off the roof, use a good, sturdy ladder that extends 3 ft. above the edge of the roof.

- Keep the roof clean so that there won't be anything to trip over.
- Be careful when sawdust is on the roof. Sawdust on a sloped roof can be as slick as ice. To be safe, call out measurements to cutters on the ground and have them clear the board of sawdust before handing it up to you.

- Never throw anything off a roof, not even a shingle, without first checking to see that no one is down below.
- In the hot sun, asphalt shingles soften and tear. Walk gently so you don't damage the shingles. In hot weather, install shingles early in the morning or late in the afternoon.
- In bitter cold weather, shingles become brittle and crack. Work carefully, and pray for sunshine.
- Shinglers who nail off a roof by hand often sit on the roof as they work. In hot weather, try sitting on a piece of foam while nailing shingles. Otherwise, hot shingles can literally burn your backside.

BUILDING WITHOUT A GABLE-END OVERHANG

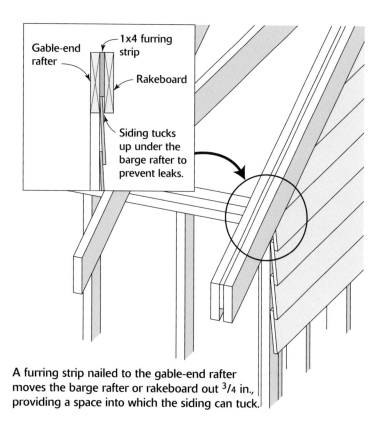

Gable-end rafter

1x4 furring strip

Rakeboard

Siding tucks up under the barge rafter to prevent leaks.

A furring strip nailed to the gable-end rafter moves the barge rafter or rakeboard out ³/4 in., providing a space into which the siding can tuck.

Unless the trusses were set on the walls at the time of delivery, they must be hoisted onto the walls by hand (see the photo on the facing page). One way to do this is to set good, strong ladders at both corners of the building. If you're dealing with long trusses, place a 2× in the center, from the ground to the top plate, at the same angle as the ladders. This way, two people can lift a truss, lay it against the ladders and the center 2×, and walk it up to the top. Another person in the middle with a notched pole can push on the truss as needed.

In preparation for installing the first truss (the gable-end truss), I nail a long, straight, temporary 2× brace on edge to the wall frame near the center of the end wall. This holds the gable-end truss stable until other braces are installed. If the truss is not too large, one person on top can drag the truss to the opposite end and lift it up against the temporary brace. Make sure that the eave overhangs are correct and that the outside of the bottom chord is flush with the outside of the end wall's top plate. Toenail the bottom chord to the double top plate, driving 16d nails every 16 in.

Trusses take teamwork. A crew of four does a good job of getting roof trusses up on the walls. Using a long push stick, the ground worker helps elevate the truss.

GABLE-END TRUSS DETAILS

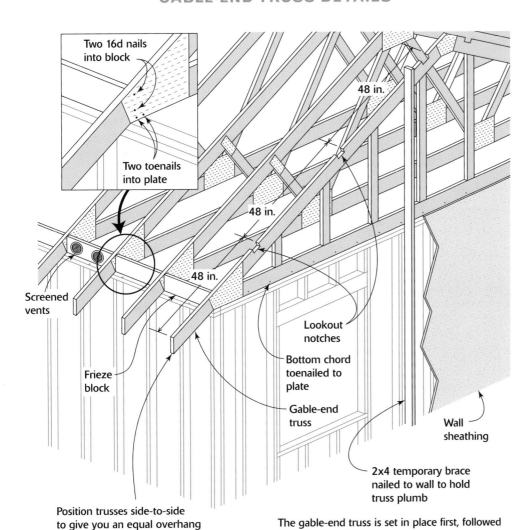

Two 16d nails into block

Two toenails into plate

48 in.

48 in.

48 in.

Screened vents

Frieze block

Lookout notches

Bottom chord toenailed to plate

Gable-end truss

Wall sheathing

2x4 temporary brace nailed to wall to hold truss plumb

Position trusses side-to-side to give you an equal overhang at both eaves.

The gable-end truss is set in place first, followed by all the regular trusses.

TIP Be aware of wind. Take care with trusses while the wind is blowing. Sheathed trusses can catch the wind like a boat's sail. Even bare trusses can be difficult to control. If it's windy, have extra helpers on hand and use extra bracing to keep installed trusses in place.

INSTALLING FRIEZE BLOCKS BETWEEN RAFTERS AND TRUSSES

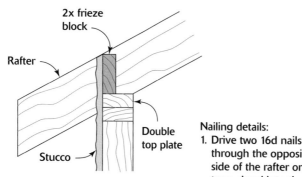

2x frieze block

Rafter

Stucco

Double top plate

Venting option: 3-in.-dia. holes can be drilled in frieze blocks and covered (from inside) with screen to provide ventilation along the eaves.

When installed plumb, a frieze block provides backing for stucco.

Nailing details:
1. Drive two 16d nails through the opposite side of the rafter or truss chord into the end of the block.
2. Nail the bottom of the block to the wall.

Rafter

2x frieze block

Siding

When installed perpendicular to the rafters, blocking provides a stop for other types of siding.

STEP 3 INSTALL THE REMAINING TRUSSES

Trusses by themselves are rather fragile. They gain strength when they're properly blocked and braced. I will now explain various blocking and bracing strategies, because this work needs to be done as the trusses are installed.

Hurricane clips and frieze blocks

A hurricane can tear a roof completely off a house. Hurricane clips, which are designed to prevent this, are required by code in some parts of the country. After the trusses are nailed in position, hurricane clips are easy to install from inside or outside the house. Drive nails into the trusses and the top plates of the wall (see the bottom left photo). Be sure to use the special short, strong "hanger" nails that are sold with the clips.

In many parts of the country, frieze blocks are required between trusses. I'm in favor of these blocks, which you can cut from the plentiful supply of 2× scrap that your crew has been collecting. Installed at the top of the wall, these 2× blocks connect the bottom chords or, depending on the truss design, the rafters of adjacent trusses. They provide extra rigidity near the truss ends (see the illustration at left).

I have seen firsthand how frieze blocks help hold truss systems together in high winds and earthquakes. They offer other benefits as well. The blocks can serve as exterior trim (with or without ventilation holes) if you plan to have an open soffit. If you are installing raised-heel trusses, as we did on this house, you'll also need to install plywood or OSB baffles between the trusses to prevent attic insulation from spilling into the soffit area (see the top photo on p. 153).

Install a pair of frieze blocks after each truss is installed. Drive a pair of 16d nails

Hurricane clips tie trusses to walls. Required by code in many areas, these metal connectors are designed to fit around the bottom chord of a truss and against the top plate of a wall. Here, a volunteer attaches a clip with an air hammer.

through the truss and into the end of the frieze block, then nail the frieze block to the top plate. You can cut a supply of blocks quickly on a chopsaw. Make sure you cut them to the correct length. If they're too long or too short, you may force the trusses off of their layout. The normal block length for trusses spaced 2 ft. o.c. is 22½ in. However, if the blocks will butt against gusset plates, you'll need to take the gusset thickness into account.

After you've nailed the first frieze blocks to the gable-end truss, swing the next truss upright. Shift it right or left, as necessary, to obtain the correct eave overhang, then toenail it to the top plate with two 16d nails through the joist chord on one side and one 16d nail on the other side (see the bottom photo at right). Install the next several trusses in this fashion. As you raise each truss, tack a series of 16-ft. 1×4s (laid out 24 in. o.c.) near the ridge of the rafter chord to keep the truss stable and properly spaced (see the top photo at right).

An efficient way to work when installing roof trusses is to have a worker at each eave toenailing the truss to the wall and installing frieze blocks while one or two crew members work on the ridge, moving trusses into position and nailing 1×4 braces to maintain proper spacing.

Plumb and brace the trusses

When bracing trusses, take time to read and follow the directions from the engineering company. These, along with local building codes, must be followed to guarantee that the house will have a strong and stable roof. Most simple gable-truss roofs are easy to brace.

After four to six trusses have been installed, plumb the gable-end truss and begin bracing the roof. Use a level to plumb the end truss, then install a diagonal 2×4 sway brace from the double top (cap) plate of the exterior wall (where the gable-end truss is installed) to an inboard truss (see the photo on p. 124). The brace should extend at a 45-degree angle from the top plate and be nailed to the top chord (or rafter) or the webbing of an inboard truss.

Securing trusses. An air nailer (top) makes quick work of toenailing the truss's bottom chord to the wall plate. Drive two nails from one side and one nail from the other. To keep trusses parallel and spaced correctly, nail temporary 1× braces spaced at 24 in. o.c. across the top chords (bottom).

If the gable-end rafter is plumb, the rafters tied to it at 24 in. o.c. should also be plumb. When all of the trusses have been installed, nail in a sway brace at the other end of the roof. On longer roofs, use additional diagonal sway braces near the center of the house to further strengthen the roof. These are important braces. In a high wind, they will help keep your roof intact.

The next step is to stabilize the joist chords by nailing a long board (a 1× or 2× will do) on top of each joist chord near the center of the span. You can move this bracing to one side or the other if you need to accommodate an opening for attic access, storage space, or room for a heating unit. Frequently a forced air heating unit will be set in this area. Nail this long brace to each chord with two 8d (for 1× stock) or 16d (for 2× stock) nails (see the bottom photo on the facing page). Additional 2×4 braces are often nailed at 45-degree angles across the underside of the rafter chords or webbing from the plate line to the ridge (see the top photo on the facing page). Nail these braces into each chord with two 16d nails. This provides lateral stability to the entire roof.

STEP 4 SECURE THE TRUSSES TO THE INTERIOR WALLS

On small houses, trusses are generally engineered to obtain their support from exterior walls without needing further support from interior walls. Still, it's not uncommon for trusses to cross over and bear on interior walls. In most regions, these trusses can usually be nailed directly to the interior wall with two 16d toenails on one side and one on the opposite side. This is not the case, however, if you live in a part of the country where the weather may be freezing one day and boiling the next. In areas with extreme temperature fluctuations, trusses must be able to expand and contract freely. Otherwise, drywall ceilings nailed to these trusses tend to crack. Check with your building department for the code requirements in your town or city. In addition, ask area builders what the local practice is.

||||||||||||||||||||||||||||||||||||||||||||||||||||||||||||||||||||||||||||||||||||||||||||||||||||||

ATTACHING TRUSS CLIPS

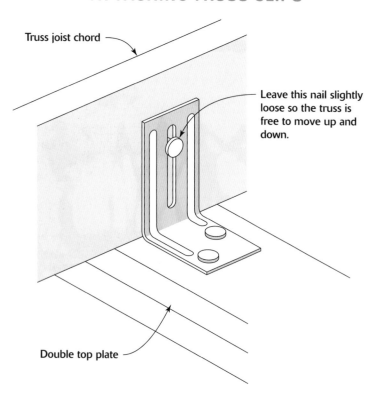

Truss joist chord

Leave this nail slightly loose so the truss is free to move up and down.

Double top plate

In areas where large temperature fluctuations are common, fasten the joist chords to interior walls with truss clips so the trusses can expand and contract freely.

Installing permanent bracing inside. Shown in the photo on the facing page, a diagonal brace from the top of a truss down to a wall plate helps hold the trusses plumb. Install a 1×6 or 2×4 catwalk on top of the trusses' bottom, or joist, chord. The brace should be nailed into every joist chord and into the end-wall top plates (photo below). Nailing 2× bracing across the webbing provides the roof structure with additional rigidity (photo above). [Photo on the facing page by Don Charles Blom, courtesy *Fine Homebuilding* magazine © The Taunton Press, Inc.]

To secure a truss to a wall while still allowing it to adapt to fluctuations in temperature and humidity, use a truss clip, as shown in the illustration on the facing page. These clips, which are nailed both to the wall plates and to the truss, feature a slot that allows the truss to move up and down as it expands and contracts—just make sure the nail is slightly loose in the joist chord.

STEP 5 ADD DRYWALL BACKING

At this point, you need to add backing (sometimes called deadwood) to walls that run parallel to the joist chords. The backing provides a nailing base for ceiling drywall (see the illustration on p. 127). It's easier to put the backing in now rather than after the roof is complete and hampered by sheathing. This is a good place to use knotty, crooked 2× stock. Nail the stock, one 16d nail every 16 in., to the double top plate of parallel walls so that the 2× backing overhangs the double top plate by at least 1 in. on both sides. Some builders use drywall clips instead of solid backing, but I like to fasten nails

TIP Be aware of overhead issues. If you're working on the ground while people are working overhead, stay alert while you are in the "drop" zone. Even though workers know not to drop things from above, it's easy to drop tools and materials accidentally.

Doing carpentry on the ground is easier than doing carpentry on top of the house.

You really have to watch your step.

We handle the trusses carefully.

Plenty of bracing is required to tie the trusses together and to the rest of the house.

When the trusses are up, you can see what the completed house will look like.

INSTALLING BACKING FOR DRYWALL

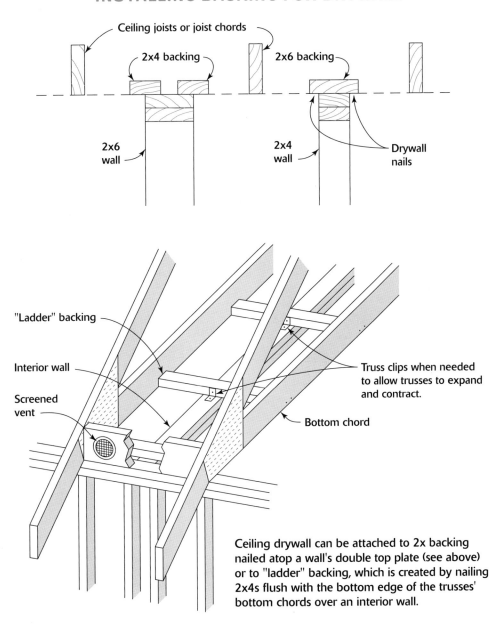

Ceiling joists or joist chords

2x4 backing

2x6 backing

2x6 wall

2x4 wall

Drywall nails

"Ladder" backing

Interior wall

Screened vent

Truss clips when needed to allow trusses to expand and contract.

Bottom chord

Ceiling drywall can be attached to 2x backing nailed atop a wall's double top plate (see above) or to "ladder" backing, which is created by nailing 2x4s flush with the bottom edge of the trusses' bottom chords over an interior wall.

into something solid. (Details on drywall installation are covered in Chapter 9.)

This process is different for trusses that are allowed to expand and contract. In this case, nail flat 2×4 "ladder" backing between the joist chords on a parallel wall. Use truss clips to attach the backing to the double top plate of the wall, as explained on p. 124. This allows the trusses to expand and contract without stressing the drywall.

STEP 6 INSTALL THE BARGE RAFTERS AND THE FASCIA BOARDS

As explained earlier in this chapter, barge rafters extend beyond the end of a building, creating an overhang at the gable ends. The rafters are supported by 2×4 lookouts that fit into notches cut in the gable-end rafters. The lookouts run back to the first inboard rafter (or roof truss). At the bottom corner of the roof,

Mitering the fascia to the barge rafter. When working on a house that will have exposed wood trim, nail a mitered fascia board to a barge rafter that is mitered at its plumb-cut angle. To keep the joint together, drive 16d galvanized finishing nails from both sides. [Photo by Tony Mason © The Taunton Press, Inc.]

a barge rafter meets a gutter or fascia board, which extends along the eave and is fastened to the ends of the rafter tails.

There are a few tricks to making sure that these exterior trim details are done correctly. If you plan to cover the trim with aluminum cladding, as we did on this house (see Chapter 7), the cutting and installation work is a little easier. On the other hand, if the barge rafter and fascia will be exposed as finished trim, you'll need to cut tight-fitting miter joints where the boards meet. Both types of installation will go more smoothly if you follow the steps described here.

Let the lookouts run long

I like to install lookouts long, then snap a line from eave to ridge and cut the lookouts in place. If you're framing with rafters rather than with trusses, the ridge board can also run long at this stage. This process ensures a straight barge rafter. Hoist a supply of 2×4 lookout stock up to the roof, set each lookout in its notch, and secure the end of each one against the face of

the first inboard truss (or rafter) with two 16d nails. Keep the top surface of the lookout flush with the top edge of the truss. Now, before driving a pair of 16d nails into each notch, move the gable-end rafter in or out to make the framing member as straight as possible. Nail all the lookouts in their notches, and leave them like this for now.

Make truss ends straight

If the truss tails have been set straight, begin to cut and install the gutter or fascia boards. If they're not straight, snap a line across the top or bottom edges, then mark plumb cuts to line up the truss ends in the same plane. This is another exception to the "never cut a truss" rule. As long as you're only making a small cutoff at the end of the truss (well away from joints and gussets), there's no chance of structural damage. Check the eave overhang called for in the plans. Measure this distance on the gable-end trusses at opposite ends of the house. Then snap a line across all the trusses, going from one end of the house to the other. Mark the cut lines on the truss ends and make the cuts. This technique also works when building plans call for exposed rafter tails that must be cut in the same plane. Use a jig or pattern, such as the one shown in the top illustration on p. 130, to mark identical plumb cuts on the rafter tails. You can make the cuts from above, while standing on the top plate of the wall, or from below, while standing on a ladder or scaffolding.

Install the gutter or fascia boards

Although both gutter and fascia boards are nailed to the rafter tails, the distinction between the two is that gutter boards are later covered with trim (aluminum or vinyl cladding or 1× finish material). Fascia, on the other hand, is a finished surface. Some builders install 1× fascia boards over 2× gutter boards or subfascia, whereas others use the 2× stock as the finished fascia.

Obviously, smooth, accurate cuts are required to install fascia boards, whereas gutter

MAKE THE ATTIC ACCESSIBLE

Code requires an access hole for the attic. This allows workers to get into the attic to install insulation and wiring. You may also want to get up there some day to check on a roof leak or just to see how the spiders are doing.

The standard attic access hole has a rough 2× frame that is 22½ in. wide by 31 in. long. This rectangular opening fits nicely between ceiling joists installed on 2-ft. centers. Usually, the hole is located in a closet or along a hallway. Once you select a spot for access to the attic, cut a pair of 2×s to fit between the ceiling joists and nail them 31 in. apart. The bottom edges of the blocking should be flush with the bottom edges of the joists. Take the time to measure the hole diagonally to make sure it's square. After ½-in. drywall is nailed in place, you will have a 21½-in. by 30-in. access hole.

If you are using blown-in insulation to insulate the ceiling, build a plywood or OSB curb around the access hole in the attic. Make sure the curb is tall enough (at least 12 in.) to keep the insulation from falling on your head every time you open the lid to the

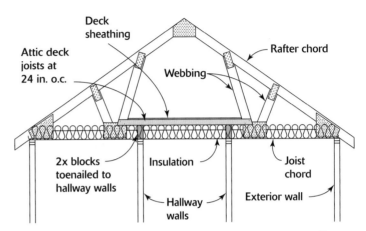

CREATING USABLE SPACE IN THE ATTIC

Deck sheathing

Attic deck joists at 24 in. o.c.

Rafter chord

Webbing

2x blocks toenailed to hallway walls

Insulation

Joist chord

Hallway walls

Exterior wall

Some usable storage space can be created in the attic, even if the house has a truss roof, by framing a floor that is supported by interior walls and sits above the trusses' joist chords.

attic. The lid can be cut from drywall and should be insulated with rigid foam board.

Instead of a simple lid for the access hole, you may want to install a pull-down stair kit. If you're using the attic for storage and need to go up there on a regular basis, a pull-down staircase is the way to go. The stairs are factory-made and designed to fit in the 22½-in. space between the joists. The rough opening must be longer, however—54 in. is common. Check the manufacturer's specifications before you frame the opening.

CREATE ATTIC STORAGE. There is some usable space in most truss-roof attics. To make use of it, don't lay sheathing directly on the joist chords of roof trusses, as trusses are not engineered for this. Instead, frame a storage platform above the joist chords, making sure that there's room for insulation beneath the platform. You can support the platform's joists on short (8-in.- to 12-in.-long) cripple studs nailed to the double top plates of nearby walls. Sheathe the platform with ½-in. plywood or OSB.

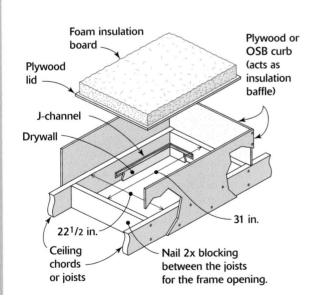

MAKING AN ATTIC ACCESS OPENING

Foam insulation board

Plywood lid

Plywood or OSB curb (acts as insulation baffle)

J-channel

Drywall

22½ in.

31 in.

Ceiling chords or joists

Nail 2x blocking between the joists for the frame opening.

A JIG FOR MARKING PLUMB CUTS IN RAFTERS

1. Mark cut lines with a small rafter square.

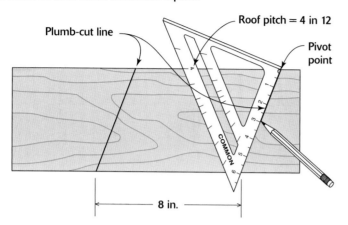

Plumb-cut line

Roof pitch = 4 in 12

Pivot point

COMMON

8 in.

2. Then nail on a 1x2 fence.

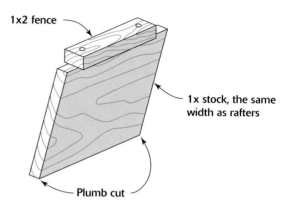

1x2 fence

1x stock, the same width as rafters

Plumb cut

If you need to make a series of plumb cuts to match and align rafter tails along an eave, make a jig like the one shown here. Use a rafter square to mark the plumb-cut angle of the roof (4-in-12 or 5-in-12) on a short length of 1x4 or 1x6, depending on the rafter size. Cut a parallelogram-shaped template with

identical plumb-cut angles, then nail a short 1x2 fence to the upper edge of the template. Once a chalkline has been snapped across all the rafter tails, use this template to mark the plumb cut on them so that they can be cut to length.

MITERING FASCIA BOARDS

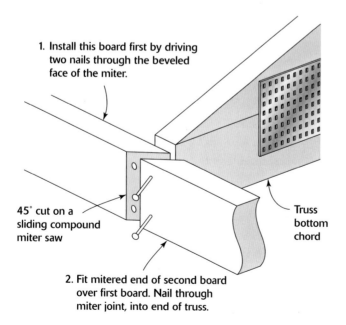

1. Install this board first by driving two nails through the beveled face of the miter.

45° cut on a sliding compound miter saw

Truss bottom chord

2. Fit mitered end of second board over first board. Nail through miter joint, into end of truss.

boards are less demanding. On this house, we installed gutter boards that were later clad with coil aluminum (see Chapter 7).

CUTTING AND NAILING GUIDELINES FOR GUTTER AND FASCIA BOARDS. Use long, straight stock for gutter or fascia boards. Both types must butt together over the solid backing of a rafter tail. Gutter boards can meet in a simple butt joint; fascia boards should meet with a mitered joint, as shown in the illustration at left.

Nail gutter and 2× fascia boards to truss or rafter ends with 16d, hot-dipped galvanized nails. Nail fascia boards with a finish hammer, being careful not to miss the nail or you'll leave hammer tracks in the wood. Have a partner hold the other end of the board. Hold the board down a bit on the rafter tail so that the roof sheathing just skims over it (see the illustration on the facing page). To line up everything correctly, tack a piece of scrap wood on the top edge of a rafter and let it project downward, the way the roof sheathing will. Drive the topmost nail high enough so it will be covered by the drip edge that will be installed later.

At the bottom corner of the roof, the level eave trim meets the pitched barge rafter. If the exterior trim will be covered with cladding, as on this house, plumb-cut the barge rafter and nail it to the plumb-cut end of the gutter board. Install the gutter board so that it runs long, just like the lookout boards, then mark the correct overhang distance on the gutter board and on the topmost lookout. Be sure to take the barge rafter's thickness into account. Snap a line between these two marks, then cut the gutter board and lookouts in place. Now you're ready to cut and install the barge rafter.

The procedure is similar if you're installing fascia instead of gutter boards; however, miter the end of the fascia board to fit a mitered plumb cut on the barge rafter (see the photo on p. 128). It's easier to make both miter cuts before nailing the boards. Miter and install the fascia first, then snap the cutoff lines on the lookouts as described previously.

Plumb-cut barge rafters

Select straight, clear stock for the barge rafters, and start with a board that's a little longer than you need. Make the bottom plumb cut on the ground. This is a mitered plumb cut, 4-in-12 on this roof, if you're working with finished trim. With one or two helpers holding the board above, nail the barge rafter to the lookouts and to the gutter or fascia board. I like to make the top plumb cut with the board in place, judging by eye where the top of the cut should be. Or you can pull a string along the top of several trusses. Pull this string out over the barge rafter to mark where it will cut. When you install the opposite barge rafter, mark the top plumb cut against the rafter you've already cut to ensure a tight-fitting joint.

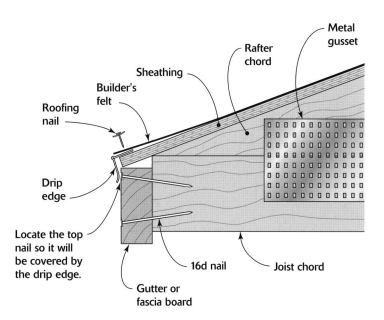

Position the gutter board on the truss or rafter end so the sheathing overlaps the top edge.

STEP 7 SHEATHE THE ROOF

Sheathing a roof is much like sheathing a floor, except that the deck is sloped, not flat, and you work at least 10 ft. off the ground. Anyone who has worked in the construction trades for more than a few years has heard stories about someone who has fallen from a roof—or has seen it happen. I was sheathing a roof many years ago on a cool morning with a bit of frost on the ground. The sunny side of the roof had no frost. Without thinking, I stepped onto the shady side of the roof and was immediately careening down a fairly steep pitch, heading for doom. Fortunately, I had my straight-clawed hammer in my hand. Instinctively using it like an ice ax, I sunk the claw into the sheathing, stopping myself just short of the roof's edge—a thrilling way to drive up my heart rate at the beginning of the day but not an experience I'd care to repeat. Take care, and stay aware.

MAKING A PLATFORM FOR ROOF SHEATHING

A safe strategy for hoisting sheathing onto a roof is to build a simple staging platform, as shown in the photo at right. Nail the platform's two horizontal supports (a pair of 2×4s works fine) to the wall framing or, if the wall has been sheathed already, to a 2× cleat nailed through the sheathing and into the studs. The supports must be a couple of feet above the bottom plate of the wall. Space them about 32 in. apart, and make them roughly level. Support the outboard end of the platform with 2× legs firmly attached to the horizontal supports. Nail a 2× on top of the platform near the outer end to provide additional stability. If necessary, install diagonal braces between the supports and the legs or the wall framing for added strength. Then set 4×8 sheets of plywood or OSB on edge on the platform; workers on the roof can grab the sheets as needed.

Sheathing work begins. Position the first row of sheathing with the top edge against a snapped reference line.

Measure 48¼ in. from the outside edge of the gutter or fascia board at each end of the roof and snap a chalkline. Lay the first row of plywood or OSB so that the top edge is right on this line (see the photo at left). Make sure the sheathing extends past the gable-end truss all the way to the barge rafter, which the sheathing helps support. Lay the slick side of the OSB down. Nail the sheets with 8d nails at 6 in. o.c. at the edges and 12 in. o.c. in the field. Be sure to nail all the boards.

Before you start the second row of sheathing, put plywood H-clips, centered between the rafter chords, on the first row (see the top photo on the facing page). Required on ½-in. sheathing (but not on ⅝-in. sheathing), these clips hold two sheets together and make the roof's surface stronger. Start the second row at one end with a 4-ft.-sq. sheet so that the courses will be staggered, just as they are with floor sheathing. Continue sheathing until you reach the top. If a ridge vent will be installed, leave a gap at the ridge so that air inside the attic can move up into the vent. If the vent is available, read the manufacturer's instructions regarding the size of the gap and check with your building inspector regarding these construction details. The gap need not run all the way to the barge rafter. Start it about 1 ft. in on the main roof.

STEP 8 SEAL THE ROOF WITH FELT PAPER

Now that the house has been framed and sheathed, it's time to seal it from the elements. As long as you are able to work safely on a roof, you can cover it with roofing felt and shingles. It's best if all the plumbing and heating vents are through the roof before you install the felt. If that isn't possible, just make sure they're installed before you begin shingling.

Roll out the felt paper

Felt paper, sometimes called tar paper or builder's felt, is the first protective layer installed over roof sheathing. This material has evolved in a fashion similar to that of a candy bar. In the old days, you could buy a good-size candy bar for a nickel. Today, you get a much smaller bar at a higher price. Similarly, the felt paper available today is much lighter, even though it's still sold as 15-lb. and 30-lb. felt. I like to use 30-lb. felt for the underlayment because it provides extra protection and the cost difference isn't that great. Roofing felt has horizontal lines marked on it. Follow a line that provides a minimum 4-in. lap as you roll one row over another.

Using H-clips between rafters. Required on ½-in. roof sheathing, H-clips increase the rigidity of the roof by locking together panel edges between framing members.

An air-operated nailgun can be used to fasten tarpaper securely to the roof before shingles are laid in place. [Photo by Don Charles Blom]

TIP Stay cool. Roofing can be hot work. Be sure to drink plenty of water, take breaks, and go down if you begin to feel weak. Remind others to do the same.

Asphalt paper is the first layer of protection. Known as builder's felt, this water-proof paper is applied over roof sheathing. Overlap each course by at least 4 in.
[Photo by Don Charles Blom]

Follow nailing guidelines

Some builders like to snap a chalkline on the sheathing 36 in. up from the edge of the gutter or fascia board and lay the first roll of felt to that line. This makes the roll lay down straight. Alternatively, you can hold the felt flush with the edge of the roof. Unroll the felt flat (with no bumps or wrinkles) and tack it down with roofing tacks. A roofing tack is a small nail with a large plastic button (generally green, orange, or red) on top (see the photo above). Or you can use a pneumatic nailgun to nail these plastic buttons in place. Stepping on felt that is not nailed well can cause you to slip off the roof, so use plenty of roofing tacks (6 in. o.c. at the

bottom and ends and 10 in. o.c. from top to bottom every 24 in. o.c. across the roof). Roofing tacks hold the felt in place, which is especially important if the roof won't be shingled for several days. Pick up any tacks that fall to the ground so that no one steps on them. Finally, trim the felt flush with the gable ends.

Whether you are tacking down roofing felt or nailing on shingles, it's important to consider whether the nails can be seen from below. When the eaves around the house are open (no soffit), a long nail penetrates the roof sheathing and is visible to anyone who looks up. Hundreds of shiny nails sticking through the plywood or OSB is unattractive. Therefore, when tacking felt around the perimeter of the roof, take care to nail the tacks into the barge rafters and gable-end rafters—not just through the sheathing into the air. When nailing shingles, use $\frac{5}{8}$-in. nails at the gable overhangs and eaves. When working over the house frame, nails that penetrate the sheathing in the attic are not a problem.

Seal twice around vents

The vent pipes that extend through the roof are flashed with special rubber or metal boots when the shingles are installed. But here in rainy Oregon, roofers take the time to make a double seal around these pipes. This is sort of like wearing a slicker and carrying an umbrella, too—but there's no such thing as being too careful when it comes to roofs and water. To provide this extra protection, cut a 3-ft.-sq. piece of felt and cut a hole in the center the size of the vent pipe. Slip the felt over the vent and seal around the pipe with a tube of roofing tar. Do the same when you roll out the long strips of roofing felt. Cut the second layer of felt around each vent and again seal it around the pipe with roofing tar. You can lap the felt over the ridge, but remember to cut it away when you shingle to permit airflow into the ridge vent.

Protect valleys and intersections

When a porch roof intersects the main roof at a right angle, valleys are created on each side of

TIP Cut elliptical holes in felt flashing. When you need to flash around a vent pipe, fold the felt in half and cut out half of an ellipse with a sharp utility knife. Because of the roof's slope, the hole is shaped more like an ellipse than a circle. The steeper the slope, the longer the ellipse.

the intersection. Valleys divert more water than a regular gable roof does, so I always provide extra protection in the form of flashing. I like to roll at least two layers of 30-lb. felt right down the center of the valley. Even better is to cover the valley area with a sheet of 90-lb. rolled roofing. Then, when you install regular roofing felt, lay each row 12 in. or more beyond the valley and keep all roofing tacks at least 12 in. from the center of the valley. This technique provides a double layer of protection prior to shingling.

When working on a roof that butts into the sidewall of a house (a porch roof connected to a gable end, for example), lap the felt on the sidewall by at least 6 in. to prevent leaks at the intersection.

Install a drip edge

Once the felt is in place, make it more secure around the edges by installing sections of vinyl or metal drip edge. Drip edge is an L-shaped metal or vinyl flashing that comes in 10-ft. sections. One leg of the L profile extends about 1½ in. up the roof; the other leg extends down the fascia or barge rafter by the same distance (see the photo at right). It has a slight lip on the lower edge to divert water from the roof.

Using roofing nails, install the drip edge under the felt at the eaves and on top of the felt at the rakes, or gable ends. Space nails about 2 ft. apart. Where one length of edging joins another, overlap the joint by about 4 in. Along the gable ends, make sure the top length of the drip edge laps over the one below. At the corners, cut a pie-shaped slice out of the top section. This allows you to bend the drip edge at a 90-degree angle and nail it around the corner. At the ridge, make a plumb cut in the vertical leg and bend the edge over the ridge, allowing the plumb cut to overlap, as shown in the illustration above.

Installing a drip edge. This L-profile flashing is installed to protect the edges of the roof. The bottom flashing goes beneath the paper and the side flashings go on top. [Photo by Don Charles Blom]

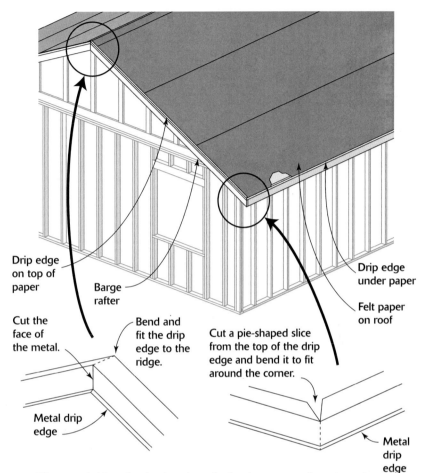

Drip edge on top of paper

Barge rafter

Cut the face of the metal.

Bend and fit the drip edge to the ridge.

Metal drip edge

Drip edge under paper

Felt paper on roof

Cut a pie-shaped slice from the top of the drip edge and bend it to fit around the corner.

Metal drip edge

The metal drip edge is placed on the fascia or gutter boards and barge rafters before shingles are nailed to the roof.

ESTIMATES FOR A ROOF

Determining the quantity of materials needed to cover and shingle a roof is rather easy. First, measure the roof to determine its square footage. Add the width of both sides of the roof and multiply that number by the length of the roof. Let's look at an example: A roof with an overall width of 28 ft. and a length of 46 ft. has a total area of 1,288 sq. ft., which I'd round up to 1,300 sq. ft.

FIGURE FELT PAPER FIRST. The first material you will need is felt paper. The coverage you can obtain from a roll of felt paper varies, but it's often 300 sq. ft. (to make sure, ask your building-materials supplier). Divide 1,300 sq. ft. by 300 sq. ft. for a total of 4.33 or 4⅓ rolls. Buy five rolls of felt paper, because you'll need the extra to compensate for overlap and to seal around the plumbing vents.

SHINGLES COME IN BUNDLES AND ARE ORDERED BY THE SQUARE. One bundle of standard-size shingles covers 33.3 sq. ft. Three bundles cover 100 sq. ft. (10 ft. by 10 ft.), which is called a square. It takes 13 squares (39 bundles) to cover a 1,300-sq.-ft. roof. Order at least two extra bundles to make up for the ridge cap, the valley lap, and waste.

In addition to the shingles, you'll need a ridge vent. Measure the length of the ridge to determine the size you'll need. Depending on the manufacturer's recommendations, vents can extend all the way across the ridge or to within 2 ft. of the roof's edge at each end.

DON'T FORGET THE NAILS. Buy ⅞-in. roofing nails for the shingles (about 1 lb. per square) and 1½-in. nails for the ridge vent (about ½ lb.). Buy coil nails if you are using a pneumatic nailer. If the eave overhangs will be exposed, buy 2 lb. of ⅝-in. roofing nails; longer nails that penetrate the roof sheathing are unsightly. You'll also need about 5 lb. of plastic-head roofing nails to hold the felt paper in place on a roof this size. Add a tube or two of asphalt caulk to cover any exposed nails and to seal around the plumbing vents.

TIP Don't let shingles get sunburned. Don't store asphalt shingles in the sun, unless you're going to use them right away. The tar strips can melt and seal the shingles together into a big, useless mess. If you must store shingles, put them in the shade or cover them with a light-colored tarp to reflect the heat.

STEP 9 SHINGLE THE ROOF

Back in the days when I was a roof shingler, I hardly ever saw asphalt or fiberglass (composition) shingles. Being a shingler meant working with wood shingles. Now in most parts of the country I see wood shingles used more often on the sides of buildings than on roofs. Composition shingles are more popular because they are faster to install and more resistant to fire.

Give some thought as to the color and style of the shingles that you want on your house. A new style of architectural shingle that casts a shadow has become popular. Light-colored shingles reflect more heat than dark ones do. For this reason, people living in the southern part of the United States tend to prefer light-colored shingles. People living further north often select darker shingles.

Lay out the shingles

With some simple layout, your shingles can look like a professional installed them. Poorly laid shingles may keep out water, but they just don't look appealing. Admittedly, not many people visit your home just to see whether your shingle pattern is pleasing to the eye, but good workers take pride in doing things right. When I was framing tract houses (500 at a time), I knew roofers who could start in one corner and shingle an entire roof without snapping a chalkline and do a neat, proper job. That's skill. The rest of us need to snap a few lines to keep the materials oriented correctly.

BASIC MEASUREMENTS. Before snapping a chalkline for the first shingle course (the starter course), determine the distance the shingles will extend beyond the drip edge. Here in Oregon, shingles typically lap over the edge by about ½ in. I worked on houses in Georgia where the shingle overhang was about 2 in. They drooped in the hot sun and provided the roof with a nice-looking detail. Just be aware that a large shingle overhang presents a greater surface area to heavy winds, making them more vulnerable and likely to tear or rip off. Check the shingle manufacturer's recommendations for overhang.

As shown in the illustration at right, a standard three-tab shingle measures 12 in. wide by 36 in. long. Each of the three tabs measures 12 in. across. (Dimensional or metric shingles are a bit larger. To install them, read the instructions printed on the package.) If you want 12-in. shingles to hang over the edges by ½ in., for example, measure 11½ in. from the outside edge and snap chalklines around the roof's perimeter.

VERTICAL LAYOUT LINES. Sometimes referred to as bond or offset lines, vertical layout lines keep shingles aligned and ensure that you don't end up with a narrow section of shingle when you get to the edge of the roof. There are different ways to establish vertical layout lines. The best method I've seen is explained in the sidebar on p. 138. My thanks to Habitat veteran Anna Carter and other volunteers, who figured out this vertical layout technique.

HORIZONTAL LAYOUT LINES. Once the vertical layout lines are in place, you can lay

out the horizontal lines. To do this, you must know the reveal—the part of each shingle that remains exposed ("to the weather") after the next course is installed. On standard shingles, this distance is usually 5 in. Therefore, on a 12-in.-wide shingle, 7 in. will be covered by the next course. Some manufacturers recommend

SHINGLE ANATOMY AND NAILING DETAILS

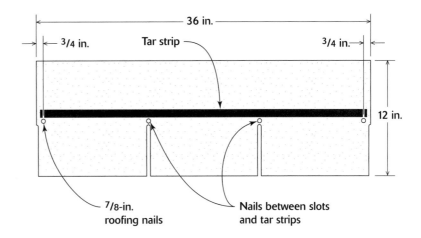

Snapped with red chalk, vertical and horizontal layout lines ensure proper shingle alignment and allow shingling work to go quickly.

VERTICAL LAYOUT FOR ROOF SHINGLES

To obtain the right layout, try this two-step method:

1. Measure across the roof from outside edge to outside edge (parallel with the eave wall), including the planned overhang distance for the shingles. For example, let's assume that the shingles will overhang the drip edge by ½ in. Measure in yards (because the length of a standard shingle is 36 in.), plus remaining inches.

2. Measure in from the left edge by a round number of yards (say, 5 yd.) and mark that distance on the roof. Then refer to the chart below to ensure that all the shingles at the edges of the roof will be at least 15 in. wide (a full tab, plus 3 in.).

EXAMPLE. Let's say the total distance across the roof, from gable end to gable end, is 10 yd. and 13 in. (including the ½-in. overhang at both ends). When you check the chart's recommendations for a roof with a 13-in. remainder (12 in. to 15 in. is the range), you'll see that the recommended offsets are 3 in. and 9 in.

From the reference mark at 5 yd., make marks 3 in. to the left and 9 in. to the left of the reference mark. You now have an offset of 6 in., or half the width of a shingle tab, between courses. Staggering the courses like this—so that the breaks between the tabs don't stack up on top of each other—prevents water from seeping beneath the shingles. Make the 3-in. and 9-in. offset marks at the bottom of the roof, near the eave, and at the top, near the ridge. Snap chalklines between the marks to establish your vertical start lines.

VERTICAL LAYOUT FOR ROOF SHINGLING

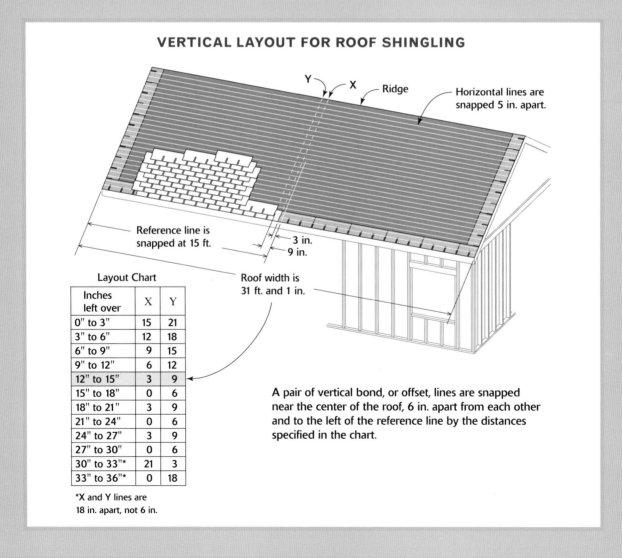

Y — X — Ridge

Horizontal lines are snapped 5 in. apart.

Reference line is snapped at 15 ft.

3 in.
9 in.

Roof width is 31 ft. and 1 in.

Layout Chart

Inches left over	X	Y
0" to 3"	15	21
3" to 6"	12	18
6" to 9"	9	15
9" to 12"	6	12
12" to 15"	3	9
15" to 18"	0	6
18" to 21"	3	9
21" to 24"	0	6
24" to 27"	3	9
27" to 30"	0	6
30" to 33"*	21	3
33" to 36"*	0	18

*X and Y lines are 18 in. apart, not 6 in.

A pair of vertical bond, or offset, lines are snapped near the center of the roof, 6 in. apart from each other and to the left of the reference line by the distances specified in the chart.

different reveals, so check the label for specifics.

Assuming your reveal is 5 in., measure 5 in., 10 in., 15 in., and so on from the starter course's chalkline (11½ in. from the edge of the eaves). Mark these 5-in. increments near both gable ends—all the way from the eave to the ridge on both sides of the roof—then snap chalklines between the marks. It's okay to use red chalk on felt, because it shows up well and will be covered by the shingles anyway. Each successive course of shingles is held to these horizontal lines.

Rather than snap a line every 5 in., some shinglers prefer to snap a line every 15 in. or 20 in., set the gauge on a shingle hatchet to 5 in., then use the hatchet to space the courses between the chalklines (see the illustration at right).

Install the shingles

Follow the vertical and horizontal lines and start nailing down shingles. Make the starter course two layers thick to provide extra protection at the roof's edge.

SPACING COURSES WITH A SHINGLE HATCHET

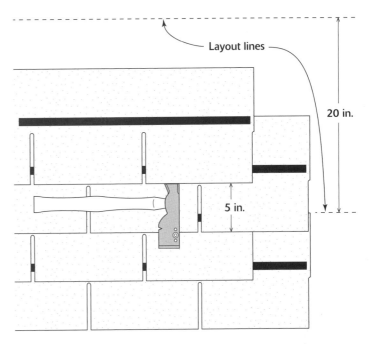

The gauge on this shingle hatchet can be set for 5 in. This way, the gauge hooks onto the bottom edge of the shingle, and the next shingle sets right on the face, or head, of the hatchet.

STARTER COURSE, BOTTOM LAYER.
All shingles (including wood) are meant to overlap, providing a double layer of protection from the elements. That's why the starter course must be two layers thick. For the first layer, lay the shingles the "wrong" way so that the three tabs face up. The stone surface should also face up (see the photo at left). Or you can buy starter shingles made just for this first course. Hold the long part of the shingle to the horizontal starter line and the right edge of the shingle to one of the vertical offset lines that you snapped near the center of the roof. With either a hammer or a pneumatic nailer, drive four ⅞-in. large-head roofing nails into each shingle just above the tar strip (see the illustration on p. 137). The tar strip is near the center of each shingle and bonds one course to the next, keeping everything in place

An inverted starter course. The first course of shingles is two layers thick, and the first layer is nailed down with shingle tabs facing up.

HOISTING MATERIALS TO THE ROOF

Here in the West, we try to order shingles the day before they will be installed. Suppliers arrive with a hoist and stack both shingles and felt paper directly onto the roof. An experienced delivery person knows to stack bundles of shingles about 6 ft. apart on both sides of the roof.

The other way to get shingles onto the roof is the hard way—hoisting one bundle at a time. If you must haul roofing shingles up to the roof yourself, make sure you have a secure ladder that is positioned properly and is 2 ft. to 3 ft. taller than the roof. It's a good idea to nail a temporary 2× tread at the spot on the roof where you will step off the ladder. This tread provides a solid foothold where you need it most.

BUST THE BUNDLE. Shingles are much easier to carry if you "bust" the bundle first. Pick up a bundle and lay it across a sawhorse. Push down on both ends until the bundle curves downward. A curved bundle is easier and safer to carry on your shoulder than a straight, stiff one (see the photo at right).

Pick up the bundle by bending your knees and draping the bundle over your shoulder. This is not always easy, because a bundle of shingles can weigh as much as 80 lb. Ascend the ladder slowly and watch your balance. Don't throw down bundles between rafters, or you could break the OSB sheathing. Just set them on the roof without a lot of force, and space the bundles so that they're easy to grab while you're shingling.

when the wind blows. Run these shingles up the gable ends, too. Remember to use shorter nails around the perimeter of the roof if the house has open eaves. Butt the starter shingles tightly to each other.

If you live in a very windy area, you can make the starter course even more secure with just a little extra effort. For the bottom layer of the starter course, cut off the three tabs on each shingle just below the tar strip. Snap a line the width of this narrower shingle around the roof's perimeter. When you install the narrow shingles, the tar strip will be very close to the edge of the roof. Nail the narrow shingles 2 in. or so

from the roof's edge with their tar strips down. When the sun heats up the tar strip, this layer of shingles will be sealed to the roofing felt below.

STARTER COURSE, SECOND LAYER. This shingle layer, and every subsequent course, is installed right side up (tabs down). Position the first row of regular shingles of this top layer flush with the lower edge of the bottom layer, with one of its short edges on the second vertical offset line. It doesn't make any difference whether you go to the right or the left of the second vertical line—all that matters is that the tabs of this top layer are offset from the tabs of the bottom layer by 6 in. Nail each and every shingle the same way. Use four ⅞-in. roofing nails and drive one nail about 1 in. from each edge and one nail above each slot. Drive all nails just below the tar strip and above the cutout.

REMAINING COURSES. Start several courses of shingles, offsetting each by 6 in. This allows other shinglers to work in both directions. Hold each new course of shingles to the 5-in. horizontal mark above the last course, alternating shingle ends on the vertical marks. This establishes a pattern with a 6-in. offset on each shingle.

At vent pipes, install a roof jack, or metal flashing, over the vent to keep out water. Install shingles below the pipe's centerline beneath the flashing. Install those above the centerline on top of the flashing (see the photo at right). The flashing can be nailed near the top corners of the tin, before shingles are laid on top of it. Don't nail the bottom corners down, though, as this could cause the flashing to leak.

At the gable ends, cut the shingles to length before nailing them in position. Mark the length and cut them from the back with a utility knife. Rather than carrying a square, I use another shingle as a straightedge to guide the cut and a third shingle as a protective base below the cut. At the top, cut the shingles flush with the sheathing that was cut back to accommodate the ridge vent.

Shingling across a valley

When a porch roof intersects the main roof at a right angle, a valley is formed. Shingles can be laid across a valley in different ways.

A woven valley is formed by weaving shingles across the valley, alternately overlapping from the main roof onto the porch roof, then vice versa. When properly done, a woven valley is watertight. Let each course of shingles overlap the valley by at least 12 in. and keep nails 8 in. or more from the centerline of the valley.

An alternative to a woven valley is a closed, or cut, valley. To create a cut valley, let all shingle courses from the main roof lap across the porch valley by at least 12 in. Don't alternate back and forth from the main roof to the

Metal flashing ensures that water stays out of the house and drains off harmlessly. Here roofing is applied over metal valley flashing. The shingles will overlap the flashing, but won't be nailed through the metal. When all the shingles are nailed down, you'll snap a chalk line an inch or so above the center of the valley and cut the shingles straight. [Photo by Daniel S. Morrison, courtesy *Fine Homebuilding* magazine © The Taunton Press, Inc.]

Save your knees when shingling. A foam pad makes a great cushion when you're nailing roof shingles. If a pad isn't convenient for you to use, try wearing cushioned knee pads.

It's hard work to hand up sheathing panels.

   We yell back and forth from the roof to the ground.

   Everyone should wear a hard hat.

   With some experienced volunteers using nailers and

others hammering, the panels go down quickly.

   After lunch, we shift from sheathing to shingling.

   The scent of cut wood is replaced by the smell of asphalt;

pretty soon, we're hoisting shingles onto the roof.

porch roof. After the shingles are laid on the main roof, lay the shingles on the porch roof so that each course laps over those on the main roof. Next, snap a chalkline down the center of the valley; use blue chalk, because most other colors stain. Cut the top layer of shingles at this chalkline. I use tinsnips or a utility knife with a hook blade to trim shingles to this line and to avoid cutting the lapped shingles below.

Install step flashing at roof-wall intersections

Use metal step flashing to waterproof the intersection where a roof butts into a wall. Usually made from aluminum or copper, metal step flashing is bent to form a series of elongated, L-shaped pieces that are lapped over each other in successive shingle courses as well as upward along the wall. The step flashing we used on this house is 10 in. by 6 in., and each leg is 3 in. wide.

The illustration on p. 144 shows how step flashing is installed on each course of shingles that runs into a wall. (It's also used where shingles meet a chimney or a skylight curb.) Each time a regular shingle is laid down, a step shingle is placed under it—on the part of the regular shingle that will be covered. Lap step shingles by about 2 in., one on top of the other. One nail above the tar strip should be enough to

Installing the ridge vent. Nailed in place over a narrow opening along the ridge, this vent keeps insects, debris, and moisture out of the attic while allowing warm air to escape.

Making ridge shingles. Cutting a regular shingle into three pieces with a utility knife is an easy way to make these smaller shingles, which will cap the ridge.

STEP FLASHING

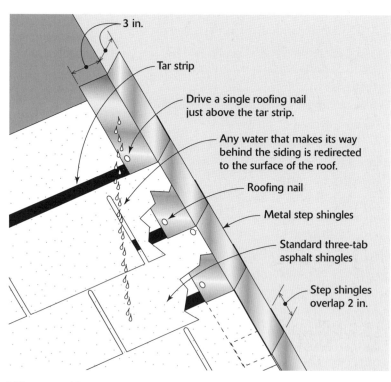

3 in.

Tar strip

Drive a single roofing nail just above the tar strip.

Any water that makes its way behind the siding is redirected to the surface of the roof.

Roofing nail

Metal step shingles

Standard three-tab asphalt shingles

Step shingles overlap 2 in.

When a roof intersects a wall, metal step shingles are used to flash the intersection. The step shingles are covered by both the three-tab shingles on the roof and by the siding on the sidewall.

Ready for rain. Finishing the roof is a big step forward. High-quality roof shingles should last 25 years or more and require little or no maintenance.

hold each step shingle in place. As each successive course of shingles is nailed in place, a portion of the step shingle on the roof is covered. Later, when the wall is covered with siding or stucco, the vertical leg will be covered as well.

Install ridge shingles and the ridge vent

At the ridge, many builders install ridge shingles on the roof ends with a ridge vent between them. An alternative is to install the ridge vent across the entire roof, even though the ends of the vent (located over the gable-end overhangs) are not functional. Some ridge vents do not require a cap of roof shingles, but others do. No matter which type of ridge vent you use, follow the manufacturer's instructions regarding its installation (see the top right photo on p. 143).

Ridge shingles are easy to make—simply cut regular three-tab shingles into three pieces, as shown in the bottom right photo on p. 143. Lay the shingle upside-down on a piece of plywood and cut it with a utility knife. Start at the top of a slot and angle inward slightly in both directions toward the top of the shingle, cutting out a small triangle of waste. These shingles cover the ridge at both ends of the roof and are overlapped to show a 5-in. reveal, just like regular shingles. The angled portion of each ridge shingle is covered by the exposed part of the next shingle.

To ensure that both the ridge shingles and the ridge vent are installed straight, I like to snap a blue chalkline about 5 in. to 6 in. down one side of the ridge. No one but the eagles may see this, but it only takes a couple of minutes to do it correctly, and it's important to develop good habits. Fasten the ridge shingles securely with 1½-in. roofing nails. Some ridge vents must also be installed with long nails. Cover exposed nail heads with a good-size dab of roofing tar.

Nice work! This peak experience gives the house its most important protection from the elements. When a roof is installed properly, you don't have to worry about it for a long time.

![Habitat for Humanity® logo]

PLAY US A TUNE

Before Katrina hit, **Habitat** affiliates in the **Gulf** were building 60 houses a year. After the storm, those same groups were building that many houses in a month! Mobilizing some 70,000 volunteers in the storm's aftermath, **Habitat for Humanity** has completed or begun construction on more than 1,200 homes as of this writing in the **Gulf Coast**, and there's no end in sight.

In **New Orleans**, hit hard by the hurricane, the **New Orleans Area Habitat for Humanity** is playing a key role in rebuilding their city. It has expanded its operations in many parishes outside the city, including **St. Bernard** parish, which sustained damage to nearly every structure within its limits,

Photo courtesy HFHI

Photo courtesy HFHI

and is also committed to the development of the celebrated **Musicians' Village**.

Seeing hundreds of **Crescent City** musicians lose their homes and livelihoods because of the storm's devastation, singer **Harry Connick Jr.** and jazz saxophonist **Branford Marsalis** teamed up with **Habitat** to do something about it.

Designed to foster the sounds and songs that make **New Orleans** unique, the **Musicians' Village** consists of single-family homes and duplexes that will house musicians as well as residents who want to be part of this musically inclined neighborhood. To top it off, the **Ellis Marsalis Center** for **Music** is being built in the heart of the community. Part performance hall, part teaching facility, the center's goal is to bring musicians young and old together to celebrate the rich musical heritage of **New Orleans**.

After so much devastation and upheaval, restoring **New Orleans** will not happen overnight. But if the joint efforts of **Habitat** and the city's citizens are any indication, the spirit of the city is alive and singing.

—*Dave Culpepper*

CLOSING IN

Windows, Doors, Siding, and Exterior Trim

Each phase of a homebuilding project offers a new set of challenges and rewards, but the work that we do in this chapter is especially exciting. The big, stick-framed box we've built is about to receive a beautiful skin, with windows and doors added to make it weatherproof. By the time we've finished the tasks in this chapter, the house will show off its finished exterior appearance. And with the inside protected from the elements, we are free to take on all the interior work ahead.

As I mentioned in Chapter 4, it's common practice in some parts of the country to sheathe wood-framed walls before they are raised rather than after. In other areas, sheathing is eliminated and diagonal steel or wood braces are installed to help walls resist shear forces. Certain types of exterior siding (such as fiber cement or sheets of T1-11 siding) can sometimes be nailed directly to the studs and do not require sheathing underneath.

Before we nail on the siding, we are sheathing this house with two materials that share the same ½-in. thickness. Structural wood panels (oriented strand board, or OSB) are used in the corners, where they provide necessary shear strength. To cover the framing between the OSB panels, rigid foam insulation board is fastened against the studs and plates. Lighter and less expensive than wood panels, rigid foam sheets are easy to handle, cut, and install. Their insulating value improves the home's energy performance, augmenting the R-value of the fiberglass batts installed between the studs.

We won't make much sawdust in this chapter. Instead, we'll learn which tools and techniques are needed to install vinyl siding and prefinished aluminum coil stock. This plastic and sheet-metal exterior is quite different from the redwood siding and trim I used earlier in my construction career. Depending

The house is almost ready for siding. This phase of construction begins with felt on the roof and sheathing on the walls.

on your budget, your personal preferences, and local availability, there are many siding and trim possibilities. Out West, where I've done the most building, fiber-cement siding is often used; it has been installed on quite a few Habitat houses in western states. There are other affordable, low-maintenance siding options to consider, too. A few of them are described briefly on pp. 162–163.

Vinyl Siding

It's not difficult to understand the popularity of vinyl siding. It's affordable, widely available, fairly easy to install, and maintenance-free. A drawback is that it takes time to learn how to install the vinyl trim pieces that go around doors, windows, and under eaves. Another disadvantage is that in some areas, like the Northwest, vinyl siding needs to be pressure washed yearly to remove fungal growth. Vinyl windows, vents, soffit material, and other components are designed to be compatible with vinyl siding, and there are plenty of

colors, surface textures, and styles from which to choose. You'll find vinyl siding on compact, affordable houses like the one featured in this book, as well as on expensive custom-built homes.

Horizontal siding is the most popular type of vinyl siding, and most styles are designed to look like wood clapboards. Clapboard widths range from 4 in. to 8 in. Manufacturers offer most of their siding with either a smooth surface or a textured, wood-grain finish. When choosing a siding color, bear in mind that it will fade slightly over time. Also, darker siding will absorb more heat and expand more than light-colored vinyl.

To estimate how much siding you'll need, refer to the sidebar on p. 154. Keep in mind that when you buy vinyl siding, you're actually buying a comprehensive system of siding components: siding panels, J-channel, inside and outside corner pieces, and other types of trim designed to simplify the installation and enhance the appearance. Siding manufacturers also make compatible vinyl soffit paneling and

GABLE WALL

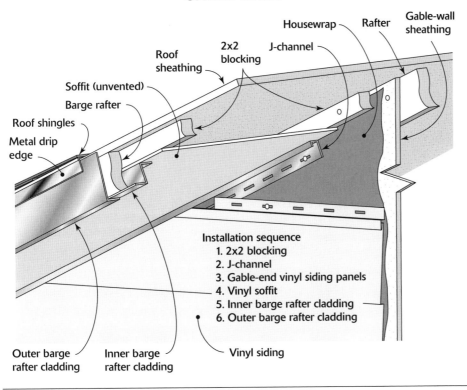

Housewrap · Rafter · Gable-wall sheathing

Roof sheathing · 2x2 blocking · J-channel

Soffit (unvented)

Barge rafter

Roof shingles

Metal drip edge

Installation sequence
1. 2x2 blocking
2. J-channel
3. Gable-end vinyl siding panels
4. Vinyl soffit
5. Inner barge rafter cladding
6. Outer barge rafter cladding

Outer barge rafter cladding · Inner barge rafter cladding · Vinyl siding

EAVE WALL

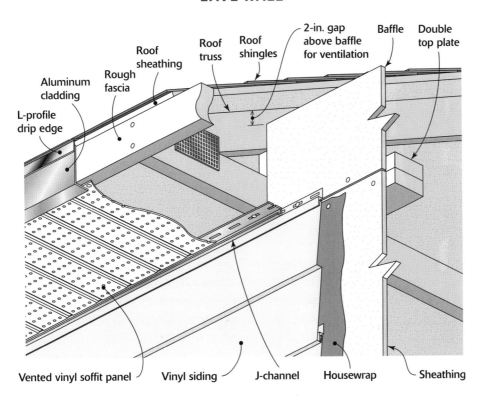

Roof sheathing · Roof shingles · 2-in. gap above baffle for ventilation · Baffle · Double top plate

Roof truss

Rough fascia

Aluminum cladding

L-profile drip edge

Vented vinyl soffit panel · Vinyl siding · J-channel · Housewrap · Sheathing

TIP Be careful with delicate sheathing. Take aim carefully when installing foam sheathing. A misdirected hammer blow can easily dent or puncture the foam. Install these insulating panels with broad-head roofing nails or plastic-cap nails. Space the nails about 16 in. apart along the edges and 24 in. apart everywhere else.

FIBER-CEMENT SIDING

Fiber-cement siding has been around a long time. The first house I worked on in the late 1940s was covered with fiber-cement siding. It was a bit brittle but just about indestructible. It fell out of favor because it was hard to work with and full of asbestos, whereas high-quality wood siding was inexpensive and becoming widely available.

Times have changed. Today, wood siding is expensive and often lacking in quality. Modern fiber-cement siding, on the other hand, contains no asbestos and offers all of its old advantages and a few new ones, too. I like it because it is simple to install, holds paint well, is fire resistant, is easy to trim out, and won't decay, rust, or mold. And if that wasn't enough, it has a 50-year guarantee! Like vinyl, it's fairly easy to work with, thanks to the new cutting and nailing equipment available today. Unlike wood, it doesn't cup, curl, or attract termites. Unlike vinyl, it doesn't burn, melt, expand, or contract.

Once you learn a few basic techniques, such as how to cut and nail it, fiber-cement siding is easy to install and goes on one plank at a time. The siding can sometimes be nailed directly to studs that have been covered with housewrap. In high wind and earthquake areas, siding often has to be nailed on walls that have been sheathed with OSB panels. These

Layout to set the levels for horizontal siding can be done with a story pole. Use the story pole to mark the siding layout on doors, windows, and trim all around the house. [Photo by Don Charles Blom]

OSB panels add lateral and structural strength to a building. In such cases, care must be taken to insure that moisture passing through the walls does not settle on the OSB and cause rot. This problem can be dealt with by creating a space between the siding and the OSB. There are different ways to create this buffer zone. To learn how to approach this part of the project, refer to the manufacturer's product and installation information, which is comprehensive and extremely useful (see Resources on p. 279).

Fiber-cement clapboard siding comes in various widths that are usually 12 ft. long and 5/16 in. thick. Both smooth and wood-grain textures are available. For best results, order the siding pre-primed on both sides. You can also purchase 4-ft. by 8-ft. panels that have vertical grooves like T1-11, or smaller panels that have a shingle pattern. For best results, order the siding pre-primed or with a permanent color already on the siding. After it has been delivered to the job site, keep it covered with a tarp whenever you're not using it to minimize moisture absorption. Store the siding flat and level, too, so it doesn't break or warp.

Cutting tips

Fiber-cement siding can be cut with a regular circular saw and a conventional carbide blade, but a diamond-tipped masonry blade with four to six teeth works much better and is probably cheaper in the long run. The biggest problem with

Space can be created between the wall sheathing and the siding either by using a rain screen or by nailing lath strips to each stud. This space allows moisture to drain and protects wood from rot or mold. [Photo by Don Charles Blom]

cutting fiber-cement with a power saw is that it creates a lot of dust. Be sure to wear a good dust mask and follow the manufacturer's recommendations to avoid unnecessary exposure to silica, which can damage your lungs.

I prefer to use a set of electric fiber-cement siding shears, a power tool designed specifically for this job (see Resources on p. 279). The shears cut cleanly, don't create any dust, and can be used for both straight and curved cuts. For small holes, such as those for exterior electrical outlets, use a jigsaw with a carbide-tipped blade. Cut round holes for pipes with a carbide-tipped hole saw mounted in a heavy-duty, two-handled drill.

Corrosion-resistant fasteners

Most companies guarantee their fiber-cement siding for 50 years. Therefore, it will last a long time—provided it's properly attached with high-quality, corrosion-resistant nails. I generally use regular 2-in.-long, hot-dipped galvanized nails. If I'm working near the ocean or another area with high humidity, I often use stainless-steel nails.

For the most part, builders use pneumatic nailers to attach fiber-cement siding to walls. I've found that a regular pneumatic nailer works better than a roofing nailer (see Resources on p. 279). Make sure that the pressure is set correctly once you get started so that you don't overdrive the nails. Nailguns these days often have a depth gauge to ensure that nails are driven flush with the surface. And there are special coil nailguns that have been developed specifically for siding. Fiber-cement siding can be nailed by hand, but you may need to predrill the nail holes to keep from breaking off the end of the plank. It's a good idea to have a pocket full of felt strips (3 in. by 8 in.). Each time you have two pieces of siding meet at a butt joint, slip a piece of felt behind the joint and let it lap down on the lower course about an inch. This will help prevent water from entering at the joint.

Trim details

As with wood siding, trim for fiber-cement siding is usually installed first, and then the siding panels are butted against

Siding can be highlighted by using different paint colors. The contrast adds to the beauty of the building. [Photo by Don Charles Blom]

it. Fiber-cement trim is available for inside and outside corners, doors, and windows, as well as for covering fascia boards and soffits. The illustrations on p. 152 show a few of the trim details available. These same details also work for wood clapboards and wood shingle siding. The trim should be fairly thick—either 5/4 (1¼ in. thick) or 2×—in order to stand proud and cover the ends of the siding.

At the outside corners, the siding can butt against the corner boards or be covered with aluminum corner pieces (called siding corners). These pieces have been used for many years as trim for wood siding and work just as well with fiber-cement siding. The siding is installed first and stopped exactly at the corner. After all the siding is in place, the siding corners can be slipped under each course. A flange at the bottom of the corner hooks a row of siding and a 6d or 8d galvanized nail is driven through a hole in the top to hold it in place.

Installing siding panels

The installation details for fiber-cement siding are similar to those for wood clapboards. The bottom-most course of siding rests on a 5/16-in.-thick, 1½-in.-wide starter strip cut from the siding or from pressure-treated wood. The bottom edge of the first course should lap about 1 in. below the top of the foundation. To install subsequent courses, follow the manufacturer's recommendations for overlapping and nailing. After you know the amount of reveal the siding will have, you can establish the height of each course. For example, a typical lap on 8¼-in.-wide

CONTINUED ON NEXT PAGE

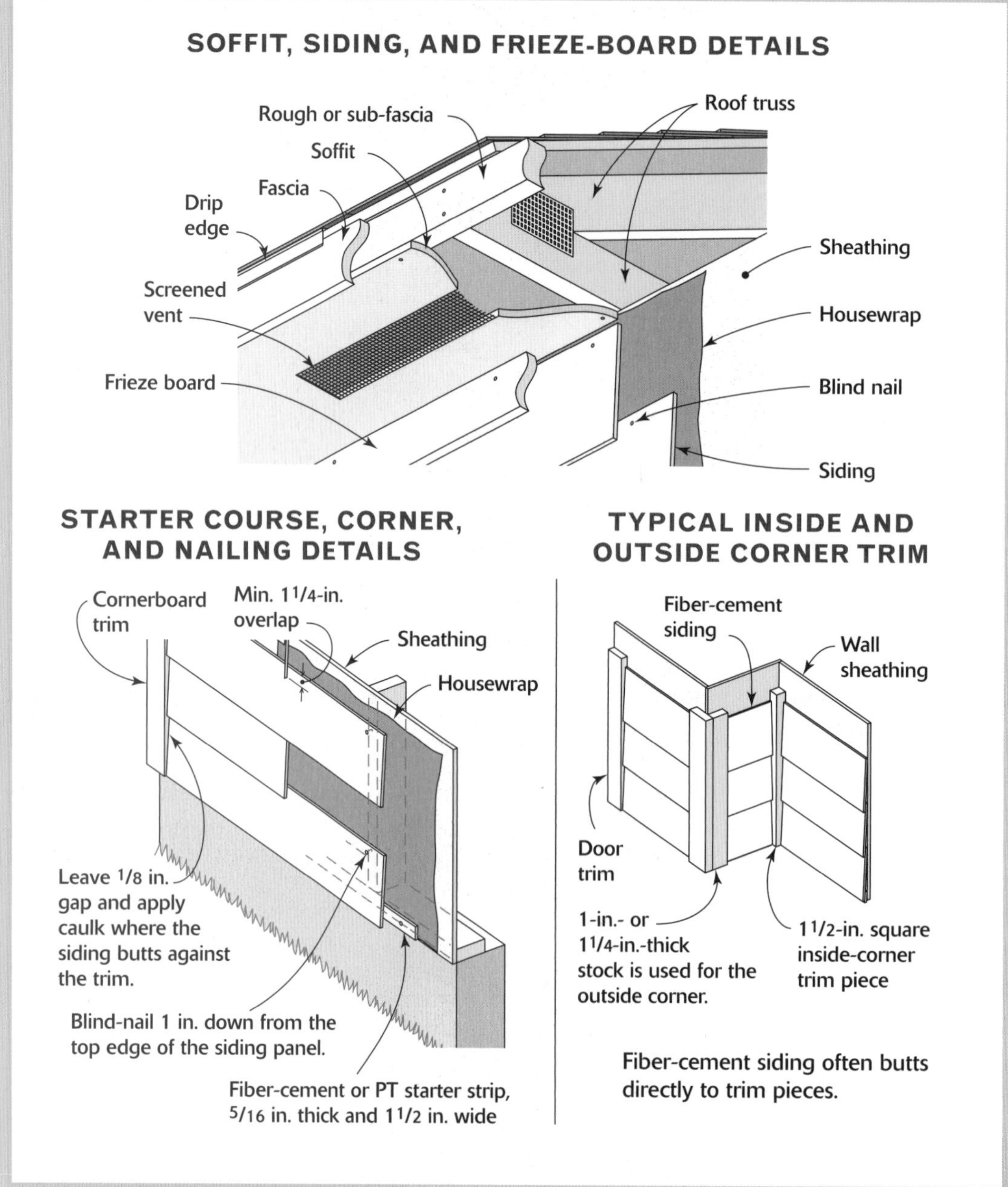

SOFFIT, SIDING, AND FRIEZE-BOARD DETAILS

Rough or sub-fascia

Roof truss

Soffit

Fascia

Drip edge

Sheathing

Screened vent

Housewrap

Frieze board

Blind nail

Siding

STARTER COURSE, CORNER, AND NAILING DETAILS

Cornerboard trim

Min. 1 1/4-in. overlap

Sheathing

Housewrap

Leave 1/8 in. gap and apply caulk where the siding butts against the trim.

Blind-nail 1 in. down from the top edge of the siding panel.

Fiber-cement or PT starter strip, 5/16 in. thick and 1 1/2 in. wide

TYPICAL INSIDE AND OUTSIDE CORNER TRIM

Fiber-cement siding

Wall sheathing

Door trim

1-in.- or 1 1/4-in.-thick stock is used for the outside corner.

1 1/2-in. square inside-corner trim piece

Fiber-cement siding often butts directly to trim pieces.

---

siding is 1¼ in., which leaves a 7-in. reveal. This reveal can be marked on each piece of corner trim and on every door and window all around the house by using a story pole. A reveal can be adjusted up or down slightly (up to ½ in.) in order to fit siding pieces around door and window openings, and to maintain a uniform distance between the top of the wall and the uppermost siding course. To make sure the last course of siding will be uniform in width, measure down from the top of the wall frequently (every other course or so) and fine-tune the reveal, if necessary.

You can mix and match siding to add a bit of style to a building. Gable ends can be sheathed with a different type of siding than the walls. T1-11 in the gable end, for example, will contrast with lap siding on the walls. Contrasts can be made even greater by painting the walls a different color than the gable end.

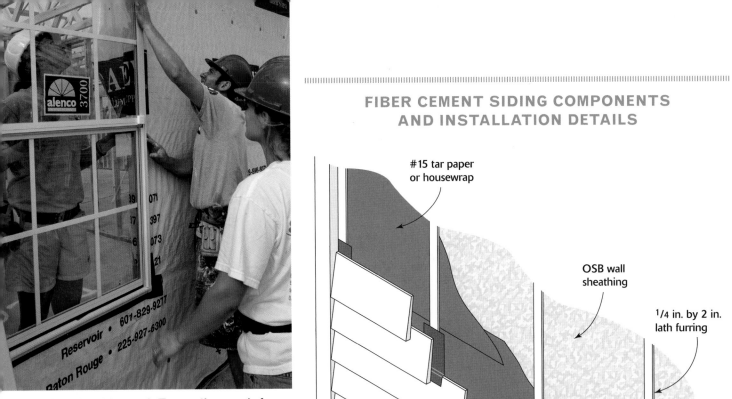

Do final sheathing work. To save time, apply foam-sheathing panels over window and door openings, then make cutouts with a handsaw. [Photo by HFHI/ Will Crocker]

other components, such as vents, electrical outlet covers, and special exterior trim. It's smart to get an overview of the full range of compatible products before you order siding. Go online to visit manufacturer's websites or call to request product information (see Resources on p. 279).

STEP 1 INSTALL THE REMAINING SHEATHING AND THE ROUGH EXTERIOR TRIM

Straight courses of finish siding and sharp-looking exterior trim depend on good prep work on the sheathing and exterior trim surfaces that will be covered with aluminum cladding. A good deal of wall sheathing will already be done at this stage. Now that finish siding is about to be installed, it's important to make sure the wall surfaces are flat and free of gaps that will cause dips or irregularities when the vinyl is installed. When installing foam sheathing, you can sheathe right over window and door openings, then use a handsaw to cut out the foam from the opening (see the photo on p. 109).

FIBER CEMENT SIDING COMPONENTS AND INSTALLATION DETAILS

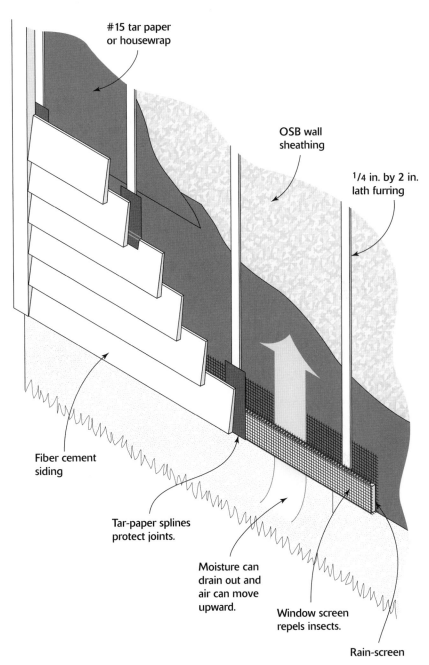

#15 tar paper or housewrap

OSB wall sheathing

1/4 in. by 2 in. lath furring

Fiber cement siding

Tar-paper splines protect joints.

Moisture can drain out and air can move upward.

Window screen repels insects.

Rain-screen

Furring strips keep the siding away from the wall. This creates a drainage plane helping to keep both siding and OSB sheathing dry.

Baffles keep insulation out of the eaves. Nail these panels to the top of the wall between the roof trusses. Leave a gap at the top of the baffle so air can pass through into the attic and out through the ridge vent.

If necessary, install wood sheathing or foam board over any unsheathed areas on which siding will be installed. These areas include the rim joist and headers above windows and doors. Along eave walls, it's also essential to extend the sheathing between the roof trusses above the top plate of the exterior wall, as shown in the photo at right. This additional sheathing acts as a baffle, preventing attic insulation from spilling out into the eaves. Cut each OSB panel so that there are a couple of inches of open space between the top edge of the panel and the top edge of the roof trusses. This clearance is essential for good ventilation; it allows air to be drawn through the soffit vents and into the attic space.

HOW TO ORDER VINYL SIDING

Horizontal siding panels are usually 12 ft. 6 in. long, though some companies make longer panels. Siding is sold by the square, or the number of panels needed to cover 100 sq. ft. To estimate how many squares of siding you'll need, calculate how many square feet of wall surface you need to cover, add 10 percent for waste, then divide by 100.

Order enough starter strips to go around the entire building; these typically come in 10-ft. lengths. You'll also need trim for each inside and outside corner. You can order trim pieces that are the same color as the siding or use a contrasting color, as we did on this house.

If the windows didn't come with an integral J-channel, or channel surround, then order enough J-channel to cover the top and the sides of all the windows and doors. J-channel is also used along the rake and soffit, as shown on p. 152. You also need to order enough undersill trim to go below each window and to cap the top edge of the last piece of wall siding on the eave walls, which is how they are often finished.

Large-head, 1½-in. to 2-in. galvanized nails are used to attach both the siding and the trim. A 50-lb. box should be adequate for a small house. Finally, don't forget about the vinyl soffit panels for closing in the area under the eaves. As shown in the following pages, soffit panels may require J- or F-channel trim.

Install fascia boards. This rough exterior trim will soon be covered with aluminum cladding. Nail the 2×4 trim boards to the rafter and truss ends.

SAFE SCAFFOLDING KEEPS YOU OUT OF HARM'S WAY

On single-story construction, most scaffold work can be done with good sawhorses and good planks. Make sure the planks you choose have a solid, even grain and small, tight knots. If a plank breaks, a fall of only a couple of feet can put you out of commission for a while. And just because you buy good scaffold planks today doesn't mean that they will be safe to use a year from now, especially if they're left out in the elements. I prefer to use manufactured decking planks made of steel and aluminum. They are more expensive, but they make a more secure working platform.

When you have to work higher up, you're better off buying or renting solid-pipe scaffolding. These 6-ft.-high units are easy to set up, and they create a 5-ft. by 8-ft. working platform. Make sure the legs are set on a firm foundation and not just on bare earth. Pipe-scaffolding units can be stacked on top of each other for working on a two-story building. If you will be working more than

10 ft. high, ask for guardrails, which are easy to install and help protect you from an accidental fall.

Some builders like to use pump jacks and ladder jacks as an alternative to pipe scaffolding. Available at most supply houses, these jacks are useful when installing sheathing, housewrap, or siding. Used in pairs, pump jacks attach to double 2×4 or single 4×4 (3½-in.) posts that are held upright with braces temporarily nailed to the roof or to the wall framing. Each pump jack can move up and down on its post to adjust the elevation of the work platform.

If you're using pump jacks, make sure the units come with a built-in guardrail that protects you from falling backward. Make sure the uprights rest on a solid base and not on bare earth. Ladder jacks are steel brackets that hook on the rungs of ladders. Once the brackets are secured to a pair of ladders, you can set planks on the brackets. If you want to move up and work at a higher level, you must remove the planks and reposition the brackets.

The walls look strange covered with foam boards and wood panels.
Vinyl siding will be a big improvement.
All the windows must be installed before the siding goes on.
It takes teamwork to get the window frame into its opening and centered properly.
Vinyl starter strips and different kinds of trim must be nailed in place before we install the siding panels.

HABITAT HELPS NEW HOMEOWNERS CONTINUE LEARNING

Providing a family with four walls and a roof is just the first step in helping them get established. Here at the Twin Cities' affiliate, we also aim to equip families with knowledge, so that they become successful homeowners. Because Habitat families are first-time homebuyers, most are unfamiliar with the basic maintenance, repair, and budgeting responsibilities that come with homeownership. To bridge this information gap, we provide more than a dozen different classes.

Many classes emphasize that "an ounce of prevention" helps protect a family's investment and reduces long-term costs. Basic maintenance classes describe how a house works from top to bottom and explain how (and why) to turn off outdoor faucets, clean out window wells, drain sediment from the water heater, test fire alarms, and check for excessive moisture in the attic.

Habitat homebuyer classes cover more than just caring for the physical house, however. Three money-management classes cover everything from basic budgeting to the pitfalls of credit cards to teaching children how to use money wisely. Other classes cover topics such as poisonous household products, city ordinances that affect property, block clubs, safety, and crime prevention.

Because Habitat has a commitment to environmental stewardship, our classes also cover recycling; ecologically friendly (and economical) practices, such as making cleaning products from natural ingredients; and energy and resource conservation. These practices often seem like common sense to homebuyers who have come from countries without the wealth of natural resources we enjoy here. And while they learn new ways of doing things in class, Habitat families often share old traditions as well.   —*Cheryl Winget*

Exterior trim

Aluminum-clad exterior trim goes well with vinyl siding because, like vinyl, it's also a no-maintenance finish treatment. Aluminum sheets have a factory-applied finish and come on large rolls in various widths. Often referred to as coil aluminum, this sheet material is bent at the job site to fit around exterior trim boards.

To prep for this treatment, rough fascia boards (also called gutter boards) are nailed to the ends of the roof trusses and to the rafter tails on the roof extension above the side door (see the photo on p. 154). Some of these trim details are covered in Chapter 5 and should be completed before the roof is sheathed and shingled. Other trim details, such as the boxed gable-end return shown on p. 173, can be done as the aluminum cladding goes on.

STEP 2 INSTALL THE HOUSEWRAP AND FLASH OPENINGS

Covering the wood house frame with housewrap, a thin protective layer, is the next step before finish siding is applied. You can use the old, reliable housewrap—rolls of 30-lb. felt paper, or you can try one of the modern housewraps, such as Tyvek®, Barricade®, and Typar®. These are lightweight, fabric-like materials that come in rolls and are literally wrapped around the walls of a house. The main purpose of this treatment is to form a drainage plane behind the siding to stop wind-driven water from penetrating into the wall cavity. No siding is completely watertight, so in areas where hard, wind-driven rain is common, housewrap can help protect the walls from moisture damage. However, housewrap is not a replacement for good flashing around doors, windows, and decks. Rather, it adds to those flashing systems, with upper layers

TIP 2 x scaffolding planks need to be strong and safe to use. Try reinforcing these boards by drilling a ¼-in. hole through the plank edge about 8 in. from each end. Insert and tighten a ¼-in. bolt with a washer on each end through the holes. This will help keep the plank from splitting.

always overlapping lower layers like shingles on a house. In addition to helping keep water out, housewrap reduces air leakage but is porous enough to allow water vapor to escape from inside the house.

Climate plays a huge role in determining how housewraps are used. We live in a country with an astonishing diversity of climates, and these varied conditions require different solutions for protecting a house and its inhabitants from the elements. Even the type of wall covering you use can affect your wrapping strategy. Talk to builders in your area (and to the building inspector) to find out what's used locally and why.

Installing housewrap

Housewrap may be attached directly to studs, on top of wall sheathing, or over rigid foam. Modern plastic housewrap is usually white or gray and comes in different widths and lengths. Don't plan to install housewrap on your own; this is definitely a two- or three-person job. The only installation tools required

are a staple gun and a sharp utility knife. Here are the basic steps:

1. Cover the inside and outside corners. This is an optional step, but one that I routinely take to provide extra protection in these critical areas, especially if the siding will be installed directly over the studs. Fold a 2-ft.-wide wall-high length of wrap in half and staple it vertically over the outside corners and into the inside corners.

2. Wrap the house from corner to corner. A 9-ft.-high roll usually fits just right on houses with 8-ft. studs. Staple the free end of the roll near a corner of the house and unroll it over the entire side of the house, with one or two helpers stapling as you go. Cover the window and door openings. When you've finished one side, simply keep rolling onto the next one until you've made your way all around the house.

3. Seal joints and repair tears, if necessary. Hopefully, you can skip this step. But if you can't create a continuous wrap around the house, make sure you overlap the wrap by at least 16 in. or one stud space. Seal the seam with the sticky, self-adhering tape made for this purpose. Be sure to get some when you pick up (or take delivery of) your housewrap. Repair a tear in the housewrap by applying a patch from the top of the wall down over the tear, so that water will drain properly. Seal the tear with tape.

4. Cut and wrap the window and door openings. To finish the installation, cut an "X"-slice in the housewrap over each window and door opening, then pull the cut ends inside the house and staple them around the trimmers, header, and rough sill. Staple the flaps right away so they don't get caught by the wind and torn.

Housewrap helps to keep wind and water out. Modern housewraps can be applied over sheathing or directly over framing, as was done here. After wrapping the walls completely, make "X" cuts at the window and door openings, then fold and staple the flaps inside. [Photo © Memo Jasso]

TIP Housewrap is shiny and slick. When installing housewrap on a bright day, wear sunglasses to protect your eyes from the glare. When leaning a ladder against a wall covered with housewrap, use rubber pads on top of the ladder and take care to position the ladder securely, because housewrap can be slippery.

TIP I like to let the housewrap hang a few inches below the siding on the foundation. This allows the bottom edge of the siding to be painted without getting paint on the foundation. Once painting is finished, the excess housewrap can be trimmed with a utility knife.

Simple flashing details

Whether or not you wrap the house, it's important to flash around the window and door openings. Especially with windows, proper flashing can prevent the water that runs down both sides of the window from entering the wall cavity through the sill area. To flash window and door openings, I generally use 6-in.- to 8-in.-wide strips of felt paper, installing the strips as shown in the illustration below. Don't forget to install the top piece of flashing after the window has been set in its opening. If housewrap is used, you can still install a top piece of flashing. Cut a horizontal slit in the housewrap above the window, then slip the top edge of the top flashing piece into the slit.

FLASHING A WINDOW

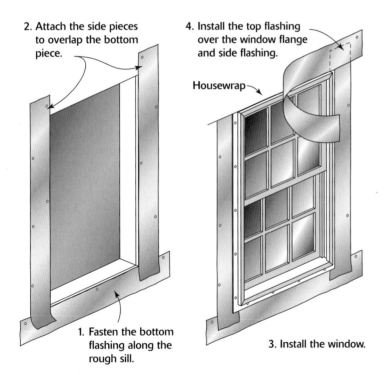

2. Attach the side pieces to overlap the bottom piece.

4. Install the top flashing over the window flange and side flashing.

Housewrap

1. Fasten the bottom flashing along the rough sill.

3. Install the window.

Cut flashing strips 6 in. to 8 in. wide from good-quality builder's felt. Secure flashing with staples or ¹/2-in. roofing nails.

STEP 3 SET THE WINDOWS AND DOORS

The setting process anchors the windows and doors in their final positions. Complete installation happens later, when we move inside the house and work on the interior trim. The windows and doors used in affordable housing are mainly vinyl and vinyl clad, though aluminum-clad frames are still installed in some areas. Some codes require that window frames be clad with white vinyl; check with your local building department. Dark-colored vinyl absorbs more solar heat and, as a result, tends to deteriorate faster. On the other hand, dark-colored aluminum cladding holds up well in sunny areas.

Both vinyl and aluminum-clad windows come with a nailing flange on the outside of the window frame; the flange greatly simplifies the installation process. The most popular styles are single hung (the bottom sash moves up and down), double hung (both sashes move up and down), and sliding (one sash slides to the side). Windows with a built-in J-channel, or channel surround, make it easy to hide the ends of vinyl and other siding without the use of extra trim.

Windows in affordable houses should definitely be double-glazed. The heat loss and gain through single-glazed windows is considerable. In very cold or very hot climates, windows with low-E coatings offer even more energy savings. For more information on energy-efficient glazing, see Resources on p. 279.

Setting a window

Flanged windows are the easiest windows to install, but windows that come with exterior trim instead of flanges are fairly easy as well. The main difference is that you nail through the exterior trim instead of through the flanges. No matter which type of window you use, it's good to have two people for this job—one inside the house and one outside. There are three basic steps involved in setting a window:

Flanged windows are easy to install. Before setting the window in its opening, apply exterior caulk to the flange surface.

1. Caulk the flange. Squeeze a generous bead of exterior caulk or sealant on the back of each window flange (see the photo above).

2. Set and plumb the window. Cut a slit in the housewrap at the top of the window. Slip the top flange of the window under the housewrap. Then set the window in its opening and push the installation flange against the wall surface. If the rough opening has been framed correctly, there will be about ¼ in. of space around the window frame on the inside. Place a couple of ¼-in.-thick shims on the inside to help center the window in the opening. Check the window for plumb and level by placing a 2-ft. or 4-ft. level against the outside of the frame, as shown in the photo at right.

3. Nail the flange to the wall. Secure the window by driving 1½-in.-long galvanized roofing nails at each corner of the window flange and every 8 in. elsewhere. Be careful not to damage the vinyl frame by hitting it with your hammer. When I'm building in rainy climates, I make one more seal all around the windows by running a strip of waterproof tape over the flange and onto the housewrap. It may be overkill, but who wants to tear off siding to repair a leaky window in the middle of a rainstorm?

Setting a prehung exterior door

Exterior doors are often prehung units that include jambs, a threshold, and wood exterior trim. I buy doors predrilled for both the house lockset and the deadbolt. Given the option, I also choose a door with a double-glazed glass window to bring more light into the house.

TIP Lighten the load. Before installing windows, you can substantially lighten their load by removing one or more sash members. It's also wise to store all screens in a safe place until the house is finished.

Plumb the frame with a level. Before nailing the flange to the wall, fine-tune the window's position so the side of the frame is plumb.

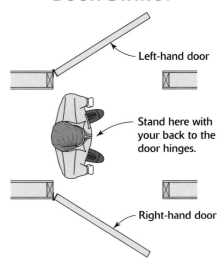

TIP If you live in a high-wind area, help protect your home by cutting pieces of plywood to fit over every window and store them in your garage. When the big blow comes you can screw these pieces in place over the windows.

Take note of which way the plans say the door should open, and make sure the door you ordered swings the right way (see the illustration at right). Most exterior doors open inward. Also, make sure the door jamb is the proper width for the wall. A 2×6 wall takes a wider jamb than a 2×4 wall does. There are four basic steps involved in setting a prehung door:

1. Flash the doorsill. The sides and top of the rough opening can be flashed in the same way as a window. With an exterior door, sill flashing is essential if you want to prevent rot beneath the threshold. I prefer to use 12-in.-wide aluminum flashing for this application, though heavy tar paper also works well. Cut the flashing about 6 in. longer than the width of the rough opening so it can cover

WHICH WAY DOES THE DOOR SWING?

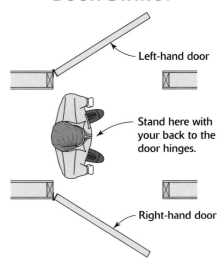

- Left-hand door
- Stand here with your back to the door hinges.
- Right-hand door

Most suppliers use the above method to determine which way a door opens.

the threshold area completely and extend several inches up each trimmer stud. Cut the flashing as necessary to create ears that fold onto the subfloor and over the exterior wall sheathing. You can keep the flashing in place with a few galvanized roofing nails.

2. Test-fit the door. When working with a prehung door, your primary concern is to set it so that it opens and closes with ease. Fortunately, this is pretty easy to do. Once you've removed any materials used to protect the door during shipping and any device used to hold the door secure in its jamb, check the fit of the door in its opening. It should fit easily (see the top photo on the facing page).

3. Set the door in place. Run a bead of sealant on the back of the door trim and a couple of heavy beads across the bottom of the rough opening on the flashing where the threshold will sit. Then set the frame in its opening. From the inside, adjust the frame so that there's a gap of about ⅛ in. all the way around the door. This will allow the weatherstripping on the door frame to seal properly. Secure the door in the opening by

ANCHORING AN EXTERIOR DOOR

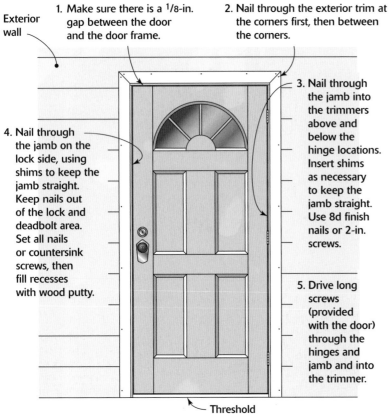

Exterior wall

1. Make sure there is a ⅛-in. gap between the door and the door frame.

2. Nail through the exterior trim at the corners first, then between the corners.

3. Nail through the jamb into the trimmers above and below the hinge locations. Insert shims as necessary to keep the jamb straight. Use 8d finish nails or 2-in. screws.

4. Nail through the jamb on the lock side, using shims to keep the jamb straight. Keep nails out of the lock and deadbolt area. Set all nails or countersink screws, then fill recesses with wood putty.

5. Drive long screws (provided with the door) through the hinges and jamb and into the trimmer.

Threshold

Keep checking as you work to make sure the door opens and closes with ease.

driving a 16d finish nail through each corner of the exterior trim and into the sheathing and studs. (Alternatively, you can drive 3-in.-long trim-head screws.)

4. Finish fastening the door. Check the door again to see that it opens and closes with ease. If it does, then drive more 16d finish nails (or screws) 2 ft. o.c. all the way around the trim. Set all nails or screws about 1/8 in. below the surface of the wood so they can be hidden by putty and covered with paint. Drive 8d finish nails or 2-in.-long screws through the hinge side of the jamb and into the trimmer near each hinge. If the jamb is not tight against the trimmer, slip in a shim to prevent the jamb from bowing. Shim and nail through the jamb on the lock side next, but be sure to keep nails away from the lock and deadbolt area. Finally, drive the long screws that are included with the door frame through the hinges and the jamb and into the trimmer. These help hold the entire assembly in place.

Test the door. Prehung doors come with jambs, a threshold, and exterior trim. Before installing the unit, I tilt the frame into the opening to make sure the fit is right.

Install the attic vent. Vinyl siding panels can't be installed until the vents, outlet boxes, and other wall elements are in place. This vent has flanges for easy installation. House-wrap and flashing go on before final installation.

MORE SIDING OPTIONS

In addition to vinyl siding, there are three more exterior finishes to consider if you're interested in affordability, low maintenance, and attractive appearance:

COMPOSITE WOOD. These planks are made the same way as OSB sheathing panels, but they look like solid-wood clapboards or horizontal lap siding when installed. This siding comes with a factory-applied primer coat, and it needs to be painted after installation. Composite-wood planks don't split, crack, or warp like solid-wood siding does, but they may not be a wise choice in extremely wet climates. These clapboards nail on walls much like cement fiber boards.

STUCCO. Two types of stucco finishes can be applied to house exteriors. Lightweight acrylic-type stucco treatments are available for application over specially prepared foam insulation board. Old-fashioned Portland cement–based stucco can be applied to masonry walls and to wire or stucco lath that's been fastened to wall sheathing or directly to studs. It's best to hire experienced professional

Lap siding, made either of cedar or cement-based material, is a good choice for a traditional appearance. [Photo courtesy HFHI]

crews to do these treatments. In hot, sunny climates, stucco stands up better than most other siding treatments.

SHINGLES. Many houses, especially in coastal areas, have cedar shingles on their exterior walls. Sometimes in Oregon we will shingle the gable ends of a house just to give it a distinctive look. I think it is safe to say that if you can nail composite shingles on a roof you can learn how to nail wood shingles on a wall. You can also buy cement fiber shingle panels that make it easier to cover a gable end or even an entire house

When you use shingles, start by covering the exterior walls with OSB panels and a good housewrap. The courses of shingles can be laid out with a story pole. The first course is doubled just as if they were roof shingles. Check with a local contractor to make sure you are using the right fasteners to nail each shingle in place. In coastal areas you will want to use a nail that doesn't rust easily.

PLYWOOD OR OSB SIDING. I have been sheathing houses with plywood panels for years. In the past, some of these products didn't hold up well over time. In wet

The exterior of the house can be closed in rapidly with sheets of textured plywood or OSB. [Photo by Don Charles Blom]

climates, the plywood delaminated. In dry climates, the surface cracked easily and paint peeled off. Houses began to look like the prairie house I lived in during the 1930s. Pretty shabby.

Texture 1-11, or T1-11, plywood panels come in different sizes and textures. The standard size of these plywood sheets is 4 ft. by 8 ft., with ¼-in.-wide grooves cut into the face every 4 in., 8 in., or 12 in. These sheets can be purchased with a textured face without grooves and even come in 9-ft. and 10-ft. lengths. These longer lengths allow you to sheathe both an 8-ft. wall and the rim joist with one piece. The same patterns and sizes are available as an OSB product. I actually prefer the OSB panels, called Smartside®, because they come paint-primed on the front side.

I have been using these panels in wet, coastal Oregon on some of the small houses we have built. You can rapidly close in the exterior walls with this material. I always prime the backside and edges before installation.

Installation is straightforward. The panels can usually be nailed directly to the studs once the housewrap is on and the windows are in place. Some people square up the framed

You can add a bit of class to a house by simply installing shingles in the gable end. [Photo by Don Charles Blom]

walls on the floor and nail on sheathing before standing the walls upright.

The siding needs to extend down over the foundation 1 in. I begin by snapping a chalkline 1 in. below the bottom sill plate all the way around the house. Start from the corner that has a 4 ft. o.c. stud layout. Use a level to make sure this first panel is nailed on plumb and level directly on the chalkline. Get this first one right and all the following panels will install easily. I like to nail off the sheets with 7d or 8d galvanized ringshank nails. Nail each panel every 6 in. around the perimeter and every 12 in. out in the field.

Make your measurements and cuts within ⅛ in. to ¼ in. around windows, doors, electrical outlets, or dryer vent. Before nailing these panels in place, run a bead of good exterior caulk around the openings and under the sheathing. Once the sheets are nailed in place, fill any gap between the panel and the window or door frame with caulk to help prevent water from entering at these points.

Trim for T1-11 or OSB sheeting is rather simple. Use roughsawn 1×4s to cover the outside corners and full 1-in.-sq. stock ripped from a 2×4 on the inside corners. Use frieze blocks between rafters when they are exposed, and 1×3s or 1×4s to trim around the windows and doors.

Windows can be trimmed in a number of ways. Here we are using 1×3s to trim and seal this window. [Photo by Don Charles Blom]

TIP Take care when cutting cement-fiber boards. They no longer have asbestos in them, but they do have silica. You definitely don't want to inhale that stuff, so get yourself a pair of electric shears that won't create dust (see Resources on p. 279) You can also buy circular saws that have dust catchers. These saws can be hooked to a shop vacuum that will catch almost all of the dust.

STEP 4 COMPLETE VENTILATION AND ELECTRICAL WORK

Before you install the siding, soffits, and exterior trim, it's important to resolve some ventilation and electrical details. For example, this house has a rectangular attic vent centered beneath the ridge in each gable-end wall. If you chose to sheathe the gable-end truss on the ground, this is the logical place to cut the hole for the vent. If the hole hasn't been cut yet, do so now, then install the vent (see the photo on p. 161).

Referring to your house plans, an electrician will be able to locate any outlet boxes that need to be installed in the exterior walls. Outdoor receptacles are placed at convenient locations; the same is true for outdoor lights.

This is also the time to cut the hole for the dryer vent. A standard dryer vent requires a 4-in. hole; it's usually placed in the laundry room, at the back of the dryer near the floor. There are several ways to cut a vent hole. The easiest way is to use a 4-in.-dia. hole saw (borrow one from the plumber, if possible). Otherwise, mark the vent location with a 4-in.-dia. circle, drill a ¾-in. hole along one edge, then cut out the circle with a keyhole saw, a jigsaw, or a reciprocating saw. Just make sure you are above the bottom plate and baseboard and away from the end stud. There shouldn't be any electrical wires down this low, but check to make sure. Insert the vent pipe through the wall, then attach the vinyl trim cover.

Be sure to seal around the vent on both the inside and the outside to keep cold air and moisture from entering the house. Vent pipes can become plugged with lint after years of use. I unplug ours by cleaning out the pipe with a broom handle and then using the vacuum cleaner.

Passive and active air vents

After all our efforts to ensure that our houses are tight and energy efficient, you need to ask yourself this question: Is there enough fresh air in the house? The answer is, well, maybe. If you live in the sunny south where windows can be kept open year round, then lots of fresh air can enter into your living spaces. I was born in western Nebraska, where Wyoming winter winds coming out of the north blew right through our house. No problem having sufficient air under those conditions. The problem is that open windows or poorly insulated houses mean high energy costs.

There are both passive and active ways to bring outside air into a closed house (see Resources on p. 279). A passive vent can be installed through the wall. Every time a bath or kitchen exhaust fan is turned on, fresh air is drawn in through this vent and into the house.

Active vents can also be placed through the walls. They come equipped with a fan that draws in fresh air from the outside. It's a good idea to place these vents away from the kitchen or bath exhaust fan unless you want the odors from these rooms wafting throughout the house.

These devices can also be set on a timer to operate only when occupants are at home. No need to run them when you are away breathing someone else's air.

Fresh air in the house is a serious matter. To explore more solutions to this problem, I encourage you to consult with your local HVAC contractor to make sure your home maintains good quality air at all times.

STEP 5 INSTALL THE STARTER STRIPS AND THE TRIM FOR VINYL SIDING

The most important thing to keep in mind as you're installing vinyl siding is that it expands and contracts significantly with temperature changes. All siding components and installation details are designed to cope with this temperature-induced movement. Review the installation information discussed throughout this chapter. Make sure you comply with the manufacturer's instructions that come with the siding. It's also smart to check with builders

Install vinyl trim. Attached along edges and corners, vinyl molding helps secure siding panels and contributes to a nice, finished appearance. Starter strips are installed along the bottom edge of the wall (left). To allow for heat-induced expansion, the end of a starter strip should be at least 1 in. away from the outside corner trim (below).

in your area for any local wisdom. This is the best way to avoid the bulges, buckles, and tears that can result from incorrect installation. Most vinyl siding should not be nailed firmly against sheathing. The installation slots in the siding, starter strips, and other vinyl components are there for a reason. Keep the nail heads proud of the vinyl so that the vinyl can move.

The tools you need to install vinyl siding are mostly tools you probably already own, but there are a few others you'll need to either buy or make (see the sidebar on p. 166). These tools are also handy for the sheet-metal work we'll tackle later in the chapter.

Starter strips

The installation of vinyl siding begins with different trim elements: starter strips, inside corners, outside corners, J-channel, and so on. The various trim details are designed to hide or interlock with siding ends and edges. As with other homebuilding phases, if you get started right, the next steps follow more smoothly. The critical first step is to put on a straight and level

starter strip right above the top of the concrete foundation wall or slab (see the photo above). This strip can usually be installed by nailing through the sheathing and into the bottom of the mudsill or sole plate. The strip's bottom edge can then extend about 1 in. over the concrete.

With a house that is covered with housewrap, it is not always easy to see where to nail the starter strip. One way to establish the exact height of the strip is to measure down from the underside of the joist chords on the roof trusses and mark the proper height at various points around the house. This will ensure that the starter strip is level and equidistant from the top plates. Connect these points with a chalkline all around the house. On long walls, keep the line from sagging in the middle by having someone hold the line to a height mark near the middle of the wall, then snap the chalkline from the center to both corners.

To secure the starter strip, drive nails in the center of the installation slots, spacing them every 12 in. to 14 in. Leave at least ¼ in. to ½ in. of expansion room between sections of starter strip

TOOLS FOR VINYL SIDING

A long, flat work surface is essential for vinyl siding and sheet-metal work. A couple of 2×12 boards on sawhorses work fine. For precise 90-degree-angle cuts and angled rake cuts, I suggest making a cutting jig for a circular saw (see the bottom center photo). The jig, which sits on a long worktable, is essentially a wooden cradle that guides the base of the circular saw. The cradle can be positioned at a right angle, or at other angles, to the siding.

Use both right- and left-handed aviation snips to make straight and curved cutouts (see the center right photo); tinsnips are also helpful. Other specialty tools you'll need include a slot punch, to make nailing slots in siding (see the top right photo); a snap-lock punch, to create crimps or tabs that lock into the finish trim (see the bottom right photo); and a zip tool, in case you need to remove a damaged panel from a wall.

TIP Don't nail it—hang it. If you remember that most vinyl siding is hung rather than nailed, you'll avoid the common error of driving nails tightly against the siding.

as you install it around the building, and drive your first nail in each piece no less than 4 in. from an end. Remember: The strip must be able to move beneath the nail heads. At a wall's outside corner, the starter strip must be 1 in. or more from the vinyl corner trim, as shown in the right photo on p. 165. Keep the strip 1½ in. to 2 in. from the inside corners.

Corner trim, J-channel, and undersill trim

The corner trim pieces, which receive the ends of the vinyl siding panels, must be installed straight and plumb or they won't look attractive. Hold a short, cutoff piece of vinyl corner post against the sheathed corner of the house and mark the edge of the flange on both sides of the corner at the top and bottom of the wall. Snap a chalkline between the marks. Set a corner post ¼ in. to ½ in. down from the soffit, and drive a 1½-in.-long nail at the top of a slot on both sides of the corner. The corner post hangs from these nails, allowing the vinyl to move. Hold the posts directly on the chalklines and drive nails about every 12 in. in both flanges, down to the bottom of the wall. Keep each nail in the center of its slot. The corner posts should extend ½ in. to 1 in. below the starter strip.

Most doors and windows have factory-made siding channels. If yours do not, install J-channel along the top and sides of the window to hide the ends of the siding. You can use a miter or a square cut at the top corners. Either way, at the ends of the top piece, leave 1-in.-long drain tabs that can be folded down over the window sides. This helps channel water down around the window (see the photo at right).

STEP 6 INSTALL THE SIDING PANELS

Thanks to the work you did in the previous step, panel installation can go quickly, especially when you have a good-size crew, as we did on this job. The first panel course is always the bottom-most course. Start against the corner on one side of the house (preferably the back corner). Pull up the first panel, snap it into the starter strip, and slide the end of the panel under the corner trim's top edge. Keep the panel seated in the starter strip as you drive nails into each stud. The nail heads should be ¹⁄₁₆ in. proud of the flange. Don't drive nails at the edge of a slot or through the vinyl itself. If the prepunched slot is not centered over a stud, lengthen the slot with a utility knife or a slot-punch tool.

Once the panel is nailed in position, check whether you can slide it back and forth manually. If the panel won't slide, find out where it's getting hung up and fix the problem. After you've checked that the panel is free to move, you can, if you like, nail it fast near the middle. Some builders prefer this technique, which

Trim around a door. J-channel trim is nailed around the window and door frames, with a tab in the top piece bent to fit around the corner.

The work goes quickly. With a Habitat-size crew, this siding job moves along at a good pace. Short offcuts from one side of the house can often be used elsewhere to minimize waste.

Some volunteers prefer contrast between the white corner trim and the brown siding, whereas others aren't sure whether it looks attractive.

We install siding panels from the bottom up.

Each new course of panels snaps onto the one below.

You can't drive the nails hard against the vinyl because it needs to move.

With snips and utility knives, we measure, trim, and cut to fit around windows, doors, outlets, and vents.

The vinyl soffit panels are filled with small holes so that air can pass into the attic space.

They finish off the eaves nicely.

Photos top row and bottom left courtesy HFHI

encourages the panel to expand and contract equally in both directions.

The clearance between the end of a panel and the inside edges of the trim pieces depends on the temperature. If it's over 90°F when you install the siding, leave the panel end about ¼ in. away from the trim piece's inside edge. If it's less than 30°F, leave a good ½ in. of clearance at each end so there's room for heat-induced expansion. For temperatures between these two extremes, gauge accordingly.

Cutting and lapping panels

When you come to an opening or reach the end of a wall, cut a panel to fit. Remember always to leave room for expansion. Cut panels to length with a tablesaw, as described earlier using a circular saw with the blade in backward. You can also crosscut with a radial-arm saw, a sliding compound-miter saw, a utility knife, a hacksaw, or even tinsnips. Plan each siding cut so that the cut ends are hidden in the corner posts, in the J-channel trim, or by the factory edge of an overlapping panel. Panels that join within a course should overlap by at least 1 in.

You'll notice that the nailing flange on a siding panel is cut back about 1 in. from the end of the panel. When two panels join each other in the same course, their nailing flanges should never butt together on the wall. When necessary, cut back the nailing flanges so that those in the same course are separated by at least 1 in.

It's best to lap the panels between—not on— the studs. Try not to install pieces shorter than 3 ft. long, especially in high-wind areas. And don't let the overlaps where siding panels meet stack over one another in subsequent courses. Rather, randomly separate these overlaps by two or three studs, so that you don't create a staircase pattern. The pattern created by the installed vinyl panels should be pleasing to the eye.

Pull each panel up snugly against the locking hem of the previous panel, but don't stretch it. Panels that were stretched tightly when they

were installed (especially in warm weather) can tear when cold weather causes them to contract. Before moving on to the next row, make sure each panel is free to move back and forth horizontally.

As you proceed upward, measure down from the underside of the trusses to each row to ensure that the siding is remaining level around the building. Vinyl siding can stretch upward and easily become out of level. Some builders snap level chalklines every 2 ft. or so around the building to serve as reference points while they install rows of siding.

Installing panels around windows, doors, outlets, and vents

Strips of undersill trim must be installed beneath windowsills. This special trim covers the horizontal edge of a siding panel and locks the panel in place. Cut each trim piece to fit between the two side J-channels, then nail it flush against the underside of the window. If the panel beneath a window needs to be notched

TIP Turn the blade backward! For smoother, shatter-free cuts in vinyl siding, use a fine-tooth paneling blade in a circular saw and turn the blade so that the teeth face backward. The same backward rule applies if you're using a chopsaw or radial-arm saw to cut vinyl siding.

Cutouts are challenging. This siding panel was notched to fit over a door and a window. It's important to measure carefully so that the cutout edges fit properly in the J-channel around the doors and windows.

MAKING AN OUTLET-BOX CUTOUT

Precise cutouts are sometimes required for certain situations, such as fitting siding panels over vents or electrical outlet boxes. Careful layout is the key here.

1. Place the siding panel directly below where it will be installed. Mark where the sides of the box hit the panel.

2. Reposition the panel to one side of the box, clipping it into the panel just below the box. Mark where the top and bottom of the box hit the panel.

3. Outline the cutout where the horizontal and vertical lines intersect, then cut the opening with a sharp utility knife.

4. The panel is now ready to install.

more than 1 in. to fit, you must fur out or shim the undersill trim. The deeper the notch in the siding, the thicker the shim you'll need. By furring out the undersill trim, you can prevent the surface of the siding from bowing in beneath the window. Try not to have any joints between panels located beneath or above windows.

To determine a notch's location horizontally in the panel beneath a window, measure from the last piece of siding to the opening and mark it on the panel (don't forget to add 1 in. for the overlap). For an accurate height measurement vertically, lock a scrap of siding into the nail flange of the piece below, then slide the scrap against the window edge. Mark where the scrap hits the bottom of the window and transfer the mark to the panel you're cutting. Finally, measure the length of the opening and transfer it to the siding, leaving ¼ in. on each side for expansion. These notched cuts can be made with a utility knife, a hacksaw, or tinsnips. Use a snap-lock punch to create crimps, or tabs, ¼ in. down from the top edge of the notched siding and make crimps every 6 in. across the length of the window. The crimps must face out to lock into the undersill trim.

The panels that fit over the tops of windows and doors are marked and notched in the same way as those on the bottom. The horizontal part of the siding slips down into the J-channel. To make cutouts where the siding fits over a dryer vent, an electrical outlet box, or another protrusion, use the techniques discussed here and on the facing page.

Installing the top piece of eave-wall siding

The last piece of siding at the top of an eave wall can be fastened in different ways. If the eaves will be left open, use strips of undersill trim and cut and fasten the final panel in the same way as the one under the window. If the eaves will be closed with soffit material (as was done on this house), then the uppermost siding panel can simply be nailed in place above the level of the soffit. The

J-channel trim for the soffit, and then the soffit itself, will cover the top siding panel.

Siding gable-end walls

Begin by nailing 2×2 blocking between the lookouts and along the barge rafter. This allows J-channel to be nailed up the rake, where it can receive the angled ends of the siding panels. Some builders prefer to hold the J-channel ½ in. down so the soffit pieces can simply lie on top of it.

To ensure accurate angled cuts where the siding panels meet the rake, make a pattern from a short scrap of vinyl siding, with the angle cut to match the roof's pitch. If you really want to save time, however, set up a circular saw guide at the proper angle on the worktable.

As you cut and fit these pieces on the gable end, be sure to leave a ¼-in. space between the siding and the inside of the J-channel. If there are gable-end vents, cut and fit pieces around the vents, just as you did for those around the windows and doors. The last small piece at the peak can be cut and secured to the wall with a small screw or nail.

Install J-channel for the soffit. The top course of vinyl siding on eave walls extends behind the J-channel that holds the soffit panels. Install the J-channel by nailing it to the bottom chords of the roof trusses.

STEP 7 FINISH THE SOFFITS

Vinyl soffit material has small holes to allow air to enter freely. Before attaching this material along eave walls, make sure that all the baffles between rafters are in place to keep insulation out of the eaves and allow airflow into the attic. On this house, we cut the vinyl soffit sections into short lengths that overlap each other and ran them perpendicular to the siding. Insert the ends of each soffit panel into vinyl J-channel trim nailed to the wall and nail the other end to the bottom edge of the gutter board.

Gable-end soffit details

Soffit work is also required to finish off the underside of the roof overhang on the gable ends of a house. Remember the J-channel trim that you installed along the rake to house the ends of the gable-wall siding panels? The inboard edge of the soffit trim can rest right on top of that J-channel. This detail is shown in the illustration on p. 149. The outboard edge of each soffit piece is nailed to the 2×2s fastened along the barge rafter.

It's common practice for some builders to build boxed returns at the bottom corners of the roof to bring the soffit around the corners of walls. One part of the return (made from 2× material) is cut to match the angle of the roof's pitch and is fastened to the underside of the barge rafter. The other part of the return should then be fastened to the angled piece and to the wall (see the sidebar on the facing page).

Nice job! To avoid hammering the vinyl, a volunteer uses a metal pin to drive soffit nails their final distance.

STEP 8 COVER EXTERIOR TRIM WITH ALUMINUM CLADDING

Aluminum trim, often referred to as coil aluminum because it comes in a coil or roll, can be shaped and used to cover rough exterior trim, such as gutter boards, barge rafters, and beams. This sheet metal comes in various widths and colors. The small nails used to install the material are available in matching colors. Softer than steel, coil aluminum can be cut with tinsnips or a utility knife. The same long, flat worktable that was used during vinyl siding installation is just as valuable for sheet-metal work. To make the precise bends that give the finished cladding its clean-lined appearance, you'll need a hand brake as well as a large sheet-metal brake, which you can borrow or rent (see the bottom right photo on p. 174).

To wrap a 2×4 gutter board, cut a 6-in.-wide strip of aluminum and bend it at 4 in. into a 90-degree angle. The 4-in. leg slips under the roof's drip cap and covers the front of the gutter board. Attach it with matching 1-in.-long nails every 24 in. along an imaginary centerline (see the left photo on p. 174). The 2-in. leg fits over the vinyl soffit, covering the nails used to secure the soffit to the bottom of the gutter board. Be careful not to drive nails so hard that you leave a hammer imprint in the metal.

Cut soffit paneling. Perforations in vinyl soffit material allow ventilation through the eaves. The soffit panel has a nailing flange with slotted holes similar to those found on vinyl siding. Cut panels to size with metal shears.

TURNING CORNERS IS TRICKY WORK

Combining an enclosed soffit with a gable-end roof overhang means that you need to construct a boxed return. The return creates the nailing surfaces required to bring the soffit and fascia trim around the corner of the house. Here's how to do the job:

1. Use 2× lumber to make the framing for the boxed return, which consists of a triangular piece cut to match the roof's pitch and a straight board that vertically extends to the gable wall.

2. Fasten this assembly to the bottom edge of the barge rafter and the back wall. The soffit paneling must be attached prior to the aluminum cladding.

3. Run electric cable through the corner soffit for an outdoor light. Slip the gutter board cladding under the roof's drip edge trim, then bend it at a 90-degree angle to cover the end of the soffit. Test-fit the cladding for the return before you nail the prebent piece in place.

4. To install gable-end siding panels, nail white J-channel trim along the rake. Trim the panel ends to match the roof's pitch.

We have to set up scaffolding to finish the siding and soffit work; by this time, the house is really looking great.

After a break to admire our progress (and clean up the spare pieces of vinyl siding), we start to cut and bend the aluminum cladding that will cover the fascia boards and the barge rafters.

A big bending tool, called a brake, creases the aluminum perfectly straight.

When it slides into place over the wood, it looks like it belongs there.

Clad the fascia. The top edge of fascia cladding must slide underneath the metal drip edge that extends from the roof. Install the cladding with special nails colored to match the prefinished aluminum.

Bend the aluminum cladding. Borrow or rent a large sheet-metal brake—it's the only way to make precise bends in aluminum cladding. The brake clamps the coil stock in a straight line while you move a lever to make the bend.

The cladding that covers the boxed return is a bit more complex, but the bends can be made with a hand brake. At the ridge peak, run one piece of aluminum past the centerline, then cut the second piece plumb to give the trim a finished appearance.

Any time you use aluminum to cover gutter boards, posts, or beams, make absolutely sure that no water can get behind the aluminum. You can do this by overlapping adjacent sections of cladding by 3 in. to 4 in. and by ensuring that a higher section of cladding (on a barge rafter, for example) always overlaps a lower section.

Put on the finishing touches. Barge-rafter cladding is installed last. For an attractive appearance and weather-tight construction, the aluminum overlaps at the peak, with the topmost piece showing a plumb cut.

GUTTERS AND GUTTER GUARDS

Gutters are sometimes required by code. When combined with downspouts and their associated fittings, gutters help keep water away from the foundation, preventing serious erosion and reducing water accumulation under the house. Gutters, downspouts, attachment hardware, and other components are available at most building-supply outlets. Also, consider buying and installing gutter guards, especially if there are large trees nearby. Different types of gutter guards are available, but they all perform the same function of keeping leaves, seedpods, and other debris out of the gutter while allowing water in. This eliminates the annual (or more frequent) chore of having to climb up on a ladder or onto the roof to clean out the gutters.

BUILDING AN OUTDOOR ROOM

Basic Design for Porches, Decks, and Landings

The porches on Habitat houses are among their nicest features. All Habitat houses have a covered porch of some sort. On the Charlotte house, there's a small porch tucked underneath the main roof, sheltering the main entry door. The side door has a landing that could grow into a larger deck sometime in the future (see the photo on the facing page). Most of the Habitat houses I've worked on out West have a porch as an attached structure. It has its own roof, which joins either the main roof or the gable end of the house (see the top photo on p. 178). In almost any form, a porch adds something special to a house. It's a place to put some flowers, kick off your shoes when you get home from work, or just sit down and relax at any time of day.

I have built hundreds of decks and porches over the years, and I've noticed that people are more inclined to use them if they are 6 ft. wide or larger. Narrower than that and all you really have is a walkway or a landing. I've also noticed that a deck with a roof—a porch, in other words—seems to get more use than a deck that's open to the elements. In northern regions, a porch can be enclosed and used as a mudroom in the winter. In southern states, porches are often screened to keep out insects.

Design Ideas for Decks and Porches

No matter what size deck or porch you decide to build, quite a few design considerations deserve attention (see Resources on p. 279). Take some time to evaluate the many decking materials that are available, including different types of solid wood and synthetic materials.

On a sloping site, it's often better to build a multilevel deck that follows

TIP Size a deck to minimize waste. Take advantage of standard lumber lengths when determining the size of a deck. For example, a deck that's 5 ft. 11 in. wide can be framed with 12-ft.-long joists or beams. A deck that's 6½ ft. wide would waste 1½ ft. of an 8-ft. beam or joist.

A porch creates an outdoor living room. A small house can live large when a porch is part of the design. On this Habitat project, the porch shelters the main entry. [Photo courtesy HFHI]

Ramps with a slope of 1 in. per ft. can make a house accessible for people using a walker or wheelchair. [Photo by Don Charles Blom]

the natural contour of the land instead of a single-level deck that requires tall support posts. Houses built on a concrete slab can have a smaller slab poured to create a porch or patio area. Just make sure the slab is 1 in. or so below the floor slab to keep water from entering the house. To promote drainage, pour the slab with a slight slope, about ¼ in. per ft. Don't forget to thicken the concrete and install a metal post base where the posts will be installed to hold the supporting roof beams.

Some Habitat houses are built with ramps to accommodate people in wheelchairs or those who have limited mobility. Ramps can take up quite a bit of room. They need to be built with a gradual slope and must be at least 36 in. wide. The slope rate is usually a 1 in. vertical rise for every 1 ft. traveled horizontally. So if the door entrance is 16 in. above ground level, the ramp will need to be 16 ft. long.

Before you begin to build, you should also know which railing design you plan to use. Drive around a few neighborhoods and you'll

POST-AND-BEAM SUPPORT FOR A PORCH ROOF

TIP Framing connectors are worth checking out. If you haven't discovered the vast variety of framing connectors that are available, try to do so before building a porch or a deck. A well-stocked lumberyard or building supplier will sell connecting hardware designed to reinforce all kinds of joints among different framing members.

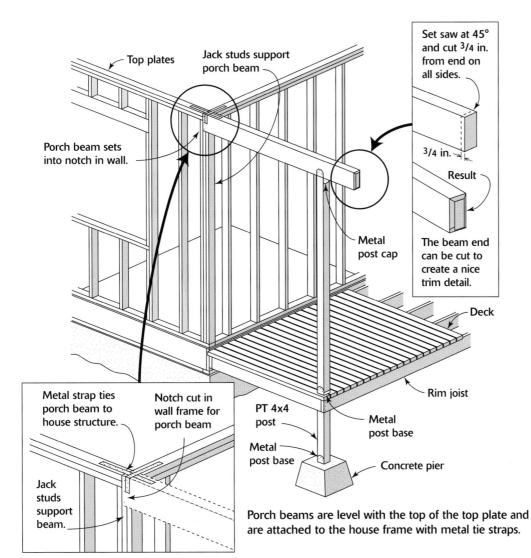

Top plates

Jack studs support porch beam

Porch beam sets into notch in wall.

Set saw at 45° and cut 3/4 in. from end on all sides.

3/4 in.

Result

The beam end can be cut to create a nice trim detail.

Metal post cap

Deck

Metal strap ties porch beam to house structure.

Notch cut in wall frame for porch beam

Jack studs support beam.

PT 4x4 post

Metal post base

Metal post base

Rim joist

Concrete pier

Porch beams are level with the top of the top plate and are attached to the house frame with metal tie straps.

certainly come upon some interesting railing designs to inspire your own efforts. Finally, consider your electrical wiring needs. Overhead light is important for security reasons, but you may also want to install some low-voltage lights on or around the porch or in nearby walkway or garden areas.

STEP 1 COMPLETE THE ESSENTIAL ROOF FRAMING

In many house designs, a section of the main roof extends over the porch. To complete the

installation of the roof trusses, roofing material, and exterior trim, the truss support beams over the porch must be cut and fastened to the wall framing. As shown in the illustration above, each beam rests in a pocket formed by a pair of jack studs framed in the house wall. The top of the beam is flush and level with the top of the wall plates.

In addition to nailing the beam to the wall framing, I strengthen the connection by nailing an 18-in. metal strap across the top of the beam and the double top plate of the wall. Beams made from rough 2× lumber can

Framing connectors are essential. Steel connecting hardware is required when building a porch or a deck. A post base (see the photo at left) is mounted on a concrete pier; it has holes for lag bolts, which fasten it to the post. A post cap connector (see the photo above) is useful for strengthening the joint between a porch post and a roof beam. [Photo at left © Memo Jasso/Brown Studio; photo above © Larry Haun]

TIP Larger decks may require more bolts to attach the ledger to the house frame. You have to think about the weight a deck might carry—a party with 50 people on a deck is a lot of weight.

later be covered with aluminum cladding, as described in Chapter 6.

If it's not possible to install permanent posts at this stage, temporary posts can be used to support porch ceiling beams. When you install permanent posts, be sure to secure them with framing connectors—a post base at the bottom and a post cap at the top that is fastened to the post and to the beams (see the photos above).

STEP 2 INSTALL THE LEDGER

On a house built over a basement or crawl space, a deck or porch can be attached to the house frame. Deck building then becomes a lot like framing a floor-joist system inside a house (see

Chapter 3). Step one in this process is to attach a ledger to the house frame. Straight, level, and solidly secured to the house, the ledger acts like a rim joist for the porch. It extends the full length of the porch, supporting its inboard side.

There are several concerns when attaching a ledger, and all of them are important. First, the ledger must be at least 2½ in. below the level of the interior floor. When 1½-in. deck boards are screwed on top of the ledger, the deck will be 1 in. lower than the interior floor, which is just about right. If wheelchair accessibility is a concern, plan to build a small ramp to bridge the distance between the deck and the doorsill.

Reserve your best boards to use as ledgers— clear lumber with straight, square edges and no major imperfections (cracks, large knots, or warping). When installing a ledger, make sure water cannot get behind the ledger and into the house frame, where it could cause rot. And make sure the ledger is secured to the house in a manner that will hold for the life of the building.

Flash the ledger

Many builders like to use flashing when installing a ledger. Find out which types of flashing builders use in your area. I tend to use heavy-gauge aluminum behind the ledger, though I sometimes opt for high-quality galvanized sheet metal or even copper—expensive though it is—instead of aluminum. Although it can take a while, ocean air and city smog will gradually take their toll on aluminum flashing, causing it to deteriorate.

The flashing is installed before the exterior siding. It can be nailed directly to the wall framing and rim joist if no sheathing has been used on the exterior walls. Otherwise, install the flashing on top of the wall sheathing (see the top illustration at right). Order flashing that is wide enough to extend several inches above the ledger and down over the rim joist. At door openings, cut the flashing just enough to bend it over and lay it flat on the subfloor. Use as few nails as possible when installing flashing, and keep them high on the wall. The ledger and exterior siding will hold the flashing in place. If you install housewrap (such as Tyvek or Barricade) over the wall sheathing, make sure the flashing tucks underneath the housewrap, as shown in the illustration.

In the dry Southwest, the ledger can be fastened directly on top of the flashing. Otherwise, use galvanized washers or PT shims to create a narrow (3/8-in. to 1/2-in.) drainage space behind the ledger. This prevents buildup of moisture or mold.

On exterior decks it is best to use treated wood or synthetic decking. It is only a matter of time before untreated wood left exposed to the elements starts to rot. In some climates, even treated wood needs to be painted every year with an oil-based solution to prevent cracking and splitting.

INSTALLING A LEDGER WITH FLASHING AND SPACERS

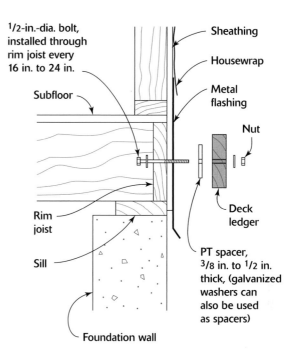

Spacers allow water to flow behind ledger.

INSTALLING A LEDGER WITHOUT FLASHING

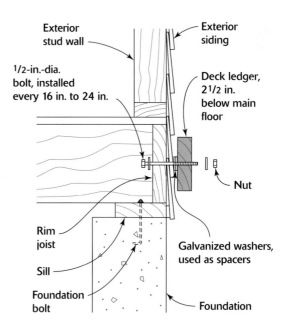

Air space behind the deck ledger allows water to drain freely. Caulk bolt holes before inserting bolts.

MAKING IT HAPPEN

Ismet Osmani and his wife, Rahime, fled Kosovo in the midst of ethnic strife and war and landed in Tucson, AZ, in April 2002. Five years later, with a four-year-old daughter and infant son in tow, they are on the path to homeownership, partnering with Habitat for Humanity Tucson.

"I used to live in a house over there, but it was burned, destroyed in the war," Ismet says of his home in Serbia. "Now we've been living in an apartment for five years, and you always have to be careful about noise and leaving stuff on the porch—it's hard."

Ismet has a degree in education and was a counselor before he immigrated with his family. Now he works as a driver for a hotel and holds down a second job in a restaurant—overqualified, perhaps, but he is glad to be working. Despite his busy schedule, Ismet dedicates every spare hour he has toward building his home. In fact, he finished his required 400 hours of "sweat equity" with Habitat long before the construction of his house was complete. When work kept him away from the house site, Ismet would often drive by to see how things were coming along.

This past summer Ismet and Rahime became U.S. citizens, an accomplishment earned through study, English lessons, and perseverance. They are extremely proud of all that they have been able to do since leaving Kosovo, and are ready to put down roots in Tucson.

"We worked hard and feel like we've accomplished a lot," he says. "We'll probably live the rest of our lives here."

—*Rebekah Daniel*

Ismet and Rahime Osami are an inspiration to their daughter—making a new life for themselves in Tucson after fleeing Kosovo and building a new home with the help of Habitat. [Photo courtesy HFHI]

Installing a ledger without flashing

Here's how to install a ledger against fiber-cement siding, wooden clapboards, or T1-11 siding without using flashing. Simply install the siding in the normal fashion, and hold the ledger away from the siding with PT wood spacers or galvanized washers. I've installed ledgers this way on a number of houses, including Habitat projects. To account for the angle of wood or fiber-cement clapboards, cut an angled PT spacer or use galvanized washers in the manner shown in the bottom right illustration on p. 181. For that technique, first install the spacers, then bolt the ledger loosely in place. Complete the deck framing, then tighten the ledger installation bolts.

Nails won't do when installing a ledger, though you can drive a few just to hold the board in position. My preference is to attach the ledger with ½-in.-dia. bolts that extend through the rim joist and are held fast with nuts and washers. Make sure the ledger is level before you begin boring holes for the bolts. Space bolts 16 in. to 24 in. apart. As extra insurance against unwanted water, apply some silicone caulk in each hole before inserting the bolt through the rim joist. Insert the bolts through the rim joist from the back, making sure you place a washer beneath each bolt's head and nut.

STEP 3 INSTALL THE FOUNDATION AND FLOOR FRAMING

Concrete piers and PT posts work well for supporting the front of the porch. In many areas, code requires that concrete porch piers be set on concrete footings, so check with your building department. For a deck that's 6 ft. wide by 16 ft. long, set three piers (16-in. square by 12-in. deep), one on each corner and one in the middle (see the top right illustration). Shorter decks can be built with a concrete pier on each corner; longer decks need more piers. I like to use precast piers that have steel post anchors set in them. The anchors hold the posts in place and resist wind uplift. Check your house plans for porch

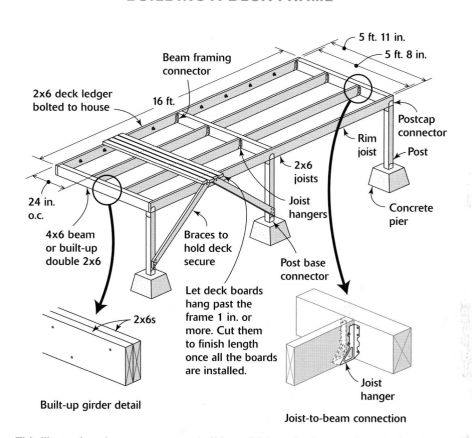

Built-up girder detail

Joist-to-beam connection

This illustration shows one way to build a solid, long-lasting porch or deck frame.

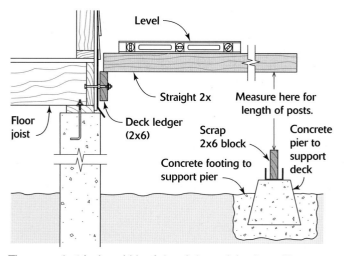

The scrap 2x6 is the width of the girder or joist that will support the deck once the frame is built. The post will extend from the concrete pier to the deck frame.

TIP Install joist hangers with special nails. Joist hangers and other steel framing hardware should be installed with the special hanger nails sold with them. Common framing nails have thinner shanks, so they're not as strong. When you buy hanger nails, make sure they have a rust-resistant coating.

width and set the piers so they are in line with the ledger board and square with the building.

Next, measure the length for the posts that will extend from the piers to support the floor framing. You can do this with a 6-ft. level or with a shorter level attached to a straightedge (see the bottom illustration on p. 183). Lay the rim joist (or a scrap board of the same size) on top of each pier and set the level or straightedge on the ledger, extending it directly out over the pier. The distance between the rim joist on the pier and the level or straightedge is the post's length. Cut those posts from PT 4×4s; make them ½ in. short (be consistent) so that the deck will slope away from the house just a bit.

Cut the two end beams (girders) first, using PT 4×6 lumber or doubled 2×6s, as shown in the top illustration on p. 183. For a deck that is 6 ft. wide, cut the two end beams at 5 ft. 8 in. The ledger and rim joist will add 3 in. to the overall width. Those beams connect to the ledger by a metal framing connector and rest, with 2 in. bearing, on the end posts. Connect any beams falling between in the same manner, but run them long over the tops of their posts. Stretch a chalkline from the ends of the two end beams across the interior beams and snap a line. Cutting the interior beams to length in this manner ensures a straight rim joist in the front.

Next, cut the rim joist to length. On a rectangular deck, the rim joist is the same length as the ledger. If you have a long deck and use several pieces of rim, make sure they break over a post. The rim rests on the posts and is nailed into each beam with two 16d galvanized nails. Toenail both the beam and the rim to the post. Then reinforce the beam-post-rim joist connections with metal framing connectors. You can nail a flat, gusset-type connector over the joint between a post and the rim joist and use right-angled connectors on the inside.

Before installing the joists between beams, make sure the post-and-beam assembly is parallel and square with the house and all the posts are plumb. Brace the porch frame so it will remain square until the stairs are attached and the decking is screwed in place. When cutting and installing joists, I recommend using joist hangers to ensure that all joist-to-beam connections are strong. The joist spacing you use depends on the decking material you plan to install. A 24-in. o.c. spacing is usually adequate for 1½-in.-thick PT decking boards. For 5/4 (1¼-in.-thick) PT decking, use 16-in. o.c. spacing. If you use any of the synthetic decking material that's becoming more popular these days, follow the manufacturer's recommendations for joist spacing.

The corner post is crucial. Holding a long level against the flat sections of a turned post, a volunteer makes sure the post is plumb.

LEARNING THE VOCABULARY OF STAIRS

Every new endeavor comes with a new vocabulary that you need to learn before you can get started. Building stairs is no exception. Once you learn the names of the different parts and how they relate to each other, you can begin to put together a set of stairs.

STRINGERS. The diagonal members (here, PT 2×12s) that support the treads and risers. Three stringers are needed for a 36-in.-wide stairway, four for a 48-in.-wide stairway. A cut or open stringer has tread and riser cutouts and can be used in the middle of a stairway. An open stairway is framed with cut stringers. A closed stringer has no cutouts; instead, cleats are used to support the treads. Closed stringers only can be used on the sides of a stairway.

RISER. The vertical part of a step. For safety's sake, the height of risers should always be around 7 in. This measurement is also known as the unit rise.

TREAD. The horizontal portion of a step, or the place where you set your foot. Treads should be approximately 11 in. wide.

LANDING. The level space at the top and bottom of a stairway (and sometimes in the middle if a set of stairs changes direction). A 3-ft.-wide stairway should have a landing that is at least 3 ft. square.

TOTAL RISE. The vertical distance that a stairway travels from the lower landing to the upper landing. This is always measured from finish floor to finish floor.

TOTAL RUN. The horizontal distance that a stairway travels from the leading edge of the first tread to the trailing edge of the last.

KICKER BOARD. The PT 2×4 or 2×6 that is secured to the bottom landing. The kicker board helps hold the stringers in place.

STAIR VOCABULARY

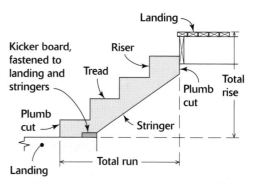

A stairway's total rise is always from finish floor to finish floor.

CUT AND CLOSED STRINGERS

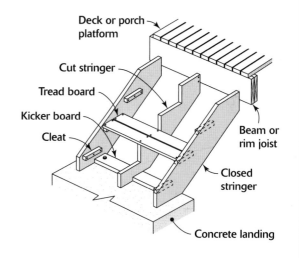

TIP Seven is the magic number. When determining the number and measurement of risers in a stairway, always start by dividing the total rise of the stair (the vertical distance from landing to landing) by 7. The unit rise (the height of each step) should be between 7 in. and 7¾ in.

STEP 4 FRAME THE STAIRS

I taught night school at a community college for 20 or so years. My students were apprentice carpenters learning how to build houses. Often, students were hesitant to take on the task of building stairs because of the presumed difficulty. It came as a surprise to most of them that building stairs—especially a simple, straight flight of stairs—is actually quite easy. If you can do some basic math and know how to use a framing square and a circular saw, you can build stairs. Although stair-building principles are the same everywhere, different states (and towns or cities) sometimes use different codes, so check to see which code requirements apply in your area.

Figure out the risers

The accepted standards for a typical stairway call for a rise of about 7 in. and a run, or tread width, of 11 in. When calculating the number of risers in a stairway, aim to stay as close as possible to those figures. If you have a pocket calculator handy (see Resources on p. 279), this calculation is easy to do.

First, determine exactly how high each riser will be. This is calculated based on the total rise, which is measured from finish floor to finish floor—in this case, from the concrete slab to the top of the porch decking. Let's call it 30 in., a fairly typical porch height. Divide the total rise (30 in.) by 7 in., the standard riser height, for a total of 4.3 risers. Round that to the closest whole number (in this case, 4) and divide your total rise of 30 in. by that number. This gives you an individual riser height of 7.5, or 7½ in. Now you have the riser height and the number of risers—4 risers, each 7½ in. high.

You can also determine the total run of the stairs; this will tell you where the concrete landing or base for the stringers should be. Do a rough sketch of the stairs, then multiply the number of treads by the tread width (in this case, 11 in.). Keep in mind that you can either run the stringers flush with the top of the deck (the top tread is even with the deck surface) or cut the stringers so that the top tread is one step down from the deck surface. The latter approach is more common; that's what we did on the house shown here.

Lay out and cut the stringers

There are two basic types of stringers for stairs. Cut, or open, stringers have square cutouts to support treads and risers. Closed stringers use cleats rather than cutouts to support treads. To

---

LAYOUT OF A STAIR STRINGER

1. STRINGER LAYOUT

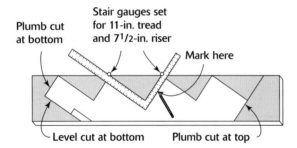

Plumb cut at bottom

Stair gauges set for 11-in. tread and 7¹/2-in. riser

Mark here

Level cut at bottom   Plumb cut at top

2. DROPPING THE STRINGER

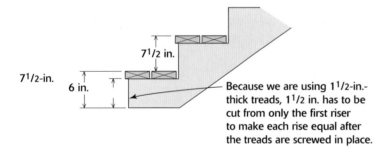

7¹/2 in.

7¹/2-in.

6 in.

Because we are using 1¹/2-in.-thick treads, 1¹/2 in. has to be cut from only the first riser to make each rise equal after the treads are screwed in place.

3. NOTCHING FOR THE KICKER BOARD

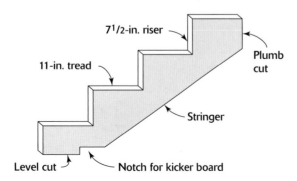

7¹/2-in. riser

Plumb cut

11-in. tread

Stringer

Level cut   Notch for kicker board

Use a square to lay out a stair stringer. Mark the square cutout areas with a framing square. The tread and riser measurements on the square align along the edge of the board.

give a deck or porch stairway a trim look, I like to use closed stringers on the sides. Cut stringers must be used in the middle. Stringers for outdoor stairways are usually cut from PT 2×12s. Stairs with three risers can be cut from 4-ft. stock, but it's a bit tight. Stairs with four risers can be cut from 6-ft. stock.

A framing square and a pencil are all you need to lay out stair stringers. Although they aren't necessary, a pair of stair gauges (small clamps that screw onto a framing square) make the layout process faster and just about foolproof. Attach one gauge at the 7½-in. measure (the rise) on the narrow part of a framing square (the tongue). Place the other gauge at the 11-in. measure (the tread width) on the wider part of the square (the blade). Now lay out the stringer, working from the bottom to the top. If you don't use stair gauges on a framing square, simply align the 7½-in. and 11-in. measurements over the edge of the stringer, as shown in the photo above. After marking the first tread and riser, move the square up,

place the tread mark directly on the riser mark, scribe the second tread and riser, then do the third. Then use the square to mark a level cut at the bottom of the stringer and a plumb cut at the top.

The bottom of the stringer must be "dropped" to allow for the thickness of the first tread. If you were to screw a 1½-in.-thick tread on the first riser (7½ in. tall), then the first step would be 9 in., which would cause a lot of people to trip every time they used the stairs. To make each riser the same height, cut 1½ in. from the bottom of the stringer. Finish laying out this stringer by marking a notch for a 2×4 kicker board. It's best to cut the kicker-board notch at the back of the stringer.

When the layout is complete, it's time to cut the stringer. Start the cuts with a circular saw, closely following the lines (see the top photo on p. 188). Then use a handsaw or a jigsaw to finish the cuts at the intersection of the tread and the riser so that you don't overcut and weaken the stringer.

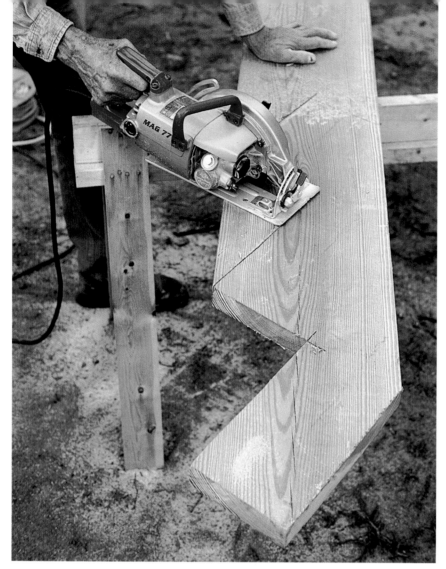

Cut a stringer the right way. Use a circular saw to cut into the corner along each tread and riser line, then finish the cut with a handsaw.

Install the stringers and treads

If you've done the stair layout and cutting correctly, the stringers should fit against the rim joist (or beam), with the level cut or cleat for the top tread located 7½ in. down from the top of the deck framing. Snap or mark a line at that level on the rim joist so you can make sure the stringers are aligned.

There are several ways to secure the stringers to a deck beam or rim joist. Sometimes the stringer butts against a post, so it can simply be nailed to the post and to the beam or rim joist. In other situations, a metal strap can be nailed to the bottom of the stringer, then to the beam or rim joist (see the bottom photo on the facing page). Still another option is to fasten a PT plywood hanger board to the top plumb-cut edge of each stringer, then nail the board to the beam or rim joist (see the illustration on p. 190).

For a set of 36-in.-wide closed-stringer stairs, cut a hanger board 14 in. high and 39 in. wide, then nail it flush with the top of the deck's

A CUT STRINGER SERVES AS A PATTERN FOR A CLOSED STRINGER.

Once you've completed a cut stringer, use it as a pattern for other cut and closed stringers in the same staircase (see the photo at right). The plumb and level cuts at the top and bottom of the closed stringer are identical to those on the cut stringer, but they are the only cuts you need to make on a closed stringer. Using the cut stringer as a pattern, mark the tread lines on the closed stringer to indicate where the cleats must be installed.

Fasten 1½-in.-sq. PT wood cleats below the tread lines on each closed stringer (see the top photo on the facing page). Drive four 2½-in.-long deck screws to secure each cleat. Manufactured metal cleats are also available, if you prefer. The treads will be screwed to the cleats after all the stair stringers have been installed.

Use one stringer to make another. Use a completed stringer as a pattern to lay out a new one.

Cleats support the treads on a closed stringer. A closed stringer forms the side of a stairway and does not require cutouts for treads. Instead, cleats can be screwed along the layout lines to support the treads.

2×6 rim joist. Then measure down 7½ in. from the top of the rim joist, mark the board on each end, and strike a line across it at that height. Drive 8d galvanized nails through the back of the hanger board and into the stringers below the 2×6 rim, making sure the top of the upper cleats on both outboard stringers and the top notch on the interior stringers land on the line you snapped on the hanger board. To stiffen the top of the stairs, cut and install PT 2×4 blocking between the stringers.

Next, cut a 36-in.-long PT 2×4 kicker board and nail it into the notch of the middle stringer and to the outside stringers. The kicker board can be fastened to the concrete landing or base with hardened nails, steel pins, or concrete anchors.

STEP 5 INSTALL THE DECKING AND STAIR TREADS

With the floor and stair framing complete, you can start installing the decking boards and stair treads. I mostly use 2×6 PT decking, because

the ready supply of redwood decking has disappeared along with the big trees. Cedar decking is available in some areas, but at a premium price. More and more people are using plastic decking material or deck boards that are a combination of wood chips or sawdust and recycled plastic. Although the up-front cost of this high-tech decking is greater than that of PT wood, the new materials don't warp, crack, or require regular finishing treatments to maintain an attractive appearance. They are worth considering.

If you're installing wood decking, keep in mind that many boards have a tendency to cup because of their circular grain structure. If you see a curve in the end grain of a board, lay it so the curve forms a hill rather than a valley. Should cupping occur sometime in the future, water will run off rather than pool. Exposed PT or cedar decking needs to be treated with a good deck finish every other year or so.

On narrow decks, the boards are often installed at a right angle to the house. I usually attach the first board on the end of the deck where the stairs are (or will be). Let the deck board overhang the end framing by about 1 in. I cut the boards slightly longer than the deck. With the boards a bit long, you can snap a chalkline and cut them off evenly so everything looks neat and proper.

I use 16d nails as spacers between wood decking boards. Placing one nail near the house and

A metal strap is useful for installing stringers. Here, the author uses a metal strap to secure the top of a center stringer to a porch beam. A temporary 2×4 cleat, nailed across all three stringers, helps maintain the alignment as the stringers are installed.

another near the edge of the porch maintains consistent spacing. Where a board crosses a joist or beam, drive two decking screws. Those steel screws have a galvanized or polymer coating that protects against rust, and their coarse threads drive quickly and hold much better than nails do. To install 1½-in.-thick decking, use 3-in. screws. To install 5/4 boards, 2½-in. screws will do. Although it takes a bit more time, I predrill the screw holes in the decking with a ³⁄₁₆-in.-dia. bit. This makes it easier to pull the boards tightly against the framing and just about eliminates the possibility of splitting a board.

When you reach about 6 ft. from the end beam, calculate how many more boards will be required to cover the distance, and check whether the distance is equal along the ledger and along the rim joist. You may need to fine-tune the spacing between boards to restore parallel orientation and to make sure the final board is of a reasonable width.

Once all the deck boards are in place, snap a chalkline across the front edge about 1 in. from the rim joist, then cut them straight with a circular saw. Tack a 1× to the deck to guide the saw and ensure a good-looking, straight cut. Take your time and do a good job. This is finish work, and it must look right.

STEP 6 INSTALL THE RAILINGS

Most codes require railings only when a deck is more than 30 in. off the ground, but you may want to build a rail on a lower deck anyway, for appearance if not for safety. The basic structure of a typical deck or porch railing consists of posts, rails, and balusters, which are also called uprights or pickets.

Even with basic PT lumber, many designs are possible. For example, you can eliminate the bottom rail, extend the balusters down, and fasten them to the rim joist. You can include a 2×6 "cap" installed over the tops of the posts and over the top rail. And you can use a chop-saw to bevel one or both ends of each baluster to give your work a sleeker appearance. There are even decorative PT balusters, along with shaped top and bottom rails that are grooved to hold baluster ends. Also available are quality vinyl railings that are attractive and maintenance-free. As I mentioned at the beginning of this chapter, it's worthwhile to investigate the design possibilities, so take a drive around your neighborhood and visit a lumberyard or home center that carries these building supplies. No matter what the design, make sure the railing meets code requirements (see the sidebar on the facing page).

TWO WAYS TO HANG STAIR STRINGERS

1. WITH METAL STRAPS

Step 2: Nail metal strap to landing.

Block between stringers

Stringer

Landing

Step 1: Bend metal strap; nail it to stringer.

2. WITH A PLYWOOD HANGER BOARD

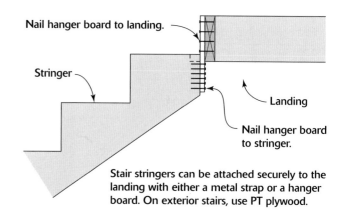

Nail hanger board to landing.

Stringer

Landing

Nail hanger board to stringer.

Stair stringers can be attached securely to the landing with either a metal strap or a hanger board. On exterior stairs, use PT plywood.

Lay down the decking. For a deck, rust-resistant screws work better than nails. Here, wood spacers are used to ensure uniform spacing between the boards. [Photo © Larry Haun]

HOW TO BUILD SAFE RAILINGS THAT WILL MEET CODE

To make porch railings and stair handrails both safe and legal, you need to know the basic rules and regulations that dictate how they're built. The specs here cover most areas of the country, but codes do vary from region to region, so always check with your local building department.

- In most regions, any deck higher than 30 in. off the ground needs a railing.
- Stairs with more than three risers (three steps) need a handrail.
- Stairs that are 44 in. wide or more need a handrail on both sides.
- The height of a handrail, measured from the nose (the front edge of the stair tread), should be between 32 in. and 36 in. The handrail should extend the length of the stairs.
- The width of a handrail must be between 1 in. and 2 in. so that it's easy to grab.
- The railing height on a deck guardrail should be between 36 in. and 42 in.
- The balusters used on porches and stairs should run vertically, so children can't climb on them. The spacing between them must be 4 in. or less, so children can't squeeze through.
- The bottom rail must not be more than 4 in. above the deck.

Attach the stair treads. It takes two boards to form one step. With open risers, an outdoor stairway is easier to keep clean.

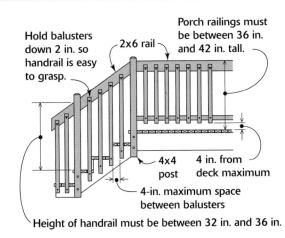

Hold balusters down 2 in. so handrail is easy to grasp.

2x6 rail

Porch railings must be between 36 in. and 42 in. tall.

4x4 post

4 in. from deck maximum

4-in. maximum space between balusters

Height of handrail must be between 32 in. and 36 in.

Building codes regulate heights of rails and spacing of balusters. Many codes require wrap around hand rails. Check with your local building department for your area's requirements.

Begin with the posts

The most difficult part about building any railing is making sure the posts are well secured
to the deck or stairs. Remember: People will
be leaning against the railings, so make them
strong. A post that extends up to the roof framing will be solid and secure. Short posts that
support only the railing are more of a concern.
Railing posts should be evenly spaced across a
deck or porch and no more than 6 ft. apart. A
good height for a railing is 36 in. to 42 in.

I like to notch railing posts to fit against the
rim joist (see the photo below). A notched post,

installed with a couple of $\frac{1}{8}$-in. or $\frac{1}{2}$-in.-dia.
carriage bolts, makes for a strong and attractive
installation. For a 4×4 post, make notches $1\frac{1}{2}$ in.
deep and long enough so the notched post can
cover the full width of the rim joist. If the top of
the railing posts won't be covered by a 2×4 or a
2×6 cap, consider letting those posts run a few
inches higher than the top rail and chamfering
the top of each post. This technique, explained
in the sidebar on the facing page, can enhance
the appearance of any railing.

Posts for stair railings can be fastened to an
outer stair stringer. Use carriage bolts rather
than screws for stronger connections. At the
base of a long stairway, where extra strength is
required, the post can be anchored in concrete
or to a steel post base embedded in concrete.

RAILS AND BALUSTERS. Once the posts
are installed, cut and install the rails. I use PT
or cedar 2×4 rails for most of my deck railings.
They can be fastened to the outside or the inside
of posts, depending on the overall design of the
railing. Some builders even notch their posts to
accept the rails. No matter which method you
choose, secure each rail-to-post connection with
two 3-in. deck screws. If your railing design
calls for top and bottom rails, install the bottom
rail $3\frac{1}{2}$ in. from the deck.

**Carriage bolts are strong and attractive. The
rounded head looks appealing, and the bolt
provides excellent holding strength for major
structural connections.**

If you like the look of the railing we installed on this house, set up a chopsaw to cut balusters 31½ in. long, with a 45-degree angle on the top to let water run off. Install the tops of the balusters 1 in. below the top of the top rail, and use 2½-in.-long deck screws to attach each baluster at both the top and the bottom. Using a gauge between balusters is helpful and speeds the process (see the photo below). Just make sure you keep the balusters plumb as you attach them. Check for plumb every now and then with a 2-ft. level, and correct gradually, if necessary.

The handrail on a staircase should be about 1½ in. wide so that it can be grasped easily as people go up and down. A 2×6 on edge can be used for a top rail. Position it so the top edge is 32 in. to 36 in. plumb from the front edge (nose) of the stair treads.

Balusters for the stairs must be individually measured for length on this stair handrail. Keep the tops of the balusters 2 in. below the top of the handrail, as shown in the photo below. Screw the bottom of each baluster to the stringer. The area under the stairs (and under the porch) can later be hidden with 4×8 vinyl or wooden lattice panels.

Space and align balusters. A 3½-in.-wide piece of 2×4 makes a fine spacer when installing balusters. A penciled layout line on the stair's handrail aligns the beveled top edge of each baluster.

CHAMFERING A POST

Chamfering the tops of railing posts or the ends of beams is a nice finishing touch you can add when building a deck or a porch. A plain, square-topped post looks clunky, but in a few minutes' time you can give the post a more distinguished appearance. All you need is a Speed square and a circular saw. For best results, use a sharp, fine-toothed blade on your saw. If you haven't tried this technique before, practice on a spare length of 4×4. Also, you may find it easier to make chamfer cuts "on the flat," with the 4×4 set on some sawhorses. It takes a little more experience

with a circular saw to chamfer a post that's already installed vertically. Here's how to chamfer a post in four simple steps:

LAY OUT THE CHAMFER LINES. As shown in the photo above, a pair of lines, spaced about 1 in. apart, should extend around all four sides of the post. The upper line represents the length of the finished post.

CUT THE POST TO LENGTH. Make a square end cut to sever the post along the upper layout line. Two cuts from opposite sides of the post should do it.

MAKE THE CHAMFER CUTS. Loosen the angle-adjustment knob or lever on your circular saw and adjust the cutting angle to 45 degrees. An exact 45-degree angle isn't necessary, but be sure to tighten the adjustment securely. Now make an angled cut along

each side of the post, following the layout line. If you have trouble maintaining a straight cut, clamp a Speed square to the post to guide the base of your saw. Another trick for ensuring a smooth cut is to retract the blade guard with your forward hand before you start to cut.

SAND THE POST SMOOTH. Use some 120-grit sandpaper to smooth out any rough areas. You can also slightly soften sharp corners.

COMFORT INSIDE

Sealing, Insulating, and Ventilating a House

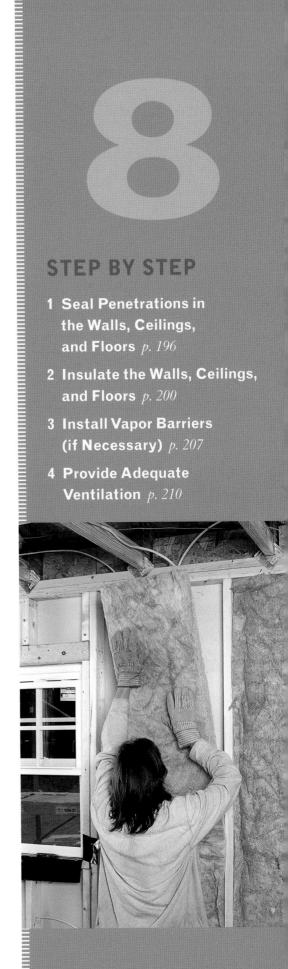

The old house I was born in still stands out there on the prairie. When I was a child, the house was simply unheatable in the wintertime. We definitely spent more dollars trying to heat the house than we did on the mortgage. Nowadays, the house has new doors and windows, insulation in the ceiling, and a real heating system—not just an old iron stove in the kitchen. But there are still plenty of cracks and gaps in the walls for those ever-present western winds to howl through.

Thankfully, we don't build houses like we used to. Today, there are materials and methods available that allow us to design and build energy-efficient houses that hold heat during the winter and keep it out during the summer. But attaining high levels of comfort and energy efficiency is not always a simple feat. In fact, it can be the most technically complex aspect of building a house.

The products that we use to seal, insulate, and ventilate houses may do more harm than good if they're not installed correctly. Common problems include poor indoor-air quality, peeling paint on interior and exterior surfaces, moldy bathrooms, and rotten wood in walls and ceilings (see the photo on p. 196). Sometimes we solve one problem (such as cold air infiltration during winter months) and cause another (high concentrations of stale, humid indoor air, for example). And thanks to the significant climate differences in this vast country of ours, what works in Maine may be ineffective in Texas.

Although there is no standard approach to building a tight, comfortable, and energy-efficient house with good indoor-air quality, it's not difficult to achieve those goals if you understand how a house works in terms of insulation, airtightness, and ventilation. This is especially true with the basic, affordable houses that Habitat builds. This chapter explains the concepts, materials,

and techniques to make your house comfortable, healthy, and energy efficient no matter what the temperature is outside. To expand your knowledge, see Resources on p. 279.

Before we dig into the technical details, here's a final thought to keep in mind as you tackle the sealing, insulation, and ventilation work on your building project: Try to keep everyone aware of these important issues. When houses were built with simple materials, they were both leaky and energy inefficient. People working in the trades didn't really need to understand the work of those preceding or following them. To build a safe, energy-efficient, nontoxic house, everyone involved in its construction must have more knowledge and work together. Otherwise, a house that was perfectly sealed and insulated can be left riddled with holes by a plumber, electrician, or heating contractor who was "just doing his job."

Sweaters, Windbreakers, and Rain Gear

Don't worry; we haven't suspended our home-building work to look through the L.L. Bean® catalog. But what you already know about sweaters, windbreakers, and raincoats will help you understand the way sealing, insulating, and moisture-protection treatments work together in a house.

Start with a sweater and a windbreaker—just what you need to wear on a cold, windy day. A house exposed to frigid temperatures and icy winds also needs a sweater and a windbreaker. Insulation, exterior siding, and housewrap provide this protection. In fact, housewraps like Tyvek and Typar act like a Gore-Tex® raincoat, blocking wind and water while still allowing vapor to pass through. This helps prevent moisture buildup, both in our clothing and inside the walls of a house.

As we work through the steps ahead, you'll see that there are different sealing, insulating, and ventilation tasks that need to be done at different stages of the construction process. Pay attention to the tasks associated with each phase

Avoid major moisture damage. Inadequate ventilation or poorly sealed walls and ceilings can lead to rot and mold, which are not healthy for a house or its occupants. [Photo © The Taunton Press, Inc.]

of construction and your house will repay you with maximum levels of comfort, longevity, and energy efficiency.

STEP 1 SEAL PENETRATIONS IN THE WALLS, CEILINGS, AND FLOORS

When you think about sealing a house, remember how much frigid air can go through a small opening in a sweater or a jacket. Even a tiny hole in a woolen mitten can make your finger numb with cold. The same thing can happen in a house. We had single-glazed, double-hung windows in that old prairie home where I grew up. In the spring, the windows were nice—we could open them wide to let in fresh breezes and the songs of meadowlarks announcing warmer weather. In the winter, though, that loose-fitting sash was a fright. My mother gave us thin strips of cloth to stuff between the window frame and the sash in hopes of slowing the icy winds that would soon roll down from the north.

Today, we have the materials and the know-how to seal a house effectively. The materials and techniques vary, depending on the type of sealing work that needs to be done.

Sealing work begins early

Sealing a house to limit air infiltration and energy loss begins early in the construction process and continues until the last bit of insulation work is done. As explained in Chapter 3, the mudsill should be sealed to the foundation with a resilient gasket material, known as sill seal, or with two thick beads of silicone caulk. Before the exterior walls are raised, it's also a good idea

Housewrap acts as a waterproof windbreaker. Modern housewraps are installed beneath the exterior siding. They block wind and water while still allowing vapor to pass through. [Photo © Mike Guertin]

CODE REQUIREMENTS FOR INSULATION

Most locales have an energy code that defines how well insulated your house must be. Check with the building inspector in your community for this information. Rather than requiring so many inches of fiberglass or rigid foam, these codes define insulation requirements in terms of R-value, or resistance to heat flow. The higher the R-value, the greater the insulating value. For example, code may require that exterior walls be R-11 or R-19. As it turns out, a 2×4 wall with fiberglass insulation designed for a 3½-in. wall has an R-value of 11. Denser batts that increase the R-value to 15 for a 2×4 wall are available. A 2×6 wall with 5½-in.-thick fiberglass has an R-value of 19. Don't try to stuff R-19 fiberglass batts into a 2×4 wall, though. Carpenters say that's like trying to stuff a 1,000-lb. gorilla into a 500-lb. bag. It just doesn't work.

Remember—code requirements set minimum standards. As far as building materials go, insulation is relatively inexpensive, so it's often cost effective to install more insulation than what is required by code. A house with lots of insulation (in the attic, for example) will not only reduce your heating bill for years to come but may also save you money up front by reducing the size of the heating or cooling system you need to install!

to apply two beads of silicone sealant beneath their bottom plates. If this was not done for some reason, you can run a heavy bead of sealant where the inside edge of the bottom plate meets the subfloor.

Once the walls are framed, it's important to install insulation in the sections that will be inaccessible after the wall sheathing is applied. As discussed in Chapter 4, these areas include the voids or spaces in the framing for corners, channels, and headers. Likewise, pay attention to areas where tubs and shower units will be installed in exterior walls. You don't want the stud cavities in these areas to be blocked off before you have a chance to insulate them.

Part of a sealing strategy may include housewrap. Modern housewraps, such as Tyvek and Typar, are wrapped around the framed exterior

CARBON MONOXIDE MONITORS SAVE LIVES

Although tight houses improve energy efficiency, they also increase the danger of carbon monoxide (CO) poisoning. CO is a byproduct of combustion from numerous sources. Woodstoves, oil furnaces, gas-fired stoves, water heaters, and fireplaces can produce hazardous levels of CO. The problem with CO is that you can't see it, taste it, or smell it—and it's poisonous. For this reason, CO detectors should be installed in any home that uses a fuel-burning appliance. Detectors are relatively inexpensive; you can buy plug-in units or modules that are permanently wired into the electrical system. Install them in kitchens, utility rooms, and wherever a CO-producing appliance is located. CO is heavier than air, so CO detectors are most effective when they are installed near the floor.

TIP Spray foam is sticky stuff. When applying spray-foam insulation, wear plastic gloves so the foam doesn't get on your hands. The foam is sticky and can stain your skin.

Expanding foam is excellent for sealing and insulating small spaces. A little foam goes a long way, so it's best not to apply too much at one time.

walls and stapled over the exterior sheathing or (if exterior sheathing is not used) directly over studs and plates (see the photo on p. 197). Housewrap is effective at stopping cold air infiltration during winter months. And at all times of the year, it serves as a drainage plane behind the exterior siding, directing water that gets behind the siding downward, instead of into the wall cavity (see Chapter 6 for details on installing housewrap).

When installing windows and doors, first you need to apply a generous bead of sealant on the flange or the back of the exterior trim. Do this just prior to installation, as explained in Chapter 6. Make sure that kitchen soffits and dropped ceilings (especially those with heating or cooling ducts inside) are completely sealed off from wall and attic spaces. Use drywall or OSB, and do it now, if you haven't already. These steps help prevent moisture-laden indoor air from moving into wall or attic areas, where it can condense and create major moisture problems.

Spray-foam insulation can handle a multitude of sealing tasks

Packaged in a pressurized can, foam insulation is extremely useful when it comes to filling gaps; sealing openings; and insulating narrow, confined spaces where fiberglass insulation doesn't easily fit (see the photo at left).

Although it's not cheap, spray-foam insulation is so helpful that I don't build a house without it. It's available in expanding and nonexpanding versions. I prefer the expanding type, because it does a better job of spreading out to fill voids. If you apply too much and the foam starts to expand beyond the intended area, don't worry. Come back later, after the foam has hardened, and trim off the excess with a utility knife. Don't try to wipe off excess foam when the material is still sticky; you'll just create a mess. Here are some of the areas in the house where spray foam can be used:

IN HOLES IN BOTTOM PLATES. Use foam to fill the spaces around plumbing pipes, electrical or cable wires, and ducts that

Insulate the shim space. You can use a screwdriver to wedge loose fiberglass insulation into the space between a window frame and its rough opening. But it's better to fill this space with foam insulation.

when it is compressed. It's better to insulate narrow spaces with foam insulation. The spaces between the window or door jamb and the rough opening can also be "foamed," but be careful not to apply too much expanding foam in those areas. Because jambs are usually only ¾ in. thick, the foam's expansive action can cause them to bow inward.

AROUND PLUMBING AND ELECTRICAL LINES THAT PASS THROUGH EXTERIOR WALLS. If your house has exterior faucets, seal the hole around each one with foam insulation. Holes for outdoor electrical lines and outlet boxes in exterior walls should also be sealed.

pass through the bottom plates of walls. It's especially important to seal off these routes, which can bring cold air into your living space, when building on a crawl-space foundation.

IN HOLES IN TOP PLATES. It's very important to seal holes in the top plates of walls. This helps prevent moist indoor air from entering a cold attic, where it can condense and cause moisture problems.

AROUND WINDOWS AND DOORS. I've often seen folks use a screwdriver or another narrow tool to stuff fiberglass insulation between trimmers and king studs (see the photo above). Although this helps to some degree, fiberglass insulation loses insulating value

CHOOSING CAULKS AND SEALANTS

If you walk down the caulk and sealant aisle at any well-stocked hardware store or home center, it's easy to feel overwhelmed by the variety of products available. For quite a few years now, the terms "caulk" and "sealant" have been used interchangeably. In technical terms, sealants are supposed to be more flexible than caulks, meaning that they are able to expand and contract with the movement of materials. But even caulk and sealant manufacturers have different definitions for these materials. For this reason, it's smart to ask local builders and knowledgeable building-material suppliers which caulks and sealants are recommended for various jobs.

Although manufacturers haven't cleared up the distinction between caulks and sealants, they have improved their labeling with regard to specific applications. For example, "painter's caulk" is an inexpensive latex-type caulk that is primarily used to fill gaps in and around interior trim prior to painting. Caulk that is labeled "for kitchen and bathroom use" is waterproof and will adhere to tile, porcelain sinks, acrylic shower units, and other surfaces found in those rooms. Silicone and urethane sealants are usually more expensive than acrylic or latex-acrylic caulks and are primarily used in exterior applications where extra durability, flexibility, and weather resistance are important. But be aware that acrylic paint does not adhere to some silicone caulks. Check with your supplier to see if your paint and caulk are compatible.

FIBERGLASS AND CELLULOSE INSULATION

The two most common types of insulation used in homes today are fiberglass and cellulose. Both are partially manufactured from recycled materials. Fiberglass is made from 25-percent recycled bottles and other types of glass that are heated and spun into fibers. Cellulose insulation is made from 75-percent recycled newsprint, which is treated with fire retardant.

Fiberglass comes in batts that are made in different widths and thicknesses. For shipping and storage, the batts are rolled up like long, thick blankets or packaged together in wall-length batts. Loose-fill fiberglass insulation is also available, but batts are much more common. Cellulose is usually blown into attic spaces and wall cavities (see the photo above). Blowers can often be rented at supply stores, but usually an insulation contractor is hired to install cellulose. Cellulose is somewhat more expensive than fiberglass but has a higher R-value per inch, so it can end up saving you more money in energy costs.

Like roof-shingle coverage, insulation coverage is calculated by the square foot. Add up the total square footage of the floor, the ceiling, and all the exterior walls. Unless you have an entire wall of doors and windows, don't subtract the wall openings. You may end up with a little extra insulation, but you can always put it in the attic.

If you're buying insulation at a home center or an equivalent store, you'll find the per-roll coverage on the label. If you're buying it from a professional supplier, you simply need to provide the total square footage and whether the stud (and joist) bays are 16 in. o.c. or 24 in. o.c. That's because fiberglass batts are either 15 in. or 23 in. wide and are sized to fit between studs and joists at conventional spacings. Long, uncut rolls work well between floor and ceiling joists. Precut sections are also available for standard 8-ft.-high walls and save on installation time.

Caulks and sealants can be useful on small openings

For filling small gaps (up to ¼ in. or so), caulks and sealants sometimes work as well as, or better than, foam. A good sealant has sufficient flexibility to maintain a seal even though the joint expands and contracts slightly. For advice on selecting caulks and sealants, see the sidebar on p. 199.

If you plan to use caulk or sealant to fill a gap wider than ¼ in., it's a good idea to insert a backer rod into the joint before you apply the sealant. Available where caulks and sealants are sold, backer rod is made from dense, compressible foam. When wedged into a joint, it helps seal the area and lets you apply a thinner bead of caulk or sealant.

STEP 2 INSULATE THE WALLS, CEILINGS, AND FLOORS

Although the reason for sealing cracks and gaps in a house frame may be fairly obvious—you don't want cold breezes (or hot air, depending on where you live) blowing through the house—the function of insulation may not be as evident. It is not to block airflow but rather to create pockets of dead air. Air pockets do the actual insulating work, whereas the insulation fibers or beads simply hold the air in place. That's why jamming fiberglass insulation into a too-small space isn't very helpful. In fact, doing so just eliminates much of the air space within the material, effectively reducing its value as insulation.

There are a number of materials used for insulation, but the three most common ones are cellulose, rigid foam, and fiberglass.

Subcontractors most often install cellulose insulation by blowing the loose material into attics with special equipment (see the sidebar at left). When binders are added to cellulose insulation, it can also be sprayed in dampened form between studs. When it is properly applied, the insulation stays in place after the moisture evaporates. Unlike fiberglass insulation, which demands careful installation to avoid gaps and air pockets, cellulose fills voids effectively, thanks to gravity (when blown into an attic) or air pressure (when blown into stud bays).

Rigid foam is often installed as insulation beneath concrete slabs and as sheathing panels beneath exterior siding (see the sidebar at right). But fiberglass is still the most common type of insulation used in this country today. Affordable and available everywhere, fiberglass insulation does a good job when it's installed properly (see the sidebar on the facing page).

Insulating walls and ceilings with fiberglass batts

The first thing to realize about installing fiberglass insulation is that you can't just shove the batts into wall and ceiling cavities any old way

Use unfaced batts in warm regions. In warm climates, where a vapor barrier on the interior of the house is not recommended, use unfaced insulation.

RIGID-FOAM INSULATION

Light, fairly inexpensive, and easy to cut and install, rigid-foam insulation has a lot going for it. This insulation board comes in different thicknesses and sheet sizes. Depending on the manufacturer, it comes in shades of blue, green, and pink. A ½-in.-thick sheet is rated at R-3; a 1-in. sheet is rated at R-5.

EXTERIOR USE. Rigid foam is often used on building exteriors. In regions where there is no danger of earthquakes or hurricanes, foam sheets are frequently used in place of wall sheathing. With this type of installation, sheets of plywood or OSB are still required at the corners of the house and every 25 ft. to provide lateral bracing for the structure; however, foam boards are used between the corner sheets and are nailed directly to the studs (see Chapter 6). Taping the seams between the sheets improves the foam's performance as a wind barrier.

I like to use foam insulation on the exterior of framed walls, because up to 25 percent of a wall's area can consist of solid wood—studs, headers, trimmers, and so on. Wood acts as a thermal bridge, allowing heat or cold to be conducted through a wall. Rigid foam helps block this conduction. Sheathing with 4-ft. by 9-ft. foam panels enables you to cover a standard-height wall and the rim joist below it.

Rigid-foam insulation gives you more flexibility in meeting code requirements. Used in conjunction with high-density R-15 fiberglass batts in a 2×4 wall, rigid foam can bring the R-value of a 2×4 wall up to that of a 2×6 wall with standard R-19-rated fiberglass (without the expense of wider framing). Using 2×4 walls, instead of 2×6s, means that your house gains an extra 2 in. all the way around the interior.

There are two important considerations if you're sheathing a house exterior with foam insulation. First, some types of exterior siding (wood shingles and clapboard, for example) are best installed over solid backing rather than over foam board. Second, if you're installing rigid foam over plywood or OSB sheathing, make sure the jambs for the doors and windows you order are wide enough for the wall. Standard-width jambs may be too narrow.

INSTALLING THE FOAM. Working with rigid foam is simple. It cuts easily with a utility knife. To nail sheets to the wall, I use either 1¼-in. roofing nails or nails with plastic heads, which are used to secure felt paper to the roof deck. In windy areas, I like to nail about 12 in. o.c. around the edges and 24 in. o.c. in the field. Make sure you fit the sheets together tightly.

and expect them to do their job. Insulation batts must fit snugly between studs or joists and cannot be jammed in tightly or packed loosely and sloppily with gaps all over the place. Kraft paper–faced batts have tabs, which should be stapled to the face of the studs every 12 in. or so.

Many installers staple insulation tabs to the stud sides of the drywall instead of the face. This makes it easier to install drywall, but when the paper tabs are stapled to the inside of the studs, a slight gap is left along both sides. Gaps are taboo when you're installing fiberglass insulation because they reduce the insulating value of the wall, especially on vertical walls.

If you plan to install fiberglass insulation in warm, humid climates (such as the southeastern United States), buy unfaced batts (see the photo on p. 201). Fiberglass insulation with kraft paper facing acts as a vapor barrier on the inside of exterior walls, potentially causing moisture problems.

For partial bays (less than 14½ in. or 22½ in. wide between studs) and small spaces, such as over headers and under windows, insulation must be cut to fit. Measure the width and length of smaller bays and cut the insulation about ½ in. to 1 in. larger (no more!) in each direction so that it will fit snugly in the cavities (see the side-bar on p. 204). You don't need to staple smaller pieces of insulation in place; the snug fit should hold them until the drywall is installed.

While you're insulating, keep in mind that another property of insulation is sound suppression. Given its relatively reasonable cost, you may want to use unfaced insulation in bedroom walls that adjoin a bathroom, living room, or utility room.

Take even more care when insulating the ceiling (see the photo below). Any heat that escapes into the attic can cause snow to melt, possibly causing an ice dam on your roof. When insulation batts butt together end to end in the ceiling, make sure the joints are tight.

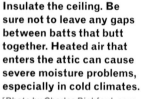

Insulate the ceiling. Be sure not to leave any gaps between batts that butt together. Heated air that enters the attic can cause severe moisture problems, especially in cold climates.
[Photo by Charles Bickford, courtesy *Fine Homebuilding* magazine © The Taunton Press, Inc.]

Because of the importance of keeping heat in the living area and out of the attic, I prefer using blown-in cellulose for the attic, even if the walls are insulated with fiberglass batts. Cellulose settles into and around gaps in the framing, forming what amounts to a giant down comforter over the entire living area of your house. And remember, it doesn't cost much to add a few more inches of cellulose—say, 14 in. to 18 in. rather than just 12 in.—but it will save on heating and cooling costs for the life of the house.

Allow for ventilation space when insulating attics and ceilings

With insulation, the only time you can have too much of a good thing is when the ceiling or attic insulation blocks the roof's ventilation. As shown in the illustration on p. 205, there must be a clear pathway for air to move from the eaves to the ridge.

In the house shown here, we nailed OSB baffles in place on the walls between the roof trusses to prevent the attic insulation (blown-in cellulose) from spilling into the eaves and covering soffit vents. When a house has a cathedral ceiling, there is no attic space to fill with insulation. Instead, fiberglass batts must be installed between the rafters. Be especially careful not to block the ventilation space between the rafters. Various cardboard and foam baffles are available to provide ventilation space and room for insulation according to the ceiling's design. Staple the baffles between the rafters before installing the insulation (see the photo at right).

While you're insulating the ceiling or attic, don't forget the attic's access cover or stairs. Rigid foam can be cut to insulate those openings. Using a compatible construction adhesive, glue several layers of foam on the top of the stairway or access hole cover.

Insulating around obstacles

If all we had to do were to fill the stud and joist bays, then insulating would be easy. Problems often arise because of all the pipes, wires, light

Baffles provide space for ventilation. On a flat roof or a cathedral ceiling, staple the baffles to the sheathing between framing members, then install the insulation.

[Photo by Steve Culpepper, courtesy *Fine Homebuilding* magazine © The Taunton Press, Inc.]

fixtures, and outlet boxes that are in walls and ceilings. For wires and pipes, cut a slice halfway through the batt and encase the pipe or wire in the insulation. It's important not to compress the batts. In cold regions, make sure that you have insulation on the back of pipes (between the pipe and the exterior wall sheathing or siding) to keep them from freezing.

For electrical boxes, split the batt so that the insulation goes behind the box, as shown in the photos on p. 205. The front part of the batt can be neatly cut with a knife or scissors to fit around the box. Once the drywall is installed, you can use cover plates with foam or rubber gaskets over outlet and switch boxes to further reduce air passage.

Many recessed light fixtures generate so much heat that you have to leave a 3-in.

WORKING WITH FIBERGLASS INSULATION

Glass fibers can irritate your skin and damage your eyes and lungs, so safety precautions are very important when working with fiberglass insulation. Cover your body with a loose-fitting, long-sleeved shirt and long trousers, and wear gloves and a hat, especially while insulating a ceiling (see the photo below). It's best to wear a pair of quality goggles, too, because eyeglasses alone don't keep fiberglass particles out of your eyes. Make sure the goggles fit properly; goggles that fit well don't fog over. Wear a good-quality dust mask or, better yet, get yourself a respirator. Don't scratch your skin while you're working (you'll just embed glass fibers), and be sure to wash up well when you are finished.

CUTTING BATTS. Cutting fiberglass batts to size is straightforward. The best tool for the job is a sharp utility knife. Note that I said "sharp." A dull blade will tear paper-faced batts, and torn paper doesn't work as a vapor barrier. A sheet of plywood or OSB makes a good cutting table. Place the insulation batt on the worktable, with the paper side down if you're using faced batts. Measure where the batt should be cut and add at least ½ in. (it's better for a

batt to be a bit snug than to have a gap at the edge or the end). Compress it with a straight board, then run the knife along the board, as shown in the photo above. Be careful with the utility knife. If it's sharp, you don't have to exert a lot of pressure. Keep the hand that is holding the board out of the blade's path.

When fitting batts around a window, you'll need to cut pieces to fit above and below the window. To speed the process of insulating walls, I measure both spaces, mark their lengths on the cutting table, and cut as many pieces as I need. Don't be sloppy with your cuts. Even small holes or gaps in fiberglass insulation can dramatically reduce its effectiveness.

INSTALLING BATTS. Batts faced with kraft paper have a foldout tab that should be stapled to the face of the studs or ceiling joists. The most common method of attaching faced batts to wood is with a hammer-type stapler and ¼-in.-long staples. Make sure the staples go in all the way, so that you won't have problems hanging drywall later. Unfaced batts are held by friction between studs or joists until the vapor barrier or drywall is in place.

Insulate around electrical boxes. First, divide the batt into two layers instead of compressing it. Slide the back layer behind the outlet box (see the photo above), then cut out the front layer to fit around the box (see the photo below). This technique also works for installing fiberglass batts around electrical wires and plumbing pipes. [Photos by Steve Culpepper, courtesy *Fine Homebuilding* magazine © The Taunton Press, Inc.]

STANDARD INSULATED CEILING

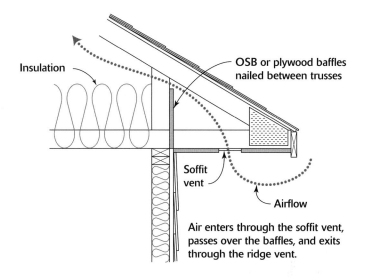

Insulation

OSB or plywood baffles nailed between trusses

Soffit vent

Airflow

Air enters through the soffit vent, passes over the baffles, and exits through the ridge vent.

CATHEDRAL CEILING

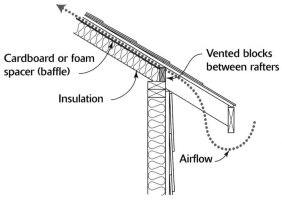

Cardboard or foam spacer (baffle)

Vented blocks between rafters

Insulation

Airflow

Air passes through the vented blocks, over the baffles, and up and out the ridge vent.

uninsulated space around them. Don't use these fixtures. It's much better to choose models that require no insulation gap. You can insulate right up to and on top of those fixtures. Some states require that fixtures be airtight, too, so check with your building inspector.

Insulating between floor joists in crawl spaces

Floor insulation is important in a house with a crawl-space foundation. Often, it is not enough

TIP Eliminate gaps when installing fiberglass insulation. Gaps around outlet boxes and along a wall's bottom or top plate can let in a lot of unwanted air. A gap of just $3/8$ in. along both sides of a fiberglass batt can cut the insulation's effectiveness by 50 percent or more!

KEEPING COLD AIR FROM ENTERING AT THE RIM JOISTS

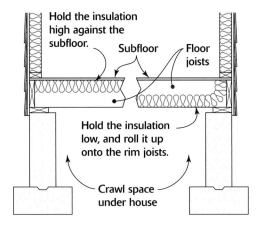

Hold the insulation high against the subfloor.

Subfloor

Floor joists

Hold the insulation low, and roll it up onto the rim joists.

Crawl space under house

To keep cold air from entering on top of the floor insulation, ensure that insulation is right up against the subfloor (above, left) or roll the insulation up the inside of the rim joist to the subfloor (above, right). Either of these techniques will help prevent a cold floor.

SUPPORTING INSULATION BETWEEN FLOOR JOISTS

Floor insulation must be well supported to do its job. Here are three reliable methods for providing support.

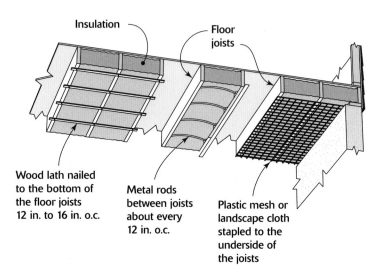

Insulation

Floor joists

Wood lath nailed to the bottom of the floor joists 12 in. to 16 in. o.c.

Metal rods between joists about every 12 in. o.c.

Plastic mesh or landscape cloth stapled to the underside of the joists

just to put insulation under the floor, because cold can pass through the rim joist. Unless batts fill the entire joist space, cold air can seep in through the rim joist and over the top of the batts, making the floor uncomfortably chilly.

To prevent this, you can either hold the insulation high or roll it up to cover the rim joist (see the top left illustration). Better yet, use a thicker batt with a higher R-value to fill the entire joist space and butt up against the rim joist.

When insulating between I-joists, make sure the insulation is wide enough to extend all the way from web to web. If you live in a cold part of the country and you're using kraft paper–faced insulation, the paper should face toward the floor. This may seem backward, but the paper acts as a vapor barrier (more on that later) and must face the heat, so to speak. If you live in an area where cooling (air-conditioning) is an issue for a majority of the year, staple the kraft paper to the underside of the joists.

It can be a pain to install batts of insulation under a floor, because there is often not much space between the ground and the joists. It's not a lot of fun to lie on your back and install fiberglass batts! Sometimes, especially in dry climates, it's possible to insulate the floor before you sheathe. The drawback with this technique is that subcontractors (plumbing and heating, especially) may not treat your work with TLC. In rainy Oregon, we wait to insulate until after the shingles are on and the house is closed in. Either way, take your time, and make sure that underfloor insulation batts are installed properly and securely around all pipes and conduits.

There are a number of ways to hold under-floor batts in place (see the bottom left illustration). In Oregon, it's common to nail strips of lath every 12 in. to 16 in. o.c. across the bottom of the joists once the insulation is installed. It's a lot of work, but it holds the batts securely without compressing them. Another way is to staple polypropylene (not cotton) twine or mesh to the bottom edges of the joists. I've also seen people staple chicken wire or hardware cloth across the joists. Still another option is to use wire supports designed specifically for the job. These wire supports, called lightning rods or tiger teeth, clip between joists and bow up against the batts, holding them in place. Installed about every 12 in. or so, they do a good job of keeping the batts in place for years to come. Just take care not to compress the batts when installing the rods.

STEP 3 INSTALL VAPOR BARRIERS (IF NECESSARY)

Unlike housewrap, a properly installed vapor barrier is supposed to be impermeable. Vapor should not pass through it. Different materials are used as vapor barriers. The kraft-paper facing on fiberglass batt insulation is designed to function as a vapor barrier. To form a continuous barrier, the paper flanges must overlap on the stud face, where they are stapled in place.

TIP Store fiberglass scraps in a garbage bag. Spare and scrap pieces of fiberglass can easily blow all over a job site. To keep this fluffy material under control, put it in a large plastic garbage bag. Partial rolls can also be stored in a plastic bag until needed.

THE AC ALTERNATIVE: A WHOLE-HOUSE EXHAUST FAN

Although it is not ideal in all climates or seasons, a whole-house fan can be a very attractive alternative to air-conditioning. A simple fan is more reliable and less expensive than a single window-mounted AC unit, and it can effectively cool an entire house. As shown in the illustration at right, the principle is simple: A single, centrally located fan pulls in fresh air through open windows and blows hot indoor air outside. By turning the fan on in the evening and opening all major windows, it's possible to quickly cool a house that has become hot during the day.

These fans work best in dry climates, or at least when the air is cool and dry outdoors. In the winter, when the fan is not being used, it must be protected with an insulated cover to prevent heated air from entering the attic space. I make a simple cover from plywood and then glue several layers of rigid foam to the top and sides.

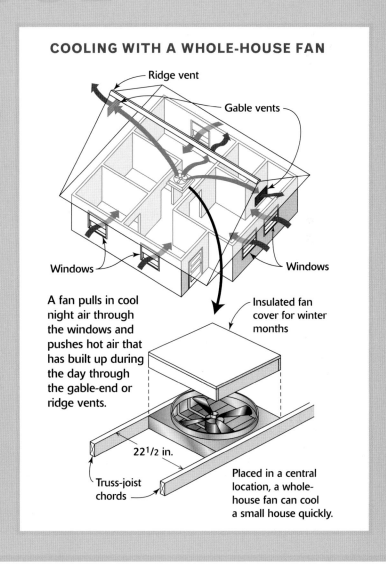

COOLING WITH A WHOLE-HOUSE FAN

Ridge vent

Gable vents

Windows

Windows

A fan pulls in cool night air through the windows and pushes hot air that has built up during the day through the gable-end or ridge vents.

Insulated fan cover for winter months

22 1/2 in.

Truss-joist chords

Placed in a central location, a whole-house fan can cool a small house quickly.

Photo courtesy HFHI

A PERFECT LITTLE NEST

When Jill Osuna was bitten by the Habitat bug, she was bitten hard. A Habitat for Humanity Tucson homeowner, she also serves as president of the Balboa Laguna homeowners association and works part time in the Habitat office as an assistant to the director of accounting.

"I love coming to work," she says. "I know what I'm doing makes a difference."

Growing up, Jill and her family moved frequently, but when Jill met her husband, a member of the Pascua Yaqui Native American tribe with extensive family in Arizona, she figured she was in Tucson to stay. Finding a home to live in, however, was challenging.

"A lot of people are selling their homes in California and New Mexico and coming here," she says. "They're only building houses for $300,000 and up, but the wages around here haven't moved. Even some middle-income families are having a hard time."

After struggling with illness due to mold and allergy contaminants in their apartment, Jill has found her new Habitat house to be a place of rest and dreams for the future. "It's our nest, our place where we're going to grow old together, a place to call our own. I call it our perfect little nest."

—Rebekah Daniel

Polyethylene sheeting is also commonly used as a vapor barrier. Thin (6 mil), clear "poly" sheet material is stapled to the face of studs, attic joists, and (on cathedral ceilings) rafters. The barrier is kept continuous by overlapping adjoining sheets and sealing the overlap with silicone or another sealant.

It's much easier to describe what a vapor barrier does than to explain why it is essential in some situations but not in others. I once had to tear out an entire wall that had rotted because the house had no vapor barrier. There was so much water trapped in the walls that you could literally wring it out of the insulation. A vapor barrier would have prevented such damage.

To understand why and where a vapor barrier is important, imagine what happens when someone takes a long, hot shower in your home when it's freezing cold outside. The bathroom is foggy with water vapor, and some of that warm, humid air makes its way into the attic and the exterior walls. The air can easily pass through openings around electrical outlets and light fixtures and even through the gypsum board itself, which absorbs moisture readily. At some point, the temperature in the attic and the exterior walls drops enough to cause condensation. This dew point can occur in the middle of the attic or wall insulation or against roof and wall sheathing. Over the course of a cold winter, a steady supply of moist interior air can easily accumulate, causing soggy insulation, mold, and rotten wood.

A vapor barrier prevents the movement of vapor from a warm area to a cold surface. In cold climates, it should definitely be installed right underneath the drywall, paneling, or other interior wall finish material. Instructions for installing a poly vapor barrier are provided in the next section.

Vapor barriers are often eliminated in warm climates, especially in areas of low humidity, such as the Southwest. But you may want to consider installing a vapor barrier beneath the exterior siding if the house will be exposed to warm, moist air outdoors and frequent air-conditioning indoors.

In mixed-climate zones—the region that extends from the mid-Atlantic states through the Carolinas and west by southwest to northern Texas—the need for a vapor barrier is minimal. In those regions, where mild winters are the rule, any moisture that does enter the wall cavities can dry from the outside in during the summer and from the inside out during the winter.

Installing a polyethylene vapor barrier

To work effectively, a vapor barrier must be installed with care. Even the smallest holes in a poly or kraft-paper vapor barrier must be sealed with housewrap tape or its equivalent. Use a durable, high-quality tape; neither duct tape nor packing tape will hold over the long run.

A friend of mine is a carpenter in Fairbanks, Alaska. They're serious about vapor barriers up there. They cut sheets of poly from rolls that are 10 ft. to 20 ft. wide and 100 ft. long, covering the entire ceiling and all the exterior walls (on the inside). They even make sure to put poly behind a bathtub installed against an exterior wall.

In any given room, there are two steps to installing a poly vapor barrier. This isn't a job you want to do solo; have helpers so that some can spread the sheet out over framing members while others staple it fast. You can begin as soon as all the insulation is in place.

1. Install the ceiling poly. Cut a piece of poly to fit the ceiling. If you have to use several pieces, make sure they overlap by at least one joist (or rafter, if you're working on a cathedral ceiling). Seal overlaps with a layer of mastic, acoustical sealant, or housewrap tape. At the edges of the ceiling, the poly should lap at least 3 in. down onto the walls. Begin stapling the poly to the joists or joist chords in the center of the room and work out toward the walls. My friend staples about 12 in. o.c. through small, precut squares of heavy paper. This keeps the poly from tearing. Fit the poly

Seal the vapor barrier to an outlet box. A bead of caulk seals a poly vapor barrier around the rim of an outlet box to reduce air infiltration and maintain a continuous vapor barrier. [Photo by Scott Gibson, courtesy *Fine Homebuilding* magazine © The Taunton Press, Inc.]

tightly into all corners so the drywall will go on easily. The drywall holds the poly tight against the studs and insulation.

2. Install poly on the walls. Make this sheet continuous so that it laps over the ceiling poly along the wall's top plate and extends past the bottom plate to lap about 3 in. onto the subfloor surface. First staple the sheet along the top plate, working from the upper center of the wall and down and out to the edges of the wall. If you need to join one sheet of poly to another, overlap them by at least one stud and seal the lap as described previously.

You can sheet right over door and window openings, then cut openings in the poly after it's

ENERGY-SAVING TIPS

While you're thinking about insulation and ventilation, you should also pay attention to a few other details that relate to energy conservation. Taken together, these small improvements can make a big difference in how well your house works.

- Locate the water heater near the kitchen and bathroom. This avoids long runs of pipe that increase plumbing costs and dissipate heat between the water heater and the faucets or showerheads.
- In cold climates, keep water-supply lines out of exterior walls.
- Use an insulated wrap for the water heater. New water heaters typically come with built-in insulation, which helps keep your energy costs low. Another money saver is water heaters that come with timers. This allows you to activate the unit during specific times of day when heated water is needed.
- Insulate all hot-water lines, and insulate cold-water lines in a crawl space. Both foam and fiberglass-wrap pipe-insulation kits are available at building-supply outlets and home centers.
- Install low-flow showerheads. A showerhead with a built-in shutoff valve provides even more savings, allowing you to shut off the water while soaping up.
- Consider using a small solar panel to preheat your water. The sun's energy is free. With a solar panel, you can reduce the energy used by your hot-water heater.

Habitat for Humanity has developed many guides to help homebuilders and homeowners save energy and money. They are available online and from HFH International (see Resources on p. 279). Take advantage of these resources and increase your understanding of how to build durable, energy-efficient houses with good indoor-air quality.

TIP Avoid single-speed fans. You'll appreciate having a vent fan that can operate at more than one speed. Multiple-speed and variable-speed models cost a little more, but they enable you to use a lower, quieter speed during extended operation.

completely stapled in place. If the windows and doors have already been installed, cut the poly along the inner edge of the jambs. If the windows and doors haven't been installed yet, wrap the poly around the trimmers, headers, and sills. Avoid loose flaps that can catch the wind and cause tearing.

To prevent leakage at electrical outlets, use airtight boxes. Available at most electrical-supply stores, airtight boxes have a broad, flexible gasket around the front edge, where a poly barrier can be sealed easily. Alternatively, you can simply cut a box-size opening in the poly and seal the poly to the electrical box with a bead of caulk (see the photo on p. 209).

STEP 4 PROVIDE ADEQUATE VENTILATION

Now that we have a tight, well-insulated house, what do we do when we want a breath of fresh air? And how can we rid the house of kitchen odors and steam from cooking, showers, and the like? Indoor-air-quality problems are magnified in a new house because of fumes from new carpets, vinyl flooring adhesive, and paint. Obviously, you can open a couple of windows to get some fresh air, as long as the weather is cooperative. But what if you're not comfortable opening windows in your neighborhood? That's a problem. And what if it's –15°F outside? What if its 105°F and humid? Opening windows when the weather is extreme or unpleasant undermines the effort you put into creating an energy-efficient house. There is a better solution, and it's called mechanical ventilation.

All houses need at least a few small fans in critical locations where large volumes of vapor are created. A mechanical ventilation system can help maintain good indoor-air quality without making a lot of noise or costing a fortune. Unfortunately, my experience is that many local building codes (and building inspectors) have some catch-up work to do when it comes to understanding house ventilation. You're better off finding a knowledgeable and reliable HVAC (heating, ventilation, and air-conditioning) contractor with up-to-date knowledge of home ventilation requirements. That said, proper ventilation for small, affordable houses isn't all that difficult to obtain.

Source ventilation is the key to reducing moisture and odors

You can start by installing adequate spot, or source, ventilation wherever moisture or odors are created. Venting moist air directly to the outside prevents it from escaping through the walls or ceilings, where it can cause damage. At a minimum, showers and stoves should have exhaust fans that are controlled by simple on-off switches or wired to come on automatically when a bathroom light is turned on or the stove is being used. For a stove installation, mechanical ventilation is usually provided by a vent hood equipped with a fan. In a bathroom, a variety of ceiling-mounted fans are available, including models with built-in lights.

Exhaust fans in moisture-producing areas should always be vented directly outdoors. That means out through a wall or up through the roof and not into an eave soffit or a crawl space. When we moved into our home in Oregon, I discovered that the clothes dryer was vented into the crawl space. Some pretty creepy looking stuff was growing down there in the dark. Even worse is venting moist kitchen or bathroom air into the attic.

Try to keep vent runs short—less than 10 ft., if possible. Avoid running vents through the attic, if possible; install them in interior soffits and dropped ceilings instead. If you can't avoid running a vent through the attic, then make sure it is well insulated. This is crucial in cold climates, where heat inside the attic can cause ice damming along the eaves. This is serious business, so pay attention to the details.

Good indoor-air quality requires air exchange

We all need fresh air to stay healthy, and in a tightly built house, some form of mechanical air exchange is essential. You can provide air exchange fairly inexpensively by using a bathroom exhaust fan controlled by an automatic timer. Look for a fan that moves air at 80 CFM (cubic feet per minute) to 120 CFM. Set the timer to run the fan about two-thirds of the time that people are generally home (it doesn't make much sense to exchange air when no one's home). The fan we have in our home is centrally located in a hallway, but check with your HVAC contractor to locate yours. Beware of bargain-priced fans. Those models are almost always noisier than other vent fans. An experienced HVAC contractor can advise you on which models run quietly and reliably.

Whenever fans are blowing indoor air outside the house, fresh air must come in to replace it. This ensures a healthy supply of fresh air and prevents negative air pressure from drawing exhaust gasses from the fireplace or furnace flues, which is a serious safety hazard. The simplest way to provide replacement air when exhaust fans are running is to open a window or two. It's not necessary for the window to be fully open; just a crack will usually do. If it's cold outside, open a window in a utility room, unused bedroom, or somewhere away from the main living area.

If you're building a house where the winters are long and very cold (in Maine or Minnesota, for example), it may be necessary to have an HVAC contractor install a heat recovery ventilator (HRV) or an air-handling unit to bring replacement air into the house at a more comfortable temperature. Those devices typically work by blowing warm indoor air outdoors while pulling an equal volume of outside air indoors. Because only a thin membrane separates the passing airstreams, some of the interior's warmth is transferred to the fresh incoming air.

TIP Improve air circulation in your house by cutting off door bottoms so they don't touch the floor. Even better, you can install a through-wall grill over a door. This allows air to move from room to room.

THE WALLS WITHIN

Drywall and Painting

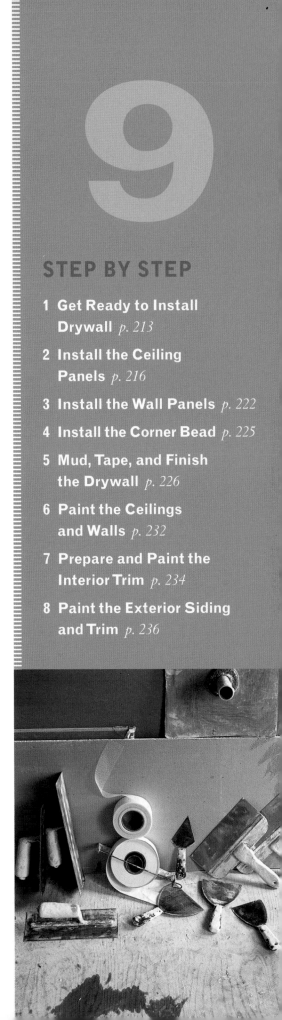

I'm not sure when drywall—also known as gypsum board, wallboard, and Sheetrock®—was first used in construction. I have seen drywall on pre–World War II houses, but we definitely didn't have drywall in my old prairie home. It wasn't until the late 1950s in California, where I was working, that drywall became the preferred wall covering in residential housing. "Knock on the Wall! Demand Genuine Lath and Plaster!" was the rallying cry of the once-mighty plaster industry, as they struggled against the newcomer—drywall.

Big plaster fought a losing battle. It took two or three weeks to cover walls with layers of plaster, and the process left the house frame waterlogged. In the winter, it could take a month or more for a house to dry out well. Cabinets installed after plastering often had sticky drawers. In addition, passage doors were hard to open, and hardwood floors expanded and buckled. It's no wonder the construction industry switched to drywall. It allowed builders to complete houses in record time.

Drywall installation can begin once you've passed all your inspections—electrical, plumbing, heating, framing, insulation, and vapor barrier. Drywall is not difficult to secure to ceilings and walls, but it takes more skill to leave the finished walls straight and smooth. This chapter will tell you how to order and store drywall, which tools and methods you need to cut and "hang" it, how to tape and finish the joints, and how to paint the walls and trim. By the time you're done with these jobs, your house will look a lot more like a home.

STEP 1 GET READY TO INSTALL DRYWALL

There's some important prep work to be done before you take delivery of your drywall order and before any installation work can begin. In addition

SIZES AND TYPES OF DRYWALL

Drywall is made by sandwiching a gypsum core between two sheets of paper. The "good" side of the panel is faced with smooth, white paper that takes paint easily. The "bad" side is darker in color, with a rough, porous paper surface. Panels (also called sheets) of drywall are packaged in pairs; to open the package, simply pull off the strips of paper that extend along each end.

The standard width for drywall panels is 48 in. For houses that have 9 ft. ceilings, use drywall sheets that are 4 ft. 6 in. wide. Different lengths are available, but for affordable housing the most commonly used lengths are 8 ft. and 12 ft. The most common thickness for drywall is ½ in. However, ⅝-in.-thick panels are often used on ceilings where the joists are spaced 2 ft. o.c. because they are less prone to sagging. Most

codes require ⅝-in. panels between the garage and the house for fire resistance. If you use ⅝-in. drywall on the walls, be sure to order wider door jambs.

Water-resistant drywall is often used in high-moisture areas, such as bathrooms. Called "greenboard" because of its green-paper facing, it is treated to resist moisture damage but is not waterproof. It's most often used to cover wall areas above tub and shower enclosures. Greenboard can be taped and painted just like regular drywall. It should not be installed on the ceiling unless the joists are spaced 12 in. o.c. to keep the board from sagging.

The short (48-in.) ends of a drywall panel are cut square, leaving the gypsum core exposed. The long edges of the panel are faced with paper and tapered so that the seams between panels can be leveled with the surrounding drywall during the finishing process.

MAKING A DRYWALL LIFTER

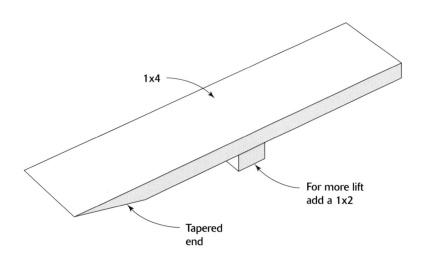

1x4

For more lift
add a 1x2

Tapered
end

A simple tool used to lift a sheet of drywall can be put together in minutes. Cut a piece of 1x4 about 16 in. long, then cut a taper on the flat face at one end. If the drywall must be lifted more than 3/4 in., add a piece of 1x2 to the bottom of the lifter.

to following the advice explained here, see the sidebar above and on p. 217 for information on sizes and types of drywall and how to order and store the material.

Make sure the studs and joists are dry

Framing lumber used today often arrives at the job site with a high moisture content. Over time, it will shrink—sometimes quite a lot. When the studs and joists shrink after the drywall has been installed, the fasteners can work loose. A loose nail or screw can create a noticeable and unsightly bump, or nail pop, in the drywall surface.

To reduce the chances that nail pops will mar your drywall work, you may need to close in the house and turn on the heat for a couple of weeks. Leave a couple of windows cracked open to allow moist air to escape as the wood dries. You can ignore this advice if you're working with dry wood or if you've had the good fortune to frame your house in clear, warm weather.

Otherwise, make sure the wood dries out. You can even run a dehumidifier inside, if necessary.

Clean and mark the floor

Take time to clean up any scraps of wood or trash on the floor. Once the floor is clean, use a piece of keel (I use red because it shows up well) to mark the stud, trimmer, and cripple locations on the floor and the joist locations on the top plate. Knowing the location of studs and joists makes it easier to nail off drywall and, later, baseboard trim.

It's also a good idea to mark the locations of electrical outlets on the floor. This helps avoid installing drywall panels over outlets, which can easily happen if you're not paying attention. If it does happen anyway, at least there will be a mark on the floor telling you where the outlet is located. You can also mark the location of the backing placed in the walls to support towel racks, grab bars, toilet-paper holders, and so on.

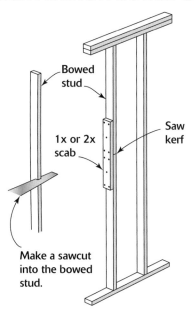

Bowed stud

1x or 2x scab

Saw kerf

Make a sawcut into the bowed stud.

To straighten a wall stud, cut a kerf into the stud at its most bowed point, pull the stud straight, then nail a 1x or 2x scab alongside it to strengthen the stud and keep it straight.

TIP Dryall has delicate corners and edges. When you store and handle sheets of drywall, make sure you protect the panels' edges and corners from getting damaged.

Several specialized tools make it easier to cut and hang drywall on ceilings and wall studs. [Photo by Don Charles Blom]

(see the illustration on p. 215).

> **TIP** Stay sharp. There are two ways to keep a utility knife blade sharp for safety and ease of use. Have some spare blades handy, and keep a small sharpening stone in your tool pocket or in a pouch on your tool belt. With a few strokes on a whetstone, a dull blade can be sharpened quite a few times before it must be replaced.

Check and correct bad studs

Even if all the studs were crowned in one direction during wall framing, it doesn't ensure a perfectly straight wall. Sight down the length of the walls or lay a straightedge across them to locate bad studs. Replace any badly bowed studs, or fix a bowed stud by making a cut into the bowed area, forcing the stud straight, and bracing it with a 1× cleat (see the illustration on p. 215).

Tool up to hang drywall

The tools you need to install drywall are pretty basic. In addition to the chalkline and tape measure you've used for the work covered in earlier chapters, you'll need the following tools:

UTILITY KNIVES AND SPARE BLADES. Most straight cuts in drywall are made with a utility knife. Have a good supply of new blades handy. A sharp blade cuts cleanly through a panel's paper facing, whereas a dull blade can tear the paper.

DRYWALL SQUARE. This large, aluminum, T-shaped square enables you to quickly and easily make straight, square cuts in drywall.

SCREW GUN. A screw gun takes the guesswork out of fastening drywall because it sinks drywall screws just the right distance into the panel. This tool resembles an electric drill and holds a replaceable Phillips-head bit.

DRYWALL HAMMER. This hammer looks like a small hatchet with a convex hitting surface. The curved face allows you to set the nail below the surface of the drywall without breaking the paper. The hatchet end is not sharp and can be used for levering or wedging drywall into place.

SURFORM® TOOL. Designed to function like a handplane, this shaping tool is very useful for trimming small amounts off the edge of a panel to improve its fit on the wall or ceiling. Avoid large Surform tools; the smaller versions are more maneuverable and fit in a pouch on your tool belt.

STEP 2 INSTALL THE CEILING PANELS

It's best to drywall the ceiling before you do the walls. This way, the top edges of the wall panels can butt up against the ceiling panels, supporting them along the edges. The long edges of ceiling panels run perpendicular to the joists or joist chords. In bedrooms and other small rooms, you'll probably be able to cover the full length of the ceiling with 12-ft. panels. If the ceiling is more that 12 ft. long, stagger the end joints where the panels butt together, just as you do on floor and roof sheathing panels. Try not to have a drywall joint land on an electrical or heat outlet, because this makes it harder to tape and hide the seam.

Measuring and cutting drywall panels

If you watch professional drywall installers measure and cut panels, you'll be impressed with the speed and accuracy of their work. Although you may not achieve speed right away, accuracy is possible from the start if you use some of the tips explained here. With accurate cuts, you'll have a much easier time mudding and taping the panels.

MAKE STRAIGHT CUTS. Instead of cutting a panel to the exact dimensions you measure on a wall or ceiling, cut it ¼ in. short. This leaves a ⅛-in. gap on both sides of the panel, allowing you to fit the piece without binding on neighboring walls or panels. Make a straight cut by scoring along the cut line; snap the cut open so the panel folds back on itself and slice through the resulting crease on the back. Mark and cut on the "good" side of the panel.

If you have a drywall T-square and need to make a square cut, guide the knife against the edge of the square (see the top left photo on p. 218). Take care not to let the knife slip and cut the hand that's holding the T-square. Just cut through the paper and slightly into

ORDERING DRYWALL AND ASSOCIATED SUPPLIES

Like shingles, siding, and insulation, drywall amounts are calculated by the square footage of the area to be covered (in this case, the walls and ceilings). Rather than measuring the ceiling and walls in every room, experienced drywallers use a shortcut calculation. They simply multiply the total square footage of a house by 3½ (3.5). For instance, a 24-ft. by 36-ft. house has 864 sq. ft. of floor space, and 864 times 3.5 equals 3,024 sq. ft. of drywall coverage. A 4×12 sheet of drywall covers 48 sq. ft. of wall. Dividing 3,024 sq. ft. by 48 proves that you need 63 sheets of drywall for this particular house.

Your drywall order

For the modest-size houses that Habitat builds, it's best to make up most of your drywall order with 12-ft. drywall panels. A 4×12 sheet of drywall is more difficult to carry than a 4×8 sheet, but it covers more area and often eliminates the need for butt joints on a wall or ceiling. To fine-tune your drywall order, subtract any greenboard you will be using in the bathroom. Also, if you decide to go with 5⁄8-in. drywall on the ceiling, subtract the floor area (864 sq. ft. in our example) from the square-foot total, then order that amount of 5⁄8-in. drywall for the ceiling.

Have the drywall delivered several days before you plan to hang it. If you're using any 5⁄8-in. drywall, stack those sheets on top of the ½-in. sheets. Storing all the drywall in one room creates a lot of weight on a few floor joists. Therefore, make a neat pile in each room, with the drywall flat on the floor, finish side facing up, or lean the sheets against the wall.

Screws and nails

Professional drywall hangers rarely use drywall nails. Screws hold better than nails, and a screw gun automatically drives the screws just the right distance, dimpling the drywall surface without breaking the paper.

If you're not a seasoned drywall hanger, you'll probably find it useful to drive a few nails to hold a panel in place against the studs or ceiling joists. Then you can finish installing the panel with screws. A 5-lb. box of drywall nails and a 50-lb. box of 1¼-in. drywall screws should give you all the fasteners you need for a 1,200-sq.-ft. house. If you're hanging 5⁄8-in.-thick panels, order 1½-in.-long fasteners.

Joint tape, corner beads, and drywall compound

You can order these finishing supplies when you order your drywall. Joint tape comes in rolls; order 400 ft. for every 1,000 sq. ft. of drywall.

Every outside corner covered with drywall requires a corner bead. These steel or plastic trim pieces are typically sold in 8-ft. or 10-ft. lengths. When estimating the amount of bead to order, make sure you account for corners where drywall wraps around window and door openings.

As far as drywall compound goes, the typical Habitat house requires about nine 5-gal. buckets. For the Charlotte house, we used an all-purpose compound called Durabond®, which comes in powdered form and is mixed with water at the job site. Other folks prefer to buy premixed compound, which comes in buckets or boxes.

Drywall is heavy! Carrying a long sheet, like this 12 footer, is definitely a two-person job. [Photo © The Taunton Press, Inc.]

TIP Remove fasteners that miss the framing. It's easy to tell when a drywall screw or nail misses a stud, joist, or other framing member. When that happens, remove the fastener and make a dimple (a concave mark with a drywall hammer) at the spot so the hole can be filled and hidden with joint compound.

Cut the drywall panel to length. First score the sheet with a sharp utility knife. A large T-square, held to the measurement mark, guides the cut (see the photo at left). Once scored, the drywall breaks right along the cut line (see the photo at right). Cut the piece free by slicing along the crease on the back.

the gypsum core—about $1/8$ in. or so. There's no need to force the blade deep into the panel. Once the panel has been scored, snap it away from the cut, as shown in the photo above right. Running a utility knife along the crease on the back of the panel will separate the pieces. If the cut edges are rough or uneven, smooth them with a Surform rasp (see the bottom left photo on the facing page).

CUT ACCURATE HOLES IN PANELS

Holes for electrical outlet boxes, heating vents, and pipes must be laid out and cut accurately. Take your measurements from a wall, ceiling, floor, or sheet of drywall already in place. I like to transfer these measurements to the drywall panel with a T-square. For electrical outlets and heating vents, use a T-square to outline the hole, then make the cut with a small drywall saw. Plunge the point of the saw into the panel from the "good" side and saw along the cut line

(see the top right photo on the facing page). The finished cut should be within $1/8$ in. of the outlet.

For a dryer vent or a round electrical outlet, measure and mark the center of the cut. Then use a compass or another round electrical box as a template to outline the hole. To make the cut, use a small drywall saw, a utility knife, or a circle-cutting tool made specifically for this job (see the bottom right photo on the facing page).

Another method for marking the location of an electrical box, regardless of its shape, is to rub the face of the box with chalk or a keel, place the sheet in position on the wall, and press the sheet against the outlet. The chalk will show you where to cut. Cut gently so you can avoid tearing the paper facing on the "good" side.

Use a drywall router to save time

Most of the time you can drywall right over door and window openings, attic access holes, and heating vents, then cut around the outlet boxes with an electric drywall router, as shown in the bottom photo on p. 220. (Get a feel for this tool by making some practice cuts on scrap drywall.)

Make sure the electrical wires are shoved to the back of all the boxes, and double-check to be sure there isn't power at any of the boxes for which you're routing holes. Tack the sheet on the ceiling or wall, then mark on the sheet the location of each outlet with a line noting the edge of the box and an "X" showing the side the outlet is on. Don't nail too near the outlet or you could break the drywall, but be sure to drive enough nails or screws into ceiling panels so they won't fall down.

Set the router bit to extend about ¾ in. past the base plate. With the router running, insert the bit into the center of the box and gently move it until it hits the side of the box. Pull

Smooth rough edges. A Surform rasp works well when you need to smooth or trim the edge of a drywall panel.

A drywall saw is made for the job. This small saw has a pointed end for making plunge cuts in drywall. It also works well for making small rectangular cutouts to fit electrical outlet boxes.

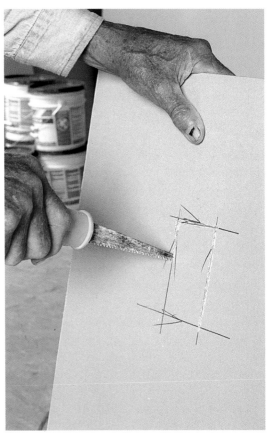

TIP When you are working with volunteers, be sure to be organized and have lots of tasks ready to go. Most volunteers come wanting to work. It is disheartening for them to arrive at the job site and have to stand around for two hours waiting for materials to arrive.

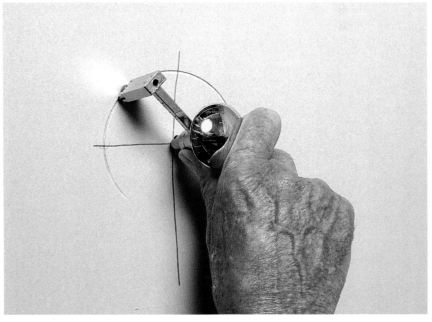

Use a circle cutter. This tool is ideal for cutting round holes in drywall for pipes or round electrical boxes.

TIP Snap lines to locate studs. If you miss framing members when driving fasteners near the center of a panel, you can snap lines to locate studs and joists. Use white chalk, which will not bleed through finish coats of paint. Or you can draw a pencil line along a straightedge.

the bit out and reinsert it just to the outside of the box. Cut in a counterclockwise direction, maintaining slight pressure against the box. The router generates some dust, so wear a good mask. A router or a large drywall saw can be used to cut larger openings as well.

Dimples are essential

Before you install the first panel on the ceiling, it's important to understand how to fasten drywall to the joists, studs, and other framing members. Whether you're using nails, screws, or both, you must leave a dimple in the panel with every fastener you drive. This small recess will later be filled with drywall compound as the wall surface is filled and finished. Screw guns can be set to pull the drywall panel tightly against the framing members and drive the screw just below the surface without breaking the face paper. If you're driving nails instead of screws, your last hammer blow should push

Make a dimple. Use a drywall hammer when nailing panels in place. The curved hitting surface is designed to dimple the drywall surface, setting the nail and creating a depression that can be filled with drywall compound.

the drywall tightly against the wood and set the head of the nail in a shallow dimple without breaking the paper surface (see the photo above).

Dead men are useful

Whether you have one helper or several, you'll find it useful to have a couple of drywall T-supports (also called preachers or dead men) to brace each panel against the framing while you drive enough screws to secure it. If possible, always start by installing a full-size sheet against one corner of the ceiling. Lift one end of the sheet into position, then raise the other end against the joists while holding the edge against the wall. Wedge the T-supports underneath the panel, then nudge the panel into its final position. Set up short ladders or sawhorses to stand on as you drive the fasteners (see the photos on the facing page).

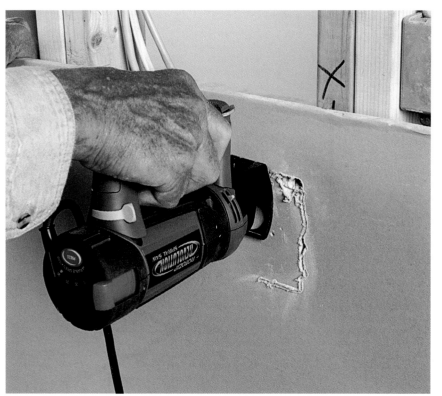

Make cutouts with a router. Equipped with a narrow straight bit, this power tool cuts holes around electrical outlet boxes after a drywall panel has been tacked in place.

Fasten according to code

Hold screws or nails back about ⅝ in. from the edges of the panel, and drive them in straight so you don't break the paper. Follow the fastening schedule for drywall that applies in your area. When ceiling joists are 24 in. o.c., nails or screws are usually driven every 8 in. along the edge of the panel and every 12 in. in the middle.

Some builders use drywall panel adhesive when attaching sheets of drywall. The adhesive is applied with a caulking gun, just like caulk or sealant. With panel adhesive, the need for screws

Use a screw gun. This electric drill is designed to drive drywall screws to exactly the right depth.

or nails is greatly reduced. Don't use adhesive over a poly vapor barrier or kraft paper–faced insulation; it's designed to affix drywall to a wood surface. Follow the application and installation instructions on the label.

Corner details

If you provided backing or deadwood while building interior walls (see Chapter 4) and installing roof trusses (see Chapter 5), you'll be able to drive nails or screws along the walls to fasten drywall panels. But if solid backing material for drywall was not nailed to the tops of parallel walls or in the corners where walls intersect, metal drywall clips can be used instead. See the illustration on p. 223 for instructions on using these clips. Unlike a drywall corner secured with nails or screws, a corner secured with clips can be more resistant to cracking when the framing material moves in response to temperature fluctuations.

Another strategy is to let the corner "float," eliminating nails where a ceiling panel meets the wall. The top edges of wall panels are

T-supports are helpful holders. Easily made on the job site, T-supports hold ceiling panels in place, allowing you to concentrate on driving nails or screws.

TIP Rent your equipment. You can buy or rent a commercial lifter that holds drywall against the ceiling as you fasten it in place, or you can make your own inexpensive supports from some scrap 1× stock. The braces, sometimes referred to as dead men or preachers, are extremely useful; I don't hang drywall without a pair of them.

Cutting drywall isn't difficult, once you learn how to score through the paper covering with a utility knife.

The panels have a gypsum core that makes them heavy and delicate. They create a lot of dust, too, especially when making cuts with a saw.

Covering the studs with drywall provides our first look at real rooms.

The metal corner bead looks ugly until it is covered with drywall compound, which we call mud.

TIP Panel offcuts come in handy. Use the cut-off ends of panels to cover small spaces, such as closet interiors, window trimmers, and closet doorways. Don't overdo it, though. Using too many small pieces creates extra work when it's time to tape and mud the joints.

then pushed snugly against the ceiling panels, holding them in place (see the top illustration on p. 224). Again, this can help prevent corner cracks at the ceiling–wall juncture due to wood shrinkage or truss uplift. If you're uncertain about how to handle drywall corners, check with experienced builders in your area.

Once all the ceiling panels are in place, run a bead of caulk where the ceiling panels butt the exterior walls to reduce air infiltration (see the top illustration on p. 224). I finish the ceiling by marking the location of wall studs with a small pencil mark on the ceiling drywall. These marks help when nailing drywall to the walls. Don't use a keel on drywall (unless it is covered with drywall tape) because it can bleed through paint.

STEP 3 INSTALL THE WALL PANELS

Hanging drywall on the walls is easier than hanging it on the ceiling. You have to work around window and door openings, and there are more electrical outlet openings to mark and cut, but you don't have to work overhead. It's important to know that some electrical wires (for the thermostat, doorbell, range hood, and so on) will not be enclosed in a box. Electricians often wrap those wires around a nail to locate their position. All you need to do is make a small hole in the drywall and pull the wires through.

Plan panel installation

It's smart to plan an installation sequence when there are a number of walls to finish with drywall. Determining which walls to cover first, and how panel layout will work, saves time and aggravation. Here are some tips to help you plan the installation sequence for walls:

HANG PANELS HORIZONTALLY. By installing 12-ft. panels horizontally, you greatly reduce the number of joints in a wall. The top panels should be hung first. Don't worry if the bottom panel doesn't extend all the way to the subfloor; this small gap will be covered by the baseboard trim. For rooms with 9-ft.-high walls, use 54-in.-wide drywall panels instead of the standard 48-in.-wide panels.

START ON CLOSETS FIRST. Check to see whether there are any closets that must be drywalled before working on long walls. Sometimes it's easier to get large drywall pieces into a closet through a wall rather than through the closet door. Don't bother cutting and installing small pieces of drywall to completely cover a closet. You can do that later with scrap pieces cut from the long sheets. At this stage, you just want to have an easier time getting big pieces into the closets.

WORK FROM THE OUTSIDE IN. I like to drywall exterior walls before interior walls. Leaving the interior wall framing open when you start gives you greater freedom to maneuver the panels. To maximize this freedom, drywall the interior hallways last.

PAY ATTENTION TO BACKING AT WALL INTERSECTIONS. As shown in the bottom right illustration on p. 224, backing can sometimes determine which wall should be covered with drywall first. When 2×6s have been used for backing where 2×4 walls intersect, there will be only a 1-in.-wide nailing surface for attaching drywall. In this situation, always install the intersecting wall's drywall after the other wall has been covered. Butt the intersecting wall's panel tightly against the adjoining wall panel to make a solid corner.

Install the panels

As mentioned earlier, the top panels should be installed first. It's important to butt the top edge

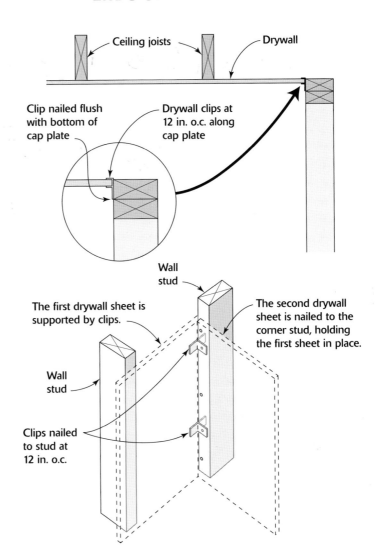

USING DRYWALL CLIPS TO SECURE THE ENDS OF DRYWALL SHEETS

Ceiling joists — Drywall

Clip nailed flush with bottom of cap plate

Drywall clips at 12 in. o.c. along cap plate

Wall stud

The first drywall sheet is supported by clips.

The second drywall sheet is nailed to the corner stud, holding the first sheet in place.

Wall stud

Clips nailed to stud at 12 in. o.c.

Drywall clips eliminate the need for backing at intersecting walls and on cap plates.

of each wall panel snugly against the ceiling drywall. To make installation easier, you can start a few nails near the top of a sheet before you raise the panel into position.

Although I drive a few nails just to hold a panel in place, I like to use screws in the rest of the sheet on both ceilings and walls. Screws hold better, resist popping when framing lumber shrinks, and can be installed quickly once you get into the rhythm of using a screw gun.

CREATING A FLOATING DRYWALL JOINT

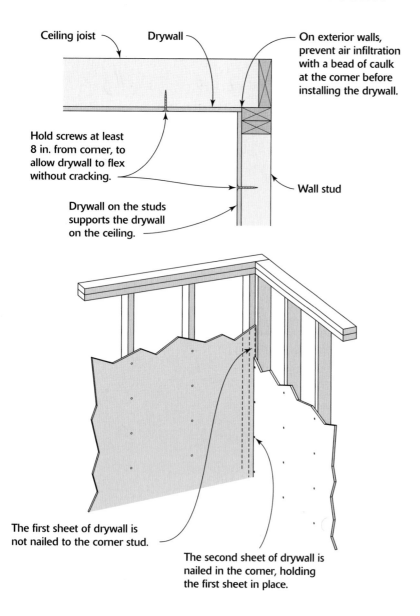

Ceiling joist — Drywall —

On exterior walls, prevent air infiltration with a bead of caulk at the corner before installing the drywall.

Hold screws at least 8 in. from corner, to allow drywall to flex without cracking.

Wall stud

Drywall on the studs supports the drywall on the ceiling.

The first sheet of drywall is not nailed to the corner stud.

The second sheet of drywall is nailed in the corner, holding the first sheet in place.

TIP Once all the drywall is installed, it is important to check to see if the thermostat or any electrical, TV, or phone outlet has been covered. You can make a visual check. You can also put a 6-ft. straightedge on a wall. If there is a hump in the wall, most likely there is a covered outlet behind.

stagger the end or butt joints, just as you did on the ceiling. The bottom panels can be placed against the wall, then raised and held in place against the top sheet with a drywall lifter, allowing you to concentrate on fastening the sheet (see the sidebar on the facing page). Long sheets can be raised with a drywall lifter at each end.

Try to keep butt joints away from the center of the wall so that the joints will be less obvious. Also, have a sheet break over a door or window rather than right at the edge of a king stud or trimmer. A joint at the edge of a door or window increases the likelihood of a crack in the drywall as the wood dries. Run panels all the way across doors and windows when you can, then cut them out later with a saw or router. You can also run a panel past an outside corner, then cut it flush with a utility knife after the panel has been fastened in place. This eliminates the need to measure and mark the panel.

If you use nails in the middle of a panel, code may require that the panels be double-nailed (see the illustration on the facing page).

When fastening a panel, work from the center to the outside edges. If you do use nails, drive the first set, then go back later and drive the second set, making sure the drywall is tight against the wall framing. When driving nails, it's always advisable to push the panel tightly against the wall.

When hanging the bottom row of drywall,

PROPER DRYWALL INSTALLATION ON 2×4 INTERSECTING WALLS USING 2×6 BACKING

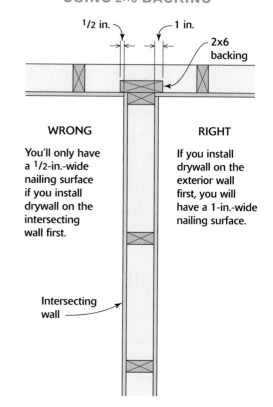

1/2 in. | 1 in.

2x6 backing

WRONG

You'll only have a 1/2-in.-wide nailing surface if you install drywall on the intersecting wall first.

RIGHT

If you install drywall on the exterior wall first, you will have a 1-in.-wide nailing surface.

Intersecting wall

MAKING A DRYWALL-PANEL LIFTER

This small lever comes in handy when you're installing the bottom course of drywall panels. By wedging the beveled edge of the tool under a bottom panel and stepping on the outboard end, you can lever the bottom panel against the bottom edge of the top panel and hold it there until you drive a few fasteners. Although you can buy a panel lifter, it's easy to make one. Cut a piece of 1×4 about 16 in. long, then cut a taper on the flat face at one end. If the drywall must be lifted more than ¾ in., add a piece of 1×2 to the bottom of the lifter.

Install J-bead

Window trimmers and headers are often wrapped in drywall. The same is true of trimmers and headers in closets where bifold or bypass doors will be installed. In these locations, drywall can replace the wood jamb as the finished surface. This is a good place to use up some of the scrap you've created. I try to select straight factory edges to go against the window frame. But other builders install vinyl J-bead trim where the drywall meets the window frame (see the illustration on p. 226). Nail the J-bead to the trimmer, then slip the drywall into the J-channel. This is an easy way to obtain a clean, straight, durable drywall edge.

I also install drywall about 2 in. up the attic access hole and cap it with J-bead. This leaves a trim surface on which the lid can rest. The lid can be made from a piece of drywall with several layers of rigid-foam board glued to the back for insulation.

STEP 4 INSTALL THE CORNER BEAD

Once all the drywall is in place, metal or vinyl corner bead is installed on all outside corners, including wall corners, window wraps, closet doorways, and the attic access hole. This bead protects corners from impact and forms a

TIP Check for covered wall outlets. When installing drywall, it's easy to overlook electrical outlets and fasten a panel right over these small boxes. As you're installing panels, look in the usual places to make sure the outlets haven't been covered. Check for receptacles every 6 ft. or so along walls near the floor and above kitchen countertops. Also check for light switches near doorways.

TYPICAL FASTENING SCHEDULES FOR DRYWALL

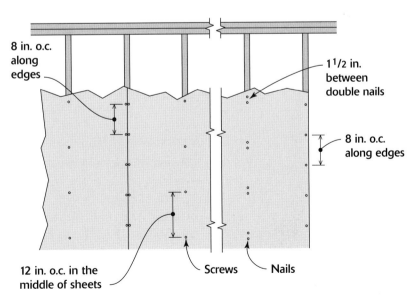

8 in. o.c. along edges

1½ in. between double nails

8 in. o.c. along edges

12 in. o.c. in the middle of sheets

Screws — Nails

When using nails instead of screws, you may be required to double-nail.

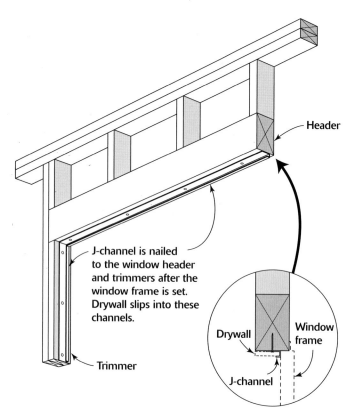

J-channel is nailed to the window header and trimmers after the window frame is set. Drywall slips into these channels.

Header

Trimmer

Drywall

Window frame

J-channel

Using J-channel around a window makes a clean joint between the drywall and the window frame.

STEP 5 MUD, TAPE, AND FINISH THE DRYWALL

I am not a professional drywall finisher, but I have taped enough wall and corner joints to know that this job is both an art and a skill. Some finishers can leave walls and ceilings as straight and smooth as glass. To the trained eye, my work looks more like antique, handmade glass—generally flat, but with some rippling and variations that give it character. The thing to remember, regardless of your skill level, is that taping drywall is finish work, so it needs to look good. Although your first efforts aren't likely to be masterful, with patience and know-how you can learn to achieve good, solid work. This section will give you the basic know-how. The patience you'll have to provide yourself.

Install corner bead. This metal trim is nailed over drywall-covered outside corners. The flanges and nails will be covered by several coats of compound. Drive nails in both flanges every 8 in. to 10 in.

TIP Dispose of waste drywall. Before you send waste drywall to a landfill, contact the **Gypsum Association** (see Resources on p. 279) to see whether there's a recycling facility in your area. Local builders may also know of recycling possibilities that can help reduce the amount of construction material sent to landfills.

straight, finished edge. Both metal and vinyl corner beads are designed to be nailed or stapled in place. Use tinsnips to cut floor-to-ceiling beads. Cut them at least ½ in. short, but hold them tightly against the ceiling. Starting at the top and working down, fasten the bead to the corner stud (below the top plates) with pairs of nails or screws opposite each other every 8 in. to 10 in. A pneumatic stapler also works well. Make sure all the beads are straight and lie flat against the wall.

Beads around windows and doors are attached just like those on corners. The header beads are cut square on both ends and then nailed in place. The side trimmer pieces are also cut square and butt into the top piece (see the photo at right).

Tool up for finishing drywall

Although professional drywall finishers rely on an assortment of equipment, including stilts to speed ceiling work, you can achieve very good results with just a few tools. You'll find them at well-stocked hardware stores, home centers, and drywall-supply outlets.

TAPING KNIVES. Mud applicators are called knives, even though they look more like overgrown spatulas. A 5-in.-wide knife is good for applying joint compound (referred to as mud). Wider knives are used to smooth and feather the edges of mud, tapering it so thin that it will be as undetectable as possible once the paint is applied. If you're new to drywall work, start with 5-in., 8-in., and 12-in. knives for best results.

TROWELS AND HAWKS. These tools are simply flat pieces of metal with handles attached. Their main purpose is to hold a small batch of compound at the ready so that you can scoop it onto the wall with a taping knife. Trowels are rectangular, while hawks tend to be square. Which tool works best is a matter of personal preference. In the hands of an experienced worker, a trowel can be used to both hold and apply compound.

POLE SANDER. Sanding finish coats of compound is often necessary to smooth uneven areas. A pole sander consists of a sanding block attached to a pole. To sand the first two coats, cover the block with 120-grit sanding screens. When one side is dull, turn over the screen and use the other side. For the final sanding, switch to a 150-grit screen.

PORTABLE LIGHTS. With one or more bright, halogen-type work lights, you'll have a much easier time finding flaws in the top coat.

DUST MASK AND GOGGLES. Don't begin to sand drywall compound without donning safety gear.

Use tape and knives for their respective tasks. Tape—either paper or plastic—is used to cover the joints. Different-size knives are used to apply and level drywall compound. [Photo by Charles Miller, courtesy *Fine Homebuilding* magazine © The Taunton Press, Inc.]

TAPING AND MUDDING JOINTS

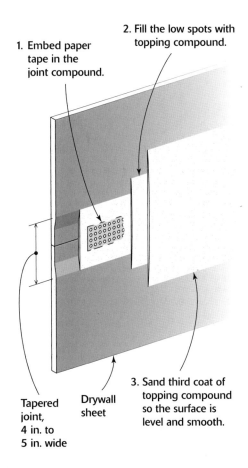

1. Embed paper tape in the joint compound.

2. Fill the low spots with topping compound.

Tapered joint, 4 in. to 5 in. wide

Drywall sheet

3. Sand third coat of topping compound so the surface is level and smooth.

Tape and drywall compound hide the joints and make them strong.

TIP Reuse joint-compound buckets. These rugged, plastic buckets are great for storing tools and materials. Wash out any remaining joint compound with water.

Do the prep work

Before you start taping and mudding, make sure that all fasteners are below the surface of the drywall. You can do this by running your hand or a wide drywall knife over the fasteners in the walls and ceiling. If any fasteners are proud of the surface, they will show when you apply the first coat of mud.

You may need to do a bit of repair work around electrical-outlet boxes. If the fit around these boxes is sloppy, use a fast-setting (as opposed to a slow-drying) joint compound that's available at supply stores. Mix a batch and fill the gaps with a small putty knife. Place small pieces of drywall tape over the mud and apply a smooth coat on top of the tape. If the gaps are quite narrow, use latex caulk to seal around them.

COMPOUND AND TAPE. Part of your preparation work is making sure you have the right supplies on hand. Joint compound is normally used as the bed for tape. If you're new to drywall work, you're better off buying premixed joint compound that is ready to apply. Topping compound is applied over joint compound; it has a finer, creamier consistency so that it can be smoothed out nicely. It's available in premixed and powdered forms. You'll also need enough tape to cover all the joints between panels, including the inside corners. Buy about 400 ft. of tape for every 1,000 sq. ft. of drywall.

Mud the joints and corners

The long edges of drywall panels are tapered, allowing the seams between adjacent panels to be filled with joint compound and taped to create a level surface. Begin by using a 5-in. knife to apply mud about ¼ in. thick along the entire seam. Roll out the tape from corner to corner, center it on the joint, press it lightly in place, and then pull it tight and straight.

Once the tape is in place, drag the knife over the top, applying enough pressure to embed the tape as you go (see the photo below). Make sure the tape is flat, wrinkle-free, and embedded in about ⅛ in. of mud. Be careful not to create

TIP Clean up as you go. When left lying around, scrap pieces of drywall crumble easily, making a paper and powder mess that can be tracked all over a job site. Avoid this by cleaning up drywall as you go. Stack usable pieces so they are easily accessible.

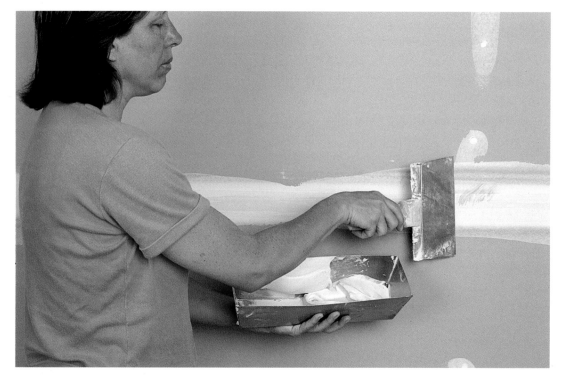

Tape the seams. Apply joint compound along the seams between sheets, then lay drywall tape over the center of the joint. Use a 5-in. knife to embed the tape in the mud.

mud buildup in the corners. Clean any excess compound from along the edges of the tape with your knife.

Inside corners and wall–ceiling joints are taped a bit differently than flat joints in a ceiling or wall. Use a 4-in. or 5-in. knife to apply an ⅛-in.-thick layer of joint compound on each edge of the corner. Next, fold the tape at the crease and press it into the corner, flattening it as you go. Working on one edge at a time, press the tape against the drywall and into the mud with the taping knife.

Outside corners covered with corner bead are easier to do (see the photo below). Using the same 4-in. or 5-in. knife, press mud along the length of the corner. The outside edge of the corner bead acts as a guide for your knife as you pull off excess mud.

The ends of a drywall sheet are not tapered like the edges are. For this reason, you should use less mud to cover the tape at the butt joints, where the ends of adjoining sheets meet. Otherwise, you can create an obvious bump in the wall. Cover the tape lightly with mud, and feather the edges away from the center of the joint so any bumps that result will be slight.

In hot, dry climates, joint-compound applications dry rapidly. Mud that dries too fast may not bond well and can crack. Try mudding a couple of joints in a room and then applying

Cover the nails. Use a 5-in. drywall knife to scoop joint compound, or mud, out of a pan and fill the dimples around nails and screws.

tape right away, rather than mudding every joint first. You may need to close up the house to retain moisture and create a slower drying time. You can also use an easy-to-sand setting compound that hardens with little shrinkage and is basically unaffected by hot, dry conditions.

It's a different story in cold and humid areas. Builders in those regions often have to close up the house, turn up the heat, and open the windows a bit to let out moisture. Portable propane heaters work well to help things dry, but they exhaust additional moisture into the air. If you're using them, leave a window open so moist air can escape. Kerosene heaters also work well, but it may take a while for the smell to leave the house.

Mud the corner beads. Apply joint compound generously along each side of a corner bead. To level off the compound, run the taping knife over the rounded outside edge of the bead. [Photo by Charles Miller, courtesy *Fine Homebuilding* magazine © The Taunton Press, Inc.]

TIP Dust can be removed from the walls using a shop vacuum with a brush nozzle. You can also use a vacuum to clean out electrical boxes and pick up the dust that accumulates where walls meet the floor.

Apply the second and third coats

Drywall compound must be applied in several thin coats because thick applications tend to shrink and crack. Also, thin coats can be feathered or tapered very gradually so that they're invisible (or nearly so) after the drywall surface is painted. Before applying the second coat, remove any lumps, high spots, or ridges of hardened compound left from the first coat. This can be done with a drywall knife or a pole sander. Be careful not to oversand, or you could damage the paper face of the drywall.

Apply topping compound over the dimples around the fasteners, just as you did with the first coat. Be even more careful as you level the compound, and use a 10-in. or 12-in. knife. Along seams, apply topping compound with a 5-in. knife, then use a 12-in. knife to remove the excess (see the top photo on p. 229). Again, take your time. The second coat should conceal the tape. Using a wider knife, feather the mud away from the center of the joints to make them harder to detect. This is especially important at butt joints. It takes some practice to get this coat right. Go over the joints more than once, if necessary, pulling the knife with a steady, even pressure to leave a smooth surface.

The same can be done along inside corners, using a 5-in. knife to mud and smooth one side of the corner at a time. This takes some skill, because it's difficult to keep the knife from marking the finished side as you mud the opposite side. For this reason, some tapers like to use a different procedure. They apply mud on one edge at a time, smooth it, and then let it dry. Once one side of the corner is dry, they return and do the other side.

Before applying the third coat of compound, lightly sand the second coat. Hit the corners, dimples, and seams with a 120-grit screen on a sanding pole to remove any bumps, trowel marks, or ridges. The third coat should be little more than a light application of topping compound to hide any imperfections and feather the seams a bit wider. To make the topping compound easier to manipulate, thin it with a little water.

The drywall in many houses, especially in the West and Southwest, is textured by using air to blow on a solution of drywall mud. [Photo by Don Charles Blom]

Smooth the joint compound. A sanding screen attached to the plate on the end of a sanding pole allows you to smooth joint compound rapidly.

[Photo © The Taunton Press, Inc.]

Sand drywall compound

Some tapers are so good that almost no sanding is required to make their drywall applications look nearly perfect. When I drywall, I can expect to spend some time with the sanding pole (see the photo above). Before you get started, make sure you have a good dust mask that seals well, because sanding drywall produces a lot of fine dust that can irritate your eyes and lungs. Goggles will help keep the dust out of your eyes. Use a 120-grit screen on the block at the end of the pole sander, and push the sander gently along the seams and corners with steady, even pressure. The key word for beginners is "gently." It's easy to get carried away, sanding through the mud and exposing the tape or damaging the drywall's paper face. If you do, apply another coat of compound to those areas and sand again after the compound has dried.

A final, light sanding can be done with a 150-grit screen, some handheld sandpaper, or even a damp sponge. Sandpaper folded into a "V" allows you to smooth out imperfections in inside corners by putting pressure on one side

TYPES OF PAINT

Years ago, painters who worked with oil-based paints, lacquers, and varnishes in poorly ventilated spaces didn't last long in the trade. A serious whiff of the solvents in those products would spin your brain and stagger your feet. Fortunately, most of the paint sold in this country today is water based, which is a lot less hazardous to use and cleans up with soapy water. The best latex paint contains a large amount of acrylic resin. Vinyl acrylic is the second-best choice. Vinyl resin is the least durable option.

Oil-based paints are still around but are mainly used by professional painters. Even among pros, alkyd paints containing synthetic resins have largely replaced oil-based paints. Alkyds are great when you want a glossy surface, but they are harder to apply than latex paints, take longer to dry, and are more work to clean up (requiring paint thinner).

Usually, there are three grades of paint: Good-quality paint has a 10-year warranty, better-quality paint offers 15 years, and best-quality paint offers 20 years. Flat-finish paint has more pigment than gloss paint, so it covers better than gloss but also wears faster. That said, when evaluating two similar products (different brands of flat-finish latex paint, for example), a higher content of solids indicates a better-quality product. However, don't compare across categories, such as flat to gloss.

One problem with paint is that it contains solvents, which release volatile organic compounds (VOCs) into the air as they evaporate. These compounds can make some people sick. Latex paints contain far lower levels of solvents than alkyds, but they can still be bothersome to some people. If fumes are a problem for you, choose one of the low-VOC paints on the market (see Resources on p. 279). To minimize indoor fumes, keep the windows open and run a good fan to promote ventilation.

or the other or right in the center, as necessary. At this point, some folks like to apply another coat to give a texture to the walls before painting. Texturing is common in the west and southwest. It is usually done by blowing a thin mixture of drywall mud onto the walls using an air compressor.

STEP 6 PAINT THE CEILINGS AND WALLS

Our prairie home seldom, if ever, had any paint on the exterior. The siding became as grained and leathery as the faces of the inhabitants. Indoors, we sometimes used a dry powder, called Kalsomine, that we mixed with water and used to paint the ceilings and walls. Kalsomine came in different colors, which added a bit to our rooms and to our lives.

After I left home, it seemed that the only interior paint color in existence was Navajo White. For years, the interior of every house we built was painted this off-white color. It was a breath of fresh air to see all the bright colors that exploded in the late 1960s and early 1970s. From bland to bright to subtle pastels and now back to Navajo White—so much for progress.

TIP Plastic wrap makes good short-term storage for brushes and rollers. When you stop painting to have lunch or simply take a break, there's no need to clean your brush or roller. Instead, just wrap it in plastic until you get back to work.

Paint prep is the key to a good paint job

Professional painters know from experience that the biggest part of a paint job is the preparation. You don't just grab a bucket of paint and a roller and have at it. Take time to remove doors from their jambs before you start painting the walls and ceilings. Number or label the doors so you'll know later where each one belongs.

Some drywall jobs create lots of dust that must be removed before you can paint. I use a vacuum cleaner to remove dust from the walls and ceilings, but a broom or a pole sander wrapped with a cotton cloth also works well. Take it easy, because topping compound is relatively soft and easily scratched. Pay special attention to dust in the corners. Remove any drywall mud or dust left in electrical outlets, and scrape up any globs of drywall compound

ON THE JOB

CHOOSING AND CARING FOR BRUSHES

My hand likes the fit of a long-handled brush. But bristles, not handles, are what make a good brush. Brushes with natural bristles, usually hog's hair, work best with oil-based products. Synthetic-bristle brushes work best with water-based paints. Soft nylon bristles are a good choice for finish work, whereas stiffer poly bristles are better for painting rough or textured surfaces, such as siding. A combination of nylon and poly bristles usually makes a good all-purpose brush. For painting large surfaces, a 3-in. or 4-in. brush with square-cut bristles is a good choice. A 1-in. or 2-in. brush with bristles cut at an angle gives you more control for cutting in trim.

A quality brush can last for years if you take good care of it. That means cleaning it thoroughly each time you use it. First, remove most of the paint from a brush by painting on some cardboard or newspaper. If you're using oil-based paints, then you must wash the brush in paint thinner. Latex and acrylic paints can be washed in lukewarm soapy water. Once the brush is clean, you can either spin it dry with a

brush spinner (available at most home centers and hardware stores) or just let it dry naturally. A wire brush and a brush comb are good to have on hand for removing hardened paint and straightening the bristles. Finally, once the brush is dry, store it in its wrapper until you need it again.

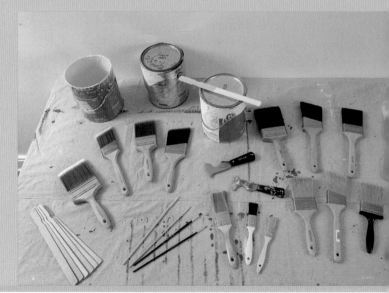

Cut in with a paint brush. A roller can't reach corners and edges. A 3-in.- to 4-in.-wide brush is ideal for painting these areas. [Photo courtesy HFHI]

that have dried on the floor. Drywall mud left on the floor can work its way up through a carpet. Then vacuum up all the dust. Cover the tub or shower with a protective sheet of inexpensive 1-mil plastic, often called painter's poly, affixed with masking tape.

Apply the prime and finish coats

My advice for buying paint and brushes is the same as for buying any other tools and materials: Talk to contractors and knowledgeable folks working behind the counter where you buy your supplies. Then buy the best you can afford. A knowledgeable paint supplier will help you choose primer and finish paints that are compatible; you'll also get advice on the best brushes and rollers to use with your paint. For some basic background information, see the sidebar on p. 231. A well-built house deserves a quality paint job. Spending more money on high-quality paint can actually save you money down the road, because good paint covers better and holds up well over time.

When using several gallons of a single color, mix them together in a 5-gal. bucket to ensure uniformity. Keep the pigment mixed by stirring well before painting and throughout the day.

Cut in around the edges

The two basic techniques for painting both ceilings and walls are cutting in and rolling. "Cutting in" means brushing paint onto areas that can't be reached with a roller. Painters usually begin working from a ladder, cutting in the corners where the ceilings meet the walls. Use a 3-in. or 4-in. brush to make a cut-in band all around the ceilings and walls, as shown in the photo at left. This band will be overlapped when the large open spaces are painted with a roller. Professional painters prefer to use a brush for cutting in, but it can also be done with a paint pad, which is basically just an absorbent sponge on a handle.

Take your time. Good brushes are easy to load with paint. Rather than painting with a full can of paint, painters like to use a bucket that's about half full. This allows them to dip the bristles about halfway into the paint, then fill the inner part of the brush with a few gentle slaps of the brush against the inside of the can (see the photo below). Apply paint in relaxed, even, gentle strokes.

TIP Avoid overloading. Inexperienced painters often make the mistake of overloading brushes (and rollers) with paint. All this does is make a bigger mess, with paint splattering, dripping, and running down to your elbows.

Load your brush with paint. A good brush can hold plenty of paint. Using a half-full paint bucket allows you to dip and load your brush by tapping it gently against the inside of the bucket.

Use a roller to fill the field

Once you've finished cutting in, switch to a roller to paint the rest of the ceilings and walls. Ask at the paint store which roller to use for your type of paint and wall surface. Many painters use a good-quality 9-in. roller frame fitted with a ½-in. synthetic-nap roller. An extension pole that attaches to the frame makes it easy to reach the ceiling. Paint can be loaded on a roller from either a paint pan or from a 5-gal. bucket with a roller screen hooked to the inside. Don't overload either the pan or the bucket with paint. Dip the roller into the paint several times to saturate the nap. Then unload the excess paint on the pan or roller screen (see the photo below).

Rolling paint on ceilings and walls must be done slowly and methodically, using long strokes. It must be done slowly because pushing a roller rapidly scatters paint far and wide. It must be methodical so that every square foot of drywall receives full and equal coverage. Try painting in 3-ft. squares, running the roller back and forth in a tight "M" or "W" formation, with each stroke overlapping the previous one by a few inches. Blend the main ceiling paint into the corners by overlapping the cut-in sections by an inch or so, but be careful not to touch the other side. In hot, dry climates, try to keep the working edge wet with paint. If you overlap a dried edge, you'll often see a lap mark after the paint has dried.

When rolling paint on walls, you can reduce the splatter by painting on the upstroke. Watch out for paint ridges left at the ends of a roller. Try tipping the roller to the side to squeeze out the excess paint as you roll. Then go back over the ridge and even out the coat. Apply a uniform, thick coat, but not so thick that the paint begins to run. When painting near the floor, turn the bend in the roller frame toward the floor to keep the roller from picking up dust and dirt. With care, you should be able to cover the walls and ceilings with one coat on top of the primer, especially if you're using good-quality paint. But don't despair if one coat looks a little

thin. Paint is not all that expensive, so just roll on another coat, if necessary.

STEP 7 PREPARE AND PAINT THE INTERIOR TRIM

One nice aspect of new construction is that you can paint all the walls and ceilings before installing the cabinets, shelving, doors, and interior trim. Even though you'll have more wall surface to cover, the work can go quickly because you don't need to worry about getting paint on all the other finished surfaces. In the next chapter, we'll see how trim and cabinets are installed. Just ahead, we'll cover what you need to know about applying finish paint or stain on interior trim.

Load you roller in a ribbed pan. To control the amount of paint in a roller and minimize spills and splatters, work the roller back and forth along the upper ribbed part of the pan. [Photo © The Taunton Press, Inc.]

Set the nails. Before painting any trim, use a hammer and nail set to drive all nails about ⅛ in. below the surface of the wood. Fill the holes with wood putty and sand them smooth.

There are several finishing options for interior trim. Instead of paint, the wood can either be stained or finished with clear polyurethane. Both options allow the grain of the wood to show. If you like the look of natural wood against painted walls and ceilings, plan to install solid stain–grade trim rather than less expensive finger-jointed, paint-grade stock. Wood doors can also be stained or coated with polyurethane or another clear finish. An application of wood stain is usually followed by a coat or two of clear finish to give the wood added protection and make it easy to clean. Tinted polyurethane finish provides the benefits of both stain and clear finish in a single application. For recommendations on stain and clear finish treatments for interior trim, consult a knowledgeable paint supplier.

With painted trim, it's a good idea to prime-coat the pieces before installing them. You can apply paint quickly when the trim pieces are set up on sawhorses. Brush primer on the back of the trim (known as back-priming) as well as on the front. It doesn't take a lot of extra time, and this technique makes the trim more resistant to warping, swelling, and shrinking in response to moisture fluctuations.

Fill holes and gaps

Once the trim has been installed, the next step is to set all the nails, then fill and sand the nail holes. Any nails that are above the surface of the wood must be driven below the surface with a nail set (see the photo at left). If you plan to stain or polyurethane the trim, fill the holes with matching wood putty. For paint prep, you can use painter's putty or ordinary Spackle® applied with a small putty knife or your finger.

Sometimes the miter joints (where the door and window trim meet) are not tight so you need to fill the gaps. There also may be slight gaps between the wall and sections of door and window casing or baseboard trim. In addition, check for gaps between shelving and walls and around cabinets and other built-ins. All these gaps can be filled with latex caulk, which is paintable and has enough elasticity to move as wood trim expands and contracts with changes in temperature (see the photo below). Wipe off any excess caulk with a damp cloth.

TIP These days, a lot of exterior trim comes primed (be sure to prime cut ends). After installation, all you have to do is apply a final coat of paint, and then the job is done.

Fill any gaps with caulk. Before painting the trim, use latex caulk to fill any gaps between the trim and the wall. After applying the caulk with a caulking gun, use a damp rag to smooth the joint.

Paint the exterior with a brush. Although exterior paint can be applied with a roller, a brush is best for working it into the siding. Tape some padding to the top of a ladder to protect the exterior siding while you paint. [Photo © Larry Haun]

and gloss on the doors. Surfaces that are finished with semigloss and gloss are more stain-resistant and easier to wipe clean than flat-finish surfaces. In addition, higher-gloss paint sets off the trim nicely.

Whichever kind of paint you choose, learn to trust yourself with a brush rather than masking between trim and wall surfaces. Masking a wall when painting the trim can be a disaster. When you remove the tape, you could also very easily remove new paint.

Instead of masking off, try using the dry-brush method when cutting in. Dip about one-third of the bristles in the paint, then wipe one side of the brush on the lip of the paint container. Place the dry side of the brush toward the surface that will not be painted and draw a straight "cut" line. Even if you get a little trim paint on the wall, all you have to do is touch up the wall. If a little bit of wall paint gets on the trim at that point, just repaint the trim.

STEP 8 PAINT THE EXTERIOR SIDING AND TRIM

On our Charlotte house, we didn't have a lot of exterior painting to do. We installed vinyl siding, soffits, and windows and covered fascia and rake boards with aluminum cladding. But we still needed to do a bit of exterior painting (door casings and doors, for example). On houses with more exposed wood, you should know how to paint the exterior correctly. Here are some guidelines you can use to make sure your exterior finishing work will look good and hold up well.

Choose an exterior finish

Wood siding, such as shingles or clapboard, is often better off when finished with stain rather than with paint. Solid-color exterior stain gives wood a paintlike appearance, but it does not crack or peel the way paint can. To let more of the wood grain show through, use semitransparent stain, which is available in many wood tones and colors.

Before painting any trim that has been nailed in place, take the time to remove all the doors and cover the cabinets with paper and painter's masking tape. I like to use what is called painter's tape, because it pulls off easily and doesn't leave a glue residue. Cover finished floors with a paint-absorbing drop cloth. Unscrew the hinges from the door jambs and store them in a box or plastic bag. Some people paint the trim with the same paint they use on the walls. In that case, there are no cutting-in problems between the wall and the trim. However, you may want to use semigloss paint on the trim and doors or semigloss on the trim

You can never have too many volunteers when it's time to paint.

We use brushes and rollers of all different sizes.

Painting a new house is great because you don't need to worry about getting paint on carpets and furniture.

People with rollers paint the walls and ceilings quickly, but it's just as satisfying to work on trim with a brush.

Whether you choose paint or stain, make sure you buy a good-quality finish that is recommended for the use you have in mind. For example, you don't want to paint a deck with porch enamel or use interior trim paint on exterior wood. The pressure-treated lumber used on many decks needs a penetrating sealer or stain rather than paint. Upright pressure-treated porch posts can be painted or stained with a solid color once the wood is clean and dry. Find out which brands and formulations knowledgeable painters and paint suppliers in your area recommend.

Do the prep work for exterior finishes

Exterior siding and trim must be painted on all sides, not just on the surfaces that will be exposed to the weather. Back-prime the trim before installation. On doors and windows with wood casings, make sure you back-prime all casings before installing the unit.

Take the time to fill all nail holes with exterior-grade wood putty. Don't caulk under the lap between siding boards. Always use a good-quality, long-lasting, paintable, exterior-grade caulk. Mask and cover any decks or railings to protect them from drips and spills. Cover the foundation or walkways to keep paint from staining the concrete. Take the time to do it right. There is no excuse for being sloppy with paint. Drops of paint on a wood deck or concrete foundation will look bad for years to come.

Apply exterior paint

Much can be done with exterior paint to give a house a classy style. There is an old house in our neighborhood that has just been repainted lavender with light-violet trim. Now, this may not be your choice of colors, but it brightens up our neighborhood in a nice way. I like it better than the Coos Bay gray that makes so many buildings look like army barracks. A good choice of colors can make a home warm and inviting. Some paint dealers have a computer program that shows you what different color combinations will look like on your house. Give your house a virtual paint job to test out various color schemes.

Once you have selected the color, try rolling paint on lap siding with a roller that matches the width of the laps. Once the paint has been rolled on, it must be brushed in to make sure every crack and crevice is covered properly. Take special care when painting the bottom edges of siding. These edges must be well coated because it is where moisture and ice gather.

Latex paint dries rapidly in hot weather, so don't roll on too much paint before you go back over it with a brush. Remember, too, that most paints require a wall temperature of at least 50°F or so for good adhesion, so don't paint if the weather is cooler than that.

Completely paint or stain the siding before you tackle the exterior trim, just as you did on the interior. Use a good brush and a steady hand to leave a neat-looking job. Doors get a lot of use, so it's best to give them at least a couple of coats on top of the primer. The metal-clad exterior doors that are often used on affordable houses come with a prime coat. You may want to use a higher-gloss paint on doors because it is easy to clean.

Instead of trying to paint doors in place, take them down and remove all the hardware. Put the hardware for each door in a small plastic bag, label the bag, and store it in a kitchen drawer. Label the door, too. The top edge is a good place to write the door's location. Drive nails or screws into the top and bottom edges, then set the door across a pair of sawhorses (see the illustration below). After painting one side, flip over the door and paint the other side. Set the door aside, resting it on the nails, while you paint another door. Wait until the first coat is dry, then apply a second coat, brushing out any streaks or drips. When you're done, remember to put a bit of caulk in the top nail holes so water can't enter.

Door jambs are also easier to paint when there's no door in the way. On some exterior entries, weatherstripping is installed on the door; on others, it's installed on the jamb. Either way, it's usually best to remove weatherstripping before painting instead of trying to paint around it. Getting paint on weatherstripping can prevent it from sealing properly. If the weatherstripping is damaged or difficult to reinstall, just buy new material. It is generally inexpensive and is important for sealing the interior of the house from the elements.

Once you are finished painting, use a small piece of cardboard to scrape all unused paint into one can. Save some paint for later touch-up work. A contractor I know takes leftover cans of latex paint, stirs them together, and uses the mixture as back-primer for the next job. Some cities have a site where you can drop off paint for recycling. Otherwise, take unused paints, stains, and solvents to a hazardous-waste facility. Give the earth a break. Don't dump toxic materials on the ground or down the sink.

PAINTING DOORS

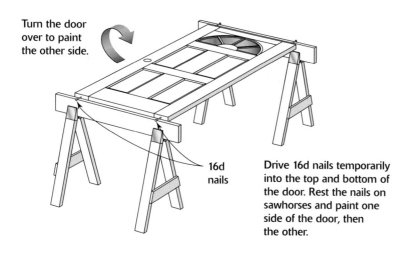

Turn the door over to paint the other side.

16d nails

Drive 16d nails temporarily into the top and bottom of the door. Rest the nails on sawhorses and paint one side of the door, then the other.

LEARNING FROM YOUR FELLOW VOLUNTEERS

When volunteers show up to build a Habitat house, they often find themselves assigned to jobs they've never done before. Still, with the proper training and supervision, they're almost always capable of rising to the challenge and making a significant and meaningful contribution to providing another family a decent home. And sometimes in the process stereotypes are broken and we learn from one another.

On the second day of a six-day blitz in 1993, during which we built 20 houses, I was roofing with Bunny Church and her friend, Stuart Phillips. It was a hot, steamy day, and we had just half a day to start and finish shingling a roof, so we set to the task energetically and with great focus. After a couple of hours of hard labor up on that roof, the temperature rising all the while we were working, we were tired, dirty, and thirsty. Suddenly, Stuart stopped our roofing production line, sighing, "I'm sorry, but I just have to put on some lipstick. Lipstick always makes me feel better."

She excused herself, climbed down the ladder to the ground, pulled her lipstick out of her pocket, then went to the Porta Potti. A moment later, Stuart emerged, still dirty and dusty, but also smiling and

radiant, her lips perfectly covered with pink lipstick. It did help!

Despite being something of a tomboy, I appreciated the lesson Stuart had unintentionally taught me—that it's okay to assert your femininity on the job. And that's one of the wonderful things about Habitat—everyone is welcome. How many roofers wear lipstick? If your heart is open, the diversity you encounter while working on a Habitat house just might enrich your life. And remember: Lipstick can make you feel better! —*Anna G. Carter*

MAKING A HOUSE BEAUTIFUL AND USEFUL

Interior Trim, Cabinets, Countertops, and Closets

When I'm feeling nostalgic, I think about the fancy, well-crafted toolkit I carried from job to job before I switched to a 5-gal. plastic bucket. That kit had a place for all my finish tools—handsaws, levels, small hammers, razor-sharp chisels with their blades wrapped in soft cotton, and planes that left long curls of wood with each pass. My brother, Jim, still has his shiny, metal miter box with its long backsaw—that's what we used to make perfect cuts in trim before chopsaws came along. Back in the late 1940s and early 1950s, those were the tools that master builders passed down to us "kids" as they taught us the craft.

Today, carpentry is different. Power tools dominate—from motorized miter saws (chopsaws) and pneumatic nailers to cordless drills, belt sanders, random-orbit sanders, and jigsaws. And many of the things we used to build at the job site, such as kitchen cabinets, bathroom vanities, and door and window jambs, are now factory-made products that arrive ready to install. Despite these changes, basic hand-tool and careful layout skills are still essential, especially at this stage of the game, when the rough frame of the house, with all its imperfections, has been covered by drywall and the walls have been painted. Now it's time to prepare floors for vinyl and carpet; install interior doors, window casing, and interior trim; and secure cabinets and countertops. Do this work right, and the inside of your house will begin to look beautiful and much more livable.

STEP 1 INSTALL UNDERLAYMENT FOR VINYL FLOORING

Because vinyl flooring is quite thin, it is common to install sheets of underlayment over a subfloor to provide a smooth, level base for the vinyl. Typically just

TIP Add character with salvaged doors. A new house gains some wonderful history when it has a few old doors. Interesting, beautifully made old doors can be found at architectural salvage yards and building-supply recyclers and at Habitat Re-stores (see Resources on p. 279).

INSTALLING UNDERLAYMENT FOR A VINYL FLOOR

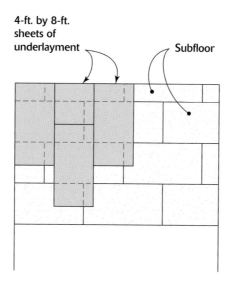

4-ft. by 8-ft. sheets of underlayment

Subfloor

Install underlayment so the joints do not break, or land, on the subfloor joints below.

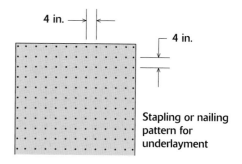

4 in.

4 in.

Stapling or nailing pattern for underlayment

Staple or nail at 4 in. o.c. along the edges and in the middle of the sheet. Make sure all staples are driven flush with the surface.

¼ in. thick, 4×8 underlayment sheets can be made of particleboard (wood particles glued together under pressure), MDF (medium-density fiberboard, a smoother version of particleboard), or plywood. I like to install underlayment in the kitchen and bathroom after the drywall is finished but before the cabinets or prehung doors are installed.

Underlayment must be installed on a relatively clean floor. Remove all globs of joint compound from the subfloor throughout the house and give it a good vacuuming. I prefer vacuuming (with a rugged wet-dry vac, not a home model) to sweeping, because sweeping can create a dust storm. Some builders apply beads of construction adhesive before installing underlayment. A clean floor allows you to do this. Adhesive won't adhere to a dirty floor.

Sheets of underlayment go down just like the subfloor. Lay them so the joints don't break on the subfloor joints underneath (see the illustration above). When you have to cut a panel to length, lay the cut end against the wall with the factory edges in the middle of the room. This will ensure a tight fit between sheets.

The best way to secure underlayment to the subfloor is with a pneumatic or heavy-duty electric stapler. Drive one staple every 4 in. along the edges of each sheet and 4 in. o.c. in both directions in the field. If necessary, snap chalklines to make a grid of 4-in. squares. A lot of staples are needed to make sure the underlayment doesn't bubble should it absorb moisture from the vinyl adhesive or other sources.

If you're nailing by hand, drive 1¼-in. ring-shank nails in the same pattern as described above. The problem with nails is that they must be driven exactly flush with the surface of the underlayment. If they are left proud (protruding above the surface), then you'll be able to see them through the thin vinyl flooring. If they're driven below the surface, they can be covered and hidden with a leveling compound—but that means more work.

After nailing the underlayment in the bathroom, fill the joint between the panel and the bathtub with silicone caulk. This helps prevent water from entering at that junction.

SELECTING AND ORDERING PREHUNG DOORS

The standard interior door used in most affordable homes is 32 in. wide and has a flat, smooth plywood "skin" that covers a hollow core. But instead of settling for standard hollow-core doors, I recommend shopping around for some frame-and-panel doors made from solid wood. Doors can be a source of beauty in your house, and it may be worth the extra cost to have some well-crafted doors in your favorite doorways. Check with one or more local suppliers, and look at the array of doors that are available. Sometimes, styles are discontinued or doors are special-ordered but never claimed. When that happens, you can find a great door at a bargain price.

Most doors open into rooms rather than into a hallway. They seldom open into closets. They can swing either to the right or to the left. The swing, or hand, of a door can be confusing. Make sure when you order doors that you and your supplier are both on the same page. Most house plans show which way the doors swing, so it's not a bad idea to take the plans with you when you order doors.

Different styles of prehung doors are used in different parts of the country. I like split-jamb, prehung doors, because they come with the trim (casing) installed, and they adjust for uneven wall thicknesses (see the photo at left). Another type of prehung door has a knockdown jamb. It comes in three pieces and also has the casing installed. A third style of prehung door has just the jambs but no casing (see the photo above). After the jambs have been nailed in place, the casing must be cut and nailed around them.

STEP 2 INSTALL THE INTERIOR DOORS

Once the underlayment is down, start installing the prehung doors. I have lived in older houses that required work on sticky doors, misaligned locks, and squeaky hinges. Quality doors open and close with ease even after years of use—if you take the time to install them with care. Remember that doors and jambs should last for the life of the house. That won't happen if you buy junk. Doors and trim are finish work and are seen and used on a daily basis, so try to buy units that are both attractive and durable (see the sidebar above).

The first step in setting prehung doors is to check the plans and see which way they open into a room. It's helpful to set each door near its opening before nailing any of them in place. This should eliminate installing the wrong door

TIP It is easier to put down underlayment and vinyl floor covering before cabinets are installed.

CROSS-SIGHTING A JAMB

Once the jambs are installed, you need to cross-sight them—that is, check to see that they're parallel or in the same vertical plane. Close the door and make sure it rests flat against the stops at both the top and the bottom. Sometimes the door hits the bottom of the stop, for example, but misses the top by ⅛ in. or more. This may happen because the door is warped, but it can also occur when two jamb sides are out of parallel.

To check whether the two jambs are parallel, stretch two strings diagonally across the door frame to form an "X." If the strings just touch in the middle, the jambs are parallel. With experience, you can also learn to check for parallel jambs by eye. Step back along the wall, about 3 ft. from the door opening, and sight across the jambs from one jamb to the other to see whether they're parallel (see the illustration at near left).

CORRECTING SKEWED JAMBS. If the jambs are out of parallel, correct the problem by moving the bottom plate a bit. Sometimes the bottom plate is not nailed directly on the chalkline when the walls are framed, causing the jamb sides to be out of parallel. To fix it, place a 2× block on the floor against the bottom plate and use a big hammer to push it back on the line (see the illustration at far right). The method may sound a bit harsh, but it works.

If the door touches the stop on the strike side at the top of the jamb but not at the bottom, the wall on the strike jamb needs to move in toward the door. If the door touches the stop on the strike side at the bottom of the jamb but not at the top, the wall on the hinge jamb needs to move a bit away from you. Normally, very little movement is needed, so even though you are using a hammer, be gentle.

As a last resort, you can use another, though less satisfactory, way to correct the problem. You can carefully pry off the doorstop trim on the lock jamb, close the door, and renail the trim snugly against the door.

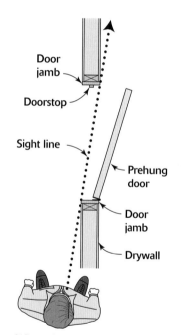

CROSS-SIGHTING A DOOR JAMB

Door jamb

Doorstop

Sight line

Prehung door

Door jamb

Drywall

When door jambs sight parallel, a door will close flush against its stop.

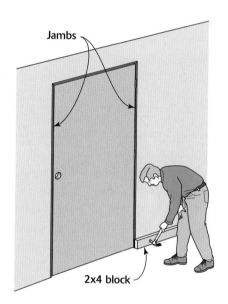

CORRECTING OUT-OF-PARALLEL DOORS

Jambs

2x4 block

One way of aligning door jambs that are out of parallel is to move the bottom plate in on one side to bring the jambs into line with each other. The 2x4 protects the wall by distributing the force of the hammer.

Install underlayment with a nailer. The quickest and most efficient way to nail off vinyl-floor underlayment is with a pneumatic nailer. Chalklines snapped on the underlayment panels form a grid of 4-in. squares that indicate where to staple.

in an opening. Whichever style of prehung door you have, the installation process is basically the same. If the floors will be carpeted, put a $^7/_{16}$-in.-thick block of OSB or plywood ($^3/_4$ in. wide by 1 in. long) under each jamb side. The block will be hidden once the floor is carpeted. Otherwise, unless you have ordered shortened doors, you may have to trim the bottom of the door so it won't drag on the carpet. The block, especially important when setting a heavy door, keeps the door assembly from settling and causing the door to stick.

Professional trim carpenters often order shortened doors from the supplier. That allows them to set the jambs right on the subfloor without having to raise them for carpeting. There is no need to buy shortened doors for thin vinyl floors. Check to see what other builders are doing in your area.

If a door is to work properly, its jamb needs to be set plumb, square, straight, and cross-sighted (both side jambs parallel to, or in plane with, each other), so pay attention to the steps in the sidebar on the facing page. Remove any nails or plugs installed at the factory to hold the jamb and door together. Set the prehung

Prehung doors are easy to install. Drive the first nail through the jamb and into the trimmer, near the top on the hinge side.

assembly in the opening and drive a 6d or an 8d finish nail through the jamb, about 3 in. or so from the top on the hinge side (see the bottom photo on p. 245).

With any luck, the trimmer on the hinge side will be plumb and you can nail the jamb directly to it without the use of shims. Use a 4-ft. level to check the hinge-side jamb for plumb and straight. Make sure the margin between the underside of the head jamb and the top of the door is at least ⅛ in., about the thickness of a nickel, all the way across the top (see the photo below). If the margin at the top is too tight (less than ⅛ in.) or too wide (more than ⅛ in.), it can be corrected by raising a jamb side. The hinge side can be raised, even with a nail at the top, with a flat bar under the jamb.

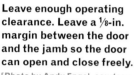

Leave enough operating clearance. Leave a ⅛-in. margin between the door and the jamb so the door can open and close freely. [Photo by Andy Engel, courtesy *Fine Homebuilding* magazine © The Taunton Press, Inc.]

Keep the jambs straight. A heavy door can bow a jamb inward at the top hinge. Straighten the jamb by lifting up the door on the lock side and then nailing the jamb securely in place. [Photo by Andy Engel, courtesy *Fine Homebuilding* magazine © The Taunton Press, Inc.]

Once the margin is correct, nail again near the bottom hinge. Remember to shim under every jamb that doesn't rest directly on the subfloor.

When setting heavy doors, the weight on the top hinge can bow the jamb outward. If that happens, place a bar under the door and raise the strike (lock) side of the closed door until the hinge jamb is straight or even bowed back slightly. Then drive a nail through the jamb on the hinge side, both above and below the top hinge.

You don't need to plumb the strike side of a prehung door. Just bring the jamb near the door so that the margin between the jamb and the door is consistent—and at least ⅛ in.—all the way around the door. Once the margin is correct, the strike-side jamb can be shimmed and nailed like the hinge side (see the illustration on the facing page). Keep all nails well above and below the lock area.

When jambs come with casing trim installed, drive 6d finish nails through the casing and into

the trimmer all the way around the door. Try not to drive nails into any grooves in the casing. This makes it hard to fill and sand nail holes.

Any space between the jamb and the trimmer can be filled with a shim before you nail the jamb to the rough framing. I am not a fan of tapered shims, because unless you use a pair of them a jamb may not be installed flat and straight. I prefer using small pieces of plywood (1/8 in., 3/16 in, 1/4 in., or thicker) for shims. I slide a 3-in.-sq. shim between the jamb and the trimmer to provide solid backing before nailing the jamb sides in place. If there is a wide gap between the jamb and the trimmer, don't fill the space with a stack of tapered shims. Instead, use a single thick shim.

To strengthen the door assembly, remove a short screw from each hinge and drive an identical-looking but longer screw through the hinge and jamb and into the trimmer. This step helps anchor the hinges and hinge-side jamb to the wall framing.

Throughout the process, continually check the door to see that it opens and closes with ease and that the jamb sides cross-sight, as described

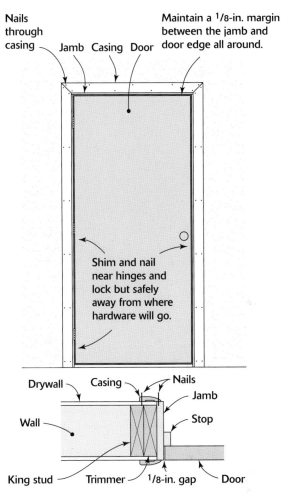

Take your time setting a prehung door. Make sure it opens and closes with ease. Shim and nail the jamb to the trimmers to hold it securely in place.

in the sidebar on p. 244. If a problem develops, it's best to find out along the way, rather than after the last nail has been driven home. If you're driving nails by hand, use a nail set to set them below the surface of the wood so they can be hidden with putty.

Install bifold and bypass doors

Bifold doors work well in small areas, such as closets and laundries. They are supported by top and bottom pivots or guided by an overhead track. I find bifold and bypass doors easy to install, but the less expensive versions are

Make a block for the bifold door bracket. Set the bracket that supports the bottom pivot of a bifold door on a small block. This block will later be covered with carpet. The door guide is installed on top of the carpet. [Photo by Charles Miller, courtesy *Fine Homebuilding* magazine, © The Taunton Press, Inc.]

A drop-down staircase provides easy access. Installing a factory-made folding staircase lets you gain convenient access to attic space. [Photo by Jefferson Kolle, courtesy *Fine Homebuilding* magazine © The Taunton Press, Inc.]

for everyday use. But if it is installed properly and used carefully, a folding staircase works quite well.

Most folding staircases consist of three ladder sections that are hinged together and attached to a ceiling-mounted trapdoor. The door is hinged and held flush to the ceiling with springs. You pull on a cord to open the door and pull down the stairs. As the door swings down, you can unfold the two bottom sections of the staircase (see the photo at left). The entire unit fits into a rough-framed attic-access hole between ceiling joists. The opening is typically 22½ in. wide by 54 in. long. Simply follow the installation instructions provided by the manufacturer.

not very durable. Many of the cheaper models have fittings that just can't take serious use. Good hardware costs more up front but may save you from having to replace the entire unit prematurely.

Step-by-step installation instructions come in every bifold and bypass door package. Once the trimmers and header have been wrapped in drywall, the opening for a bifold should be the size of the doors. A 3/0 bifold door is installed in a 36-in.-wide opening. The opening for bypass doors should be 1 in. less than the size of the doors. For example, a 5/0 bypass door needs a 59-in.-wide opening.

If the floor will be carpeted, nail a plywood block (usually about ½ in. or ¾ in. thick) under the brackets that support the bottom pivot of bifold doors (see the photo on p. 247). If you are working on a slab, drill holes in the concrete and set sleeves in the holes. Then glue the block in place and screw it into the holes. The carpet will cover the block. A similar block needs to be placed in the center of bypass doors to hold the bottom door guide.

Install attic stairs

Some people like to install a folding staircase to give them access to attic space. A factory-made folding staircase doesn't meet the code requirements for a regular stairway, so it's not designed

Temporary ledgers simplify installation. A pair of boards can be screwed to ceiling framing, supporting the ends of the drop-down staircase until it's secured. [Photo by Jefferson Kolle, courtesy *Fine Homebuilding* magazine © The Press, Inc.]

The stair unit comes out of the box completely assembled. When attaching it to the joist chords and header, use the screws that come in the package—not drywall screws. Drywall screws are relatively brittle, do not possess much shear strength, and can break under a heavy load. To support the unit during installation, screw temporary ledgers (supports) to the ceiling joists that surround the opening. The ledgers should project about 1 in. into the rough opening. The ledgers hold the stair unit while you secure it in place.

The unit is installed much like a prehung door. You need to shim between the sides of the stair jambs and the supporting joists before driving the screws through predrilled holes. Once a few screws are in place, open and shut the door now and then to ensure that it opens easily and that the reveal, or space, between the door and the jambs is even all the way around.

The bottom section of the stairway must be cut to length, with the ends of the legs (or stringers) cut at the correct angle so they rest solidly on the floor. To find the angle, swing the staircase down and unfold all but the last section. Extend a 1×4 board alongside an upper-section stair stringer so that the 1×4 reaches the floor. Place another board on the floor and against the 1×4, then mark the cutoff angle on the 1×4. Once you cut that angle on the 1×4, transfer it to measured cutoff lines on both bottom-section stringers and cut them to length.

STEP 3 INSTALL THE WINDOW AND DOOR CASINGS

If you've installed prehung doors with the casing (trim) attached, then some of your trimwork has already been done. If not, then the time to trim the windows and doors is now. Remember: Accuracy is critical for good finish work. All joints between pieces of wood should be tight, with no space showing.

Doing a good job depends on having the right tools, measuring carefully, and using a few finish carpentry tricks. Make sure you have a

Here, an experienced Habitat volunteer drives and sets a nail with one lick and seldom splits the wood. [Photo by Charles Miller, courtesy *Fine Homebuilding* magazine © The Taunton Press, Inc.]

good chopsaw that is fitted with a finish-cutting blade. A pneumatic nailer is a tremendous time-saver when installing trim, and it ensures that installed pieces won't be marred by hammer blows (see the photo above). However, you can still do the job the old-fashioned way if you have to—with a hammer, finish nails, and a nail set. If you cut a joint that doesn't fit well, cut it again and make it right. Don't rely on putty or caulk to fill any but the smallest of gaps. Caulk shrinks as it dries, so relying on it to hide shoddy work isn't a good solution.

Install windowsills

When trimming around a window, it's fine to cover the trimmers and header with drywall, as described in Chapter 9. But don't use drywall for the sill; it won't hold up. Besides, a wood sill adds a bit of warmth and style to a house. It looks even nicer when you surround the window with a wood jamb and casing.

WOOD AND MDF SILLS HAVE DIFFERENT ADVANTAGES. Standard, ¾-in.-thick stock works fine as a sill, but I

TIP Practice using a chopsaw. For better results when cutting trim on a chopsaw, make some practice cuts in scrap material. Practice making the same miter, square, or beveled cuts you'll be making when installing trim. Test the results with a combination square to make sure your square and 45-degree cuts are accurate.

TIP Use clamping blocks to protect trim. When you need to clamp trim to a workbench (when making coped cuts, for example), place a wooden block between the clamp and the workpiece. This prevents the clamp from marring the trim.

think thicker stock—1 in. or even 1¼ in.—looks better. If you want to see natural wood and your budget allows it, trim with oak, pine, or spruce, and seal it with clear finish. If you prefer a painted finish or your budget is very tight, choose medium-density fiberboard (MDF). Like wood, MDF can be shaped into many styles of trim. It cuts much like wood does and, once painted, looks like solid wood but without an evident grain pattern. Just remember: MDF must be kept away from moisture, which can cause it to swell and come apart, so don't use MDF in the bathroom or utility room, or around the kitchen sink area.

CUT THE SILL TO SIZE. When a window is trimmed on the sides with drywall, each end of the sill should extend about 1½ in. beyond the drywall corner on the side of the window opening. When a window is trimmed with wood casing, take into account the width of the window opening, plus the width of the wood casing on both sides, plus 2 in., then cut the sill to that length. That way, the side casings rest on the sill and the sill extends 1 in. beyond the casing on each side. A sill should be wide enough to cover the rough sill and extend at least 1½ in. from the wall. You can vary the projection distance to suit your needs. The sill I have by my writing desk extends 3½ in. beyond the wall; it's wide enough to hold a book or a vase.

NOTCH THE SILL. Once the sill is cut to length, cut a notch in from each corner to leave what's known as a horn for the casing to rest on (see the illustration below). For the depth of the notch, measure in from the edge of the drywall to the window frame and mark your cut lines on the sill. Or you can hold the sill at the window opening and mark the cut lines with a combination square. That will give you an accurate cut line, even if the jamb sides are not square.

Whether you make the cut with a handsaw or a jigsaw, clamp the workpiece securely to a sawhorse or workbench so that it will be easier to make exact cuts. Remember that this is finish work. Take your time and do it accurately. The sill should fit snugly against the window frame. If there are small gaps between the sill and the drywall on the sides, fill them with paintable caulk.

Don't leave the front edges and corners of the sill sharp. Instead, use a block plane to make a bevel or chamfer on the edges, or round them over with a bit with sandpaper. This will improve the look and feel of the sill. It also makes the trim less hazardous to small children. Secure the finish sill to the rough sill with construction adhesive and drive two 6d or 8d nails at each end.

Once the sill is in place, cover the trimmers and header with ¾-in.-thick stock, as shown in the illustration at left. The side (and head) jambs are cut flush with the plane of the wall, set on the wood sill, and nailed in place. The head jamb fits snugly between the two side jambs. Make sure all your cuts are square and fit tightly together. Nail them in place with 6d finish nails.

TRIMMING A NAIL-ON VINYL WINDOW WITH WOOD

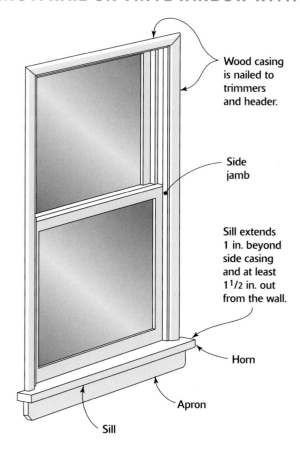

Wood casing is nailed to trimmers and header.

Side jamb

Sill extends 1 in. beyond side casing and at least 1¹/2 in. out from the wall.

Horn

Apron

Sill

Measure and cut the casing

Often referred to as door and window trim, casing hides the joint between the drywall and the door or window jamb. Spend some time at your local lumberyard and you'll see all the styles and grades of casing, including the type that's installed at the factory on many prehung doors. Solid wood casing can be used if you want to leave the wood natural. Paint-grade trim—made from MDF or from shorter pieces of wood that have been finger-jointed together—is also available and costs less. Some people prefer a plain, narrow, simple style, whereas others prefer wider, more complex profiles. Purchase 14-ft. lengths to minimize waste. Another option is to buy 7-ft.-long pieces that have a 45-degree miter precut on one end. These pieces are used to trim around doors.

PLAN FOR A REVEAL. When running casing, carpenters commonly leave what's called a reveal, which simply means that one piece of wood is held back a bit so you can see the edge of the piece beneath it. The idea is to create a shadow line, which produces a sense of depth and adds visual interest. This is done even on simple trim in an affordable house. To mark the setback for the casing on the jamb, use an adjustable combination square. Set it at about $^3/_{16}$ in. to $^1/_4$ in. in from the inside edge of the jamb—whether it is on a door, a window, or an attic access—and mark a pencil line in several places (see the illustration at right). With a little experience, you'll be able to mark a setback by eye, without a square. The casing is cut and nailed to that line.

MARK AND CUT THE CASING. Now it's time to cut the side and head casings to length. Cut and nail the casing with its thinner edge facing in, toward the door opening. The baseboard trim butts into the wide edge of the casing at the floor line. To find the length of a piece of side-jamb casing, measure from the floor to the horizontal reveal line at the top of the door or window. That measurement is the distance to the short point of the miter cut.

Another way to obtain this measurement is to hold a piece of casing alongside the door or

MARKING A REVEAL ON DOOR AND WINDOW JAMBS

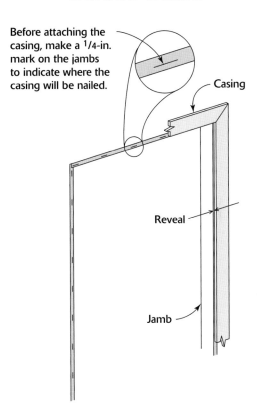

Before attaching the casing, make a 1/4-in. mark on the jambs to indicate where the casing will be nailed.

Casing

Reveal

Jamb

across the head jamb and mark the short end of the miter cut at the $^1/_4$-in. reveal line (see the bottom left photo on p. 252). Make a diagonal mark on the casing to show which way to make the cut. Just make sure the mark will be cut off, so it won't be visible once the casing is installed. Take the casing stock to the chopsaw and make the cut. Side casings are cut in pairs, one for the jamb on the right and one for the jamb on the left. Take your time. Work slowly. Make sure you are cutting in pairs.

The same technique can be used for windows with sills and jambs. Measure from the sill to the horizontal reveal on the head jamb (for side casings) and from one vertical reveal line to the other on the side jambs (for head casings). All these marks are made from heel to heel, or short point to short point, of the miter cut.

In theory, once you know the length of one piece of casing, you should be able to set up

TIP Back-cut trim for tight-fitting joints. By shaving a slight bevel on the back or hidden part of a joint, you can force the visible front edges more tightly together. To accomplish this finish carpentry trick, make the back-cut with a sharp chisel, a utility knife, or a belt sander equipped with a fine-grit sanding belt.

at the saw and cut every piece for doors and windows of the same size. This can eliminate repetitive measuring and lots of time spent walking back and forth to your saw. In practice, side casings may vary slightly in length. But small gaps at the floor line will be hidden by carpeting or cut to uniform distance to accommodate wood or other finish flooring. Find out what carpenters are doing in your area.

Nail the casing to the jambs

Nailing trim around doors and windows can be difficult when the wall extends past the jamb. If drywall edges protrude just a little, they can usually be knocked back enough by hitting them gently with a hammer. Just make sure the casing will completely cover the flattened, compressed drywall.

Sometimes, I start by installing door casing inside a closet, where people won't readily notice mistakes. Think of it as a warm-up exercise. Begin by nailing a piece of side casing first, holding it to the reveal marks. (Other people start with the head casing first.) If you're nailing

Leave a reveal. Install the casing so its inside edge sits back a uniform distance (¼ in. or so) from the corner of the jamb. This creates a pleasing reveal.

Mark the casing; don't measure. Mark the short end of the casing's miter cut by holding the casing in place on the jamb.

the casing by hand, drive a pair of nails at the top and then about every 16 in. down the casing. Drive 4d nails through the trim and into the jamb, and drive 6d nails through the thicker part of the trim and into the wall frame. A pneumatic finish nailer makes this job much easier, and you won't have to use different size nails.

Next comes the head casing. Check the joint between the head and the side casing. If it looks good, add a bit of glue to the ends of the two pieces, then nail the head casing to the wall along the horizontal reveal line (see the photo above). If the joint is open a little, cut the miter again and fine-tune the angle of the chopsaw, if necessary, to get a better fit. If the joint is open more than a little, cut another headpiece; start a little long and make sure you have the angle right before cutting it to length. If all else fails, fill the joint with putty before painting. Repeat this process for the second piece of side casing.

Casing installed around an attic staircase or access hole can be cut and nailed in the same way. The only difference is that you'll have miter joints at all four corners.

Install the window aprons

Just as you'd imagine, the piece of trim called an apron is installed beneath the windowsill. It covers the joint between the drywall and the sill and is usually cut from casing stock. Nail it in place with its wide edge up against the sill to support it.

The apron does not run the full length of the sill. If the window sides are covered with drywall, cut the apron 2 in. longer than the window opening. For windows with wood jambs and casing, the apron should line up with the outside edges of the casing on both sides of the window. You can cut the apron square or give it a slight back-cut of about 6 degrees (see the illustration at right). Then nail the apron directly below the windowsill (see the photo below).

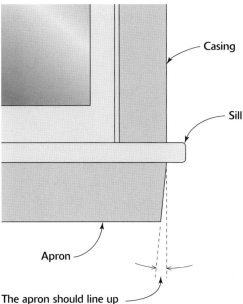

INSTALLING A WINDOW APRON

Casing

Sill

Apron

The apron should line up flush with the outside edges of the casing on both sides. The apron can either be cut square or have a 6-degree back-cut.

Install an apron. This piece of trim is nailed below a windowsill; it covers a gap in the drywall and gives the sill some visual weight.

STEP 4 INSTALL THE CABINETS

I started doing finish work as a helper to a cabinetmaker. In the 1950s, there were few factory-made cabinets available. Every cabinet that we installed in every house was built piece by piece on the job.

Today, there is no need to build cabinets on site. Home centers and cabinet shops carry many cabinet styles that are built to order. The price depends on a number of factors, including the amount of solid wood used in the construction; the style of doors and drawer fronts; and the quality of the hinges, handles, drawer slides, and other hardware. Most base cabinets are sized to provide a countertop height of 36 in. But other sizes and styles are available to accommodate wheelchair access and

TIP Use only the best bit. You'll need to drill pilot holes for screws when fastening cabinets to the wall and to each other. A combination countersink/counterbore bit (available at hardware stores and home centers) is the best bit to use when fastening together stiles. This type of bit is available in sizes that match common screw sizes. It is designed to bore the pilot hole for the screw, as well as the recess that will countersink or counterbore the screw head.

Using a block plane, shave off just a little bit of wood on the windowsill to make it fit better.

The windowsill is installed before the other pieces of trim.

It's exciting when the first cabinets are installed in the kitchen, but they can be heavy and hard to move.

The work starts with a level layout line.

It takes teamwork to hold them in place until they are fastened to the wall.

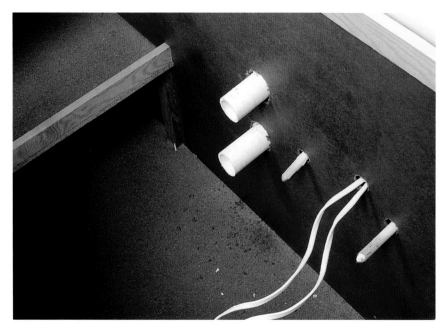

Make room for utilities beneath the sink. Holes must be drilled in the back of sink cabinets to make room for pipes and electrical wires.

floor are in place. That makes it much easier for the vinyl-floor installer. Just be careful not to mar the floor while installing the cabinets. Baseboard trim is installed after the cabinets because it butts into the base cabinets.

Today's kitchens are filled with many appliances, such as a refrigerator, stove, microwave oven, garbage compactor, and dishwasher. Most appliance suppliers are more than happy to look at your house plans and help you design a kitchen in which every cabinet and appliance fits into its allotted space. Once you settle on a cabinet style, you can choose different sections—one for dishes, one for pans, one for utensils, and so on. After cabinets are delivered to the job site, they are installed one section at a time.

folks with special needs. A local woodworker in his small shop builds the cabinets we use in Habitat houses here on the Oregon coast. They are made from pine or birch and particleboard. Although simple in style, they're also beautiful and, thankfully, rather inexpensive.

Kitchen and bath cabinets can be installed any time after painting. Base cabinets should be installed after the underlayment and the vinyl

Install the base cabinets in kitchens and baths

Cabinet installation details are the same, whether you're working in the kitchen, the bathroom, or any room. Some people prefer to install wall cabinets first so they won't have to reach over the base cabinets. Perhaps because I am tall, I generally install base cabinets first. Either way, it's best to begin in a corner. Corner cabinets tend to be large and are trickier to install because

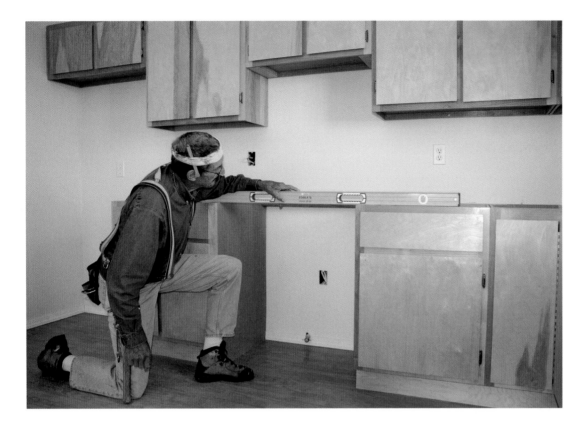

they have to fit against two wall surfaces. But once you get a corner cabinet installed plumb and level, you'll have an easier time with the rest of the job.

PLANNING AND PREPARATION ARE IMPORTANT. Before you screw any cabinets to the wall, it's a good idea to line them up and see whether they will fit into the allotted space. It's not unheard of for one or more cabinets to be manufactured in the wrong size, so this test-fitting exercise is important. At this stage, and during the installation process, it's important to allow adequate clearances between cabinets for the major appliances. For example, you should leave between 30⅛ in. and 30¼ in. of space between base cabinets to fit a standard 30-in.-wide range or stove. Your final prep step is to label all cabinet doors and drawers, then remove them until you've finished the installation process.

START WITH A LEVEL LINE. Begin the installation process by marking a level line on the wall, where the top edges of your base cabinets will fit. If you suspect that the floor surface isn't exactly level where the cabinets will be installed,

INSTALLING A BASE CABINET

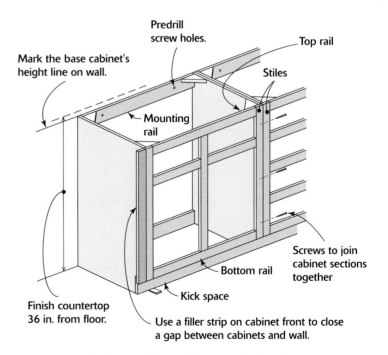

Mark the base cabinet's height line on wall.

Predrill screw holes.

Top rail

Stiles

Mounting rail

Finish countertop 36 in. from floor.

Bottom rail

Screws to join cabinet sections together

Kick space

Use a filler strip on cabinet front to close a gap between cabinets and wall.

Make sure base cabinets are level and set to a height line marked on the wall.

TIP Inexpensive sensors, both electronic and magnetic, are available to help locate studs behind drywall. As a sensor is moved along the drywall, it detects the location of the wall studs and indicates when it finds one.

use a level to find the highest spot on the floor, then measure up the wall near that spot. The standard height of base cabinets without a countertop is usually 34½ in. or 35¼ in., depending on the manufacturer (see the illustration on p. 255).

DRIVE INSTALLATION SCREWS INTO STUDS. Base cabinets are screwed into wall studs or the 2×4 backing described in Chapter 4. If stud locations were not marked on the floor, you can locate them by tapping lightly on the drywall with a hammer and listening for a solid sound. To make sure you've found a stud, drive a nail through the drywall in a place where the cabinet will cover the holes. Once you locate one stud, other studs should be 16 in. or 24 in. o.c. Use 3-in. flat-head screws to install cabinets. Don't use drywall screws, because they tend to be brittle and aren't designed to support heavy loads.

GET CABINETS LEVEL. Make sure the top back edge of the cabinet sets directly to the wall line so it's level. Predrill holes for the installation screws through the mounting rail and into the studs. Then screw the cabinet to the wall. Now place a 2-ft. level across the top of the cabinet from the back edge to the front edge. As necessary, wedge shims under the cabinet to get the top of the cabinet level in all directions. You can glue the shims in place to make sure they don't shift around. If any part of a shim projects beyond the front or side of a cabinet, cut or chisel it flush. Use this leveling technique when installing all base cabinets.

JOIN CABINETS TOGETHER. Separate cabinets, both base and wall types, are joined together where their stiles meet. A stile is a vertical member in the rectangular face frame that forms the front of most cabinets. Horizontal frame members are called rails (see the illustration on p. 255). With face-frame cabinets, the stiles of adjacent cabinets are clamped together, drilled, and screwed.

As you join and clamp one cabinet to another, make sure each cabinet is level and at the proper height. A pair of clamps should be sufficient to hold two stiles together until you screw them to each other. Drill countersunk pilot holes for two screws, one near the top hinge and one near the bottom hinge. A third screw can be driven near the center of the stile, if necessary. With a countersunk pilot hole, the head of the screw should be just slightly below the wood surface.

CUT HOLES IN SINK CABINETS. A base cabinet that will hold a sink needs to have holes drilled or cut at the back for water supply and waste lines. A kitchen sink base will also have

INSTALLING WALL CABINETS

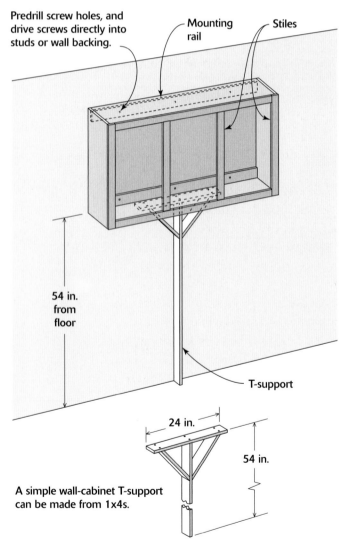

Predrill screw holes, and drive screws directly into studs or wall backing.

Mounting rail

Stiles

54 in. from floor

T-support

24 in.

54 in.

A simple wall-cabinet T-support can be made from 1x4s.

Make sure wall cabinets are plumb and set to a line 54 in. from the floor.

an electrical line coming in, if a garbage disposal unit and/or a dishwasher will be installed (see the bottom photo on p. 254). Measure from the floor and the adjoining cabinet to locate the centers of the access holes. You can use a jigsaw or a drill with a hole saw to cut the holes. Drill slowly and leave a neat-looking job. Seal any holes around pipes with expanding foam or caulk.

FILL GAPS WITH STRIPS. At times you may need a vertical filler strip to close a gap between the edge of a cabinet and an adjoining wall. A filler strip is like a stile. It is cut to the width of the gap and then screwed to the cabinet stile, as shown in the illustration p. 255. If the space allotted between walls is too small for the cabinets to fit in, the overhanging part of a stile can often be trimmed to make more room.

Check the manufacturer's plans for the sink cutout. The countertop manufacturer can cut out the sink hole. Otherwise, the dimensions and cutting details for this hole should come with the sink you plan to install. If your countertop supplier can't make the cutout, do it yourself with a jigsaw equipped with a fine cutting blade.
[Photo © Larry Haun]

Install the wall cabinets

Wall cabinets are usually installed with their bottom edges 54 in. from the floor, or 18 in. above a countertop (see the illustration on the facing page). Mark a level line for the wall cabinets with a soft pencil, so that it can be erased or easily covered with paint. If there is a kitchen soffit make sure the cabinets are secured to the walls, with their tops fitting snugly against the soffit.

Before hanging wall cabinets, remove the doors and shelves to make the cabinets lighter. Just as with base cabinets, start in a corner and install every unit level and plumb. Use a T-support or something similar to hold a cabinet in place until it is attached to the wall (see the photo at left). Wall cabinets should be set directly above corresponding base cabinets. Drive screws at both the top and the bottom of wall cabinets and into the studs or backing blocks placed in the wall frame.

If there is no backing in the walls, make sure that the screws for the wall cabinets go directly into studs. Kitchen cabinets filled with dishes can be heavy. A friend called me recently and asked me to come by to see whether I could tell her why one of the kitchen cabinets in her new house was sagging. It turns out the installer missed the studs when screwing the cabinet to the wall. To make sure that doesn't happen, find the location of studs, then transfer those locations to the inside of each cabinet.

Use temporary supports. Simple T-supports are helpful for installing wall cabinets.

ATTACHING A COUNTERTOP TO A BASE CABINET

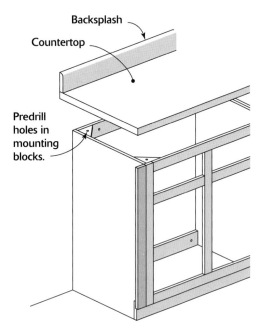

Backsplash

Countertop

Predrill holes in mounting blocks.

Use 1¹/4-in.-long screws to drive up through the mounting blocks into the countertop substrate, taking care not to break through the finish surface of the countertop.

TIP Take the saw to the work. If you have a chopsaw that's compact and light enough to carry, move it into the room where you're installing trim. This can save you time and energy when making the many required cuts.

An electronic stud finder will locate studs quickly and accurately. But if you don't have one, there are other methods you can use. Look on the floor for keel marks that were used to locate the studs before drywall installation. Electrical-outlet boxes are nailed into studs. Tap gently on the wall and listen for a duller sound when you tap over a stud. Or drive nails behind the cabinet to locate a stud. When one stud is found, other studs should be 16 in. or 24 in. from it. Once the studs are found, mark their locations inside the cabinets on the mounting rail. Predrill screw holes in the cabinet mounting rail, set the cabinet in place, and drive a screw into each stud. If the screw misses the stud, check again for its location until you get it right. And feel free to use a few extra screws in wall cabinets. Just make sure they go into studs.

STEP 5 INSTALL THE COUNTERTOPS

Many types of countertops are available these days, but the most common type of affordable countertop is plastic laminate applied over particleboard or MDF. Laminate countertops come in many colors and styles. Remember if you choose this type of countertop that scratches show up more on dark surfaces than on lighter ones. Also, be aware that very hot pans can leave burn marks on laminate countertops. Sometimes, a countertop is also needed in a bathroom, but often the bath vanity comes with a countertop and a sink already attached.

A countertop ends where it meets a wall or stove and extends 1 in. or so beyond the end of the last cabinet. When I'm ready to install a countertop, I go to a supplier, pick a color, and give the clerk the exact measurements of the base cabinets. I prefer the style of laminate countertop that comes with a backsplash. If you provide the size and location of the sink, the supplier can cut the hole for it, often at no additional cost (see the top photo on p. 257). Otherwise, a hole can be cut on the job site with a jigsaw or a reciprocating saw (sabersaw) equipped with a fine-tooth blade. Just follow the directions that come with the sink. Put some duct tape on the base of the saw to keep it from scratching the laminate surface.

In many Habitat houses, the kitchen layout provides for straight countertop surfaces rather than L-shaped countertops, which are more difficult to install. If you need an L-shaped countertop, the supplier will make the necessary miter cuts and provide special hardware for joining countertop sections from underneath. Before joining mitered sections, put waterproof silicone caulk on the two mating edges. Test-fit each countertop section, placing it on top of the base cabinets and seeing whether the unit fits properly. If the backsplash doesn't fit tightly against the wall, fill small gaps with silicone caulk after attaching the countertop. If necessary, especially on a crooked or wavy wall, scribe a line on the backsplash and then use a belt sander to remove material from the backsplash to make it fit against the wall.

ATTACH THE COUNTERTOP WITH SCREWS. Usually, base cabinets are built so the top can be screwed directly to them. For some cabinet and countertop combinations, though, a supplier may advise you to put strips of 1× material on top of the base cabinets so the countertop nosing won't prevent cabinet doors and drawers from opening.

Prefinished countertops must be attached with screws from below. Attach the countertop by driving 1¼-in.-long screws up through the 1× mounting blocks installed by the cabinet manufacturer (see the illustration on the facing page). Predrill a screw hole through the mounting blocks, but be very careful not to drill or drive the screws so deeply that you break through the finish surface. It's easy to strip a screw driven into a countertop's particleboard or MDF substrate, so don't try to drive installation screws extra tight. Complete the job by running a neat bead of silicone caulk between the backsplash and the wall.

STEP 6 INSTALL THE BASEBOARD AND CHAIR RAIL

The old house I grew up in had full 1×12 baseboards. In our part of the country, they were called mopboards. In those days, people used big mops to clean their floors with soap and water. The baseboard not only covered the joint between the plaster and the floor but also protected the walls from being banged by the mop.

Today, baseboard trim is made from real or manufactured wood, and there are many styles available. In the last Habitat house we built here on the coast, we used 1×4 baseboards made of preprimed MDF. Once it was installed and painted, it looked great, but it was so solid that you could hardly drive a nail through it by hand.

In other houses, we have used 3-in.-wide trim that's about ⅜ in. thick at the bottom and slopes up to a slender top edge. The thin edge

CUTTING A COPED JOINT

If you're installing baseboard trim that has a rectangular profile, butt one board into another at an inside corner. For baseboard trim that has a shaped profile, it's customary to make inside corners using coped joints. Coped joints can also be used on inside corners when installing chair rail, base shoe trim, and crown molding.

Start by setting a piece of trim upright in the chopsaw and make a 45-degree cut so you can see the face grain of the wood. The long point of the miter cut is toward the back of the material. Then, using a coping saw (or a small jigsaw) fitted with a fine-tooth blade, carefully cut along the outline of the exposed end grain. Tip the saw back a few degrees to give the wood a slight back-cut. This will allow the leading edge of the coped cut to fit tightly against the previously installed baseboard, creating a tight-fitting joint. Use scraps of trim to practice cutting coped joints until you can do them perfectly.

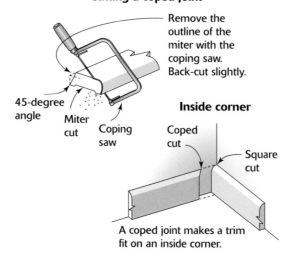

FITTING BASEBOARD AT CORNERS

Outside corner

Mitered corner

45-degree cuts

Baseboard

Base shoe

A 45-degree cut on each piece of baseboard and shoe should make for a neat fit at a 90-degree outside corner.

Cutting a coped joint

Remove the outline of the miter with the coping saw. Back-cut slightly.

45-degree angle

Miter cut

Coping saw

Inside corner

Coped cut

Square cut

A coped joint makes a trim fit on an inside corner.

A chopsaw is a great tool for cutting trim square or with a miter cut. [Photo by Don Charles Blom]

Right-handed people generally prefer to install baseboard counterclockwise (right to left), starting at a door. This makes it easier for righties to cut a coped joint. Lefties tend to install baseboard clockwise for the same reason. Set baseboard right on vinyl or wood flooring, but hold it up about ½ in. if you plan to install carpeting later so that you can slip the carpet under it. When working in rooms that will later be carpeted, use small blocks of OSB as temporary supports under baseboards as you nail them to the wall.

To get my trim skills up to speed, I like to start running baseboard in a closet. Try making a rough plan of each room on scrap paper and record the measured length of each wall. Drywall is often left a bit rough near the floor line, so it's hard to measure accurately at that point. Hold the tape off the floor a couple of inches to get a more accurate measurement. This will save you time walking back and forth to the chopsaw with a new measurement each time you want to make a cut.

The first piece right inside the door is measured to length from the door casing to the wall and cut square on each end. Often, that piece is quite short (2 in. or so). If it fits snugly in place, you may not need to nail it. Instead, spread some glue on the back and just press it into position. The next piece of trim will hold the short

TIP Short trim splits easily. Short pieces of trim must be predrilled so nails won't split them. If a short piece of trim fits snugly in place, you can simply glue it without using nails.

makes it harder for dust to collect on the top. Baseboards still cover the joint between the drywall and the floor and keep the wall from getting banged by a vacuum cleaner. Order long stock from the supplier so you can eliminate joints on most walls.

Install the baseboard trim

Before installing baseboards, use a putty knife first to clean any excess joint compound from the corners. Then clearly mark (or re-mark) the location of the studs on the floor. If the gap between the bottom edge of the drywall and the floor is greater than 1 in., take the time to fill it with strips of ½-in.-thick OSB or plywood. Otherwise, the bottom part of the trim can easily be canted inward during installation. If you'll be nailing the baseboard by hand, protect your knees with a pair of kneepads.

Paint-grade MDF is a material commonly used in baseboard and door trim. It is not advisable to use this material in bathrooms, kitchens, or laundry rooms. MDF absorbs water easily, causing it to expand. It will then have to be replaced.

Inside baseboard corners are coped. The coped cut fits the profile of the trim piece that runs into the corner. [Photo © The Taunton Press, Inc.]

Outside corners are mitered. Two pieces of baseboard cut at 45-degree angles should meet to form a neat, tight 90-degree corner.

MARK THE BASEBOARD AT OUTSIDE CORNERS AND ON LONG WALLS.

I prefer marking trim for outside corners in place rather than determining the length with a measuring tape. Position a piece of trim along the wall. Make a mark where the top of the trim meets the corner. The cut will be the short point of the 45-degree miter. The two mitered pieces of baseboard meet at a corner and make a 90-degree angle (see the photo at left).

If an outside corner is not square, adjust the cut to make the miters fit (see the sidebar on p. 262). A bit of glue on the corner will help hold the joint secure. Drive a 4d nail through the face of one baseboard and into the end of

TIP Pneumatic gun nails are labeled in inches rather than by "d". So rather than looking for an 8d nail, you need to look for a 2-in. gun nail. These nails are thin with a square point, which allows them to be driven into wood without splitting it.

one until the glue sets. Use 6d finishing nails for ½-in.-thick trim and 8d nails for ¾-in.-thick trim. Space the nails about 16 in. apart, and drive them into either the bottom plate or the studs. Driving each nail should pull the trim tightly against the wall.

The second piece of baseboard is coped to fit against the first piece and cut square to butt against the next wall. On the end that will mate with the short piece of baseboard, cut a 45-degree miter that is long on the back (so you can see the cut surface). Now use a coping saw to cut the outline of the profile left in the exposed end grain (see the sidebar on p. 259). The cope-cut end will fit snugly against the first piece of baseboard (see the bottom photo on the facing page). Trim for inside corners that will be painted can be fitted together with a miter cut rather than a coped joint. If the fit isn't perfect, you can fill it with a bit of painter's putty.

As an alternative to making coped cuts for inside corners, some builders install manufactured corner blocks, which are available in several styles. Each block is simply glued to an inside corner; baseboard trim can then be cut square to butt against an edge of the corner block. A similar type of block is available to fit on outside corners that are covered with a rounded drywall bead rather than with a square one.

INSTALLING BASEBOARD ON THE WALLS ABOVE CARPETED AND VINYL FLOORS

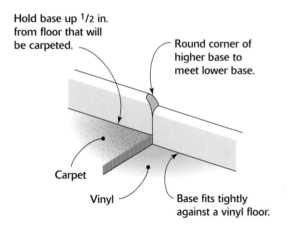

Hold base up ½ in. from floor that will be carpeted.

Round corner of higher base to meet lower base.

Carpet

Vinyl

Base fits tightly against a vinyl floor.

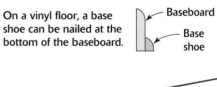

On a vinyl floor, a base shoe can be nailed at the bottom of the baseboard.

Baseboard

Base shoe

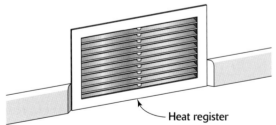

Heat register

Where baseboard runs into a heat register, cut the baseboard back 15 degrees on both sides to soften the ends.

FITTING BASEBOARD IN IMPERFECT CORNERS

The joints in baseboard should be close to perfect. Minor touchups with latex caulk can be done before painting. Unfortunately, it's not so easy to make perfect joints at corners when the drywall is not straight or a corner is not square.

On inside corners, drywall can be tipped back, causing a coped or mitered baseboard joint to open. This can be remedied by putting a shim behind the tipped trim so that it sets straight up and down. Instead of a shim, I sometimes drive a drywall screw into the bottom plate to hold the baseboard square (see the illustration at right).

I use two short pieces of baseboard with mitered (45-degree) ends to check outside corners for square (see the photo right). If the mitered joints fit perfectly, the corner is square. If not, note whether the joint is open at the heel (the back corner of the baseboard) or at the toe (the front edge). If it's open at the heel, set the chopsaw at a 44-degree angle (or less, if necessary) before making the cut. If it's open at the toe, set the saw at a 46-degree angle (or more, if appropriate). Rather than waste long pieces of material, make practice cuts on scrap until you get the right fit.

PREVENTING BASEBOARD FROM TOEING IN

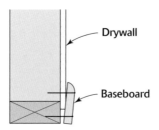
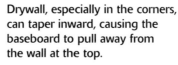
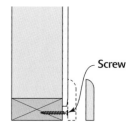

Drywall, especially in the corners, can taper inward, causing the baseboard to pull away from the wall at the top.

To prevent this, drive a drywall screw into the bottom plate behind the baseboard to hold the baseboard plumb.

TIP Offset closet doors make sense. Instead of framing a closet doorway in the center of the closet space, consider offsetting the doorway to one side. This will leave space at one end of the closet to make cubby-holes for folded clothing and shoes.

the other to help hold the miter firmly together. Predrill the nail hole so you don't split the wood.

To cover a long wall, join two pieces of baseboard with a 45-degree scarf joint. It's best to break the joint over a stud. Cut the first piece of trim, and install it with the long point of the miter at the back of the material. The second piece is cut with the long point of the miter at the front of the material. The second miter laps over the first to make a tight joint.

The last piece of baseboard in a room should have a coped joint on one end. The other end will have a square cut that butts into the door casing.

FINISH UP. Pieces of baseboard will be at slightly different elevations where carpeting meets vinyl flooring. Join the two pieces of baseboard with a square cut, and use sandpaper to round the corner of the higher piece so that it meets the lower one (see the illustration on p. 261).

Other situations require a bit of finesse. For example, you can't run baseboard in front of a heat register that goes all the way to the floor. In that situation, bevel each end cut 15 degrees instead of making a right-angled cut (see the illustration on p. 261).

Cabinet manufacturers sometimes supply a prefinished baseboard that matches their cabinets. This base material is cut and nailed under the front of the cabinets in the toekick space. Once installed, it hides the joints between the cabinets.

If that cabinet trim is not available, you can cover the toekick area with a regular piece of baseboard trim. You may also want to install base shoe, or shoe trim, a small, quarter-round type of molding that is often used with baseboard trim (see the illustration on p. 261). Shoe trim hides any space that may exist between the baseboard and hardwood or vinyl flooring. Because it's so small, it's quite flexible (much more so than baseboard), so it can be bent to fit the contour of a wavy wall or floor. It is not needed with carpeting because carpeting fills the space between the baseboard and the floor.

If you've hand-nailed all the interior trim, you now need to drive all the finish nails below the surface of the wood with a nail set. Once set, the holes can be filled with putty and sanded in preparation for painting. Caulk along the top edge of the baseboard trim and along the casings to fill any gap between the trim and the wall. Remember that caulk shrinks, so some gaps may need a second application. Take your time when caulking baseboard. Leave joints looking neat, not messy.

Chair rail adds character

Chair rail is another type of traditional trim that is installed horizontally and often used in kitchens, dining rooms, and sometimes hallways. In days past, chair rail protected the wall from being marred by the backs of chairs. Today, it is mainly used to add character to a room. Chair rail is cut and installed just like baseboard (see the photo above). Join two pieces with a coped joint at inside corners and a mitered joint at outside corners. Nail the chair rail directly to the wall studs, with the top of the rail 36 in. from the floor.

Chair rail provides visual interest. Running horizontally at chair rail height, this trim can add a bit of character to a room. In this installation, the chair rail also serves as apron trim beneath the windowsills.

MAKING A CLOSET INTO A MORE USABLE SPACE

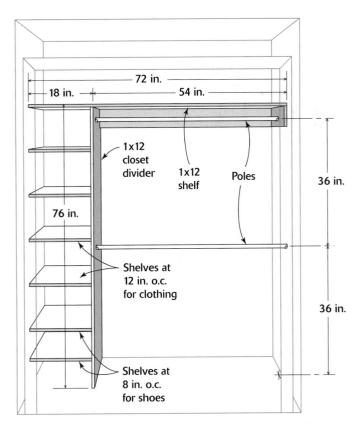

A double pole and shelves create storage room in a small closet.

STEP 7 TRIM OUT THE CLOSETS

Most closets in affordable houses get nothing more than a shelf and a pole. It's my opinion that we can do much better without a lot of effort or expense. Very little extra material is needed to add shelves for socks and underwear, to make a place to hang belts and ties, and to make cubbyholes for shoes. Experience tells me that people like and use such storage. Even if you don't want to build special storage bins, you can buy them. Many people now use the wire shelving available at home centers.

Install shelves and poles

To install a basic shelf and a pole in a closet, measure 66 in. from the floor and mark the back and sides of the closet (see the illustration on the facing page). Then cut cleats (also called rails or ledgers) from 1×4 stock and nail each cleat so its top edge is on a line. Drive two 8d finish nails through the 1× rails and into each stud.

Cut the shelves from 1×12 pine or melamine (particleboard covered with white plastic laminate). A standard closet shelf extends from wall to wall. I like to secure the shelf with a couple of nails driven into the cleat. It's a good idea to predrill the nail holes.

In a small closet, where the shelf and pole are just 3 ft. long or so, no mid-span support for the shelf or pole is necessary. Each end of the pole rests in a socket that is screwed to a side cleat.

In a larger closet, both the shelf and the pole need additional support from metal brackets. Place a bracket against a side cleat to determine the location of the pole sockets. This ensures that the sockets and brackets will support the pole at the same level. Attach the top part of the bracket to the 1×4 horizontal cleat on the back wall, then nail a 10-in.-long piece of 1×4 perpendicular to the cleat and over a stud to support the bottom of the bracket (see the illustration on the facing page).

Shelves customize a closet. Attaching shelves to a closet wall creates more storage space while giving you more flexibility in locating the closet pole.
[Photo by Roe A. Osborn, courtesy *Fine Homebuilding* magazine © The Taunton Press, Inc.]

Wire instead of wood. Wire shelving is versatile in design and easy to install. You can add shelves, baskets, drawers, and shoe racks, to name a few options. [Photo by Roe A. Osborn, courtesy *Fine Homebuilding* magazine © The Taunton Press, Inc.]

Add smaller shelves to a closet

Rather than always running a shelf pole all the way across a closet, you can shorten the pole and add a column of shelves at one end, as shown in the illustration on p. 263. With this design, you can make a typical 6-ft. closet much more useful for storing all kinds of clothes, including shoes. Cut the 1×12 divider 76 in. long, lay out the shelf locations, then attach 1×2 shelf-support cleats to the divider.

I usually place the two lowest shelves 8 in. and 16 in. off the floor for shoes. For socks and underclothes, I place a shelf every 12 in. above the first two. Fasten corresponding cleats to the side of the closet wall where the shelves will be installed.

In a 6-ft.-wide closet, install a vertical divider 54 in. from one side or the other. Toenail the divider to the floor. Nail the top shelf (which extends all the way across the closet) to the top of the divider, making sure the divider is plumb.

Remember that cleats along the back and end edges should also support the top shelf, as discussed previously.

Cut the shelves to fit between the divider and the closet wall, then nail them to the cleats to further secure the divider.

On what will be the clothes-hanging side of the closet, attach a 1×4 cleat to the divider at 66 in. to support the pole. Or you can install two poles, one at 72 in. and one at 36 in. The pole sockets are attached to the cleats and the divider.

If you'd prefer to buy shelving rather than make it, you can find plastic-coated 1×12s with shelving holes already drilled in them at most home centers. The shelves sit on small shelf pins that fit into the holes drilled into the divider.

INSTALLING A BASIC SHELF AND POLE IN A CLOSET

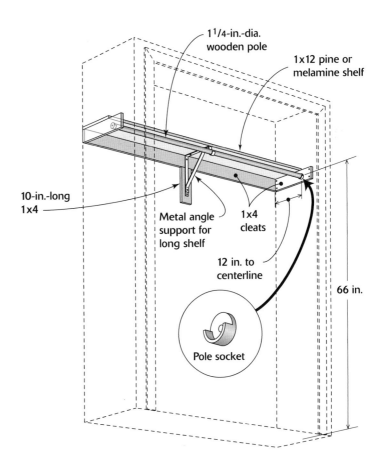

1¹/₄-in.-dia. wooden pole

1×12 pine or melamine shelf

10-in.-long 1×4

Metal angle support for long shelf

1×4 cleats

12 in. to centerline

Pole socket

66 in.

The inside of a closet can be arranged to hold much more than clothes on hangers. A bank of shelves can eliminate the need for a chest of drawers. [Photo by Don Charles Blom]

This allows you to adjust the height of shelves, just as in a kitchen cabinet.

On the pole side of the divider, put a few hooks to hang belts. On the cleat holding the shelf on the other end, install a hook or two to hold clothes you don't want to put on a hanger. Now you have a much more usable closet with little added expense or labor.

Trim out a closet with coated-wire shelving

The rubberized wire shelving found at home centers offers many accessories to help organize a clothes closet. The wire frames are strong and open, and you don't have to paint them (see the photo on p. 265). Besides the traditional shelf-and-pole setup, you can install baskets, drawers, and tie, belt, and shoe racks. The possibilities for arranging your closets with these components are really endless. The only drawback is that they're more expensive than building simple storage spaces with wood.

I haven't installed a lot of this type of shelving, but it isn't difficult. The instructions that come with the components are easy to follow. Just be sure to make accurate measurements so the shelving is installed straight and level. Some people put backing in the wall frame before drywall is installed so the hooks that hold

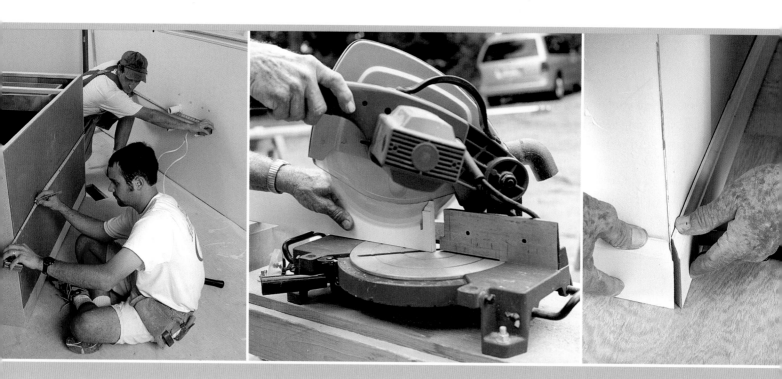

Bringing pipes and electrical wire through the back of a base cabinet calls for careful measurements.

We tackle the baseboard trim after all the cabinets have been installed.

Cutting exact angles is easy when you have a chopsaw. A tight-fitting miter really looks nice.

the wire units can be screwed into solid wood. Otherwise, you can screw the hooks into studs and use the drywall anchors that come with the shelving units in places where you need support but don't have a stud.

Install shelves in linen closets and the laundry room

A complaint I hear from many homeowners is that they just don't have enough places to store their belongings. Certainly, most of us could stand to reduce the clutter in our lives, but adequate storage space is in short supply in small, affordable houses. For that reason, it makes sense to get the most out of whatever storage space you do have.

Just as in a clothes closet, you can do a lot with a linen closet by building shelving like that shown in the illustration on p. 263. I like to install the first shelf at 18 in. to 20 in. off the floor, then place shelves every 12 in. to 16 in. up from there. Use 1×2 cleats on each side of the closet, and attach the shelving to the cleats.

Take advantage of all the space in a linen closet (usually around 24 in.) by using full-depth shelves. Melamine shelving is available in various standard widths up to 24 in., or you can buy 4-ft. by 8-ft. sheets of the material and cut it to the desired width.

Laundry rooms are often just large enough to hold a washer and dryer. Few affordable houses have a large utility room with space for lots of shelves. In a small laundry room, I install a couple of shelves over the washer and dryer for items such as soap and bleach.

I install the first shelf at 5 ft. off the floor and another one above the first. Or you can buy a simple wall cabinet and attach it to the wall.

Another strategy to consider is using built-ins to gain space. Most home centers sell an ironing board in a cabinet that fits neatly between two wall studs. You may want to build a bookcase that fits into the wall. I often like to build a small box with a shelf to place in walls here and there. This provides a place for a vase with flowers or other knickknacks.

COLORFUL CHARACTER FOR A HOME

We once rehabbed a house for a couple with seven children. The father, Eddie, had never had his own bed as a child. As we worked together fixing up the house that would become his family's new home, it was clear that he was overwhelmed with pride.

Eddie had a colorful personality, and he loved color in every aspect of his life. Each room in his soon-to-be completed house was to be painted a happy color—hot pink for his girls, electric blue for his boys. And on the outside? Bright-yellow vinyl siding.

After the house was finished, Eddie and his family came to our church to thank the congregation for sponsoring the rehab of their new home. Striding down the aisle with his wife, Shandra, and all their kids, Eddie—who's at least 6 ft. 3 in. and rail-thin—was all smiles. What a happy man he was that day. But he wasn't the only one smiling. As Eddie and his family made their way to the front of the church, past the 900 people sitting in their pews, I couldn't help noticing his shoes, and I smiled myself. They were fire-engine red. Color, obviously, is important to Eddie.

—*Anna G. Carter*

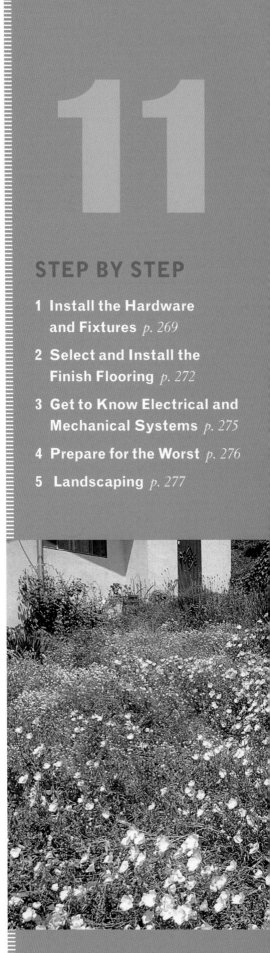

FINAL DETAILS

From Locks to Smoke Detectors to Landscaping

It was the great Yankee catcher, Yogi Berra, who said of baseball, "It ain't over 'til it's over." The same is true of building a house. Even as you finish the interior painting, install the cabinets, and complete all the plumbing and electrical work, there's still plenty to do before a new house is ready to welcome its first inhabitants. Although most of these final tasks are small compared to the major construction stages that have already been done, there are a surprising number that belong on what some contractors refer to as a punchlist. Such tasks range from installing the toilet-paper holder and mounting a fire extinguisher to nailing up house numbers and putting in the medicine cabinet. Taken together, these little assignments can demand just as much of your time—and possibly more—than some of the bigger jobs you did earlier. The step-by-step format in this chapter will help you divide these details into manageable chunks of work.

STEP 1 INSTALL THE HARDWARE AND FIXTURES

Most finish hardware will be seen and used for the life of the house, so take your time installing items such as door locks, drawer pulls, and towel bars. Once they're installed neatly and accurately, they'll look attractive and work well for a long time. Keep in mind that safety items, such as grab bars, also need to be installed securely so that they'll be safe to use.

Choose and install exterior-door locksets and deadbolts

These days, security is a concern in many areas. When a house is first closed in, it's a good idea to buy an inexpensive door lock to seal it off. That way, you can

TIP Buy your welcome mat early! To reduce the amount of dirt that gets tracked into a house after new carpeting and vinyl and wood flooring have been installed, set up some sort of dirt-catching mat. Put it by the front door near a sign that says, "Please wipe your feet or remove your shoes."

Find a comfortable seat. A small workbench or even a 5-gal. bucket allows you to sit down when installing latches and locksets. [Photo by Don Charles Blom]

Use an easier handle. A lever-type door handle is easier to open than a round knob is, especially for older folks and those with arthritis or carpal-tunnel pain. [Photo © Rex Cauldwell]

have a bunch of keys made and give a key to any contractor who needs to get in. There is no need to install the finished locks until after the painting is done and just before the final inspection.

With door locksets, you'll find a wide range of prices for different products. The quality range is just as broad. You don't need to buy the best lock on the shelf, but you shouldn't buy the cheapest, either. The exterior lockset is used many times every day, and a bargain-basement lock won't hold up over the long haul.

LEVERS, KNOBS, AND KEYS. Instead of buying a lockset that opens with a round knob, consider one that opens with a lever, as shown in the photo at left. This type of lockset and handle is much easier on the hands of older folks and people with arthritis. Also, be sure to buy exterior locks and deadbolts that open with the same key. If a supplier doesn't have enough identical-key locksets in stock, order them. This will eliminate the hassle of having different keys for all the exterior doors.

INSTALLING A LOCKSET

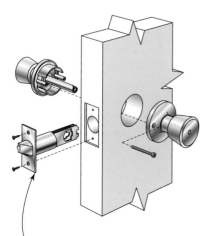

Install the latch assembly first, and screw the latch plate to the edge of the door. Once the latch assembly has been installed, you can install the handles and screw them together. It's often necessary to use a sharp chisel to deepen the mortar for latch assembly.

For good reason, fire-safety code requires that deadbolts open with a lever (not a key) from the inside. You wouldn't want to look for a key with fire licking at your heels.

INSTALLATION DETAILS. Prehung exterior doors are drilled at the factory to receive both a lockset and a deadbolt. If you buy your doors this way, you should have an easy time installing the lockset. The installation instructions that come with each unit aren't difficult to follow (see the illustration on the facing page). When installing locksets, I like to sit on my workbench with my tools and hardware on the shelf below. This is easier and more comfortable than kneeling or bending over (see the photo on the facing page).

The spring-loaded latch assembly and deadbolt are installed first. The factory-cut mortises for the latch and deadbolt plates, as well as those in the door jamb for the strike plates, all have rounded corners. If the plates in your hardware set aren't rounded also, you'll need to cut the mortised corners square with a sharp chisel to make the plates fit. You may need to deepen the latch bolt mortise to ensure that the plate fits flush with the surface of the door edge.

Once the latch and deadbolt plates have been screwed to the door edge and the strike plates have been screwed to the jamb, you can install the knobs or handles. On exterior doors, standard practice is to orient the keyhole so that the key can be inserted with the smooth side down. Most folks find that this makes it easier to fit the key in the lock when unlocking a door in the dark.

Install the interior-door hardware

Interior-door handles and locks are installed in essentially the same manner as those used on exterior doors. Most interior doors just require a handle and a latch, or what is commonly known as a passage-door lockset. However, for bedroom and bathroom doors you may want a privacy lock—an interior lockset that locks when you push or turn a button.

TIP Childproof latches are inexpensive lifesavers. If you plan to store poisonous compounds, such as drain cleaner and bleach, under the sink or in any base cabinet, keep them out of children's hands by installing childproof latches on cabinet doors.

Bath fixtures can be mounted on a 1×4 and then screwed securely into wall studs. [Photo by Don Charles Blom]

Install the bathroom hardware and fixtures

One of your primary concerns when installing fixtures in a bathroom is to make sure they won't come loose in a month or two. A toilet-paper holder, for example, should be screwed into solid wood and not into drywall alone. This is why we installed backing in the bathroom walls when we framed the walls (see Chapter 4). If, for whatever reason, there is no backing in the wall, try to mount items by screwing them into studs. If you simply can't avoid fastening into drywall alone, use an expansion, or toggle, bolt that goes through the drywall and opens in the back. You could also mount the fixture on 1×4 trim and then screw the board into the wall studs.

A recessed medicine cabinet is installed in the hole left in the drywall, which is usually directly over the sink. If the cabinet is surface mounted,

Vinyl flooring offers beauty, durability, and easy maintenance. Available in roll or tile form, vinyl flooring offers all three advantages, making it a wise choice for kitchens. [Photo by Reese Hamilton, courtesy *Fine Homebuilding* magazine © The Taunton Press, Inc.]

position it so the bottom edge is 4 ft. from the floor, then screw it into studs or backing.

The toilet-paper holder should be screwed either into backing near the toilet, at 24 in. above the floor, or into a nearby vanity cabinet at the same height. Towel bars should be installed near the tub and vanity at 54 in. above the floor (see the photos on p. 271). If you want to install a toothbrush and cup holder, they should be located 4 in. above the sink or 40 in. from the floor. It's also a good idea to put a small clothes hook or two on the back of the bathroom door.

Various types of shower curtain rods can be installed in different ways. I like the ones that mount in sockets that are screwed into wall studs, much like the pole in a clothes closet. Or you can use the type of rod that is held by pressure between the two walls that surround the tub-shower. Cut the rod to length with a hacksaw, locate it just above the top of the shower walls, then expand it until it holds itself in place. Don't forget to hang a beautiful shower curtain to add some color to your bathroom.

STEP 2 SELECT AND INSTALL THE FINISH FLOORING

Things are looking good. The house is painted; the doors, cabinets, and countertops have been installed; and all your faucets and light switches are working. But one major transformation remains—the finish flooring.

Installing finish flooring is one of the last jobs to do or have done, and for good reason. Now that you're down to the detail work, fewer workers will be coming through the house, so there is less chance that the flooring will be damaged. There are many options, even for affordable homes, so this is a great opportunity to make choices that express your personal style.

Know the pros and cons of carpeting

Carpeting is not my first choice for a floor covering. In general, inexpensive carpeting

doesn't last long, so it tends to be a significant part of the waste stream clogging our landfills. Fortunately, efforts are now being made to recycle some of the millions of yards of carpeting that are replaced every year.

If you really like wall-to-wall carpeting, I recommend using it selectively—in bedrooms, for example. It's not a good flooring choice in bathrooms, kitchens, and entryways. Don't install wall-to-wall carpeting where it will get wet and be difficult to keep clean. In those situations, carpeting can collect dust and harbor dust mites and mold, becoming a potential health hazard. It's worth it to buy good-quality carpeting. Avoid light colors, if possible.

Carpeting is most often purchased from a supplier and then installed by a subcontractor. Talk to your carpet subcontractor about the quality and durability of any carpet you're considering. A tightly woven carpet with a low nap is the easiest type to clean. Find out whether your choice of carpeting and carpet padding are manufactured with low levels of volatile organic compounds (VOCs), which can adversely affect allergy-prone individuals. Low-VOC carpets, pads, and adhesives cost a bit more, but your health is on the line.

As with other types of finish flooring, carpeting should be installed only over a clean, dry substrate. When installing carpeting over a concrete slab, make sure the concrete has had a chance to cure and dry. Laying carpet on a damp slab is an invitation to mold and rot.

Vinyl floor coverings come in many designs

When I was growing up in my family's prairie home, our kitchen floor was covered with a thick linoleum that was common years ago. It had a beautiful floral pattern in bright colors—except in the high-traffic areas, where it had worn bare within six months of installation. Fortunately, today's vinyl floor coverings are much tougher than old-fashioned linoleum, and they come in a dazzling array of colors, patterns, and designs. I usually shy away from light colors because they tend to show dirt and require more cleaning.

Vinyl works well in kitchens, bathrooms, mudrooms, dining areas, and entryways because it's durable, waterproof, and easy to clean. Whatever you install should be able to withstand the wear and tear of a family for at least a few years. Better grades are usually worth the extra money because they last longer.

As with wall-to-wall carpeting, vinyl flooring is usually installed by a subcontractor. In most cases, an underlayment of ¼-in.-thick plywood or OSB is installed over the subfloor to provide a flat, firm base for the vinyl. Make sure the adhesive the contractor uses to bond the vinyl to the underlayment has a low VOC content. Once the vinyl flooring is in place, take care when moving the refrigerator, stove, or other heavy object across the floor. The feet on those appliances can scrape or tear a vinyl floor.

Engineered-wood flooring is easy to install. Plied construction, tongue-and-groove joints, and a factory-applied finish make engineered-wood flooring easy to install and very durable. Different plank widths and a wide range of wood species are available. [Photo by Scott Phillips, courtesy *Fine Homebuilding* magazine © The Taunton Press, Inc.]

Wood and plastic laminate floorings are very durable

When my family moved into our present home, the living room floor was covered with an ancient yellow shag carpet. There were things growing in that carpet that even our dog didn't like. I replaced the carpeting with a nice, prefinished floor made from bamboo. The cost for the floor, not counting my labor, was less than the cost for a decent carpet. We have a couple of area rugs that can be taken outside and given a good shaking now and then.

PREFINISHED WOOD FLOORING. In the old days, wood flooring was installed "in the raw," one tongue-and-groove strip at a time. Then it was sanded and finished. The sanding process covered everything with fine sawdust, and the oil-varnish finish filled the air with unpleasant (and often hazardous) fumes. Although it's still possible to install wood floors that way, more and more people are choosing prefinished wood flooring. The installed cost is about the same for both flooring treatments,

but you don't have to deal with dust or fumes. You also don't have to wait for the multiple coats of finish to be applied. In addition, the factory-applied finishes on better-quality flooring are very durable.

I love wood floors. I prefer them over carpet. They are attractive, affordable—the installation price of a wood floor is often lower than that of carpet—and easy to clean. So it's great to see such a wide selection of wood flooring available at home-improvement centers and flooring dealers. Good instructions are also available from manufacturers and in-store experts for installing prefinished flooring. As with traditional solid-wood floors, prefinished flooring is made to fit together with tongue-and-groove joints.

Prefinished hardwood floors come in many styles and woods. Some of the more popular choices are oak, maple, cherry, ash, and fir. You can also select the stain or clear finish and the edge detail. Most prefinished wood flooring is made by gluing wood plies together. Referred to as engineered wood flooring, prefinished wood

Install a "floating" floor. Both plastic-laminate flooring (shown here) and engineered-wood flooring can be installed without nails. The individual sections of flooring "snap" together in an interlocking joint. The finished floor "floats" on a resilient pad laid over the subfloor. [Photo by Don Charles Blom]

flooring is manufactured in strip, plank, and parquet form. Strip flooring can be up to 3½ in. wide, planks are wider, and parquet flooring comes in square pieces. The overall thickness is usually ½ in. or less. Some prefinished strips and planks have slightly eased or beveled edges to make handling and installation easier. Basic, square-edged flooring is also available.

Wood flooring can be installed with a pneumatic nailer, attached to the subfloor with adhesive, or simply "snapped" together with an interlocking tongue and groove system. These floors "float" on a resilient pad. Manufacturers have even developed flooring that simply snaps together without glue. If you want to do the installation yourself, check with the manufacturer or with your flooring supplier to determine which type of installation is appropriate, and be sure to follow the installation instructions that come with the flooring material.

PLASTIC-LAMINATE FLOORING. Like engineered-wood flooring, plastic-laminate flooring is a plywood construction, but the top, or "show," layer is man-made rather than natural. Different colors and patterns are available, including some very realistic wood tones. The surface is extremely durable, though it can't be sanded and refinished like some types of wood flooring. Shop around and you'll find plastic-laminate flooring for about the same price as good-quality vinyl flooring. It's easy to install, too. This type of flooring works well in kitchens and bathrooms. I have it in my writing room. The supplier taught me how to lay it by "snapping" the edges together. I installed about 100 sq. ft. without driving a single nail.

STEP 3 GET TO KNOW ELECTRICAL AND MECHANICAL SYSTEMS

Houses are a lot like automobiles. Both work well if they're cared for and maintained. In order to maintain your car, you need to know simple things, such as where and how to add oil or brake fluid, how to put air in the tires, and how to check the radiator. Sure, you could have

Be safe while wiring. Always shut off an electrical circuit before you work on any outlets or switches included in that circuit.

a mechanic take care of this routine maintenance, but it can quickly get expensive—and besides, it's satisfying to understand the basics of your daily transportation. The same goes for a house. There's no need to call a plumber every time you have a leaky faucet or an electrician every time a circuit breaker needs to be reset. Now that you've finished building an affordable house, you can maintain it affordably with a little basic know-how.

Do electrical checks

For safety's sake, one of the first things you should check is that all switch, outlet, doorbell, and exhaust fan covers are securely in place. As a homeowner, you should also know the location of the main electrical circuit box. It contains wires leading to every part of the house and the circuit breakers, which are the switches that control the electricity on individual circuits. Open the box door covering the circuit breakers and make sure the electrical contractor has labeled what each breaker controls. This circuit map should be on the inside of the door. You should be able to identify the separate breakers for the stove, refrigerator, and furnace, as well as lighting and receptacle circuits for different parts of the house. There will also be a large single breaker that completely shuts down the current throughout the house. With well-labeled breakers, you'll be able to shut off power when you need to do wiring work on a specific switch or outlet.

TIP Store a wrench near the gas line's shutoff valve. Shutting off the main gas line quickly can save lives during an earthquake or a hurricane. Buy a wrench that fits the gas line shutoff valve, and store the wrench right next to the valve so that it's immediately accessible should an emergency occur.

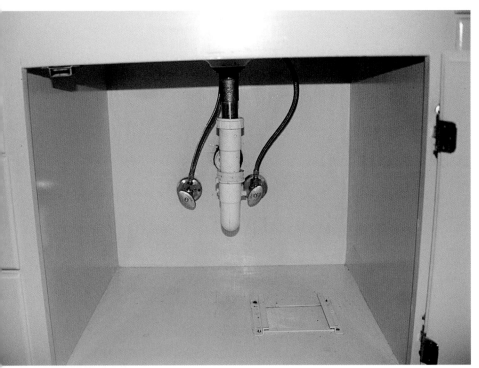

Don't forget the shutoff valves. Located beneath a sink, these valves allow you to shut off hot and cold water lines going to the faucet so that repairs can be made. [Photo © Larry Haun]

TIP Change smoke detector batteries. Incorporate this maintenance task into your New Year's Day routine to make sure that all smoke detectors in the house receive fresh batteries at least once a year.

If an outlet doesn't work, one of the first things to check is whether it's a ground-fault circuit interrupter (GFCI) outlet. GFCI protection is required for outdoor receptacles (outlets) and electrical outlets in the kitchen and bathroom—places where the presence of moisture might pose an electrical shock hazard. If overloading or an electrical short is detected, a GFCI circuit breaker will shut down at the main service panel, cutting off power to all outlets on the circuit. GFCI protection can also be provided by a GFCI receptacle that's wired to other receptacles. Both GFCI devices have test and reset buttons. Find out which type of GFCI protection you have, where the devices are located, and which outlets they control. By pressing the test and reset buttons, you'll see how they work.

Many electrical codes also protect houses using AFCIs (arc-fault circuit interrupters). Fires sometimes start when electricity arcs between two points. If an arc occurs, an AFCI automatically cuts off the flow of electricity. Power can be restored by resetting the breaker in the main control box in the house once the problem has been fixed.

Know the water and gas lines

In the same way that there's a main electrical shutoff switch in the electrical circuit box, there are also shutoff valves for the water and, in some places, the natural gas supplies that come into a home. Find out from your plumber and heating contractor where these valves are, and label them clearly. Water and gas lines can break, and being able to shut off the flow of water or gas could mean the difference between a minor problem and a catastrophe.

Turning a valve on the gas meter with a crescent wrench can often shut it off. There is a shutoff valve on the main water pipe coming into the house. There are also localized shutoff valves under sinks and toilets and near washer–dryer units (see the photo at left). These allow you to turn off the water to a particular appliance so that you can fix a dripping faucet or make other repairs.

Be familiar with heating and air-conditioning components

The filter is an inexpensive but very important part of most forced-air heating systems. A central air-conditioning system also relies on a filter to trap dust and dirt that may otherwise be blown into living spaces when the system is operating. Make sure you know where these filters are located and how to change them. Replacing a furnace or central AC filter usually takes no more than a minute or two. Always have one or two new replacement filters on hand. Check your working filter against a new one, and replace the old filter once it's discolored by trapped material. A well-functioning filter is good for your health and the health of your HVAC system.

STEP 4 PREPARE FOR THE WORST

Earthquakes, tornadoes, and hurricanes don't come our way very often, but their brute force can be devastating—even fatal—if we're not prepared. Look at what Katrina did to Louisiana and Mississippi. Disasters don't just strike "other people." Sometimes they happen to us.

I remember inspecting a house in California after the 6.8 Northridge earthquake. The house hadn't collapsed, but the hot-water heater had been thrown 20 ft. out into the street. Other heavy appliances were scattered throughout the house. A good HVAC contractor knows which measures are required for securing equipment in areas where the risk of natural disasters is higher than normal. Steel strapping and other hold-down hardware are available at most home centers. Check with your building department to see whether there are special requirements in your area for securing heaters and other appliances.

Smoke detectors and fire extinguishers save lives

Smoke detectors can and often do save lives, especially when a fire breaks out while you are sleeping. Most codes require that smoke detectors be installed in every bedroom and hallway. Some detectors are designed to be wired into your electrical system (with battery backup in case of power outages), whereas others work on battery power alone. You need to know the location of these units so you can check them every three to four months by pressing the test button that's clearly visible on each detector. If the unit is operating properly, it will emit a high-pitched sound.

A while back, a friend was visiting and left a small towel on top of the stove, not realizing that one of the burners was on. In just a minute or two, the towel was ablaze. A handy fire extinguisher quickly put an end to what could have been a major disaster. Fire extinguishers are inexpensive and have been put in all the Habitat houses I have worked on. Install one in the kitchen where it is easily visible and accessible so that anyone can locate it quickly. Drive the mounting screws into a stud so the fire extinguisher is securely attached.

STEP 5 LANDSCAPING

No one wants a lawn that looks like a junk-yard, but who wants to spend half a lifetime

Rather than a lawn, try growing a garden in a few raised beds. Not only will you have veggies and flowers for your family, but there will be plenty to share with your neighbors. [Photo by Don Charles Blom]

Leave the lawn cutting to the parks and recreation department. Yards can be made attractive by using bark, chips, and a few native plants. [Photo by Don Charles Blom]

DID YOU KNOW?

According to a survey in *Builder Magazine,* Habitat for Humanity is the 16th largest house builder in the United States.

- Since its founding in 1976, Habitat for Humanity has built or rehabilitated more than 60,000 houses throughout the United States.

- More than 1,200 Habitat houses have been built by all-women crews.

- According to the *Chronicle of Philanthropy*, Habitat for Humanity is the 17th largest nonprofit organization in the United States.

- The average Habitat house built in the United States costs just over $64,500, encompasses 1,100 sq. ft. of living space, is held together with 40,790 nails, contains 600 pieces of lumber, and is finished with 50 gal. of paint.

- Habitat for Humanity has more than 1,700 affiliates in the United States (including Guam and Puerto Rico) and 600 international affiliates in more than 90 countries.

Photo courtesy HFHI

landscaping a yard to look like a city park? A well-tended yard can play a key role in making a house look and feel like a home, so what are we to do?

For many homeowners the answer has been to think beyond a traditional lawn. Lawns are high maintenance. To avoid a visit from the homeowners association, you have to own, operate, and store a lawn mower. Watering a lawn is costly, and care of one often involves pesticides and chemical fertilizers, some of which can pollute our water systems and may affect our children's health.

I have to admit that I'm not a big fan of lawns for the front or back yard. This may come from growing up in a place where my "lawn" was hundreds of miles of the open prairie. Lawn maintenance was the responsibility of grazing cows, horses, buffaloes, and prairie dogs.

There are many ways to make a yard attractive and welcoming. Something as simple as a curved sidewalk is a good place to start. Many people like to put down a liner that keeps weeds from growing and cover this with tree bark, mulch, or different kinds of rock. Native trees and shrubs can be planted to add greenery.

It makes sense to landscape with native plants. They flourish with little care and are truly a natural part of the landscape. Better to use plants that call the land around you home.

For me, the solution has been to remove the sod lawns on my property and replant native plants and an organic vegetable and flower garden. That way I can grow all kinds of delicious foods (see Resources on p. 279), and if I feel the need to walk on manicured grass, I can visit a golf course.

Also think about creating a special place in your yard where you can read or meditate. Try placing a bench under a tree where you can kick off your shoes, rest, and watch your children play. Even a few well-placed rocks can turn a common corner into an area of interest. Enjoy your new home!

RESOURCES

POWER TOOLS

BOSCH
1800 W. Central Rd.
Mount Prospect, IL 60656
877-267-2499
www.boschtools.com
Large selection of both corded and
battery-powered tools.

HITACHI
3950 Steve Reynolds Blvd.
Norcross, GA 30093
770-925-1774
www.hitachipowertools.com
Power tools plus air-operated nailguns.

PACTOOL
26139 United Rd.
Kingston, WA 98346
800-297-7487
www.pactool.us
Tools for cutting and installing fiber-
cement siding.

MILWAUKEE TOOL
13135 W. Lisbon Rd.
Brookfield, WI 53005
262-781-3600
www.milwaukeetool.com
Power tools, including battery-operated
combo kits of different tools.

RIDGID
400 Clark St.
Elyria, OH 40035
800-474-3443
www.ridgid.com
Chopsaws and many other corded and
battery-operated tools.

MISCELLANEOUS

HABITAT RESTORES
www.habitat.org
Store locations where you can recycle or
buy used building materials.

MAKITA USA
14930 Northam St.
La Mirada, CA 90638
714-522-8088
Good source for tools to cut fiber
cement siding.

PACIFIC LASER SYSTEMS
2550 Kerner Blvd.
San Rafael, CA 94901
800-601-4500
www.plslaser.com
Lasers for leveling, plumbing, squaring.

PROCTOR PRODUCTS
P.O. Box 697
Kirkland, WA 98083
425-822-9296
www.proctorp.com
Easy-to-use jacks for lifting heavy walls.

RINNAI
103 International Drive
Peachtree City, GA 30269
Toll Free: 800-621-9419
Tel: 678-829-1700
www.rinnai.com
Rinnai's Smart Technology product line
includes a wide range of environmentally
friendly residential and commercial gas
appliances for efficiently heating water,
air, and food.

STABILA, INC.
332 Industrial Dr.
Box 402
800-869-7460
www.stabila.com
Quality hand levels for plumbing and
leveling.

**TILE PARTNERS FOR
HUMANITY**
3845 Holcomb Bridge Road, Suite 400
Norcross, GA 30092
770-416-0200
www.tpfh.com
Partnership between the tile industry
and Habitat for Humanity International,
a nonprofit organization working to
eliminate substandard housing around
the world. Industry partners provide tile,
setting materials, tools, floor preparation
materials, cleaners and sealers, labor and
installation.

VALSPAR
1101 S. Third St.
Minneapolis, MN 55415-1211
612-332-7371
www.valsparglobal.com
The Valspar Corporation provides coatings and coating intermediates.

WHIRLPOOL
2000 North M-63
Benton Harbor, MI 49022
269-923-5000
www.whirlpoolcorp.com
Whirlpool Corporation manufactures
major home appliances.

BOOKS

Fine Gardening Editors. *Landscaping Your
Home.* Newtown, CT: The Taunton
Press, Inc., 2001. Creative ideas on
how to landscape.

Haun, Larry. *Homebuilding Basics:
Carpentry.* Newtown, CT: The
Taunton Press, Inc., 1999. How to use
basic carpentry tools to frame a house.

Haun, Larry. *The Very Efficient Carpenter.*
Newtown, CT: The Taunton Press,
Inc., 1992. A detailed, step-by-step
manual with three one-hour videos
on how to frame an affordable house.
redwing44@verizon.net

Shapiro, Howard-Yana, and Harrisson,
John. *Gardening for the Future of the
Earth.* New York: Bantam Books,
2000. How to create natural bounty in
your own backyard.

Susanka, Sarah, with Kira Obolensky.
The Not So Big House. Newtown, CT:
The Taunton Press, Inc., 1998. Just
because a house is small doesn't mean
it can't be beautiful.

WEBSITES

BACKYARDS
www.nwf.org/backyardwildlifehabitat
Creating places in your backyard for
birds and other wildlife.

BUILDING NEWS
802-257-7300
www.buildinggreen.com
Publisher of *Environmental Building
News.* Source of much information on
building materials, construction techniques, and building design.

CERTIFIED FOREST PRODUCTS
503-224-2205
www.certifiedwood.org
Certified lumber from forests that are
managed for the health of the planet and
not just for profit.

ENERGY STAR HOMES
www.energystar.gov
How to build homes that use less energy
for heating and cooling.

**ENVIRONMENTAL BUILDING
SUPPLIES**
503-222-3881
www.ecohaus.com
Green and sustainable building
materials.

GARDENS FOR EVERYONE
www.backyardgardener.com
How to grow good food in small areas.

HABITAT FOR HUMANITY
www.habitat.org
Help for building affordable, decent,
energy-efficient houses.

SMART GROWTH NETWORK
www.smartgrowth.org
How to protect environmental resources
and yet build places where people want
to live.

WOMEN IN CONSTRUCTION
www.nawic.org
Information on women working in
construction.

INDEX